SUMMIT OF THE MIND

All India Cross-Disability Convention

SUMMIT
OF
THE MIND

All India Cross-Disability Convention

Major H.P.S. Ahluwalia
Dr. J.P. Singh

Rehabilitation Council of India

in Association with

KANISHKA PUBLISHERS, DISTRIBUTORS
NEW DELHI-110 002

KANISHKA PUBLISHERS, DISTRIBUTORS
4697/5-21A, Ansari Road, Daryaganj
New Delhi -110 002
Phones : 2327 0497, 232 8 8285
Fax : 011-2328 8285
E-mail : kanishka_publishing@yahoo.co.in
kanishkabooks@gmail.com

Summit of The Mind: All India Cross-Disability Convention

First Published-2004

Edition-2023

ISBN : 81-7391-634-9

PRINTED IN INDIA

Published by Madan Sachdeva for Kanishka Publishers, Distributors, 4697/5-21A, Ansari Road, Daryaganj, New Delhi-110002, Typeset by Sunshine Graphics, Delhi, and Printed at G.S. Printers, Delhi.

PREFACE

This book marks a moment that will go a long way in creating a congenial atmosphere that complements growth among people with disabilities. It is a veritable celebration of life as it describes the emotions and experiences of the participants in the All India Cross-Disability Convention, 'Summit of the Mind'. It is a document of belief that collectively we will realize the dream to reach the top where there will be no barriers—physical, social, emotional or economic.

Several of the most theoretical and scientific debates can be resolved only by a practical and extensive application of ideas, scientific findings and interventions in providing services for people with disabilities, ensuring full human rights and dignity. Realizing that the time has come to bring government and non-government organizations together to brainstorm how their energies can be synergized, 'Summit of the Mind' was organized. It called for a free flow of ideas and the channelling of forces for constructive sharing of technical know-how, infrastructure and innovative devices so that we learn and think together. Together, we shall overcome and reach the 'Summit'.

The summit strongly brought to the forefront the need for collective efforts in changing the attitudes of both family and community and for providing social and economic opportunities for employment and independent living. It explored disability issues, revealed the hurt in being labelled and segregated and discussed the dilemmas and battles that parents, family and friends have faced in bringing up disabled children. The openness and eagerness with which People with Disabilities shared their life's bittersweet experiences enriched one and all.

This book is a compilation of all the ideas, viewpoints, interactions and strategies that emerged during the three-day convention. I am sure it will prove useful to every individual and will be of special interest to researchers and practitioners involved in the development and growth of People with Disabilities.

Major H.P.S. Ahluwalia

ACKNOWLEDGEMENTS

I would like to thank all the people who have contributed to the success of this convention. In particular, I would like to thank Dr. A.K. Mukherjee, Prof. C.L. Kundu, Shri Lal Advani, Prof. P. Jeyachandran, Dr. M.N.G. Mani, Mrs. Rita Chatterjee, Shri M.S. Chhikara, Mr. J.L. Kaushik, Ms. Veena Choudhary, Ms. Anita Aggarwal, Mr. S.P. Parashar, Ms. Ritu Gosain and every participant for their interaction which contributed enormously to the success of the 'Summit'.

Dr. J.P. Singh

CONTENTS

Part II
PAPERS

LIST OF CONTRIBUTORS

Padma Bhushan Major H.P.S. Ahluwalia, Chairman, RCI, Indian Spinal Injuries Centre, Sector-C, Vasant Kunj, Opp. Vasant Valley School, New Delhi.

Dr. A.K. Mukharjee, Director General, Indian Spinal Injuries Centre, Sector-C, Vasant Kunj, Opp. Vasant Valley School, New Delhi.

Shri C. Gopal Reddy, Secretary, Ministry of Social Justice and Empowerment, Shastri Bhawan, New Delhi.

Prof. V.K. Gangarade, Vice Chairman, Gandhi Samriti and Darshan Samiti, Rajghat, New Delhi.

Maj. Gen (Retd.) Ranbir Bakshi, M.C. Chariman, RAPHAEL, P.O. Box No. 157, Dehradun, Uttranchal.

Dr. Satyanarayan Jatia, Hon'ble Minister, Ministry of Social Justice and Empowerment, Shastri Bhawan, New Delhi.

Dr. J.P. Singh, Member Secretary, RCI, 23-A, Shivaji Marg (Near Karampura Complex), New Delhi.

Mrs. Aloka Guha, Chairperson, National Trust, 4, Vishnu Digamber Marg, New Delhi.

Ms. Annie Shyam, Spastic Society of Tamil Nadu, Opp. T.T.T.I., Taramani Road, Chennai (T.N.).

Dr. Bhushan Punani, Executive Director, Blind Peoples Association, Dr. Vikram Sarabhai Road, Vastrapur, Ahmedabad, Gujarat.

Prof. G. Guru, M.P. Bhoj (Open) University, Campus II, I.T.I., Gas Rahat Building, Govindpuri, Bhopal (M.P.).

Dr. C. Tulsi Das, Deva Integrated School for the Handicapped, B-21/100, Bind Bhavan, Kamachh Chungi, Varanasi (U.P.).

Prof. H.P. Dikshit, Vice Chancellor, Indira Gandhi National Open University (IGNOU), Maidan Garhi, New Delhi.

Dr. K.C. Panda, Ex-Principal, Regional College of Education, Chhayataru, D-25, Maitri Vihar, Chandrashekher Pur, Bhubaneshwar, Orissa.

Dr. D.K. Singh, Swargiya Dr. Yamuna Prasad Singh Seva Nidhi, Pirpainti, Bhagalpur, Bihar.

Dr. N. Vijayaditya, Director General, NIC, CGO Complex, New Delhi.

Mr. R. Rangasayoo, Ali Yavar Jung National Institute for the Hearing Handicapped, Kishenchand Marg, Bandra (W), Mumbai, Maharashtra.

Dr. K.N. Pavithran, National Institute of Speech & Hearing, Palace Road, Poojappura, Trivandrum, Kerala.

Ms. Swati Lahiri, Indian Institute of Cerebral Palsy (Formerly Spastic Society of Eastern India), P-35/1, Taratolla Road, Calcutta (W.B.).

Mr. Ashwini Kumar Aggarwal, National Association of Blind, Sector-V, R.K. Puram, New Delhi.

Dr. K.K. Sai, Scientist G, R&D Electronics and Promotion of Hardware Manufacturing, Ministry of Communication & IT, Electronics Niketan, 6, CGO Complex, New Delhi.

Dr. M.N.G. Mani, Director, International Human Resource Development Centre for the Disabled (IHRDC), Shri Ramakrishna Vidyalaya Post, Coimbatore (T.N.).

Prof. J.S. Grewal, Director, M.P. Bhoj Open University, Campus II, I.T.I., Gas Rahat Building, Govindpuri, Bhopal (M.P.).

Swami Atmaramanandaji Maharaj, Sri Ramakrishna Mission Vidyalaya, Coni, Coimbatore (T.N.).

Rita Mari, Guidance Home for the Adult Deaf Girls, Director, M-11, Ist Avenue, Ashok Nagar, Chennai (T.N.).

Mrs. Indumathi Rao, CBR Network (South Asia), 134, 1st Block, 6th Floor, 3rd Phase, III Stage, BSK, Bangalore, Karnataka.

Mr. Ankur Saxena, P.G. Department of Social Work, C/o A-3/7, Urmi Apts., Behind Convent School, Fatehgunj, Baroda, Gujarat.

Mr. Bhasker Yogendra Mehta, National Association for the Blind, Near Satyam Auto Service, Shreenagar Road 10, At & Po. Idar, Dist. Sabarkantha, Idar.

Ms. Anjali Agarwal, Samarthya, B-181, Mansarovar Garden, New Delhi.

Mr. Hiramath, Flexitorn, 114, 6th Cross, 6th Block, Kora Mangla, Bangalore, Karnataka.

Mr. M. Ramaswami, Mangalam South Unit, Adjacent, North Post Office, R.S. Gardner, Thirupati (A.P.).

Mr. Thakur Vijay Prasad, Thakur Hari Prasad Institute of Research and Rehabilitation for the Mentally Handicapped, Vivekanand Nagar, Dilsukh Nagar, Hyderabad (A.P.).

Shri Prasana Kr. Pincha, Action Aid, Ramakrishna Mission Road, Birubari, Guwahati, Assam.

Ms. Maria Kamalam, Institute of Rehabilitation Science, Holy Cross College, Tiruchirapalli (T.N.).

Mr. Sanjib Kumar Das, AROGYAM, Research and Rehabilitation Centre for Handicapped, AT/P.O. Chitrada, Dist. Mayurbhanj, Orissa.

Mr. K. Kanan, Samatvam, 124, MIG Flats, Prasad Nagar, New Delhi.

Prof. P.C. Upadhyay, Prof. of Mechanical Engineering, Institute of Technology, Banars Hindu University, Kamachha, Varanasi (U.P.).

Dr. M. Jayaram, Director, All India Institute for Speech & Hearing, Manus Gangothri, Mysore, Karnataka.

Shri Rakesh Arora, Director, Planning Commission, Yojana Bhawan, Parliament Street, New Delhi.

Ms. Samita Jayawant, All India Institute of Physical Medicine and Rehabilitation, Mahalaxmi Building, Haji Ali Park, Mumbai, Maharashtra.

Dr. (Mrs.) Uma Tuli, Chief Commissioner of Disability, 6, Bhagwan Das Road, New Delhi.

Mr. G.L. Karna, Hony. President, Society for Disability and Rehabilitation Studies, 6, Mahanandi (Old), Jawaharlal Nehru University, New Delhi.

Mr. Sanjiv Sachdeva, Samarthya, B-181, Mansarovar Garden, New Delhi.

Dr. P. Hanumantha Rao, Sweekar Rehabilitation Institute for Handicapped, Upkar Circle, Picket, Secunderabad (A.P.).

Prof. P. Jeyachandran, Vijay Human Services, # 4, Lakshmipuram, 3rd Street, Royapettah, Chennai (T.N.).

Ms. Anuradha Mohit, Consultant, NHRC, Indian Spinal Injury Centre, Sector-C, Vasant Kunj, Opp. Vasant Valley School, New Delhi.

Ms. Usha Dalvi, Ali Yavar Jung National Institute for the Hearing Handicapped, Kishenchand Marg, Bandra (W), Mumbai, Maharashtra.

Ms. Sumitra Mishra, E-2, Tarun Nagar, Part II, Opp. Arihant Nagar, Gurukul Road, Memnagar, Ahmedabad, Gujarat.

Mr. J.P. Gadkari, Karnataka Parents' Association for the Mentally Retarded Citizens, AMC Compound, Off. Hosur Road, Near Kidwai Memorial Hospital, Bangalore, Karnataka.

Dr. S. Hariharan, Principal, Co-operative Medical College, Kallore, Kochi, Kerala.

Mr. Anil Upendra Joshi, Sweekar, 9, Kasturba Gandhi Bhawan, 349/2, Bajaj Nagar, Nagpur, Maharashtra.

Shri S.C. Tripathi, Secretary (EE&L), Ministry of Human Resources Development, Shastri Bhawan, New Delhi.

Ms. Aparna Nandurkar, Ali Yavar Jung National Institute for the Hearing Handicapped, Kishenchand Marg, Bandra (W), Mumbai, Maharashtra.

Mr. L. Shanmugam, Integrated Education Implementation Committee, Service Centre for the Disabled, P.B. No. 56, St. Mary's HSS, Madurai (T.N.).

Dr. R. Ranganathan, Department of Special Education, Andhra University, Visakhapatnam (A.P.).

INTRODUCTION

India has probably anywhere between 60 million people with disabilities at all ages and living in diverse socio-economic environments. Their needs are dependent on a variety of factors including the family attitudes, the community attitudes, the socio-economic environment and even genetic endowment. Therefore, a host of services are required to deal with such variety of problems encountered by persons with disabilities.

The contribution of non-governmental organizations to the development of disability welfare in India is stupendous. The efforts of these NGOs in serving persons with disabilities are evident from the fact that the number of disabled persons served by the NGOs in the country is more than that of the beneficiaries being helped by both the central and state governments. Therefore, NGO movement in the field of disability is a formidable force and its strength needs to be capitalized by the government agencies for providing better services to persons with disabilities.

Need to involve NGOs in disability welfare is reflected in the policy framework of United Nations and in various international bodies. The Persons with Disabilities Act passed by the Parliament in 1995, amplifies the need for treating services for persons with disabilities with human dignity. Many conferences held in India since 1995 formulated action plans for implementation of various schemes to augment services for persons with disabilities in education, rehabilitation etc. The review meeting of the UN-ESCAP decade of the disabled conducted in Bangkok in 1999 resolved that the countries in the Asia and Pacific regions should promote the literacy level of persons with disabilities and it is mammoth task.

The recently concluded Osaka Forum has extended the UN-ESCAP decade of persons with disabilities to another 10 years and the international community is expected to address the needs for barrier-free, rights based and inclusive society. These declarations have lot of ramifications in the Indian scenario. The programmes for education initiated by the governments at both Central and State levels should ensure that children with disabilities are included in all activities. The Sarva Shiksha Abhiyan, which aims at providing education for all, should certainly include children with disability.

The Rehabilitation Council of India Act too emphasizes that the RCI should collaborate with various service providers to develop appropriate human resource to help persons with disabilities. The RCI has recognized more than 160 institutions in the country to offer manpower development programmes in various disability areas and more than 80 per cent of these organizations are managed by NGOs. Therefore, NGOs are the main stakeholders in realizing the mission of RCI. Still the mechanism of information sharing of the NGOs with RCI are not commendable. Therefore, the RCI opines that the time has come to bring the NGOs working in disability sector together and brainstorm on what they can offer together in synergizing the efforts in serving persons with disabilities in India.

RCI believes that the mental barriers between various organizations serving persons with disabilities should be removed and a congenial atmosphere be created so that the efforts become complementary rather than competitive in nature. It is in this context that the RCI is proposing to organize a three days' get-together with NGOs in India to deliberate on various issues pertaining to education, rehabilitation, creating awareness, capacity building, research, technology, etc. RCI treats this meeting as the "Summit of Minds".

Manpower Report of RCI estimated that a total of at least 3,63,000 professionals would be required to serve the 10 per cent of the disabled population all over the country in the Ninth Plan period whereas at present only about 21,000 professionals have been registered with RCI. Though the numbers of training institutions have increased from 22 to 160 wherein around 4,000 professionals are produced per annum. It will take more than a century to train adequate number of professionals unless innovative, imaginative and resourceful approach is adopted to accelerate the pace. This shows that although we have marched ahead the road forward is long, arduous and may call for allocation of resources, both human and material. The time has come to see that 3,000 NGOs working for the welfare of the persons with disabilities should chalk out strategies to achieve the vision of RCI in providing quality services at the doorstep by creating sufficient human resources for meeting the entire life-cycle need.

The volunteerism in India is as old as its ancient civilization. There are approximately one million voluntary agencies working in various sectors in the country. Of these more than 3,000 voluntary agencies are engaged for the welfare of the disabled. The Tenth Plan document has emphasized rightly that voluntary agencies can be a viable force for helping the people at large. Since these organizations have wide experience and are working for a longer time in the field, there is a strong need to have a close interaction between these voluntary agencies and Rehabilitation Council of India to achieve its vision of providing quality service at the doorstep.

For this reason, a convention has been called for a free exchange of ideas to carry out the programmes for the welfare of the persons with disabilities.

निराशा नहीं आशा

श्री वी. के. गंगाराडे

जब हम साथ-साथ चलतें हैं तो पग-पग दीये जल जाते हैं। विकलांगता शब्द कोष से ही हटा देना चाहिए क्योंकि विकलांगता कैसे है। हम सब लोग इस देश के नागरिक हैं और संसार के भी नागरिक हैं। अगर नागरिक हो गया तो नागरिक भेद-भाव कैसे हुआ। नेताशाही और नौकरशाही में नागरिक खो गया है। तो अभी आपने नागरिक ढूंढना है। अहलूवालिया साहब आप कभी मत सोचिये आप विकलांग हैं। मुकर्जी साहब आपने कहा Hope and Despair बहुत पुरानी बात है 1971 की, जब गांधी जी के सौ वर्ष हुए तो राष्ट्रीय सेवा योजना का कार्यक्रम शुरु करना था। मुझे कहा गया कि क्या आप इसको संभाल सकते हैं? मैंने कहा सरकार में रह कर नहीं, तो पूछा गया आप सरकार में क्यों नहीं आना चाहते? मैंने कहा मुझे सरकार में आकर मास्टर की Voice बोलनी पड़ेगी। विश्वविद्यालय में रहकर मैं अपनी आवाज बोल सकता हूँ। वहां पर एक विदेशी सलाहकार थे। मैंने उनसे कहा यह देश आशा पर जिन्दा है। आशा ही इस देश की सबसे बड़ी संपदा है। उन्होंने कहा कैसे? हमने कहा देखिए आप लोग मि. लिखते हैं। हम लोग श्री लिखते हैं। हर नाम के आगे 'श्री' मतलब लक्ष्मी, विद्वान, बहुत जानने वाला। मैं स्वयंसेवी संस्थाओं को बुलाऊँगा। हम आपसे कुछ नहीं चाहते हैं। सौ व्यक्ति स्वयंसेवी संस्थाओं से आए। पूरा राष्ट्रीय सेवा कार्य समय पर हो गया। हमें स्वयंसेवी की ताकत को जगाना है। उसे इकट्ठा करना है। उसको संगठित करना है। सबसे पहले स्वयंसेवी संस्था में मैंने एक पूरी किताब लिखी हुई है 'NGOs in India' जो भी व्यक्ति काम करे उसको साधक बनना चाहिए। फिर शोधक बनाना चाहिए क्योंकि हम लोग काम तो बहुत करते हैं लेकिन उस पर मनन या शोध नहीं करते हैं। साधक और शोधक का साथ होना बड़ा जरूरी है। तब ही आप सेवक बन सकते हैं।

गाँधी जी को एक बार एक पत्रकार ने पूछा कि जब आपको कठिनाई होती है तो आप क्या करते हैं? जब भी मुझे कठिनाई होती है तो मैं गीता पढ़ता हूँ जिसके श्लोक पढ़कर मुझे ताकत मिलती है। गाँधी जी बार-बार कहा करते थे गीता के छठे अध्याय में पाँच श्लोक हैं जिसका अंग्रेजी अनुवाद है "Raise yourself by yourself, you are your best friend, you are also your best enemy" यह कहावत है "God helps those who help themselves"। एक अंग्रेज ने एक बार सेवाग्राम में गांधी जी से सेवा का मंत्र पूछा। कुछ देर बाद अंग्रेज ने गांधी जी से फिर पूछा आपने मुझे बताया नहीं सेवा किसे कहते हैं? गांधी जी ने कहा क्या तुम्हें अभी तक समझ में नहीं आया सेवा किसे कहते हैं। गांधी जी ने कहा मैं मानव की सेवा में भगवान को देख रहा हूँ। जब तक मैं ये सेवा नहीं करूंगा तब तक भगवान मुझे नहीं मिलेगा। जब पहली बार आदमी चांद पर पहुँचा तो न्यूयार्क के मेयर से पूछा तुम्हारा क्या perception है। उसने कहा "How soon can I deposit my garbage on the Moon" फिर लोगों से पूछा तो उन्होंने कहा कि क्या चांद पर हमें कार पार्क करने की जगह मिलेगी?

गांधी जी कहा करते थे सबसे पहले दिमाग को ठीक करिए। दिमाग से फिर आप दिल में पहुँचेंगे। फिर आप समाज का ढांचा ठीक कर सकते हैं।

सबसे पहले मैं यह कहना चाहूँगा कि विकलांग व्यक्ति को अपने आप को विकलांग नहीं समझना चाहिए। कभी भी निराशावादी नहीं होना चाहिए। हमेशा आशावादी होना चाहिए स्टीफन हॉकिंस, विश्व के एक महान वैज्ञानिक अभी देश में आए थे। उनका दिमाग ठीक है लेकिन उनकी सिर्फ एक उंगली ही कार्य करती है। उनके बराबर कोई भी गणितज्ञ हुआ नहीं है। इसलिए कभी भी अपने आप को कमजोर मत समझो। किसी परिवार को भी यह नहीं सोचना चाहिए कि हमने उस जन्म में कोई पाप किए होंगे इसलिए ऐसा बच्चा पैदा हुआ। महाभारत के समय में भी संचार माध्यम बहुत थे। जब दुर्योधन इन्द्रप्रस्थ में गया जो जहाँ उसने फर्श समझा वहां पानी निकला, द्रोपदी ने क्या कहा 'अंधे के पुत्र अंधे ही होते हैं'। उन दो शब्दों ने पूरा महाभारत रच डाला। यह एक Communication का असर था। अगर आप विज्ञान और तकनीक का असल भी देखें तो पाँडव कितने बड़े वैज्ञानिक थे। इसलिए कभी विकलांग को विकलांग मत कहिए। उनका भी साहस बढ़ाइए। हमें उनका मनोबल बढ़ाना है। इस प्रकार का सम्मेलन हर वर्ष होना चाहिए। मैं अपने वैज्ञानिकों से

अनुरोध करूंगा कि क्या वे विकलांगों के लिए या विकलांगता के क्षेत्र में कुछ शोध, कुछ खोज कर सकते हैं जिससे उनकी विकलांगता कम हो सके। जिस प्रकार अंधे बैंत के सहारे चलते हैं तो कितना अच्छा हो जाता है। मैं मनोवैज्ञानिकों को भी कहूंगा कि घर में किस प्रकार का वातावरण बनाये रखा जाये जिससे उनमें निराशा पैदा न हो।

Depression (निराशा) महिलाओं में बहुत अधिक होता है। इसमें भी हमें शोध करना चाहिए। अगर आप सभी यह ठान लें कि हमें यह कार्य करना है तो कोई ऐसा कार्य नहीं है जिसे हम नहीं कर सकते।

इस संस्था को दस वर्ष हो गये हैं इसे अब आगे कदम बढ़ाना चाहिए। आप अलग-अलग विशेषज्ञ समितियां बनायें जो अपना ध्यान उसी कार्य में लगायें जो उनको दिया गया है। मै मंत्री जी से निवेदन करूंगा कि जो संस्थाओं और परिषद् का निवेदन है उसे अमल में लाइए।

सेवा ही संकल्प

डा. सत्यनारायण जटिया*

सेवा भी एक इबादत है। आज का यह समारोह ऐसे सभी सेवा करने वाली संस्थाओं, संगठनों और महानुभावों का एक आतिथ्य सम्मेलन है।

जहां तक वैज्ञानिक आधार की बात है, जहां तक इस सेवा का प्रकल्प शुरू करने का विषय है वह तो है। सेवा के प्रकल्प में संकल्प की आवश्यकता है। सेवा में संकल्प ही चाहिए। अपने काम को प्रसन्न्तापूर्वक करना ही सेवा है। जो भी काम मिला। काम कोई छोटा या बड़ा होता नहीं है। इसलिए हमारे यहां कहा गया है कि सेवा ही पूजा है। पूजा वो पूजा है जो बिना किसी संशय के होना चाहिए हम जानते हैं कि सेवा कि लिए धैर्य चाहिए। ऐसे कहा जा सकता है कि उस की याद आई है, सांसों जरा धीरे-धीरे चलो। धड़कने भी इबादत में खलल करती हैं। सेवा करते समय हमें किसी भी प्रकार का अंहकार नहीं करना चाहिए। सेवा करते हुए किसी भी बात का अभिमान नहीं करना चाहिए। कुछ संगठन के लोग आकर झगड़ा कर देते हैं, आपको पता नहीं है हम कितनी बड़ी सेवा कर रहे हैं। आप समझते नहीं हैं। हमने कहा हम समझते नहीं हैं इसलिए तो आप इतना बोल रहे हैं। अगर हम समझ लिये होते तो इतना मौका ही नहीं मिलता आप से बात करने का। आप क्या समझाना चाहते हैं बताइये। वे गुस्से में बोल देते हैं। गुस्सा विवेकशीलता को खत्म कर देता है। यह भी एक विकलांगता है तो वो दिखाई देती है। किंतु शरीर ही व्यक्ति के व्यक्तित्व का प्रतिबिंब नहीं है। किसी भी शरीर की रचना में शरीर, बुद्धि और आत्मा काम करते हैं। किसी भी व्यक्ति के बारे में बात करते हैं, विकलांगता के बारे में बात करते हैं तो यदि मानसिक विकलांगता भी है फिर भी इसकी कुछ विशेष क्षमतायें हैं ही। मैंने प्रायः देखा है कि जिसमें

* माननीय मंत्री, सामाजिक न्याय एवं अधिकारिता मंत्रालय, भारत सरकार

कोई क्षमता नहीं होती, जो शक्ति है वह दूसरी ओर चली जाती है। वो कहीं ना कहीं लक्षणता के रूप में प्रकट होकर आती है। हमने वामन अवतार का नाम भी सुना है। उन्होंने तीन पग में दुनिया को नापने का काम कर लिया था। तीन पग में कर लिया मतलब वो सृष्टि के बारे में जानने की क्षमता रखते थे। सृष्टि में कहाँ क्या हो रहा है यह पता करने की समझ थी। अष्टावक्र के बारे में भी यही है। इस दृष्टि से कुछ लोगों को विलक्षण दृष्टि प्राप्त होती है। उस का सही प्रयोग करा जाये यह जरूरी है। कोई भी व्यक्ति बिना किसी शिक्षा या अभ्यास के कार्य नहीं कर सकता। यदि किसी व्यक्ति को जन्म से ही एकांत में छोड़ दिया जाए, तो वो जिसे देखता आया है उस जैसा ही बर्ताव करेगा। मनुष्य होने के बावजूद भी उसे शिक्षा की आवश्यकता होती है। प्रशिक्षण की आवश्यकता होती है। प्रशिक्षण के माध्यम से ही उसकी प्रतिभा निखर के आती है। तो शिक्षण और प्रशिक्षण बहुत जरूरी है। यह अनुसंधान का विषय है कि उसको किस प्रकार की शिक्षा और प्रशिक्षण की आवश्यकता है और कोई भी व्यक्ति किस प्रकार से सीख सकता है। जैसे कि जो नहीं सुन सकते हैं उन्हें संकेतों से समझाने का काम हो रहा है। उन संकेतों से भी जो मैं बोल रहा हूँ समझाया जा रहा है। इसी प्रकार सूरदास जी देख नहीं सकते थे लेकिन वर्णन सुनकर भी हम वही देख रहे हैं जो खुली आँखों से दिखाई दे रहा है। लेकिन हम आँख बंद करके देखने की कोशिश करें तो दृष्टि बहुत दूर जा सकती है।

जो अनुभव में आ गया है वही श्रेष्ठ है। गीता के ग्यारहवें अध्याय में कहा गया है कि अभ्यास ही श्रेष्ठ ज्ञान है। अभ्यास से ज्ञान और ज्ञान से अनुभव और त्याग से शांति प्राप्त होती है। कुछ छोड़ने से कुछ प्राप्त होता है। क्या प्राप्त होता है यह व्यक्ति पर निर्भर करता है। कहते हैं गैर-सरकारी संगठन ऐसे संगठन हैं जो कुछ काम नहीं करते। जो काम करते हैं उनकी चिन्ता करिए दूसरे तो वैसे ही अपना काम बना लेंगें। जो काम करते हैं उसकी चिंता करनी चाहिए। मैंने देखा है कि ऐसे गैर-सरकारी संगठन आगे आते नहीं हैं वो अपने से ही संसाधन जुटाते रहते हैं, अपना काम करते रहते हैं और सरकारी उसकी प्रक्रिया में आने के बाद सरकारी प्रक्रिया से गुजरना पड़ता है। वहां पर एक System है। वह यह नहीं देखता क्या सही है क्या गलत है। जो कागज पर लिखा है वही सही है। इस System में सही क्या है यह पता करने के लिए एक विधि बनाई जाये, यह मेरी कोशिश है। हम ऐसी संस्थाओं

को ढूंढ-ढूंढ कर आगे लाने का प्रयास करें जो अच्छा काम कर रही हैं। हमारे पास संसाधन बहुत सीमित हैं लेकिन जितने भी संसाधन हैं उनको सम्मानपूर्वक उन तक पहुँचाना चाहिए। कुछ अनुभवी लोगों को आगे आना चाहिए जो निरीक्षण के द्वारा पता लगा सकें कि सही क्या है। अगर सही पता लग गया तो ऐसी संस्था को मदद करने में कोई प्रतिकूलता नहीं होनी चाहिए।

इससे पहले मैं श्रम मंत्रालय में था। जब सामाजिक न्याय मंत्रालय में भेजा गया तो सोचा सामाजिक न्याय क्या होता है ? सामाजिक न्याय का अर्थ क्या है ? मैंने कहा सामाजिक अन्याय का ना होना ही सामाजिक न्याय है। न्याय का अर्थ है अन्याय किसी भी रूप में न होना न्याय है। सभी भारत के लोगों के लिए संविधान में कहा गया है। हमने ही करना है। किसी के प्रति दुर्भाव न हो, किसी के प्रति द्वेष न हो, किसी के प्रति विसंगति न हो। हमने बनाया है। उसी को अर्पित कर दिया है, तेरा तुझ को अर्पण क्या लागे मेरा, क्या तेरा और क्या मेरा। हम 50 वर्ष से कहते आ रहें हैं। अभी भी समझ नें नहीं आया तो कौन समझायेगा। हमें ही समझना है और हमें ही करना है।

शिकायतें बहुत हैं लेकिन जिनको शिकायतें करने की आदत हो गई है उनके बारे में मुझे कुछ कहना नहीं है। किंतु अपने पर भरोसा रख करके, कौन बैठा रहे अंदेशाएं फरदा लेकर, मुतबिन हूँ तेरी विस्वत का सहारा लेकर अपनी क्षमता पर भरोसा है। जिसको अपनी क्षमता पर भरोसा हो वह प्रश्न नहीं उठाया करता। सभी प्रश्नों का उत्तर यही है कि अपनी क्षमताओं का पूर्ण रूप से सदुपयोग करने का रास्ता निकालें।

आज के सम्मेलन में बहुत महत्वपूर्ण विषय रखे गये हैं। पुनर्वास करना, उनकी क्षमताओं के अनुरूप पुनर्वास करना। हमारे देश में मुश्किल यह है कि जो भी क्षमताएं हैं हम उनका ठीक से समायोजन नहीं कर पाते। जिस बात में मनुष्य की रूचि होती है उसमें कभी थकान नहीं होती। जिसमें रुचि नहीं होती उसे जबरन करना पड़ता है। इसी प्रकार जिन स्वयंसेवी संस्थाओं की सेवा में रुचि है वो अपना कार्य सुचारू रूप से कर रही हैं।

हमारे सामने चुनौतियाँ हैं और उनका सामना करने का साहस हमें जुटाना होगा। विकलांगता भी एक चुनौती है। इस क्षेत्र में जागरूकता पैदा करने की आवश्यकता है। दूर गांवों में जाना होगा। मैंने देखा है कि मेरे जिले में 35,000 विकलांग लोग हैं। अभी तक हम 7,000 लोगों तक पहुँच पाये हैं। 35,000 लोगों तक पहुँचने के लिये क्या करना चाहिए ? हमने कहा एक वर्ष

में सबका पता लगाओ और इस को पूरा करो। गांव में जाने के लिये साधन नहीं हैं। विकलांगों की सेवा करने के लिये स्वयंसेवी संगठन तय कर लेंगे तो जायेंगे। इसलिए संकल्प के साथ काम करने की जरूरत है।

संसार की स्मर स्थलों में धीरता धारण करो, चलते हुए इष्ट पगों पर संकटों से मत डरो, अति धीरता के साथ अपने कार्य में तत्पर रहो, विपत्तियों के वार सारे वीर बनकर सहो, भय बाधाएं मुक्त हो जायेंगी, होगी सफलता, आत्म में कृति फैलेगी हमारी चंहु ओर।

दीगरीगंध में हमारे माननीय राष्ट्रपति जी और प्रधानमंत्री जी ने कहा है कि इस देश को विकसित देश बनाना चाहते हैं विकलांगों के प्रति उन लोगों की बहुत चिंता है। देश के राष्ट्रपति जिस बात की चिंता करते हों, प्रधानमंत्री करते हों, आप लोग करते हों, वो बात कठिन होगी, मैं ऐसा नहीं मानता। इसी विश्वास को लेकर जो समर्थ लोगों को दे दिया है उनका दायित्व है कि जो क्षमता उनको मिल गई है, बाकि के लोगों को दें, जिनके पास नहीं हैं। प्रकृति ने तुझे जीवन दिया है, तू भी तो कुछ दे। परोपकार के फल का जीवन ये, परोपकार के जीवन में भी सेवा का भाव देखना।

मैं एक परिपूर्ण सिंधू
है ये मेरा अपना समाज
मेरा इसका संबंध मर्मय
व्यक्ति यह है मेरा समाज
इससे पाया तन मन
इससे मैंने पाया जीवन
मेरा तो कर्तव्य यहीं कर दूं
सब्र कुछ इसको अपर्ण।

जो कुछ भी कहता हूँ, मेरा कुछ भी नही हैं, वो समाज का है, इसलिए समाज से मैंने प्राप्त किया है उसी को लौटा रहा हूँ। हम यह चाहेंगे कि कोई भी व्यक्ति इस अक्षमता के, इस विकलांगता के साथ रह रहे हों, उनकी शिक्षा, प्रशिक्षण और पुनर्वास हमारी जिम्मेवारी है। सरकार तो इस क्षेत्र में प्रयत्नशील है लेकिन लोगों को इस बारे में जागरूक बना देना एक कठिन काम है। जिसकी अर्थिक क्षमता बढ़ जाती है उसकी घर में भी कदर होती है। किसी की Ability इस बात में नहीं है कि वो स्वस्थ है पर इस बात पर है कि वो अपनी क्षमताओं का उपयोग किस प्रकार कर रहा है। मेरा देश अभी गांव में

है और गांव में संदेश जाना बाकी है। आप लोग ही यह संदेश गांव-गांव तक पहुंचा सकते हैं। जो भी इस प्रकार का प्रयास करेगा हम उसकी सहायता करेंगे। इसमें कोई कठिनाई नहीं है। सरकार जो कार्य करना चाहती है उसका लोगों को पता ही नहीं होता। यदि आप इस प्रकार का आयोजन करके लोगों तक पहुंचाने के कार्य करते हैं तो इस बात का अभिनंदन किया जायेगा। सरकार ने 85 संस्थानों पर जिला पुनर्वास केन्द्र स्थापित किये हैं। राष्ट्रीय संस्थान डिग्री और डिप्लोमा चला रहे हैं। हमने कोशिश की है उनको कहीं रोजगार उपलब्ध कराया जा सके। लोगों को जागरूकता बढ़ने के कारण उनका लाभ मिलने वाला है। पुनर्वास में अनुसंधान की आवश्यकता है। पुनर्वास में सूचना प्रद्यौगिकी के प्रयोग की आवश्यकता है। हमारी तीन दिन की कार्यशाला का क्या निष्कर्ष निकल कर आये, बहुत कड़ा निष्कर्ष निकालने की जरूरत नहीं है। निकालें तो अच्छा है। जो भी बातें निकल कर आयेंगी वो सरकार के कार्यक्रम और नितियां होंगी। वो हमारा मार्गदर्शन करने के लिए उपयुक्त होंगी।

आपका यह संकल्प नये क्षितिज बनाये और उसमें सभी लोग सुखी और समृद्ध हों यही कामना करता हूँ।

क्षितिज तक प्रत्येक दिशा में हम उठें प्राण भरने,
नव सृजन को साध लें हू उठें निर्माण करने।
साधना के दीप शुभ हो ज्ञान का आलोक छाये,
नष्ट तृष्णा के तीर हो धाम अपना जगमगाये।

PART I

PROCEEDINGS

THE FIRST WORD

Padmabhusan Major H.P.S. Ahluwalia

It gives me great pleasure in welcoming Hon'ble Minister for Social Justice and Empowerment, Dr. Satyanarayan Jatiya Ji, Prof. V. K. Gangarade, Gen. Bakhshi, Mrs. Rajwant Sandhu, Dr. Mukherjee, Dr. Uma Tuli, Mrs. Aloka Guha, Dr. Jubei, Director, St. Raffel Hospital and distinguished participants to this unique Convention, the Summit of the Mind. We are extremely fortunate to have with us Hon'ble Minister who is not only a great poet, a scholar but also a grass roots level worker. It is very easy for us to relate with him, so much so that for this Convention, when I went to him without any appointment (I should not have done that), he was leaving for the Parliament but he was so gracious as to meet me and also readily agreed to inaugurate this Convention.

The month of May is generally considered hot and dusty but for the Mountaineers it is an auspicious month as all major climbs including Mt. Everest fall in this very month. My climb to Mt. Everest was also in this month on 29th May, 1965. Therefore, I firmly believe that this meeting of minds would enable us to scale greater heights. It is our perception that the problem of education, employment, social attitudes, peer acceptance is common to all disabilities. For this reason, the Rehabilitation Council of India has brought all the NGOs looking after various disabilities together on one forum which has not been done before. I hope this Convention will be a trendsetter and will expand knowledge and understanding of all the disabilities. The major task before us, in my opinion, is manpower development. You are perhaps, aware that the manpower report of RCI has identified gaps in the requirement of manpower in the rehabilitation field. It recommended training of approximately half a million specialists. Indeed, for any country, it is a daunting task to prepare human resource of such a great magnitude. In spite of the efforts of the academic institutions, government and the NGOs, we still have a backlog of very high proportion. We can have any number of training centres but where are the teachers? How do we solve this problem? In my opinion, Information Communication Technologies have great potential to accelerate the human resource development. Relying on satellite based communication systems, we will be able to utilize the expertise in the most efficient manner. Experts from a central location will interact with learners, carers and others at various centres throughout the country and all centres will be served simultaneously by one group of experts. This will not only ensure speed but also quality in the standards of teaching. RCI is in the process of providing infrastructure to down link via satellite. The government has already given sanction to begin with 25 equipped centres and I can assure you they will be functional by 22nd of June. I won't be surprised if the next meeting of the minds is via satellite engaging thousands of minds from all parts of the country, I will assure that it happens sooner than later. As you are aware RCI has given equal importance to the needs of all categories of people with disabilities. In certain areas our performance has been outstanding. There are areas where improvement is needed. The courses on autism, learning disability and multiple disability need to be strengthened. I would request you to share your thoughts, experiences and even frustrations with us. It is quite possible that some of you have found answers to these problems while others are trying to grapple with them. Therefore, I would be happy if you could generously share your experiences with us.

Being a person with disability I am aware of the fact that if we keep on talking of long-term goals without taking into consideration the needs of persons with disability at the grass roots level, we would in some way be failing in our duty. It is for this reason that RCI has established seven Zonal Committees for better coverage through a decentralized system. Each Zonal Committee has a Media Sub-Committee and their basic aim is to address the issues at the grass roots level. We have employed traditional and distance educational strategies for various types of courses, particularly for in-service professionals or care givers. Courses which bring immediate benefit to the person with disability are extremely popular so are the other courses like Foundation Course for Elementary in-house teachers, B. Ed. (Special Education). Other courses for parents and teachers would be launched shortly by MP Bhoj Open University and IGNOU. I believe there are 3000 NGOs working relentlessly for the empowerment of people with disability. India is known all over the world for the good work done by NGOs. I wonder why only about 200 NGOs have come forward to deliver RCI recognized courses. We invite each one of you to be a partner with us.

Next month RCI will be completing 10 years of its existence. During this decade RCI has had many achievements to its credit. So the important task for this Convention is to suggest strategies looking forward which must take into account the lessons of the past and see how our perception of disability undergoes a significant change to ensure that every person with disability becomes an asset to the community. Please spell out a clear programme of action with tenable goals in a reasonable timeframe. I wish each one of you great luck in scaling the roar Everest in empowering the persons with disability. In the end, I once again on behalf of the Rehabilitation Council of India team and on my own behalf, thank the Hon'ble Minister for inaugurating this auspicious Convention and I thank each one of you, NGOs for your enthusiastic response.

Thank you.

ISSUES IN MIND

Dr. A K Mukherjee

The disability issue should be analyzed along with the socio-economic development of any nation because they are all inter-linked. At the beginning of the 21st century, we stand at the cross-roads with hope and despair. Hope because there has been a great development, despair because the progress has been either inadequate or not reachable. Today India's GDP, which is one of the important signs of growth, stands at around US $ 450 billion considering 8 per cent growth rate as envisaged by the Planning Commission it will take 30 years to reach the present level of China. Is our development comparable to many fast growing nations in the South East Asian region? The answer is an obvious no. Besides the literacy rate in India today, more than 300 million illiterate Indians today are marching towards future. If this trend continues what happens during the vast multitude of 20 years. This will be another warning for the nation. Prof. Prahlad, an international management Guru who visited CII only three weeks back, referred to those groups who are rural, illiterate, poor and form the bottom of social pyramid, as a segment which determines India's success and future. To make an effective change, there is need for a strong leadership with clear vision to identify a road map for sustainable development. This can happen only if an effective partnership between government, private and voluntary agencies is established. The voluntary agencies are also called as the third force. There is a need for India to harness the third force to move faster for growth and prosperity. The word 'volunteerism' comes from the Latin word 'voluntes' meaning thereby the inner will. From the time of antiquity, the ancient Indian culture has propagated the philosophy that "service to the mankind is the service to the God and that is why the Vedas said that there is no other way". Over the last 20 years there has been an explosion in international civil society networks. As per Elvin Toffler, a famous futurologist, not really a horoscope reader, the rise of NGOs is due to non-responsive political system. They represent otherwise the unrepresented voices of people concerned with a specific problem. They should also form a fundamental partner of any government system. The Hunting of Class, the book on classes of civilization mentions three waves for social development for any nation. The first wave is agricultural revolution, the second is industrial and the third is knowledge based revolution. The third wave leads to pluralism where non-stick actors, who are NGOs influence policies and programmes in a civil society. This is legitimate power in a democratic setup. In the international scene the first NGO against the anti-slavery Act was registered in 1839. Since then there has been a rapid expansion of NGOs among middle and lower income groups primarily. One NGO was coined by the United Nations in early 1950s and during the last decade of the last century the growth of NGOs in the social sector is the highest, standing at 78.5 per cent and next highest percentage of increase is in the health sector. In 1997 more than 7 billion aids flowed to the developing countries through the NGOs. The survey in 1996 recognized that India has the largest number of NGOs in the world, almost 10 lakhs. There is a growing concern about the accountability among the NGOs. The newest form of accountability offers the more participatory form and is known as judicial accountability meaning thereby balanced and voiced approach. This system does not correct any bad decision but it can publicise the wrong decision and encourage the organization to reconsider the decision. The disabled people form the world's largest minority. As per WHO, India has the second highest load from disability and this is on the increase, survey in 1991 and 2001 shows 1 per cent increase in the number.

For this country 1 per cent is very high. Planning Commission report of 2002 recognizes the deficiency in addressing the disability issue into three factors. They are inadequate resources, the lack of integrated approach and social insensitivity. The Tenth Plan has emphasized basically the need of the rural disabled and more support to voluntary organizations. In India, Government has allocated Rs.510 crore in the Tenth Plan for NGOs working in the disability sector which is double the amount in Ninth Plan. While there are 10,000 NGOs as per the Planning Commission report in the social sector, 1/20 th of NGOs have received financial support from the Ministry of Social Justice and Empowerment in the disability sector. While in some of the States NGOs are totally missing, the States like Arunachal and Assam have received grant for one NGO each.

RCI in a decade has made enormous contribution in human resource development and is also playing a pro-active role to enhance the effectiveness of NGOs in the disability field. The countdown has begun for a massive national movement and RCI has given a wake up call for all with the following objectives: To bring under a common platform the largest number of NGOs working for the disabled, to share the strengths and weaknesses of RCI programmes, to identify priority programmes for RCI from the NGOs perspective, and to establish functional relationship between NGOs and RCI within the framework of RCI Act. What would developed India look like in a decade's time? Our President Dr. Abdul Kalam believes "knowledge powered rural development is the essential need for transforming India". But the question is how and when the country can reach that stage. For that country needs the vision which can be measured, monitored and can be achieved. In this context may I humbly suggest following points for your consideration:

I believe there is a need for establishing a National Commission on Disability. In fact, Dr. Jatiya has been a pioneer for establishing the National Commission on Labour. There is a need for a functional advisory body. Many times many good programmes of the government are not known to us. They may be on white paper which government can take up in future. Recognize an apex coordination body for NGOs which does not exist in the country today. Grant for more NGOs, encourage NGOs in the weaker States and the target must be fixed for all government programmes, extensive use of information technology, awareness programmes from Panchayats to State Legislators, encourage State and Rural NGOs meeting, support RCI from the leadership not only in this country but in the SAARC region. India should also project now as an international leader and may host the global meeting on disability. People of the world will know what we are. As the need for globalisation has struck South East Asia, India should pass its ride into future. May I remind this august body a unique astronomical phenomenon at the time of 7th May, the sun, the mercury and the earth have come in one line, this will not be repeated more than dozen times in this century. Trust me, RCI has brought government, NGOs and the people interested in disability on one platform. In Roman history, the mercury is also the messenger of law. I hope RCI does not follow the astronomical tradition and we will be meeting very soon as the Chairman of RCI has mentioned. It is a great moment to welcome the rest of the 21st century.

ABILITY IN DISABILITY

Mrs. Rajwant Sandhu

The Ministry of Social Justice and Empowerment is the nodal Ministry concerning all matters relating to disability. The traditional approach for NGOs has been to deal with single disability like blindness, hearing impairment, locomotor impairment or mental retardation. However, in the present day scenario regarding incidence of disability, development of new technology and spread of educational services has shown us that many problems are common to all disabilities and therefore a cross-disability approach is the imperative need of the hour if we are to use our material resources optimally. The Ministry is very happy that the RCI has convened this All India Cross-Disability Convention to consider common issues and challenges in the new millennium. Challenges also give us opportunities to develop new programmes and deliver new services and perhaps this Convention will be able to identify challenges and opportunities. The Government of India has been endeavouring to develop programmes for the education and rehabilitation of persons with disabilities. The work began soon after independence and is continuing in both Ministry of Human Resource Development and our Ministry. The Ministry of Health and Rural Development have also taken active interest. As an example I can cite that 3 per cent of all poverty alleviation funds are earmarked for persons with disabilities. However, these funds are not utilized adequately. I hope this Convention will also consider the issue of access to resources. Our Ministry is operating a number of schemes that directly benefit persons with disabilities. Under ADIP, aids and appliances are delivered to large number of persons with disabilities, specially to those who cannot afford to procure them on their own. The National Institutes of the Government of India have been helping in manpower development, distributing aids and appliances, organizing camps, conducting research to develop new approaches to the emerging challenges in the field of disability. We plan to set up more than 130 district disability rehabilitation centres to deliver services in a decentralized manner. This is an attempt to increase outreach. We have also set up five composite regional centres again with the objective of training at the decentralized level and to deliver important services effectively to persons with disabilities. The RCI Act was enforced in June, 1993. It is nearly 10 years since the enforcement and the last decade has witnessed significant changes in the human resource development. Rehabilitation and special education both require services of trained professionals. Twenty years ago there was hardly any institute imparting regular training to serve persons with disabilities. Today it is heartening to see that over 22,000 professionals are registered with RCI. RCI is probably the only body in the world set up by an Act of Parliament to standardize, regulate and monitor the training of professionals in rehabilitation and special education. During the Tenth Plan period we are sure we will see far-reaching changes and much wider facilities and activities are offered to persons with disabilities. We also have to ensure that people with disabilities are mainstreamed. For this purpose the cross-disability approach is of crucial importance as no comprehensive rehabilitation can be provided unless multi-disciplinary and cross-disability approach is adopted. I hope that the recommendations of this Conference will enable us to prepare a road map for developing new programmes and to meet the emergent needs of persons with disabilities so that in this new millennium there are new opportunities and human rights of persons with disabilities are fully recognized and the beginning of empowerment is available as a matter of right. Let us resolve at this Convention that every person with a disability shall be recognized as a person who has a potential as a citizen equal in all respects in this country. Just as we are trying to abolish gender differences so let us also try to resolve all differences among men and women on the basis of disability. Let us discover ability in disability and develop respect and regard for all those who have ability and who can contribute despite their disabilities to the enrichment of our society.

Thank you.

EXPRESSIONS

Maj. Gen. (Retd.) Ranbir Bakhshi

It is a great pleasure and honour for me to be a Guest of Honour at this important Convention most appropriately named as "Summit of the Mind". The staggering figure of 10 per cent population of our country suffering from some form of disability calls for a unified action by all agencies working in this field to ameliorate the sufferings of the handicapped. All such organizations be they government or non-government can put in maximum effort to relieve the suffering of the disabled, if they imbibe the latest concepts and techniques adopted by some of the organizations working in this field. Today much water has flown under the bridge in the field of disability mainly due to widespread awareness and awakenness of the society. It is imperative, therefore, that we all keep abreast of the emerging techniques and latest innovations in different facets of disability management, be it providing relief, training or rehabilitation. For different types of benefits either having a government backing through legislations or being made available through charitable trusts and organizations, it is advisable that development of human resources in the field of disability be planned and executed judiciously and meaningfully.

The themes being discussed in this Convention are most appropriate and are befitting with the need of the hour. I have no doubt that the participants would freely exchange their views, ideas and share their experiences so that at the end of the Convention each one of us is more educated and better equipped to carry out our responsibilities more efficiently and more effectively.

DR. J.P. SINGH

I would like to thank the Hon'ble Minister for his speech and assure him that we will try to come up to his expectations. All the participants will remember your enlightening speech and will discuss for the next two days, the way you have guided us.

Equally enlightening was the speech of Madam Rajwant Sandhu. Her words will guide the Convention so that we come out with the recommendations which are useful to the government, to the society and in particular to the people with disabilities. My sincere thanks are due to her and I hope that her wisdom and experience will always be available to RCI.

When I requested Prof. V.K. Gangarade, he agreed to our request and graced the occasion and we thank him for the same.

Gandhiji was always champion of the weak, no section of the society is weaker than the people with disabilities. For centuries they have been denied the necessities of life. Gandhiji fought for the rights of the untouchables. We have learnt lot of things from Gandhiji's philosophy. The condition of many people with disabilities is worst, they have no means of living. Prof. Gangarade, Vice-Chairman, Gandhi Smriti and Gandhi Darshan Samiti has expressed Gandhiji's concern for the weaker sections of the society. His empathy for disabled will help the delegates to reach worthwhile conclusions. Therefore, I would like to express my sincere thanks to Prof. Gangarade for his valuable remarks.

Maj. Gen. Bakhshi, he is the seniormost person here today, he has been a source of inspiration and his continuous effort in supporting the cause is worth praising. He has taken the initiative of promoting all our programmes in Uttaranchal and he is pursuing the State Government to do something in the State. I thank you Sir, for taking this responsibility of the Council. We will see that Himalayan region is not left out and whatever is possible is done.

I will be failing in my duty if I don't thank the speakers in advance, chairmen, co-chairmen and others who are equally distinguished and who have consented to contribute to the deliberations of this Convention. I also thank all the delegates who have come here spending their money and I hope they will enjoy the Convention and their stay in Delhi despite the heat. I am sure with your co-operation the Council will be able to provide services at the doorstep of person with disability.

Before I conclude I would like to thank the staff of RCI and everyone else who participated in making this convention successful and I am sure the effort would be fruitful. The media, print and electronic, I cannot forget them. They have always helped the Council in creating awareness. I would like to thank them. In the end I would say that in unity lies the strength of power and when 500 minds get together we cannot but reach the Summit of the Mind so appropriately that every person with disability remembers and enjoys this unique occasion.

I

REHABILITATION IN THE NEW MILLENNIUM

CHALLENGES AND OPPORTUNITIES

Chairperson: Mrs. Aloka Guha
Co-Chairperson: Mr. T. Bardolai

DR. BHUSHAN PUNANI

When we talk about millennium challenges, the first thing is to come out of those traditional programmes, activities, which we have been doing for many years. The disability movement is a people's movement. We cannot isolate the sector and talk in isolation. We have to involve each and everybody in our programme in a very participative manner. We are looking for an inclusive society, where everybody has a right for everything like anybody else. Friends, this is possible only when we have participation of individual themselves, their family members, their community and of course the stake holders who are concerned with people with disabilities in any manner. We have to take rehabilitation as a matter of right, as a matter of human right. We just cannot talk of education in isolation. It is the right of the child, right of the individual to be educated and we have to take right issue, to the best possible manner, to the best extent possible so that everybody accepts the right of the individual.

Friends, we are getting used to few things. We always talk that there is a failure of the programme, we blame the system, we talk of lack of opportunities. We always think that the PwD Act is not being implemented which I am sure we are going to talk the whole day. We talk of limited resources and we talk of apathy of officials and service providers. These are the thoughts we are getting used to. But in the meantime we forget that we have tremendous challenges within the system. We have lot of opportunities within the community. There are so many resources which are available in the system even today. But the stake holders themselves have demonstrated that they have lot of potentials. They have gained lot of strength. They can themselves play a very important role if they are given the opportunity. There is wealth of knowledge. There are thousands of workers now who are professionals, personnel, who are devoted workers and if their experience is used we can do wonders. We have tremendous unutilized, wrongly utilized resources, infrastructure, establishment and knowledge. We can do much better with the resources available if we have better plans, better perspectives. As you all know the U.N. is ceased with the idea of taking up the Convention of the Human Rights of the disabled. All people are born equal, we cannot differentiate them by their birth. We have the same rights to survival, to education, to growth, to development and that commands there should be a convention on the rights of the disabled. Standing on this platform I urge everybody that we must prevail upon our government, our system, our NGOs, our organizations that India must express solidarity with the U.N. on the Convention on Human Rights. I hope you agree to that. That is the only way. Unless we take disability as a human right, we cannot make a dent, what we have not been able to do for 100 years, we may not do for the next millennium as well unless we take such bold outline. Some of you who are present will agree that the work being envisaged in Biwako framework is very much in line, very much in consonance with the policy India is pursuing at the moment. Our request, our challenge should be to adopt this millennium document as a policy document for India and already I think the process has been started. Government is planning to have a national consultation but as a group, we as professionals, we as NGOs, we as government officials must prevail upon the government that this document must be adopted, must be taken up as a policy document so that we can adopt many good things which according to me are very much in consonance with our thoughts and our policies.

Friends, I am going to make a very bold submission here, a very big challenge. We have been talking for many years, for many programmes, for many activities but still we do not have an independent Ministry which talks only of disability. In fact we have to talk of millions of people, we have to talk of huge resources, unless there is a focussed coverage, unless the people sitting there, understand the needs of people with disabilities, unless they are sensitized, unless we have something to identify this is our Ministry, these are our departments at the State level. Friends, this group must put a challenge before the government, before everybody that disability sector should have its own Ministry, its own departments, its own people, its own professionals, who understand disability better than what we do now.

In line with that, the next challenge according to me is that let us not talk of single category coverage, single activity, one room NGOs, these things are no more viable. When we are talking of millions of people to be covered in a short span of time, we have to develop a comprehensive, cross-disability, multi prong programmes to cover each and every person with disability, each and every combination of disability and these NGOs, these organizations must have a very high standard of accountability, transparency, viability and these NGOs must not act away from the people for whom they are working. There should be active participation of family members, service providers and most important persons with disabilities, not only in taking the services but in the management and policy formulations of these NGOs. Unless these drastic steps are taken, nothing much will be happening, we have to take all these measures at the earliest. We have to work on networking of the huge number of NGOs with the State Departments, State officials duplication, and top unutilized potentials to avoid. We have to pool our resources, we have to share our information, exchange our expertise and that will bring lot of synergy. 2 plus 2 is five, that is how the synergy is defined. Unless we are able to network, interface, and exchange our views, I am sure we cannot progress as much as we could be progressing. This networking should not be within the sector alone but outside with the whole developmental system. Unless the developmental system thinks of disabilities as the area of coverage, I am sure we are not going to make any tremendous progress which we are talking as challenges. In line with the networking of NGOs, the great potentials of the parents, DPOs. This is one area we have not progressed as much we should have done. Seeing our social fabric, seeing our love they neighbour, we have to encourage the parents to come forward. We have to encourage the people with disabilities to come forward, to form their organizations because they will understand, they will have more sensitivity about the concepts than anybody else. They will ensure the participation of PwDs, as I spoke earlier, they will understand the issues better. That will be expertise from within. This will have lot of demonstration effect on our developmental work and that is the only way we can empower the individuals, families and the parents, the community. That is the way we can progress better.

Now, I am raising a very interesting issue. It is very sad that when we come to developmental field, even for our staff the government says 'no' we do not pay the salaries, we give the honorarium just to avoid the legal tangles. We pay them the fixed salaries, why? How can the people face the challenge unless they are properly paid. Unless they are paid the salaries at least, this group I am sure has a challenge. Why disability sector should bow down to such dictates that staff will be paid honorarium not the salaries, not the scales, not the allowances. I am sure the time has come when we have to re-think of the ideas, thoughts, which are imposed upon us because of the legal factors. Is the legality concerning only our field? That is what we have to discuss.

Friends, again shifting to the disability sector, I am not going to talk much about barrier free environment that is a must. Unless we provide access to the built environment, and sensitivity of all concerned, may be builders, architects, local authorities, corporations, committees, I am sure access is never going to be possible. But a good beginning has been made. Let us take it forward and I suggest as a challenge there should be an authority which ensures barrier free environment in each and every manner and in a time frame which is decent and which is achievable.

Shifting to other area, RCI has done commendable work for standardizing courses for professionals and personnel in the field of disability. But lot needs to be done for the people themselves, for the disabled people themselves. If you want to improve the quality of training, quality of services, better equipment, better technology, better access and want to have minimum standards of intervention, the only way is to standardize courses, the training programmes which are being run for people with disabilities and have a system of their evaluation and monitoring of progress because, according to me, it is very important to have best quality programmes. I think the quality programme which meets the minimum standards that can be done and that is the mandate to RCI not only the programmes for professionals and personnel, but also the programmes which are for individuals, should be standardized and now the time has come that that process must be started.

Shifting to a very very important area. I am going to make a very bold submission. Pardon me, if you don't agree, and if you agree, please at the end of these five statements, do clap because that is going to change the whole situation. There is something called Kangaroo day, when they have a clean up operation. You clean up everything around you. There are things which you don't need, which are not required any more, which are not relevant, which are not effective, which are irrelevant throw them out. Unless you make space for new things change cannot occur. We have to accept this concept in the disability sector and I am going to make a very bold submission to our chairperson, all those things which are irrelevant, which are not relevant any more, all those concepts must be thrown out of the window. All the programmes which are ineffective, which have not fulfilled the aspirations of people with disabilities, must be discontinued. We have to give a second thought. Why should we provide training in caning the chairs, making of chalks, as the trades are no more existing? Please do not run programmes, vocations which are not relevant, don't run them for the sake of running, just because grant is available, just because donation is available, let us discontinue all those things which are no more effective in the present context. All the machinery, equipment, which is occupying your space, is not benefiting anybody in any way, please throw that away. Don't waste your infrastructure on that. You have to have a system which is functional, which is relevant, which is efficient. Last but most important, all those people who subscribe to out dated thoughts, who are not willing to live with the modern thoughts, who are not able to understand and appreciate the new concepts and new ideas, I am sure they have no business to hang around. I don't think we should have people who are not able to deliver the goods, in the present context, they must go or they must improve. There is no other option. Unless these drastic steps are taken, this millennium will be like the previous millennium.

Friends, another very bold submission all those institutions which isolate people by design, by the old system, those must be dismantled. They must give place to new concepts, new thoughts, new institutions. All those projects which advocate segregation, which take away people from the community to live there in isolation, they must go. They have no right to exist. That is against the issue of rights, against the issues of integration, against the issue of inclusion. All those who shelter the capable, people who don't need to be sheltered, people who are productive, people who are effective, why they should be sheltered. There is no business for these centres to continue because they are creating more disolance than rehabilitation. They must go, they must disappear from the face of this earth. All the training activities, which never result in income generation, employment or self-employment, economic rehabilitation, must disappear. In the name of rehabilitation resources are wasted. All such centres must be discontinued. They must disappear to give way to new concepts, new thoughts. All the services that never reach the target group, that are not resulted oriented, they must be discontinued. I leave it to you to vote if you agree, please clap, if you don't agree just forget. It is up to you, if you want to usher in a new era that ensures human rights, that ensures inclusion and complete development of not a chosen few but each and every person with disability, if that is the case this millennium will have the challenge not otherwise.

PROF. G. GURU

First of all I would like to express my gratitude to RCI for inviting me to this Convention to express my ideas. I would like to inform you that such a Convention was held about 5,000 years ago in the Mahabharat period and the topic of discussion was who is the greatest thing. More than 1,000 luminaries of that period had gathered there to give their ideas. Some told that the Sun is greater because it sustains the world, Vishnu is greater because it sustains the world, like that many topics were discussed. But in the end, some one said every one is greater in his own way. Nobody is better than the man. Mahatma Gandhi followed the same tradition, service to mankind is service to God.

The Theme of the discussion is Rehabilitation in the New Millennium: Challenges and Opportunities. The world is led by intelligence. Behind every action there is a thought. So automatically this discussion is a timely one. What are the challenges of the millennium we are facing? What are the opportunities? If we have proper perception, then only we will be able to do any work in the disability area. I have taken the subject of "Perception of Development in the New Millennium and fulfilling the needs and aspirations of people with disabilities" Now what is the significance of time? All of us while witnessing the unfolding of the world which is a state of dramatic transformation, social, economical, political, cultural as well as environmental. One of the saying was that whatever changes have occurred during the last 25,000 years of human history, within that 25 years much more demonstrative things are going to occur. The present generation is going to change the world twice. This is the significance of the time. This is significance of the debate that we are going to do. What are the challenges we are facing? What are the global trends that affect our development anywhere in the world? The developmental processes in the last century had led the attention of many numbers of people. I will just go to global trends in population growth and consumption pattern. In 1950 the population was 1.5 billion and became 6 billion in 2000. But what is the consumption pattern? In 1900 the consumption was 1.5 trillion dollar and after 50 years, it became 4 trillion and in 2000 it became 25 trillion. Though the population is increasing in one way, so far as the consumption is concerned, it is increasing in leaps and bounds. What is happening? Twenty per cent richest people in the world are actually consuming 80 per cent of the consumption rate and rest of the 80 per cent people are consuming 20 per cent. This disparity, this inequality is a major problem faced by the mankind and causing. Polarisation of human society into haves and have-nots. The 20 per cent richest people of the world have 40 per cent of the land area and are consuming 85 per cent energy of the world. What is happening now, the capital is ruling the entire mankind. The decisions are taken at the highest level, the arrival of the age of cybernetics and the emergence of quaternary sector of economy leads to the fundamental changes in the economic activities. We are all in the age of cybernetics. Manipulation of the land in the agricultural civilization thousands of years ago. After industrial revolution it is manipulation of the machine and now in the age of cybernetics it is the manipulation of information. Even in west, they are collecting all sorts of information. They are taking the decision how it will go to their advantage. Whatever programme we are implementing has failed and there are several other factors coming. What are the tensions to be confronted/overcome in the 21st century? International Commission on Education of the 21st century has identified certain tensions. We are in the new millennium. So what are the tensions local and global, the universal and individual, tension and modernity, long-term and short-term consideration, the need for competition, and the concern for equal opportunity, external way of knowledge, and human based capacity to assimilate it? It is said that whatever knowledge base is there now within three months it gets doubled. The tension is spiritual and material. Automatically whatever action we take, we have to know about tension we have to confront and overcome to succeed in our effort. What constraints you are going to face? This summarizes what Mahatma Gandhi said, constraints are "politics without principle, wealth without work commerce without morality, education without character, science without humanity, leisure without conscience, and worship without sacrifice". Working at the grass roots level we are facing such constraints and we have to overcome these to succeed.

What are the opportunities before us? What should be the Planetary goal of development in the new millennium. It is the sustainability of man and environment by promoting harmony with human society and environment. That is locally, nationally, regionally, and globally. This is the planetary goal of development. For any local action we have to evolve a global perception, otherwise we will not succeed at all. Whatever I do global perception must be there. What is sustainable development? The World Commission on Development defines sustainable development as seeking to meet the aspirations and needs of present generation without compromising on the needs of future. This is the major problem scientists and authors are calling it the metalistic village of culture because so far as petroleums are concerned, they are going to end in the next millennium. Keeping that in view we have to actually work for the solargic village culture because Indian villages are ideal for such a development. What is the metalistic solar agriculture? Harnessing of solar and biomass energy. Ecological and sophisticated organic gardening and farming. Miniturization of technology and harnessing of the eco system. Present technology is dividing the people into haves and have-nots. It is production based. So far as the new millennium is concerned, it should be development based. Therefore, there should be harnessing of eco system. Community is the cultural centre of growth and learning. Assimilating the cybernetics concept in every village the people should be connected to the world of cybernetics. What is the state of human development? There are four models. Economic growth model, human resource development model, welfare approaches model and basic needs approach. What are the defects here? Economic growth model deals with expanding GNP rather than enhancing the quality of human life. Human resource model treats human beings primarily as an input in the production process. Welfare approaches model looks at the human beings as a beneficiary and not as an agent of development. Basic needs approach focuses on providing basic needs material to the required population growth rather than enlarging human needs.

In the new millennium the focus is on human resource development, enlarging human choices, it encompasses earlier concerns and growth beyond analysing all issues from of people's perspective. This is the summary given by Human Resource Development Report of UNDP. We must focus on different abilities of persons with disabilities. The hidden talents of the disabled persons should be tapped. We are telling that they are people with different abilities. Different abilities are much more intensive as compared to abilities in the normal people. Whatever evolution phase is occurring in the nature, it has significance. Existence of disability is there. They have to play an important role in the evolution stage. The International Commission on Education for the 21st century in their report envisages a vision that all societies in the world have to move towards necessary utopia through building four pillars of education, learning to learn, learning to do, learning to be, learning to live together. This concides with our national goal. Our policy on education for all as well as the global goal is education for all and health for all by 2015. To realize this goal, India within the next 10 years has to work to cover all special schools, *i.e.* at primary level, one million teachers, 2,50,000 teachers for middle level and 1,00,000 teachers for secondary level. What is the basic human need for satisfactory existence? It has been summarized by the Indian document on Environmental problems and concerns in the Society as physical needs of food, health, shelter and clothing and the social needs of education, creating employment, individual freedom, ability to participate in the prevailing social system. These things must be fulfilled for all disabled persons. Then only we can realize our goal. It becomes the fundamental obligation of the society and the statutory responsibility of the State to make all necessary efforts to meet the basic human needs of the entire population including the persons with disabilities. A very challenging task before us, it can go through the document. We should make effort at every level to see that our political system secures effective citizen participation in decision-making, our economic system generates resources on self-reliant basis and our social system provides solutions for the tensions arising from development, our production system must respect the obligation of providing the basic needs for development, our technical system to research continuously for new solution, our administrative system must have flexibility and capacity for self correction and our national foreign policy should strive for intense understanding in fostering sustained trade. Sustainable development of India—historical necessity of mankind. The history we have predicted with the present chapter of world history, which had western beginning, will have to have an Indian ending, if it is not to end in self destruction. We are in a better position. We have great future.

DR. TULSI DAS

What I am going to present today does not directly concern the handicapped or challenged or disabled, but I am more concerned with the rehabilitation professionals themselves. This is based on my views when I visited Russia, France and Holland as visiting professor and there met many rehabilitation professionals. Based on that they used to ask me Dr. Tulasi what you have in India which is special for us. What is special with India? For us who are from the grass roots level we have to have some programmes, not only training programme but some coping skills for the professionals themselves to work more effectively with the children outside. So I call the inside state of mind of rehabilitation professionals as internal environment which I think is very important in the present scenario, when there is lot of confusion, lot of changes are taking place and we have to work under great hardship, not like super power countries like France or Holland where social securities exists. So in such a situation what we should have as a rehabilitation professionals when working with any kind of disabled or with anybody in the present scenario. I would like to stress on those points, may be further research is needed. We need some programmes for ourselves, along with the training of children, for one's internal growth. Human beings first tried to understand the Nature and then tried to adjust as per the demands of the environment. Then he started moulding it for selfish goals. Now he wants to dominate, create and formulate artificial environment. He wants to change everybody, and everything. There power game between human beings and environment has resulted in scientific advancements such as cloning of human beings and detection of genome. However, we also see aggressive instincts being developed and breakage of human values taking place.

Seventeenth century is known as the age of enlightenment, 18th century as the age of reasoning, 19th century as the age of progress, 20th century we call it the age of anxiety, then this 21st century is definitely the age of confusions. We call it the age of confusion because there are lot of confusions starting from electronic age to coming age, we don't know what is going on. I told, as in the west also, why do we need a change in our internal environment. This was also on my doctorate thesis which was acclaimed by one of the noted psychologist of the world, Dr. Wilped. In this we are talking about Lord Vishnu who is sleeping on the hood of a serpent, where the outside environment all around is so dangerous but still he is calm, happy and relaxed. I work with many kinds of children with rubella, with AIDS, children with leprosy. Cured cases of leprosy. I feel that we need something. It is just not only the money that we need. In the Vishnu-Shayanam photograph you see that outside environment is turbulent but he is quite serene and calm. Similarly, coping skills levels and family levels of rehabilitation professionals need equal attention just much as we expect from them in the rehabilitation of the handicapped. Then the situation I think, will improve much more. Some of the programmes which we can conduct and which we are conducting at different places in India are related to handicapped. I train them in coping skills. It is not the financial state of rehabilitation professionals but it is their coping skills to produce calm and peaceful state of mind, for working in such highly stressed environment of handicapped children, who can be not just mild or moderate but can be severe, profound or multiply handicapped. We find the same example in Mahabharata. It is now very well known concept even in scientific literature. Everybody knows, Arjuna. In this picture the Archer Arjuna when he put down his bow and arrow and says that he can't face the bow, then at that time the sermon that Lord Krishna gives actually changes his mental environment. Due to which he comes out of that conflict and then he could face that challenge more effectively and with more vigour, with more happiness. I call it the karamyoga concept. We need karamyogis. Now we have karamyogis who are not karamyogis of the last century, but entrepreneurs who can do things on their own things. We cannot be dependent on the government all the time. We have to develop our own programmes outside as well as inside. Some of the ancient methods from Upanishads on which I have worked in the last years, we can take and use it very well, not only with children, again and again I repeat, because we all talk about children outside all the time. One thing is clear, we can't be honest to others if we are not honest to ourselves first. Similarly we can't keep on changing others but to change ourselves as per the need of the outside. Like chanting of sounds from Vedas can very well be utilized not only for children but even for rehabilitation professionals. From the Bhagavad Geeta the attitude of Karamyoga. From Patanjali Yogasutra's we can take do's and don'ts of daily living, postural exercises, some parts of yoga, and meditation. Meditation actually happens it can't be done. From Ayurvedas we can take out methods of longevity, how to have more healthy attitude, vegetarianism concepts from Jainism, from Buddhism we can take vipasana and the middle path of living. In this we want a change and change goes to the level of frustration, whether there is any kind of disability. So how we can live up to that. That is the middle path. Sufism is very good for us to learn methods to develop our inner self. There are also some cults and movements like Sikhism, Tibetan scriptures which have suggested an effective way of living and promoting our mental health which is very important. My point of view is not orthodox or spiritual. Thanks to the Indian Association of Clinical Psychologists and other Social Scientists around the world who have now accepted the terminology of spiritual health in recently held National Conference at Ranchi. It has no data to support but I can discuss it. This article will not turn the wheel back to the stone age but it will lead to high success rate, and a feeling of satisfaction in the rehabilitation professionals, less job turn over in the field of rehabilitation of the cross disability in the new millennium.

OPEN DISCUSSION

SPEAKER (UNIDENTIFIED)

Dr. Bhushan Punani you have mentioned number of people thrown out of window. In case of mental retardation particularly of those with profound cases, all this training, if you look from the economic point of view, and in terms of employment, it will be a waste. But if we take in terms of human values, it is a must.

DR. PUNANI

My only point was that it is possible to follow as normal means as possible but there are special needs. The problem is in the name of special needs we do everything for everybody. We should change that attitude and, wherever possible have them in the mainstream in the normal way, that should be our first and only option. After that only we can think of other needs, special needs. The target should again be we shall bring them to normal life as far as possible.

DR. ARUN SHARMA

I am looking after an NGO, Medicare and Research Foundation. My request is to Dr. Punani, we give reservation from Parliament to the lowest level in the funded activities to the disabled. What is your opinion in that respect when 8 to 10 per cent of the population is suffering from disability. It is a huge population and if the same percentage, 4-5 per cent seats are reserved right from the Parliament to the lower level, panchayat level, etc., then they will look after the things in a better way rather than depending upon other able persons all the time, or begging etc. What is your opinion on that.

DR. PUNANI

In fact when you talk of SC/ST and other backward classes, that is a constitutional issue. Disability has not become a constitutional issue so far. It is a legislative issue. There is a technical difference in that we started many years before, giving rights to people who are SC/ST as per the constitution and then things happened automatically. I agree with you and that while we can't talk of constitutional provisions at this stage, we have to have the issue of rights. Rights not only in the form of a Disability Act. In the true spirit, right to everything including education, rehabilitation, integration, special support, is the mandate of each and everybody and not only for the Ministry of Social Justice & Empowerment and Welfare Departments. It is a mandate for each and everybody of us and for that we are already going in for an amendment which definitely will ensures some of the things. If we have to achieve these targets let us not equate with other reservations. That is not the way. The correct way is to see that what we already have is it effective, is that happening, and who will make that happen. It is not always government, it is all of us. The classical example is Kerala Parents Association's case decided by Supreme Court reserving 3 per cent seats in all educational institutes which is going to be the precedent for the whole country and is going to ensure that the law becomes effective.

SPEAKER (UNIDENTIFIED)

Thirty-six per cent of people in the country are working manpower and 8 per cent out of this 36 per cent are working in organized sector, both public and private. Even if 100 per cent seats are reserved, only 8 per cent of people will get jobs. What about the 92 per cent? Automatically there has to be social effort, voluntary efforts. No government above can solve this problem. I was working for 22 years in a vocational education programme and this is the situation. It is the self-employment venture. This is not only applicable to our disabled population but there is another difficulty. Now we have entered global market economy. Goods and services of international standard are required. Our disabled persons have to compete. This is the greatest challenge we are facing.

MR. P.K. DAS

The papers submitted by Dr. Punani, Prof. Guru and Dr. Tulsi deserve appreciation and we happily welcome. But my submission is Dr. Punani is telling that if we should throw away all the old ones which are not effective today, if we have to go for the new millennium. Naturally if you want to go. At the same time he said good salary, and all these things for the staff should be arranged. If we have to depend upon NGOs, how can we just collect funds, because government is always emphasizing on the voluntary basis. The condition of the people, the economic standard of the people is not very sound. Do please tell how the balance will be made for going a step forward and doing things in proper manner.

DR. PUNANI

I knew this question is going to come. That is why in my opening remarks I did mention there are tremendous community resources, there are tremendous unutilized resources at the moment. Our problem is most of us have put on blinkers and we do not look at the other side. Unless we throw the ineffective, effectiveness never comes in. It is not always a question of money, it is also a question of managing in a better and effective manner what you have. The surprising thing is that effective things are most cost effective, less expensive, easy to manage and easy to access. For example, taking a child to a special school may cost you a few lakhs by the time child completes the education. Taking the same child to a normal school may cost you one-tenth of that cost but the problem is are we going to accept that our special child is not special for education, but special for support services, and can access the services available next door. In fact more effective will be less expensive, easy to manage, provided we change our thoughts, change our outlook, our approach, our programmes and change our considerations. To me it is not the four walls you construct, but the four walls which are already existing where we have to integrate our child like any other child in the neighbourhood.

PROF. JEYACHANDRAN

Some gentleman talked about 10 per cent of disabled population. I think there is lot of discrepancy in the thinking. I would like to have Chairman's clarification about the percentage of disabled population. If the Chairperson can give available information, the field workers would know where we are.

CHAIRPERSON

Ten per cent looks completely exaggerated and completely outdated. It came back from 10 to 7, 7 to 5 and any available data points to 2 per cent to 3 per cent maximum. By the end of October we shall be coming out on the Sample Survey on Disability alone, in some States it has already been completed, and it includes mental retardation. All indications are that we are not talking of any figure beyond 3 per cent.

MR. RAVI

Dr. Punani has suggested the setting up of a Department of Disabilities. He has also advocated that the human rights of PwDs should be pushed forward. As a human rights activist, somehow, I find it very difficult to reconcile to this. All movement of human rights being ruling back the State. How would you react to my suggestion that what is required is not so much a Department of Disabilities rather a National Commission for Rights for the Disabilities. Commission gives access to human rights activitists to push forward the rights and it puts pressure on the State, puts pressure on the society. Would not the Commission be more useful than the Department?

DR. PUNANI

Thank you very much for your suggestion. You will be glad to know that National Human Rights Commission has already appointed a full time Rapporteur on Disability and Ms. Anuradha Mohit has taken up this role. Only thing is Commissions have a very limited role, when it comes to service delivery and coordination. They are more like watch dogs. What is happening should not be happening is their role. But if we have to deliver the services, we have to bring about more programmes. If we have to make human rights really effective we do need a mechanism, we do need a machinery. In that context I have suggested three things simultaneously, members having an independent department which is more sensitive, more educated, and more concerned about disability and also at the same time taking disability as a human rights issue because that is the only way we can ensure many legal, constitutional and social support in an organized manner. At the same time I do support your contention if there can be a National Commission on the rights of the disabled. I am sure I will be in full agreement with that.

CHAIRPERSON

I have the privilege of releasing a book by Dr. J.P. Singh, Technology for the Blind: Concept and Context.

I now have to wrap this session summing up what the three speakers have been talking about. In the century of confusion, keeping in mind the tensions we have to overcome by assimilating and interiorizing consciousness, in remembering the seven social skills enumerated by Mahatma Gandhi and by linking ancient Indian traditional concepts from the multi fabric richness of India, what we need now is populistic development. I have identified five challenges. One, the statistical imperatives, the number of disabled persons that we have to address and the response to the challenges that we have to move from uni-disciplinary to trans-disciplinary professionals and methodologies and bring cross-disability which will give us some more geometric progression rather than an arithmetic one. The problem here is upscaling. We have always said that there are enough models, small adhoc programmes, islands of excellence, we need now to upscale and give huge coverage to a variety of training methodologies, satellite training, etc. The one answer to that is information. The second challenge is the financial constraints. Do we have the resources for reaching the 50 odd million people we need to reach? The answer is obviously no. If we have a vertical model of development. You set up through the rehabilitation sector, one layer, second layer, third layer, reaching the community. Again there the answer is the through convergence and through multi-sectoral linkages, mainstream and again mainstream. The answer is inclusion in the existing resources which are hugely available, grossly unutilized and sometimes misutilized for disability and disabled people. For the complete and holistic development of people with disabilities starting from the

Anganwadis and going to primary schools, inclusion should happen in employment giving the new trends in the employment sector. The third challenge is the participation of people with disabilities and their families in every aspect that concerns them. We all know the David Werner's call 'nothing about us without us'. Total and full participation not only in implementation but also in the decision-making programmes that concern them. The fourth challenge is creating access, a barrier-free environment, not only free from physical barriers but attitudinal barriers and probably more important from information barriers. The fifth challenge identified today is social security. How do we ensure quality of life which is ensuring equality, social justice and dignity? Perhaps this is the biggest challenge of them all and this is where we need synergy, we need fundamental obligations, fundamental commitment not just from government, not just from NGOs, not just professionals but the entire civil society itself.

This was the finals of the Special Olympics in Helsinki, the international final. It was a race run by young children between 9 and 12 years of age, there were 8 contestants. As the pistol was fired all 8 contestants set off from the starting line. Seven went ahead, one young boy sat down, he was refusing to move. The other seven sprinted towards the final line but one by one all stopped and turn around and they looked at this boy who had sat down and without discussing amongst themselves they all came back and said to this boy 'get up'. He said 'no'. They picked him up, forced him to stand up, linked hands in one chain and they all together ran towards the finishing line. The entire crowd of 5,000 people stood up and cheered. There was not a single dry eye in the audience because that day these children with mental handicap, taught us the triumph of human spirit over the human body, they also taught us that winning is not about one person, but reaching the finishing line everybody, everybody together, getting there at the same time.

II

HUMAN RESOURCE DEVELOPMENT
GRASS ROOTS AND HIGHER LEVEL

Co-Chairperson: Prof. K.C. Panda

Let me express my gratitude to all of you and RCI for having thought of me to chair this session, 'Human Resource Development—Grass roots and higher level'. As you all know the field of disability has a long past but a short scientific history in terms of its expansion and in terms of human resource development. Particularly, if you look at the Education Commission's Report of 1964-66, the number of institutions were limited to single number in terms of training human resource for meeting the needs of the disabled children. Subsequently, the situation improved but we people have a fancy of having drinks and rest, therefore, it did not get a major breakthrough till the International Year of the Disabled Persons. Thereafter, systematic thinking went on in developing some of the structural outlines following the 1986 policy on Education to see that the human resource development is speeded up and particularly at the NGO and government sector, encouragement was given. Now, at the moment, there is a greater need of different personnel not only at the school level but at the tertiary level as well as at the grass roots level. We have in our midst today Prof. M.N.G. Mani, who is a stalwart not only in the field of visual impairment, but also in programme planning and policy decisions. It would be a pleasure to listen to his thoughts and his contributions as well. The next speaker friend is, a friend of mine, Prof. J S Grewal, we worked together in NCERT, he is now Director of Bhoj University. For a long time one of my colleagues Prof. G. G. Prabhu of the NIMHANS and myself were the expert group for RCI for developing programmes at different levels. At that time I was very much opposed to any distance learning programme as it may not really deliver the delivery in an efficient manner. But as time changes and the technology advanced, I think the distance learning system is the need of the day to meet the challenges of the large number of human resource.

DR. M. N. G. MANI

It gives me great pleasure to be here this morning to talk about human resource development. Somebody asked our late Prime Minister Rajiv Gandhi a question when he was touring. Mr. Prime Minister the population of India is a big concern, how are you going to tackle? Without any hesitation he said, I am not bothered about the population of India, because we are going to convert them as human resources. That is the great spirit of human resources and that is why the Ministry of Education was changed as Ministry of Human Resource Development. Today, I am going to outline the challenges and issues in the area of HRD. When I talk about HRD, one phrase comes to my mind, that is, so little achieved and so much to accomplish. This is the condition today. HRD should not be viewed in pieces. We have to view HRD in totality, in national perspective. We should not look at HRD in the field of education, in the field of rehabilitation, at the diploma level or at the graduation level. We have to have national perspective when we talk about HRD. Again when we talk about HRD, the objective is not to produce simply manpower, that should be utilized. In the first session, Dr. Punani spoke about the unutilized resources. I think, that is what we are facing in the area of HRD today ineffective utilization. When we talk about that we are trying to reinvent the wheel. Let us not try to do that. Let us complement the efforts of each other. With these general principles, let us talk about HRD in Special Education. But before that we have to understand the country first. What is the condition of India? How India looks like? 17 per cent of world's population is in India. In terms of land area it is 2.4 per cent of total land area. Coming to the languages, 325 of the 2,820 languages of the world, yet local dialects vary after every 8 to 10 kms. It is India. At present 44 per cent of the adult population is still illiterate. Now let us examine the magnitude of the problem. I want to approach Special Education in the light of human resource needs in the entire country. These are the statistics that we get from the report of the Ministry of Education. It says that in our country today, 11.38 crore of children are at the primary level, 1-5. The coverage is 26 per cent. So if you use these statistics, our estimate is in this age group, there are 12 crore children in this country. When it comes to upper primary, age from 6-8, the enrolment is 4.28 crores and the Ministry projects this as 59 per cent. That means in this age group we have about 7.5 crore of children. Altogether we have 20 crore of children in the age group of 6-14 years and this is 1/5th of the population of our country. Enrolment upto the upper primary level, 1 to 8 is 82 per cent. Now drawing a parallel from the general education scenario and also using the statistics of 10 per cent, Dr. Aloka Guha told that, it has come down to 7 per cent, 5 per cent, now 3 per cent. Where is the authentic statistics? Whatever number we use, the number is huge. Going with the statistics of 10 per cent population of disabled, we have about 2 crore of children with disabilities, who are in need of education. Their enrolment at the rate of 82 per cent compared to general education scenario, should have been 1.6 crore, right now. What is the present status? It is not more than even 5 lakhs. If we look at the number of children who have been covered in the special schools and general schools, the coverage is less than 2.5 per cent. Therefore, there is a gap of about 78 per cent when we compare the general education and the special education. Coming to the teachers. There are about 32 lakh teachers working in primary and upper primary schools as general class room teachers based on the Government of India statistics and not my own. The teacher pupil ratio is 1: 43. In the light of these what would be the human resource development needs of the country. Everybody is talking about inclusive education. Assuming that we are integrating, including children with disabilities from mild to profound categories, in the general schools and assuming that special teacher is available to look after hundred children in a cluster, it is very liberal estimate, still we need 2 lakh teachers to work with children with special needs. The ratio is very conservative. By reducing the ratio which is necessary for educating children with disabilities, if we work on the ratio of 1: 15, we need 4 lakh teachers. That is why RCI Manpower Development Document, the figures projected are realistic. RCI projected a figure of 7.64 lakhs of human resource, particularly the professionals in the Tenth Plan period. If you compare it with general education, the document is not unrealistic. What I have analysed is only the primary education and upper primary. Now when we talk about HRD, we are talking about three groups, the group which is from 0 to 5 years. The need is not reflecting that. Who would serve these children? Similarly from the age group 18 to 60 years, which is in the need of vocational opportunities. Age beyond 60 years, which requires medical care and other types of rehabilitation services, etc. If we combine the needs it is enormous. HRD again it does not include only the teachers. It includes the grass roots level workers, and the higher level policy makers also who need awareness tc disability. This is the projection of RCI document that we need 3,62,000 professionals to serve the disability area. That was not achieved, training institutes were not available. In the Tenth Plan period, it has projected 7,24,000 professionals needed. This number, again if we go with the statistics already available in the Government of India, is not unrealistic at all. Efforts are needed to provide training programmes starting from the short-term courses to long-term skills training. That is why the Manpower Document of RCI is giving us a realistic picture. When you talk about the trends, we are talking about the conventional system. If we just go out of the conventional system and if we include other categories also, our HRD requirement will be still larger. Let us talk about recreation therapy, which is needed to assist about 20 per cent of people with disabilities who belong to the elderly category. Similarly new categories are emerging with recognition of new categories like autism and multiple disabilities. What about the emergence of inclusive education? Millions of class room teachers have to be trained and focus on children with learning disabilities. This is going to make the HRD task gigantic. We have to take into account all these areas when we talk about our human resources. Who needs to know about disability? The obvious answer is all need to know about disability. If we classify high level, middle level, and grass rootss level. High level public servants, bureaucrats, legal bodies, Vice-Chancellors, educational authorities, customs officials, transport officials and so on. When it comes to middle level, we are talking about teachers, doctors. RCI programme for doctors, that has a tremendous impact. The doctors trained through the PHC programme, they have referred more than 1 lakh persons with disabilities in my own State of Tamil Nadu to education and rehabilitation programmes. We have to train the psychologists, rehabilitation managers, elected persons of Panchayats. I am very happy that the vision of RCI is not related to teachers and other professionals. It has gone beyond that. Thanks to the Chairman in orienting the elected representatives in Panchayats, Assemblies, that has found impact. Grass roots level workers, parents, Anganwadi workers, health workers, volunteers, disabled persons themselves. This morning one of the speakers, pointed out that we have to make the people understand themselves, that is what Swami Vivekananda said. We have to make them understand themselves. So we have to organize programmes for disabled people also—Personality development programmes. The need of the hour is to develop the national perspective in the field of HRD in special education and rehabilitation. Three strategies are emerging. Let us not discuss elaborately on this. Biwako framework says everybody should be included. All programmes in the government, whether it is State Government programme or Central Government programme should include disability. There is no category as disability. They are all human beings and whatever schemes you come up with, disabled people also should have a share. This is the ideal scenario. This will happen only when there is a political will. That is why we have to make the people understand that PwDs are also part of the inclusive barrier free. Rights based society. The second approach is the disability focus approach which is happening in most of the places who don't have the resources. Of course, the quality may be there. Educating a child with disability in a special school, we don't have resources. It may require lakhs of lakhs of rupees. That is why we have to have a combined approach. There specialists are needed for consultative roles and disability issues are assimilated in the general system. So we cannot get away with the specialists. When people talk about inclusion they say no specialists are not needed. We need specialists. Let us not approach the problem like this. We need specialists may be for a cluster, may be for a block, we have to have specialists also. Whereas most of the educational aspects and CBR aspects can be taken care of by the general education system and the community. We have to have a shift from welfare approach to social development approach. This is practical and for making this effective we need micro planning. That is the present status of the human resources, a substantial number of untrained persons are working in the field. Trained persons working on adhoc basis are poorly paid when compared to other fields. There is a disparity with regard to qualification also. We have to make the government understand these issues so that the disability issue is absorbed in the general system.

Issues before us

What additional categories of disabilities can be covered? At what levels the programmes can be organized, degree level, diploma level, certificate level. We have to have the micro planning. How to encourage R&D? In this field we need lot of Research & Development but unfortunately it is very much missing. How to encourage, how to address the infrastructure needs? What would be financial requirements for serving persons with disabilities. Find out the human resource needs in the country with respect to the RCI recognized programmes. Promote courses on information technology. Yesterday Chairman pointed out that we have to make use of information technology in the field of special education also. Work with the organizations which are working for HRD to include special education as a component in the pre-service training itself. There are so many organizations in the country which are working for HRD. We have to collaborate with them. Develop packages for in-service programmes and indigenous literature. NGOs have to implement the PHC programme because still 17,000 doctors have to be trained. Without the support of NGOs, particularly in the northern region, we will not be able to achieve this target. More and more NGOs should come forward to take part in HRD programmes and we must also prescribe minimum standards for institutions who run the distance education programmes. To sum up, improve access for knowledge acquisition through various modes of learning, not only through formal mode, informal mode, distance education, that is challenge number one. How are we going to tackle that? Challenge number two, adopting the existing systems and upgradation. The third challenge is strengthening of links in the field of training and work. Collaboration and Networking is going to be the watch word in the future. Collaboration between the government organizations, collaboration with the international organizations, collaboration with the NGO's and NGO's. Today lot of resources are there and we have to collaborate, that should be the watch word to facilitate harmonious development of special education and rehabilitation. With the constructive work of NGOs and their networking, I think the work for persons with disabilities will never have red light it will always have green light in front of us. Let this Summit open a new chapter, that is what we call collaboration. When we go from this place, let us go with one message, we have to collaborate for welfare of persons with disabilities.

CHAIRPERSON

It was a very illustrative presentation emphasizing some of the salient challenges which we face in the field of HRD both at micro and macro level. Now I request Prof. Grewal to enlighten us on this issue.

PROF. J. S. GREWAL

My paper is based on my experience and I had the opportunity in 1994-95 to teach this paper on human resource development at the University of Cape Course in West Africa. It was at that time, that I came into contact with the concepts of HRD. It was a M. Phil course. I taught the course for 3 months, then I guided certain dissertations in the area of HRD. I think on this premises Dr. J. P. Singh, assigned this topic to me at a very short notice. I could summaries some of the components of HRD. I have divided my paper in four parts. Firstly the introductory part, followed by what are the basis of HRD, HRD at grass roots level and HRD at tertiary or higher education level, integrated to HRD and implications of HRD concept as a whole for the disabled population.

As Dr. Mani described, it was Prime Minister Rajiv Gandhi who used the term HRD and since then this term has been used very frequently. But the real person who worked in this area was Prof. Maqbul Haque from Pakistan he tried to assess the HRD indices of all the countries of the world by taking into consideration certain parameters. This movement has spread like any thing and now there is a Maqbul Haque Foundation which continuously develops and monitors the HRD index for all the countries. Even for different States of our country, they have taken upon this task to assess the components of HRD and then monitor the progress which has been taking place. HRD, I already said, started as a movement. Its theory is simple, statistically and psycho metrically he has worked out the formula for it. Every year HRD Index report is published and circulated by the Maqbul Haque Foundation throughout the country and a number of reports have come.

Secondly, I would say that education is no longer only a training or a social activity which is taking place in the social sector. Education is very mixed up with economics. The concept of education and economics is very much intermingling now as far as this particular aspect is concerned. We should have a balanced HRD policy based on certain facts. In the morning it was said that disabled population is 10 per cent, somebody said 7 per cent, 5 per cent. It was even pointed out that there is going to be a National Sample Survey report. I do not know what shape it will take but definitely the disabled population is for the welfare of which you are working and you are giving education, training, vocational aspects and thus you are developing this population. There are six bases of HRD, the ethical and human dimensions, it is said that we must go beyond the economic and psycho metric means of education. Education is a human rights, it leads every individual to creativity, improved participation in economic, social and cultural roles in society, and hence more comprehensive contribution to human resource development. Second base is health and nutrition. Every thing is linked to education and health. Education improves health. It is said that each year of schooling causes, out of every 1,000, 9 fear deaths. Now the thesis of nutrition aspects is we should know as workers of disabled population the extent to which nutrition state is affected by being disabled. It is basis on this statement that we have launched two Ph.D level thesis. We have taken up in the State of Madhya Pradesh in the tribal areas, in urban areas, we have given two dissertations to home science students. They are taking into consideration the mentally retarded, the hearing impaired, visual impaired and going to the pre-school centres where the disabled students are studying and taking their measurements, weights, their social economic factors. Results or findings will come after a year or so. What is the nutritional status of our disabled children? I am saying that this is a factor for HRD. We must have data for it. It is not sufficient to summarize on the basis of reports of UNICEF, UNESCO and other international bodies.

Economic Development

Economic development is another indicator of HRD. It is said that four years of primary education increased 9 per cent of productivity. 8.7 per cent of productivity is increased by forges of primary education. Those who are primary level educated, they have 27 per cent more earnings. Those who have secondary education 15-17 per cent returns they have increased. Education as a factor causes technological change. The purpose here is that schooling promotes modern attitudes and rationality. A country's pursuit in development and use of new technologies has implications in terms of employment and skill requirements. Both these aspects are important as HRD activity. In our country primary education is 8 years. In other developing countries the primary education may be 7 or 8 years. We have made higher secondary as a terminal stage. We have an assumption that only after higher secondary people can develop their human resource potential. But if you take into consideration other developing countries, we also have lot of studies that there is a drop-out rate at primary stage. It is alright that there is a drop-out rate, we write textbooks and impress others by saying this. But how we can resolve this? In developing countries like Africa they have tried to resolve, they say primary education is sufficient for HRD. They have reasons for this. Many of the students will not come and join higher secondary or secondary because secondary education is very costly to them. Even for primary education studies have been conducted on the availability of textual material. Three textbooks are shared by one student, the fees at the secondary stage is very high. They cannot afford to go to secondary stage. They say whatever you want to give them, give them at the primary stage, otherwise you will not be able to catch them. That is why they have tried to include subjects like integrated production skills. In our country, we try to follow different concepts. Firstly, crafts education. Basic education is not a term point only for the Education of Vardha Scheme of education. Basic education means primary education. Then work experience.

Then socially useful productive work. Work education in the national education framework of school education. Education concept is highlighted and even implemented. Textual materials are available. These are the subjects which are very near to HRD. This is pre-vocational education. Social cultural changes, in social cultural changes secondary education is for attitude change. Attitudes for being modern, education relates to savings, planning, economic planning, productive activities. Social aspect of education at secondary stage is that it should educate the women folk, marriage age third which is very low. Rather low because the studies indicate that at the age of 20, 50 per cent of the women or girls get married in Africa and 40 per cent in Asia, and 30 per cent in Latin American countries. Early marriage, more children, more children less economic well being, less human development activity of the children which has to be raised, brought up and provided education. Women who are educated have small families. So education has social factors, it is also an important factor. It also promotes other things like population control, family planning, health and hygiene, nutrition and motivation of children. We have been carrying on the activities of population control for many years. Now it is pointed out and believed that curricular efforts have not succeeded. We have not been able to enthuse the message of population education through textual material. These efforts have failed, we should go to more approaches like campaign approach, and more practical activities. Inequalities in HRD are caused by political factors. It is believed that the democracy is the best in the political order system to promote equality, every body gets opportunity. There is equalization of opportunities. Geographical imbalance is there. They have overcome gender factor. Income and political factors. Coming to HRD at lower level. Here I want to tell you agriculture as one of the subjects. We emphasize that agriculture is major occupation of our people and 75 per cent people live in villages. But agriculture as a subject has not been encouraged to the extent it was required. I had an opportunity to work on an appraisal mission and there I came across that agriculture as a subject started right from primary one. Taking care of animals, cultivation, backyards, creating all sorts of attitudes among the people so that they can earn their livelihood. Agriculture as a subject. Integrated vocational skills. If the subjects like agriculture is not there as a social productive activity, economics is also included. Basic primary technology and art. These subjects have never been encouraged in the past. Then business and entrepreneurship. There are maximum number of women who are taking to trades in African countries. They are the persons who are undertaking economic activities under entrepreneurship. HRD at higher levels. We know that there is an upsurge of educational institutions at higher level providing engineering, medical courses, so many institutions. Unplanned expansion which is taking place. But how far it is relevant to the needs. I can cite here the example of newly formed State of Chhatisgarh. They have started a three year Medical Degree course, purposely, the Chief Minister of the State said that if you get a four year M.B.B.S. the doctors will leave their jobs and the manpower needs of that area will not be met. Purposely he has introduced a para medical course. HRD needs selective expansion, promoting equality, improving quality and correcting imbalance. If all these things are taken into consideration, courses are expanded, and funding should be available. Private universities are being set up and various States bills have been passed. In the end I would say the achievements in HRD, we should start with the primary education, meaningful secondary education, diversified higher education, but relevant to the needs of the people. All these activities are taking place but you are the persons who are providing to the disabled population in or the other way, vocational training to the disabled will answer the question of problem of HRD for disadvantaged population.

CHAIRPERSON

It was a comprehensive presentation. The audience will excuse me for not allowing any question answer session.

Let me summarize briefly what Prof. Mani and Prof. Grewal presented before us and if time permits my own thinking on these issues. Prof. Mani has initially provided a very wider spectrum including presenting before us the challenges and issues in HRD emphasizing three major points, that is, access to knowledge through various modes, upgradation and updation of institutes for quality control, and linking trainers and trainees to the field work as well as thinking of collaboration between various organizations. At the same time he has also emphasized that while thinking of HRD in special education, the age group should form a major factor. 0-5 age group, 6-18, 18-60 which has different needs patterns developmentally. At the same time, he also suggested that we should try to move away from the traditional modes of preparation to modern modes of preparation which can meet different needs in terms of preparing large number of personnel to help us in executing the programmes. At the same time he did make us cautious, two important things are necessary macro planning as well as micro planning. But all this is dependent upon the political will. Because initially in early 1960s we concentrated on four major categories of disabilities. Now after the PwD Act, we have more categories of disabilities. Are we now in a position to meet the supply of human resource to meet the needs of various categories, even learning disabilities, emerging from time to time. There may be a possibility of another category in terms of stress and tensions which is likely to be created and which needs the role of better clinical psychologist and counselling techniques to deal with them. One of the points he very strongly emphasized, which I have also agreed in the past, research and development. In this country we should not base our thinking on training procedures and methodologies from western thinking. Because Indian society is not only multi-cultural but also multi-lingual. Therefore, the programmes for preparing HRD should be anchored in the ecological framework in which the training is being organized. When that is possible and how that will be possible. As you all know in a formal structure which I mean the public sector or private sector, the red-tapism prevents implementation of very well conceived, very well designed, well planned programmes to take off. It is not I am amidst NGO colleagues, I am saying this, but if we read our hon'ble President's Book "Vision for 2010" towards the end of the book, he has made two cautious remarks. Those teacher educators and teachers who are incharge of delivering goods are a miserable lot in terms of the life they lead. They can derive satisfaction if they upgrade themselves. This has bearing on continuing education programmes, in-service programmes and exchange of information between various organizations at different forums. At the same time he did emphasize that in the long run NGOs have to take up large responsibility in collaboration with governmental agencies. Therefore, we the people interested in the area of disability have to take it as a challenge in the coming years. Prof. Grewal has also tried to enlighten us and say that he is not expert but experts are not only knowledge based, it is an experienced based expertise in the field of special education. He has very clearly outlined the special education movement, its various components, the socio, ethical dynamics, as well as the imbalances which exist now. I have a couple of observations to make. I will just cite one personal experience for your benefit. I worked in the United States in the field of disability in 1968 to 1972: I was very much committed that in our country there should be development of special education in a large perspective. When I moved to NCERT in 1976 I tried to, because not much thinking on special education was available at that time, I tried to incorporate special education contents in traditional B.Ed. and M.Ed. curriculum. And submitted a proposal for introduction of Bachelor in Special Education and when I presented that to a body of 200 academicians, that we need to develop HRD in special education, at that time my thinking was to have B.Ed. in special education. Before I completed my sentence I was stopped by shouting that we have enough B.Ed. education in our country, we don't want special education. I am on record. I humbly submitted it is not a special restaurant or a hotel, exact term I said, because I had no fear at that time, special education is education for the neglected disabled children in this country. Therefore, we need teachers and at one stroke the course was approved. Unfortunately bureaucracy did not allow things to grow, it could not start. It started thereafter. As a reaction to that I wrote a paper on the role of bureaucracy in impeding development, particularly in the field of HRD which was published in the Vision Journal in 1978. So I had much anguish in the field. Though I have retired for nine years, I still continue to have my commitment in this field. I did work for all the Chairmen since inception of The Rehabilitation Council of India as a technical expert in this field of mental retardation and associated disabilities, and I have seen all the Chairmen supporting the new venture. Although during the last three four years, particularly the last couple of years, it has taken up a very very geometrical progression. My concern is that human resource development should be viewed in a wider perspective. That is awareness building among parents, because they are the first human resource, among administrators, among anganwadi workers dealing with early childhood period, the critical period of life in the child's development. Brain development in the first three or four years of life is limited in the first critical period. Then it is difficult to catch up. We cannot go back no matter whatever you do, you cannot reverse the damage that is done. Therefore, there is a need of professionals for early intervention programmes, pre-school programmes, and care givers programme and parental awareness programme, who will start bridging the gap between the child and the family before he comes to school, whether it is special school, inclusive school, special class, integrated school, no matter what it is. Let us have a early start. Then the other part, which I would like to insist upon you is that there should be a continuity in our programmes of preparation, a kind of vertical mobility. People who are trained at the early level moved to the higher level through modular programmes not repeating the regular programmes again, building up the programmes. RCI over these few years has done a very remarkable job. I am grateful to the present Chairman and previous Chairmen for really taking the course from the traditional mode to the distance mode, from a very content based course to skill based course, trying to develop uniform in structure and also arriving at some techniques of quality control. Even though the quality control has to be ensured more. HRD in terms of professional teacher preparation is one side. The other side is there should be a cross-disability specialization because very rightly you have said it is a cross-disability convention. Any body who specializes in one area of disability can also have competence in other areas by planned programmes and RCI is thinking in that particular line. The other areas of concern should be therapeutics. There is a dearth of professionals whether it is Physiotherapy, Occupational therapy, counselling or even any kind of speech and communication therapy, whatever it may be. Those specialists are in dire need. The Manpower Development Report of RCI, I was also associated with MR section, it projected a very realistic figure but I would go a little forward in saying that statistical data are good servants but very poor masters. In the absence of any reliable sample survey statistics in this country, whether it is national sample survey, UNICEF survey, which combined mental retardation and mental illness together, which is 100 per cent wrong. Unless the special survey to which Mrs. Aloka Guha referred to, by September, we will know the realistic figures. With sufficient caution we have to plan our HRD programmes. But caution may not be necessary because the problem is so large, the number of people to be trained is so large, that any preparation would not be surplus. Therefore, we should not be worried about statistics and we should go ahead and many of our NGO colleagues should come forward to take up such programmes meeting the conditions of RCI and see that they do contribute to the furtherance of the special education.

III

ROLE OF NON-GOVERNMENTAL ORGANIZATIONS IN REHABILITATION PROGRAMMES

Chairperson: Swami Atmaramanandaji Maharaj

We are now into the Plenary Session III and theme is Role of Non-Governmental Organizations in Rehabilitation Programmes. The role to be played by the NGOs needs hardly to be emphasized. The role they are expected to play is immense. Its immense because the number of NGOs involved in the field of disability is very minimum. Professionally qualified, qualitatively acceptable, perhaps there are about 150 recognizable or mentionable institutions, out of which 125 I believe are NGOs. There are many number of small institutions or individuals working in the field but this is handful. In the context of the main theme of this convention the Challenges and opportunities before the NGOs and the government organizations one of facing the challenge of having to deal with almost sixty to 70 million of disabled people. The role that the NGOs have to play is to convert these challenges into opportunities and finally succeed. With these opening remarks I call upon Mrs. Indumathi Rao of the CBR Network South Asia, Bangalore to place her views before us all.

MRS. INDUMATHI RAO

We all know that we are dealing with the problem where the

magnitude is vast and its impact is severe on the individual, family and community, when the person is differently abled. We are also aware that we are talking about two countries in a country, one is India and the other is Bharat, India is seen in the cities like Delhi, Calcutta, Mumbai, Bangalore and we continue to see Bharat in remote villages where disparity is appalling and we feel very guilty. The conservative estimates say that there are 4-5 per cent of persons with disabilities. Prevalence of disability according to census data of 2001. We have analysed the data for 538 districts of India, age-wise and disability-wise and we are talking about a very number of differently abled people in the country. If you also add the aging population where more than 80 per cent who are above 80, will have one or more than one disability, we are talking about a very vast gigantic figure. We also have some supporting things in terms of policy documents like PwD Act. The Government has also set up National Institutes like NIMH, NIVH, NIHH, NIOH, etc. We also have NCERT which gives guidelines for inclusive education. There has been lot of glorification of NGOs. As an NGO we feel very happy when the government says that the NGOs are the main players. Let us see what kind of partnership we have with the government. We have contributed for human resource development, professionalisation, advocacy, networking, community based rehabilitation, portage, inclusive education, application of latest technology. NGOs in 70s have really done a lot. NGOs are developing. There has been a tremendous change in the NGOs profiles, NGOs capabilities. I would like to say one more word on the capabilities of NGOs, the capacity of NGOs is gaining lot of recognition at the information level, at the national level, at the international levels. NGOs are not mere recipients of government grants and implementing the services. They are contributing to filling up the gaps which the government is not able to do without the support of NGOs. The contribution of NGOs, I see lot of development, initiated basically in urban areas and NGOs moving into rural areas but by and large the NGO culture, NGOs efforts have been urban based. It is not only urban based if you analyse, we have an example of 500 NGOs which have been listed by the Planning Commission and if we analyse the data, the data is also very interesting. Like we see only 1 per cent of NGOs, out of 580, are in early intervention programmes. Seventy-seven per cent are involved in education and only 3 per cent are involved in vocational training and placement. Less than 1 per cent are involved in networking and advocacy and again less than 1 per cent are involved in gender focus. Around 17 per cent are involved in human resource development. We have to see why there is so much development. By and large the NGOs are initiated by parents, and the parents who were educated in 70s and 80s. When we look at the 90s scenario, we see lot of community based groups, self-help groups that are initiated by the local people. What is really affecting the scenario is that there is not real convergence, understanding and trust between the NGOs and the government and what are the priorities. Where is the map for the NGOs based on the need and what kind of support the government gives, funding infrastructure and various other issues. But we don't have data on what kind of NGOs are required, what is the magnitude of the problem of disability, how much money is available, which NGO is expected in each district, how we should go about it. When we see the number of NGOs working in different areas of disability, we find that only less than 27 per cent of districts in India have presence of NGOs and they are based in district headquarters and if you go to the remote villages there are no NGOs. So it is very important for us to see that this development has to be checked to make an impact in the field of disability. The need of the hour is that we have need based distribution of services. What is the money available and in what sectors and that is very very important to NGOs like us to identify and prioritise our efforts into the districts so that NGOs are spread in all the districts and do not concentrate in urban areas or at the district headquarters. The relationship has to be based on mutual trust and respect and the NGOs should not be seen as implementing government programmes but to look at the NGOs programmes as replicable major government programme. So this also calls for more convergence. There are issues that are bothering NGOs, whether they are centrally sponsored schemes or schemes sponsored by international agencies or by the grant in aid schemes of the State Governments. The major problem that NGOs have is certainly money and which is a very important problem. We see insecurity among NGOs in terms of resources. The major problem we have identified is, what would happen once the government withdraws funding. This is the problem with the centrally sponsored programmes. When the international agencies support what happens to their project when it is over, then it has to be translated into programme, who will sustain those programmes. Having said that NGOs or the people are part of the community like after raising hope after starting services, they cannot close down the services. It is not possible. What happens is NGOs start services with a very high level of enthusiasm but we see NGOs struggling a lot to sustain them because none of these programmes guarantee on-going support. According to a study done by NCDP, less than 25 per cent NGOs in India receive any grant from the government. That way we are very happy that there is a good will and gesture of volunteerism but on the other hand we also see that there is no fair distribution of government resources. We see NGOs in the remote villages, community based organizations or people with disabilities have initiated their own groups, they have a long way to go to get access to climb in the bureaucratic ladder to access government resources. It is very important for us to realize that none of us is as good as all of us. The time has come for networking. Only through network will we be able to look into those issues and collectively plan and prepare both kind of energies. We have to analyse that and channelise our energy to lead to a society which is just and fair to all persons with disabilities. Time has come to break the barriers of labour. Time has come for us to look into partnership, which is meaningful and purposeful.

Suggestions: Government must publish need for starting NGOs in different districts. This kind of baseline is very important and according to me it is very much lacking. We have no idea on what kind of NGOs are required and what kind of resources are available. This is not only the responsibility of central government. It is also very important to see that the State governments also publish this data. NGOs should chose the geographical area based on the need. We cannot start the services where we are because it is convenient to us. We need to take up lot of hardships and move out and to see that we start the services where these are needed most. There is also need for proper documentation of NGOs. NGOs work is not well documented in the disability sector. We need to really move in this direction and make it available to the government, policy planners and the society. NGOs should move in a very big way consciously, intelligently, deliberately to see that our managements, our governing councils, at all decision-making levels, we have people with disabilities deciding every thing. We cannot say something else and do something else. We need to practice what we preach. Because it is very very important that we move with rights approach. We have to protect the rights of our organization because there are lot of studies in India which shows that people with disabilities and women with disabilities, have no representation on the board of management or in the staff. So time has come for introspection and to see that there is no gap between what we say and what we do. We have to introduce more accountability and it is very important to establish credibility. The big fish among NGO sector, have to really take the responsibility to support small fish in the pond because what we see is that there are big organizations who really take the big chunk of resources and small ones struggle even for basic support from the government. Micro level decentralization of resources, at the Panchayat level, will ensure that small community based organizations will have access to majority of resources. With that I would like to conclude my presentation. I am very thankful to RCI for organizing this seminar where for the first time I find that a government organization is having relationship which is based on mutual trust and respect.

CHAIRPERSON

Thank you Mrs. Rao. Your last suggestion that NGOs need better accountability is a very important point and I feel so far as funds disbursement is concerned, this factor has to be taken very seriously. Constraints of funds is definitely there. At the same time willingness of NGOs to become accountable is very important. I would say that one of the challenges before NGOs today to make their services, make their funds properly utilized. Try to maximise utilization with the limited resources that are available. Other points which she has referred to I will try to sum up at the end of this session.

MR. ANKUR SAXENA

At part of the theme Role of NGO's in rehabilitation programmes I am presenting a case study of Sunday School, a project of Friends Society, Baroda, The evolution of NGOs. As globalization and international trade impact, societies, NGOs, have become increasingly influential in world affairs. They are consulted by governments as well as international organizations and the United Nations has created associated status for them. The development of NGOs can be placed within the context of historical evolutionary developments. So there is a need to clarify the current position. Korten describes this development of NGOs in three phases or generations beginning with a focus on relief and welfare, then moving towards local self-reliance and finally to sustainable systems development.

India has a glorious tradition of organizing voluntary work for social good. NGOs, are thus, no more regarded marginal actors they were perceived to be through the 1970s and much of the 1980s. In the changed situation, they are rather considered to be the key players who can have a substantial impact on development. In line with the growing critiques of the state and market mechanisms, NGOs are considered as the third sector possessing a vast potential for change and development by virtue of their comparative advantages. Our society is at the level of self-reliance.

Friends Society is a non-governmental organization started functioning in 1969. Friends Society stands for the mobilization and rehabilitation of voluntary efforts of persons, especially the differently abled persons for conducting need based community service projects and developing their personality and rehabilitating them. I would like to present the case study of Sunday School. It is non-institutionalized differently abled school for children of the Baroda city. The main objective of this school is provision of supplementary education, medical rehabilitation, mobility acceleration and social integration of its beneficiaries. This school started in 1978. At present there are about 60 differently abled children attending the Sunday School and the age group of these differently abled children are from 6 to 12 years. The classification of the children is we have 40 physically handicapped, 3 mentally retarded and physically handicapped and 17 mentally retarded attending Sunday School every Sunday. Some of the activities undertaken through Sunday School are medical rehabilitation done through physiotherapy, check ups by orthopaedic surgeons and paediatricians, counselling session for family members of the children with guidance in correct handling and child rearing practices, educational activities include exposure to banks, railway station, yoga camps, etc., art therapy like drawing painting, clay modelling, mehandi work, origami is carried out to improve the fine motor co-ordination of the children, monthly parents meeting regarding rehabilitation and development status of child. In addition, we are celebrating festivals. Gujarat is famous for navratra festivals. The main aim is to mainstream them in the society. Other activities include activities of daily living, instrumental activities for daily living, reading, writing and arithmetic skill development, extra curricular activities like sport, culture, vocational and social activities, community integration. We give more emphasis on the parents meeting, particularly mother's come to Sunday School with their children. Volunteers from social work come to Sunday School to teach the students. What should be the role of NGOs in rehabilitation programmes? NGOs should know about all the available schemes of the Government of India, NGOs should be aware of all the acts and legislations for ensuring the rights of disabled people, NGOs should integrate the disabled people in the society by the acting as a bridge between government and mentally retarded children, NGOs should strengthen hands of government by co-ordinating with various government departments to ensure that disabled people are given all the benefits of government programmes, NGOs can help to create good awareness about the rights of the disabled, NGOs can help to prevent discrimination in society against the disabled people, and NGOs can mobilize the disabled people to get assistance from programmes available for the disabled people. There is smile on the mother's face and that is a matter of satisfaction for us.

CHAIRPERSON

We are happy to see that a young man like you has taken a life of dedication. We would like to see more such young people coming forward in this task of serving the disabled.

MR. YOGENDRA MEHTA (Translated from Hindi)

Earlier speakers have told us about the problems, challenges before us. The job of NGOs is like that of heart to purify the blood. If all the NGOs are good, they are doing good work, then there will be no problem because no bad NGOs would enter the field. People treat us as God so we have to live as God. They call us mother, because mother give us love. Do we love our disabled clients? Mother gives us medicine, do we give such medicine to our disabled clients, mother does not complain but earns silently to feed us. If we do all this we can be mothers of our own disabled child. As Indumathi Rao said it is time for introspection, we have to give love and affection to disabled, whether they belong to SC, ST or any other class. We should consider whether are we able to give to the children what they need from a father. If the answer is yes, then let us move forward. Or let us try to improve. Have we accepted our disabled children or disabled people as our good friends? If yes, it is very good. If no, then we must try to become their good friends through NGOs because only the NGOs are good friends of the disabled. Like Krishna and Arjun, we NGOs should go to the disabled to understand their problems, their needs. Mind should be dominated by heart. Why I say this because without heart you can't get involvement. If you don't have devoted involvement, you can't be *karamyogi*. You can't make the disabled happy, healthy and prosperous. In order to achieve all this, we have to involve our heart with all these activities and all our problems remind you very well, all our problems can easily be solved if our heart is involved in our work. Once I was going in a bus when the conductor and some other passengers forced a mentally retarded child to get down from the bus. But I interfered. Conductor asked me whether he was my relative. I told him that he is my relative not in blood relation but as a human being. It is rightly said that the disabled should be involved. Nothing for us without us. NGOs should be ever changing. Dr. Punani has rightly said that what is not relevant should be thrown out only then there would be space for the good. Government is also disabled system. I would like to cite an example. I and Dr. Punani went to meet a Secretary, who said that blind children cannot study with normal children. I asked why? He said because blind is also deaf. We should try to make such officials understand the reality. If we want to achieve the all-round rehabilitation of all the disabled in this country, we should not follow the example of Ram. We cannot exclude disabled. We have to follow Krishna's attitude in our developmental programmes. One teacher asked me, that I don't have teachers to teach the blind. I asked him do you teach the man. He said yes. I told him that blind is a person first and blind later. Let us be outspoken to protect our rights, to get our rights. Remember, truth is never sweet. We must undertake research for new aids and appliances. We must strengthen financial position of our NGOs. We make buildings, but we don't buy books, why, because there is no money. We have to change our role otherwise people will forget us. We have to reach to the lowest level where the disabled person is living. We also have to work towards disability prevention. There was a NAB Convention on Prevention of Blindness in which we all worked together. The law of humanity should guide all the laws for mentally retarded, multiple handicapped. If our NGOs can become an eye opener even that is needed and that we should do. Government is ready to accept our impartial advice and therefore I feel instead of talking too much let us begin our real work and then this summit of mind will be converted into summit of humanity.

CHAIRPERSON

His talk has come from his heart. The willingness to serve despite challenges, despite several severed hurdles, the willingness to sacrifice as great part of welfare for others. Data, statistics, technologies, strategies, these are all necessary. Without love, affection and dignity to the disabled whom we are trying to serve, our effort shall remain incomplete. At the same time I would assure Mr. Mehta that NGOs need not take on the role of Sri Krishna in the sense of being aggressive with the government, not necessary. What we have to be aggressive against is mass of ignorance. Insensitivity towards disabled. Various factors have contributed to the general apathy of the people. Afterall government is not a monolithic body. We may be having our own relatives and friends working in the government. What is it that prevents us from becoming pro-actively aware of the problem of disability? I think the problem of disability has become invisible by the other problems being faced by the country. So much so that we do not know when disability would occupy centre stage in the national consciousness. This is one of the very important roles the NGOs will have to play. It is a challenge before us to awaken awareness about the disability in the entire society. Some months ago, when I had an opportunity to speak in the Spastic Society of India in Chennai, I had made this point that media has to be taken help of. The same way that pulse polio immunization was popularized and made successful all over the country, media should impinge something similar on a massive scale upon public awareness at all levels, at all age groups. The print media, the electronic media, the audio-visual media, writers, dramatics, cultural groups, have to take on this public awareness, insensitivity head on. That is where we have to be aggressive. Not against the government department. We lack information for the direction we have to take for convergence. We all need to know what RCI expects from us. Which are the areas where our services are needed? It is with this view that RCI in fact started the Zonal Advisory Councils. The NGOs can very well approach the Zonal Advisory Committees instead of bombarding RCI. Lot of information will be available through the ZACs so that the NGOs can work more effectively. All NGOs involved in the field of rehabilitation and disability have to learn to get down to the level of people they serve to understand their needs individually and collectively. They have to learn to see things through their minds. Just as a good teacher in school is best when he gets down to the level of student. Similarly NGOs shall be more effective when they succeed in getting down to the level of persons they wish to serve. Their needs are diverse, problems are many, age groups are different, community backgrounds are different, India is a very vast country, region to region this problem differs. Solutions will also have to differ. We are bound to succeed as the response to this Convention is tremendous evidence that our will power is still strong and the government, NGOs all are feeling the necessity of working together to achieve our goals. Now I request Dr. D. K. Singh to present his views.

DR. D. K. SINGH

Today we have gathered here to talk about role of NGOs in cross-disability rehabilitation. NGO's are India's greatest asset and are involved in promoting health, education, social welfare. The lives and needs and expectations of people with disabilities in India like rest of the world, are changing. Therefore, the policy of the welfare State must also change to the new situation.

I graduated from Patna Medical College in 1952 and was selected for higher studies in USA but my father said you have been born and brought up in a village, you have to go back to the village for work, upliftment and all round development of the under-privileged, poor, tribals and disabled. This was a big challenge for me but I thought I owe something. I must go there to serve people. There was no electricity, no roads, and other necessary amenities in the village but I obeyed my father and started private medical practice and voluntary work at the same time. I began visiting patients in different villages on horse back. I was surprised to see the poverty and suffering of the disabled. One day in 1954 while I was waiting for a boat to cross a river, I saw a leper begging. His fingers and toes were eaten up by deep ulcers. I still remember his name was Sheikh Chedi. I told him to get himself treated. He was reluctant. He said there was no body to look after me. There was no money and felt it was a curse of God. I assured him free treatment and told him to come to my clinic. He came to me and stayed at my hospital for three months. His wounds dried up and he was able to walk freely. I gave him a new set of clothes, Pyjama etc. and helped him in starting his job of fishing. Other lepers saw how his wounds healed and they developed faith in treatment. I kept treating them and about 250 lepers were treated and rehabilitated between 1954 and 1974. Their entire expenses were borne by me. I started organizing free eye camps from 1974 each year in winter. This impetus arose in me when I saw almost physically fit men and women between the age of 40 to 70 completely disabled due to blindness, mostly due to cataract. These patients were unable to move around and found it difficult to even go out to urinate or defecate. They were abused by their own children and few would lend a helping hand. This suffering was disgraceful. After proper investigation, diagnosis and surgery they were provided with spectacles and they could see. The brightness in their eyes and a smile on their faces makes us understand what eyesight means. An average of 150 patients per year were treated. All the expenses till 1984 were borne by me. In 1978, I took up another good cause when I saw little children limping around. I diagnosed they were all polio patients. I contacted the State and Central Government. They said polio vaccine were not available. So I imported 1,000 doses of polio vaccine from Russia and immunized the children in this area. In 1965 as a sole delegate from India to the World Asthma Conference in East Town, England, we discussed about disability and the chronically ill bronchial asthma patients with severe airway obstruction. In the U.S. we saw big size nebuligers in which the patients would put their heads in side and breath for 2 to 5 minutes. This would keep them fit for next two days. They were also disabled because of their illness.

I would recommend the following: disabled people with locomotor, visual, speech, hearing or mental impairment should be included in decision-making bodies of the government, representation of women should increase from present 3 per cent in executive bodies of the government or NGOs. Industry related skills, for example, art, crafts, making of stationery items, TV & Radio repair, computer handling and repairs should be taught and handled by disabled people, low cost aids and appliances and service for their repairs and maintenance should be made available, hostel facilities should be given to such disabled working people especially women, government should allocate more funds for the disabled sector. Many NGOs are facing problems as they remain starved of funds and resources. Working with RCI in mutual interest and purposive co-operation will edge to better service condition, proper use of resources, improved training of staff and more effective and efficient service, and the struggle for survival of NGOs is fierce. The thought of having co-operation, co-ordination and joint vision is becoming an unattainable dream.

DR. ALOKA GUHA

I want to share with you what role has been envisaged for NGOs in the National Trust which in itself is a culmination of synergy between government and non-government. After Bhaskar Bhai's emotive presentation, it is very difficult to talk about mind, brain without the heart. I would try to combine all three. As you know there are three Legislations in India. The last decade has been a very busy time for rights legislation. In the 1999 came to National Trust for Persons with Autism, Cerebral Palsy, Mental Retardation, and Multiple Disabilities.

We have been discussing figures in all the sessions and I don't think any body has exact figures. Perhaps we are talking about 50 million people with disabilities. If we take autism and cerebral palsy, it would be 2 or 3 per thousand. It is suggestive and not an exact figure. The point that has been raised again and again and the reason why the National Trust was set up is because it is understood that there are very very close links in poverty and disability and poverty is seen both as consequence and a cause of disability. If we look at the cycle we have here poverty which leads to poor literacy, poor health care, leads to disability which leads to limited access to education, health, and which in turn leads to unemployability. Again leading to isolation from the market place to economic strain and we are back to poverty cycle. Cycle of poverty and disability is something that is challenge for this millennium, certainly a challenge that will only be answered by inclusion and access for four categories of disabilities. In the National Trust NGOs have a very very strong role to play. It is like an NGO itself. In the National Trust the chairperson comes from the NGO sector, under Section 4 (a). The second role is as a member under Local Level Committee (LLC) which is a major instrumentality of the National Trust. Under Section 13: In its objectives it is very clearly mentioned about the role of NGOs. In approved programmes in Section 11, registered organizations, again NGOs have a major role to play. The last is Annual General Meeting which is hosted by us every year in which our Annual Report is passed by our stake holders before we send it to Ministry to be placed in Parliament. So in many ways National Trust runs in a democratic way like an NGO to whom we give registration. Fifty per cent of our Board consists of NGOs and four out of those 9 persons are parents of four disabilities represented in the Trust. So we have equal fifty fifty representation, government having 9 seats, NGOs having 9 seats, chairperson being from the NGO. You must have understood how very very strong is the role of NGOs in the National Trust. This is the implementational role. Starting with awareness generation in every corner of the country from Tripura to Salem to Activation of National Trust in itself in meetings, legal guardianship, as a watch dog and participating in the Local Level Committee. One-third of a Local Level Committee is consisting of NGO. Advocacy for inclusive programmes. What you see here is a group of District Collectors, we call them to Delhi from different parts of the country and organize sensitization programme for them. Assimilation exercises; we give the Collectors wheelchairs, crutches etc. to feel themselves, what is disability. We have 22 types of publications translated into 13 languages and we have circulated and sold over 85,000 copies in the last 1½ years. These copies are available outside. In the implementation of skills our NGOs have strongest role to play. NGOs are registered to implement our schemes. One scheme of reach and relief, which is sub-divided into two parts. One is the Care Givers Scheme which we have done at three levels, State, district and community level. Then we have three types of Centre based schemes, day care, respite care short-term and residential care. This is a care givers training programme, this is the home based services for the first time in India, providing care givers in a six months home based training programme which is recognized by RCI and where the applicant is of 10 or 12 standard, comes from the community and stays in the community. I have heard enormously promoting response from them. If you ask them what is mental retardation, they may not be able to give you an exact definition but they will give you very very clear characteristics of mental retardation. That kind of services we need in our remote and rural areas today. We work at 34 information centres. This year we are launching six Annual Awards of the National Trust, Award for the best Local Level Committee (LLC), Award for the

Best Information Centre, Award for the Best Care Givers Training, Best Day Care Centre, Best Respite Centre, Best Residential Centre. Rs. 50,000, a shield and a certificate. This information will be available through our information centre and through our web site. We, the larger organizations, have to take the facilitator role for smaller organizations. We tried this through Blind People's Association (BPA), funds are routed through BPA and they support more organizations, thereby maintaining accountability, good technical expertise, and uniformity in service delivery. We had 9 teleconferences through IGNOU. In Rajasthan, out of 30, 18 LLCs are very active. 269 LLCs are there in 578 districts. We have given registration to 344. We trained master trainers at NIMH at their cost. Then they went to district level and trained the district level trainers. District level trainers trained the community level care givers. 1,600 care givers have been trained. We have 203 projects going on. We should break information barrier. If we do that we will have attitudinal changes and access will be easier for barrier free.

Don't walk before me, for I may not follow;
Don't walk behind me, for I may not lead;
Just walk beside me, and be my friend.

CHAIRPERSON

Role of NGOs is under four heads. Creating awareness, creating right type of professionals, to adopt and adapt our strategies, procedures and our activities, adopt the standards set up by RCI, recognize the distinction between needs of geographic areas, different disabled persons in different areas, recognize that what we mean by educating the disabled should not be limited to formal education. We have to recognize that the mass majority of disabled shall be benefited most if they are provided skills based money earning vocational skills. It is a challenge and the role that the NGO must play because of which the government has to come forth. The government and NGOs have to work together. My appeal to NGOs is to keep this commitment alive. The willingness to sacrifice for the sake of the disabled as educated people. I should not be misquoting from Swami Vivekananda who said I hold every educated Indian who having been educated at the cost of millions does not pay back to them. Let us also keep alive our strong motivation, our transparency. I wish all the NGOs success in their activities and I hope that we shall succeed working together.

IV

INFORMATION COMMUNICATION TECHNOLOGY IN REHABILITATION

Chairperson: Dr. N. Vijayaditya
Co-Chairperson: Dr. Bhushan Punani

As far as Information Technology (IT) is concerned, this particular field can be extensively used, there are lots of ways in which this technology can be utilised. So that we can help disabled people in a variety of ways. Recently I have been reading an article from US, where he was trying to embed micro processor chip behind the ear so that hearing impaired people can hear properly. He was trying to connect this chip to brain so that interpretation becomes much much easier. Lot of work has been going on. Also in the area of electronics, we are going from micro electronics to neon electronics which is going to be very minute, which is very small and even not visible. Definitely we have to look at it. I think one needs to do lot of work in this area so that this particular technology can be effectively used. Of course to use any of these products you may require knowledge. We are supposed to be very good in software. We are known worldwide for software. I got a letter from a Government department that the websites prepared by NIC should have a provision so that these websites can be used by the disabled people. I asked my officer what are the requirements for this, why can't we do this. She said she would examine and it is good disabled people should be enabled to have access to websites. But there are certain enabling clauses which have to be implemented by the government so that it is compulsory for them to do that. I understand recently that United States Government has introduced an amendment to their particular scheme to facilitate the people to provide information which can assist the disabled persons to make use of the information which is put on the website. All the NGOs are there, I would like to emphasize here. We need to look at it and ask the government about the amendment which has to be made so that the electronic information that is available can be effectively made use of by all the people concerned. We need to work for this amendment so that it comes in a faster manner. If you look at the Internet and video conferencing, this is a mechanism to provide information only, dissemination of information. How to chat with each other, how to make use of the voice mail system. In every disability you should be able to introduce this technology. These technologies help us to extract knowledge from the individual and is an asset to the organization. I am quite sure we have enough capability in this country to work in this particular direction. I remember one day Major Ahluwalia asked me, they are conducting spinal surgery, etc., why can't we enable other institutions which are there. We actively participated with them and this was done at Vasant Kunj connected to other centres, where the doctors could participate. People working in this area have to gain knowledge what is going on in the world. This is one technology which can be done and can be used effectively.

CO-CHAIRPERSON

You have already given valuable information. One thing I would like to add from the rehabilitation point of view, it is not only the computers and IT which matters, this technology has great scope in compensating sensory losses, like person with deaf-blindness, there are systems available where information technology can play a role to access the outside information and to compensate for some of the losses. Only point I would like to remind the speakers, that in our country while this technology is growing very fast in the sector of disability it has not grown as well. The biggest constraint at the moment is the cost. While IT in general has become affordable, it is not so in case of disability sector. Still we do not have as much systems within the country where we can go for mass production. Still we depend upon imported technology. For example, software for the visually impaired. Even today you have to import it paying US $ 800 whereas it is not costing more than 10 dollars. The only point of reference is the Ministry of Social Justice & Empowerment should come forward, should sponsor some research to indigenous technology for people with disabilities so that it is affordable. The irony of the situation is that we have technology, we have systems, but they are for the institutes, only for few. Unless it becomes affordable, my request to the Chairman is that how this technology can be made affordable. The point is very well taken that there is technology, it helps, it compensates for the loss, very good for exchange of information, for sensitization. But the question is can we afford to give this technology to each and everybody. According to me we can't give to a select few because for most of the technology we have to depend on import.

MR. R. RANGASAYEE

Ours is a National Institute and we recognize diversity in the population, diversity not only in degree of disability but in terms of their socio-economic conditions as well. Therefore, we have methods and approaches where at no cost hearing screening can be taken. At no cost hearing intervention can be done, at no cost hearing assessment can be done. These are our boundaries and within diversity we are defining the boundaries. This is an emerging area and improved technologies have led to reducing the cost in many countries. For example in the area of bio-chemistry where a bio-chemical test will cost 100 dollars, today is available in the form of a chip in two dollars. In fact, in developed countries tele-rehabilitation has been used very successfully. In a way assessment is done through tele mode. Teleconferencing techniques have been used to provide therapy to people, sitting in one room they have 10 terminal through which they control. This is the highest level at which they are handling. The minimum level at which they are handling is very nice. Through a telephone they call up a person who is emotionally disturbed, who is placed elsewhere in open employment. They call up and talk to him, this is happening. If you look at what inspired me three four years ago, I was telling one dental surgeon whose father had a stroke and he was not able to swallow. He had typical difficulty in swallowing. There was a need to tell the dental surgeon to give cold treatment on the tonsils. This much I had to tell him. We have lost lot of time. I know that Malasiya is doing much better in hardware than we are doing.

There are many definitions of tele-rehabilitation. But basically it is described by use of video cameras, computers, video phone, internet and telephone to provide rehabilitation services to those who live away from the rehabilitation experts. In our conventional mode we expect somebody to reach us, but in this we reach them, that is the difference. It also reduces the number of trips to the rehabilitation experts. This provides beneficiaries life long learning opportunities in the process of rehabilitation. The need for tele-rehabilitation is virtual reality technology, this is something which reduces the gap between invention by the time it is used for the benefit of the persons with disability. That time should be reduced. Virtual technology has emerged in this area. It can reach the beneficiary with speed, accuracy and effectiveness in terms of rehabilitation of people with disabilities. It can effectively reach the unreached people, to empower the family and community, increase the number of beneficiaries across political borders and also to save cost. In Mumbai lawyers went on one day strike. Why, because the companies are consulting the lawyers in US and they are getting signed scripts from US. These lawyers are going jobless. This can happen in any other area as well. Which means the fund flow, the money flow, can be missing. To increase the number across the political border as well as to save cost. If we don't do, we will be left out to draw the benefit. More so for the professionals. Elsewhere it shows that hearing impairment, learning disability, autism, dysphasia, stuttering, and in many other areas, even in educating hearing handicapped, there have been specific studies which have appeared and they have been encouraging. The scope of tele-rehabilitation is limited to our imagination. Tele-rehabilitation need not be a tool in the hands of people with disabilities for rehabilitation purposes. The use of tele-rehabilitation is possible where there are telephones and mobile phones. The scope of tele-rehabilitation include tele-monitoring, screening and therapy, video conferencing, video tele-communication as well as text screen. Special purpose graphics can make the text response final. Today in India we have 9.4 lakh internet users, about 5 crores telephone users, and other two million mobile phone users are there and there are large number of families of people with disabilities who have access to these. Application of tele-rehabilitation can be in screening of disability, diagnosis, therapy or intervention, research, training of trainers as well as in self-employment area. Emerging areas in tele-rehabilitation programmes are tele-assessment, tele-therapy, tele-play, tele-clinic, tele-coaching, tele-home care, tele-group therapy, and tele-monitoring. I have listed needs from the audiological point of view for hearing testing, for auditory response. It can be used for research, it can be used for testing, through telephone, some of the private hospitals do have these facilities. Hearing testing can be done if we appropriately use this technology. The interpretation may have to change but there is a need. If you look at the market economy, they will not be interested in substituting advanced technology because they will need money. But in our country it can be used for people with disabilities at our cost. If you are good, people from all over the world will contact you. What can be done in India. Video camera and video phone, video camera can be used in store and access mode. For example, certification of disability is a major activity going on and I believe more than 60 per cent need not come to hospital or need not come to district level for their certification. If we can arrange to send somebody with the video camera who can go along with evidence and take those films and bring and plays, what is called store and access mode, this can be very successfully used. It needs to be tried, what kind of medical assistance is required. You may not even need a clinic. You can function from your room from telephone from tele-clinic, still be a consultant to hundreds and thousands of people. There are more strengths and opportunities than weaknesses in this area. Tele-rehabilitation has great potential to increase the reach. Telephones and mobiles can be used, video camera can be used for certification, e-mail services. This I thought will use for the professionals who are running away from India. You use this tele-rehabilitation method and whole world will be yours. Simply because you are in Delhi your facilities no one need to come to me, people from Delhi will contact me in Mumbai and get my advice. This is what across the geographical boundaries, all political boundaries also, the tele-rehabilitation is bound to happen and if we use this as our tool in our economic and social milieu, if we apply innovatively, I am sure this tele-rehabilitation approach can make lot of meaning in this country.

CHAIRPERSON

In this country we did make some progress in this field.

MS. SWATI LAHIRI AND SMITA WORAH

The topic of our presentation is "Information Communication Technology for Persons with Disabilities—our experience and new developments". We see technological advances in our daily lives. It has tremendous effect on the lives of people with disabilities which can not be undermined. More attention needs to be paid to develop technologies to assist persons with disabilities to become independent within their abilities. However, in order to use technology meaningfully for persons with disabilities, the conducive infrastructure needs to exist. This is in terms of collaboration between NGOs working in the field of disability, institutes of technology and the government. All three can put their resources together and improve the life of persons with disabilities. Indian Institute of Cerebral Palsy (IICP) has been working in the field of multiple disabilities for two decades. While providing services, IICP has realized the importance of technology and how it can assist the disabled. IT opens the world for any body sitting before a terminal and adds another dimension to education, teaching aids and visual communication for leisure skills and communication itself. The application of software and hardware, helps the people with multiple disabilities, in realising that the cognitive and physical constraints can be overcome. In education this can be used as teaching aids. It makes learning easy in the class-room. Software which audio visually reinforces the concept of colour, shape, sizes, and directions can be taught and is useful for young learners. It gives the idea of scanning the right one. We have another software which is used to teach the number skills and its basic concepts at higher level. Most of the students who have severe physical access problem can use these features, like adapted mouse, etc. Computers can be of great help as a medium of communication for the students with severe problems of physical access and for students for non-speaking. This group needs help to write independently. To communicate with the world around them. A thorough and careful assessment has to be carried out of the situation. Accessibility options in Indian environment can help the people with disabilities. Different adaptive hardware options can be used to help persons with severe disabilities. Computers have special softwares for Braille, for voice recognition systems which can enhance the educational skills of persons with disabilities. Students studying at National Open School and Indira Gandhi National Open University can take advantage of these special software. The persons with disabilities can pursue higher education if they are given these facilities. IT for leisure. Many persons with disabilities may not be able to pursue leisure skills such as go out and play physical games. They can receive that extra exposure and extra information through IT. They can use the media like surf the internet, send e-mail, chat with friends and play CDs, play games. Multimedia can change their lives. Most of the adaptive devices and software are so far being imported. As a result they are very expensive. Moreover no support is available for these products. Fortunately some IT institutes are showing interest in this area and are taking up research projects. IICP is also pursuing following projects in this area. Firstly developing a multi-media software which will allow facilitators and users to use standardized pictures and icons. Attach pre-recorded voice for enhancement of language and composition of text. IICP will field test this software with facilitators and users. The data base can be in different languages and can be developed according to individualized needs. Developing a hardware and software system for education of students with cerebral palsy and communication difficulties in collaboration with IIT, Kharagpur.

CHAIRPERSON

The last point what she made that the technology should help and not the technology should dictate what to do. It is very important. You should know what you want the technology to perform. The issues raised and points made are very valid.

MR. ASHWINI KUMAR AGGARWAL

I stand here to represent the National Association for the Blind (NAB), Delhi Branch which has always pioneered the important role of bringing information technology to support the VI persons to dismantle the disability that we face. My paper in detail will be coming to you. I am giving the things in a very brief form and I would like the audience to spend some more time in putting queries so that I can exactly share the experience NAB Delhi has gained over the last 10 years in the field of information communication and technology. Chairman Sir, you have just mentioned about your website being made accessible to visually impaired persons. NAB has always been, along with most of the other agencies, producing CDs and various information technology which is being put in the market to ensure that these are accessible. We have been calling upon the government authorities, recommendations after recommendations that the information technology whichever is coming it should come in the form of accessible format. How a visually impaired person accesses information technology. We have four softwares which are very crucial to help a visually impaired person to access the information technology. First and foremost which is of paramount importance is screen reading software. This is text to speech utilization technology. They are text to speech engines. The basic advantage is that you get complete control of whatever is there on the screen that can be put forward in the form of audio through multi-media into the synthetic voice. This helps us to manoeuvre whether we want to read sentence by sentence or para by para or text. Graphics with text markings are fully accessible to us. Second software that is of crucial importance is that optical connector recognition software. Here we have to understand as such, we don't have to make any major change in respect of hardware in order to access the information from the computers. The multi-media which is available in all the computers, we have to only load the screen reading software the cost of which is there, as Dr. Punani mentioned, I would like to discuss separately. OCRS helps through the use of scanner whatever the print material is there to scan it, it is deciphered and through the screen reading software the print word is accessed by the visually impaired person. Third software is the Braille transcription software which also helps us to access information through Braille. Most of the modern Braille presses are already using the number of software which are there. These softwares help us to provide the books fast, do editing fast and simultaneously the multiple copies that are produced are more accurate, less error prone and they are easily accessible to blind persons. So this gives us or empowers us to have more Braille books for the visually impaired persons in the country. What this Information Communication Technology (ICT) is giving to the visually impaired person? One of the major areas in which it has made dent is the education. Now the visually impaired person can access the Braille books, the E-text library which NAB Delhi is soon going to develop with help from Lee Foundation, would allow E-text of books which the visually impaired persons anywhere in the country would be in a position to request to us, we are going to convert that into E-text and provide the book in the E-text format which would allow the person to read it through the computers. The same information in the E-text format can be utilized for producing Braille books. The fourth technology which has come is the digital format, like wrist watches with audio output, or talking calculators or talking thermometers. This very technology has been utilized in the form of Daisy format. Earlier we were having our talking books on audio cassettes. We had to access information manually whereas we could not maneuver to go to a specific chapter, specific page, specific section, this has been dismantled. Now we are into the age in which we are going to introduce digital technology and NAB Delhi has already introduced it. We are going to play an important role to ensure that all the talking book libraries in the country have access to the technology and utilize it accordingly. Another good thing I would like to share is that IIT Delhi is collaborating with NAB Delhi to produce a Daisy player which is economical. One can procure under the Scheme of Assistance to Disabled Persons for Purchase/Fitting of Aids/Appliances (ADIP Scheme). But at present the Daisy books can be played on PCs, which is a limiting factor which needs to be dismantled. Second area in which ICT has helped us is in acquiring employment opportunities. We have visually impaired people, may be small number, who are going into programming. With the help of screen reading software we have visually impaired persons who are working as programmers whether with RBI or in the private sector and more people are there in the pipeline who are going to be programmers. Similarly medical transcriptors, call centre managers. There are people who are involved in more jobs who were slightly getting outdated because of automation. They have again been rehabilitated with the use of ICT. A bank officer can access his information, his circulars, and other matters with the help of screen reading software which he could not have otherwise.

A person who is practicing as a lawyer, they have been able to access the information, refer the cases which are there because most of the material on the cases being available on the E-text format. These things have helped in employment of visually impaired persons in empowering them to open new avenues for them. Leisure activity or entertainment is rather crucial. There are certain games which our children right from initial stages are utilizing and they are getting friendly with the ICT. These are the three areas which are of paramount importance. I would like to share some of the things about the training NAB has been imparting. We should start training to the visually impaired person as early as possible. We at NAB Delhi invite all of you if you have a chance to visit us, and see how a five or six years old kid completely maneuvers the computer. The earlier you familiarize the child with the use of computers the better the child is. This is our experience. There are children in our centre who are studying in regular schools in inclusive setting making use of ICT both in the school as well as in their homes to do their home work. One of the child is using his computer in the classroom and whatever work is given by the teachers he does it there itself and the teacher checks it also. These things are possible may be a small beginning has been made, but over the years we will find that inclusive education as such can also be looked into with the help of ICT. NAB Delhi has already gained such an experience and we are ready to share with other agencies as the time comes. While training visually impaired persons, it is of paramount importance that exposure to alternative control other than mouse is important. The mouse should be removed while a person is training the visually impaired person. Our experience with visually impaired persons as faculty has always been very positive and effective. Another important task which I would like to stress is on post-training utilization. NAB Delhi has been playing a very important role in ensuring that after the training, the trainee is properly utilized. To ensure that we have a scheme where we provide interest free loans to visually impaired persons as soon as they complete the training. So that they are in a position to get the computers right away. Second thing is we are holding regular workshops and interactive sessions with our trainees, ex-trainees, so that they are continuously updated with their work.

DR. K. S. SAI

We are engaged in the development of gadgets on the medical side as well as for the handicapped. Most of you would know that the Department of Information Technology, which was earlier called Department of Electronics has been engaged in the development of a number of gadgets under R&D projects. We have been developing information technology related aids for the visually handicapped and there were number of projects during the last 8-10 years. But what happens under R&D projects we have been interacting with a number of R&D goods in electronics, whether it is IITs or CSIR laboratories. When a scientist gets involved in such a thing he develops a prototype which will be a working model and he is happy for solving the problem. But if you can really go to the field and it is used by the handicapped person extensively so that stage generally does not come. Unless you deploy in a large scale, consciously make an effort from the people who use it, the project invariably becomes success in a way that it has achieved what the researcher had in mind. But the failure is that it never reaches the field. There must be a departure from this trend. As a part of Jai Vigyan Mission project, the aim of which is to see that some result reaches the field level funding was no problem under this project. We took up that opportunity and launched a project which was comparatively a larger project but this time we said we will not stop at the laboratory level but whatever is developed is really deployed in the field on a larger scale. So we launched the project jointly with Rabble Media Limited, Calcutta and IIT Kharagpur for the development of Braille transcriptor system and a variety of aids, IT related aids for the visually handicapped. Predominantly the emphasis there has been on text speech related systems. There are two schools developing gadgets for the visually handicapped. One school very strongly believes that Braille is there to stay and we must help the visually handicapped persons with the Braille as far as possible. Always the similar question printed matter *vs* Braille? Even for the normal people also I don't think we can ever dispense with the books. However, e-books may be there in the computer we would definitely like to hold a book in our hand and read it. Similarly for the blind people also Braille is actually their life line. And definitely they would like to continue with that. From that point of view we thought that technology should be brought to that level so that Braille material is more easily available to them. As on today the situation is, if you look at the blind school children one major problem with them is the Braille reading material. Why this problem? Because today what we have with us is that the child himself or herself takes the notes in her own hand using the style as Braille writing material or get access to the more difficult textbooks which are printed by the Braille presses of the Government of India. The Braille presses from the Government of India can not turn out large number of Braille books. This is the situation where PCs are available in most of the schools also or even if they are not, they are at affordable prices. From the PC you can get an embosser which works in an inexpensive way and easy is an kind of thing to operate, then this problem can be solved. With the help of Mediatronics, Kolkata and IIT, Kharagpur, this webble people what they have done, all of you know the blind persons would have used what is known as Brailler which is basically a manual mechanical Brailler with the normal hammer, which we have in normal typewriters. They have removed the hammers, they have removed the bottom portion of that thing and replaced it with a complete electronic circuit and motorised the whole thing. That has been interfaced with a PC with the result it is now possible to take out a Braille print using this Braille embosser. Any file available in the PC can be taken out as a Braille output. India is a linguistically and culturally rich country and all the States have their own languages and other things. If you want a Brailler to take an output in Indian languages it is next to impossible because it is provided only in English. In this particular project the IIT, Kharagpur has developed the software and if you have a file in any Indian language and using ILAY it is possible to take the Braille print out in any Indian language. The system has been deployed in 30 schools all over the country. All these people are using different Indian languages, 12 languages have already been developed. It is possible to generate a file in the computer and using the ILAY, it is possible for a blind school teacher to generate class notes, or question paper or whatever she wants and give the output to her children. Earlier we used to depend upon typewriter and the typist to give a print out in typed form. Once the laser printer has come we can easily take out the print and use it. Similarly with the help of this small gadget which is available, any file in the PC can be taken out in any of the Indian languages by the school authorities themselves. There is also a Braille to text kind of software which has been developed. For example, if a visually handicapped person wants to communicate with the normal person there is no way because he cannot write in the normal text characters. His Braille sighted people would not know. Braille-text software helps to take out the print out in normal text which can be used by the sighted people. These two things that is from the PC, output can be taken out on an automatic Braille embosser and Braille key board which can be used by a blind person the output can be taken out as a normal printed text. This is in demonstration mode outside and can be seen. We are also trying to develop a tactile device. Tactile device is a replaceable device which are of 20 character and have Braille cells. It can be connected to computer and as sighted persons use monitor to see a text or whatever is there in the file, if they want they can take the print or can scan the pages. This opens a large number of opportunities. This is like a library situation. The sighted librarian can connect, whatever is there in the e-text format or whatever format, to the computer. Eight blind students each of them can read a different file with the help of this tactile device. For example, if I want to read a novel of Charles Dickens, the librarians open a Charles Dickens file for me. Similarly each individual can handle the tactile device at his own speed individually. Also with the help of direct keyboard that has been developed, 8 such people can be connected to a computer, the sighted person will be there as a teacher and the students will be having the Braille keyboard with them so that when the teacher asks a question, each one can type their answer independently with his keyboard. Automatically on the screen of the teacher the answer comes. It is an e-class room type of environment. Using this technology it is possible for the student to answer whatever question is asked by the teacher and automatically the teacher can evaluate the answers. In addition, a number of other things are going on. Today we have scanners, page scanners. Using the OCR or text, it is possible to read the whole file. Unfortunately, these page scanners do not allow any book to be loaded on to them. We are also developing a software for the blind persons to help them read a book like sighted persons. The day is not far when such a scanner would be available. Hope within the next 3-4 years of time this project would also be realized.

MR. R.P. PAL

I was very carefully listening to Dr. Sai and that now visually handicapped persons can use computers, multi-media computers, voice mail and audio signal. Can they use voice mail or audio signals instead of braille which is very costly. In the multiplicity of the language, I know that at IIT, Bombay, my friend Mr. Bhattacharyya has been working on languages highway which makes 86 languages, inter convertible. You talk French, you want in Marathi you will get it. With that convertibility on the back, can you use audio man to activate your inputs to your computer that will enlarge access to information and all other websites. The problem is not to receive, receiving is very easy but your inputs to the computer can be audio accessed.

MR. AGGARWAL

As regards inputs to visually impaired persons, input from an ordinary keyboard is very comfortable for a visually impaired person which we have experienced with very young children. As regards voice input, it has not been very successful.

DR. SAI

From speech to text, I think technologically it is too far off. There has been so much expenditure all over the world. But speech to text, because there are variety of speeches people speak, I think that will be far off.

MR. PRAKASH

The presentation made by both the experts is really excellent. I am suffering from visual disability right from birth and using the computers with the help of Jaws for windows. I would like to add something to what has been presented here. There are three other software also. Coresal 1,000 with the help of this software you can read the printed material. Scanner will read the book. You can go to any page, any para, any section with ease. Other one is OBR, Optical Braille Recognition Software. You can take out the print out of old Braille material which may not be quite clear. There is no need for data entry. The third software is TGD, Tactile Graphic Designer. You can convert any graph into Braille with the help of computer. These softwares are available in my organization at Rajkot and Jamnagar. We have got lot of experience with these softwares.

DR. SAI

All these softwares are available outside the country and are expensive. Most of our schools, blind persons cannot afford it. They are not available in Indian languages. For the blind persons predominantly what is needed at the grass roots level is something available in Indian languages. I would request all of you to see our demonstration. The Braille embosser and duxbury software will cost you around Rs. 4.5 lakhs. What we have developed can be afforded by most of our schools, printer along with software is available at a cost of Rs. 1.2 lakhs. If you have computer, you will be able to generate your own braille material from the Indian languages.

DR. SANGITA AGGARWAL

I have integrated children with CP and other disabled children and I am a strong believer in mainstreaming. Whenever I attend such conferences I find that IT related equipments/software are available in IT institutions and other institutions, but there is no such facility available in government schools. Are we not depriving our disabled children in the government schools from such facilities. Is there any scheme for this?

SPEAKER

This is a very good point and it can be one of the recommendations that when we are talking about inclusive education, we should ensure that this technology goes to general schools also, wherever children with disabilities are there. As a teacher in the school, you must bring this matter to the notice of the higher authority and request them that this thing needs to be done. Those who are working in the disability area, they have to pressurise the higher authorities of the general schools also that they have to do it.

DR. SAI

Those who develop technology should remember that it should be easy to use, and must be inexpensive.

SPEAKER

The normal computers with minor adaptations, like adapted mouse, can be used by the disabled children. If you have computers they can be used. Otherwise there are other teaching aids also available which can be used specially for the CP children. These teaching aids should be included under ADIP Scheme so that the family of the disabled child can purchase it as the schools can't afford it.

SPEAKER

I would like to mention here that the Simcomputer was developed, which is hand held computer. It is supposed to be less than Rs.10,000/- and that needs to be looked into in this context.

MRS. INDUMATHI RAO

Tele-rehabilitation is taking a shape of revolution all over the world. One company has been started in Bangalore for tele-medicine. The project will be started in 300 districts. We need NGO partners who are working in remote areas in the country. We would be happy to associate with you in our programme. We have prepared a software on hearing testing and vision testing and there are 300 doctors. This is the only company of its kind in South Asia. Please write to us for details.

PROF. GURU

I am in M.P. Bhoj University. We have to translate material in many Indian languages. Is there any software to translate from one Indian language to another?

DR. SAI

Such a translation work is possible for European languages which is easily available. I think for Indian languages it is under development. IIT, Kanpur is working on that translation from English to Hindi but the accuracy rate is 80-85 per cent.

MS. GEETA JAINA

We are working with Perkins Brailler but we are facing lot of difficulties of speed. If you remove these problems, it will be of great help to us. Further, it is not possible to provide Brailler in all the institutions and schools due to its high cost, because India is such a big country.

CHAIRPERSON

I would like to thank all the speakers for their excellent presentation. Thank you very much.

V

PROMOTION OF CROSS-DISABILITY APPROACHES

Chairperson: Dr. P. Hanumantha Rao
Co-Chairperson: Prof. P. Jeyachandran

MS. ANURADHA MOHIT

I realize that each of us present here is an embodiment of experience, commitment and commitment is for the empowerment of people with disabilities. The ultimate goal of all our actions, all our thinking, all our activities is the empowerment of people with disabilities and one is looking for ways of accelerating the process. I think that is my understanding with all of us who are concerned with two basic issues. One is how to reach how many and in as little time as possible because the uncovered or the people who have not been reached are so many and spread to the length and breadth of the country. There are so many models available and each model has its own strength and all these models have contributed in their own way in advancing the agenda of empowerment and reaching the unreached. I know that all of you are aware but just to once again bring into focus the issue of cross-disability approaches, I take you back to the history. It was the blind people who organized themselves an organization for the blind as the history of special schools is very old. Special schools I can compare with the factories. The industrialization brought the labour force together in the factories and labour unions got evolved. Similarly blind schools brought blind people together and union of the blind people came into existence. After that the tradition was to bring deaf people in the schools for the deaf. Second movement which emerged is of people who are hearing impaired. We have not seen many strong organizations of locomotor disabled people, of people with intellectual disabilities and others. That is a historical fact. The situation changed with the emergence of Disabled People International (DPI). DPI marks two very distinct trends. Number one, DPI is the first cross-disability movement, before that we had World Blind Union, the single organization of the blind people in the world and the Welfare Association of the Deaf. Again all organizations of the deaf through out the world came under this banner. Then came the organization for the mentally retarded, known as Inclusion International. These were the historical organizations in existence with different names. World Blind Union had different name, it was International Federation of the Blind, and there was a historical organization known as Rehabilitation International, which is a forum where the professionals meet, professionals in the area of rehabilitation. It is a very large and powerful organization. A number of disabled persons who are actively participating in the process of rehabilitation and they are professionals, they were also members of the Rehabilitation International more as professionals than as people with disabilities. But they felt the need of adequate representation of people with disabilities in the Rehabilitation International. Unfortunately, Rehabilitation International, the leadership was not open to the idea of giving more representation in the decision-making to people with disabilities. This is the historical fact which led to the split of the organization and out of that was born the DPI. The founders of DPI had a clear vision, the vision was to advance the rights of people with disabilities and lend a very strong voice to the movement of people with disabilities and the movement which would be led by the people with disabilities. That is why the slogan of DPI is nothing about us without us. This is the slogan given to the world by the DPI. Slogan is taken by the movement from the farmers organization in France, the first agro revolution ever to place was in the 14th century and a very famous film gives a reflection of this. When the society was moving from a slave society to the farming society. That was the period when the farmer's first rising was seen by the world. So the cross-disability is a concept given to us by people with disabilities and what was the purpose. I said the overriding purpose was to advance the rights of people with disabilities. But how do we do that? The decision was that the cross-disability would be the diplomatic arm of the disability sector. It would use diplomatic channels to advance the rights movement and bring the issues of rights on the political agenda. It is a political wing of the disability movement. Cross-disability historically is a political wing, the political way of advancing the rights issues. By politics I do not mean the mainstream party politics, but definitely there is a political way of doing things. Political way of doing things is quite different from the way we provide services. We secure rights of people with disabilities by providing services. How does a person with disability enjoys the right of education? The right of education ultimately depends on the opportunities available for education and that in turn depends on infrastructure which includes the manpower, the human resource and the RCI's main job is to develop human resource required to service the sector. This is another way of securing rights but the people with disabilities, when they talk of cross-disability organizations, when they created the first cross-disability organization in the DPI, their understanding of cross-disability movement was quite different. They saw their role in advancing the rights by using the political forums. Which are the political forums? Political forums are the political parties, political parties meet in the Parliament, and all parties together, when they form government, they meet at the level of United Nations. UN is a forum of the governments. The governments all around the world come together, one forum known as United Nations Organization. It is again a governmental body. That means DPI gave itself the task of dialoguing, negotiating with these forums. At the domestic level it is the government, at the sub-domestic government it may be the regional government, local government. Then moving on the union, regional, like in our region we have UN-ESCAP and then going on to the UN. So cross-disability, political movement, good dialogue with these bodies for the advancement of their rights. Why did they decide to do so? Because the rights which are recognized by the people have no meaning unless there is a body which is responsible to guarantee those rights. How does this happen? The Constitution of our country says, every citizen has a right to work, freedom of expression, freedom of movement, co-mingling. How do we exercise these rights? There has to be a body which would guarantee the enjoyment of rights. And what is the system? The system is that we as people collectively give our common assignment, our common tasks in the hands of a body called government and for it to function what do we do? We give it the financial resources. How do we contribute financial resources? We contribute financial resources by way of taxes, direct taxes and indirect taxes and by way of our labour. We work to produce profit for the country. We contribute tax and the money which we generate is handed over to government to develop those systems, those infrastructures, those services which are absolutely necessary for the enjoyment of the rights given to us under the Constitution. That is the role of that body which has to guarantee the right. Rights are not defined in the heavens. We all are born without any rights. The rights are assigned to us, collectively by us through our constitutions and through our laws, through our responsibilities. When we say rights and responsibilities, it does not mean I have a right to education but a responsibility to pay the fee. That is not the concept of rights and responsibilities. The rights and responsibilities means if you have a right then someone has a responsibility to make sure that you are able to enjoy your right. That is the concept of rights and responsibilities. Even those who are engaged in discharging their responsibilities, they too have same rights as anybody else. If a person joins the Government, or gets into the Parliament, that does not mean that this person has only responsibility and does not have rights. This person also has rights.

The same rights. So, therefore, the question of rights of affording opportunities of exercising rights lies with the government. Therefore, the world over people with disabilities realized that they are the best advocates of their own rights. They have the capacity to articulate, what their rights are and how those rights must be guaranteed to them. They decided that we need just like others, for example, any child would require a teacher to learn. For advance education, every person would need to go to a professional school. To exercise the right of movement, we need the transport systems, somebody has to make the roads, bridges, railways, the buses, the airways. The same way for people with disabilities, professionals, the service providers have to do their jobs but as far as their rights are concerned they feel at least they have the capacity to say what they need. We decided that we both non-disabled professionals and the disabled people, we have a role which is inter-linked but independent. Which is inter-dependent but autonomous. So the professionals come together under RI, the disabled people for the political cause go to the DPI. The question is which is the better approach. The cross-disability or single. When we think in terms of RCI, because it is a forum of RCI, and you look at their role, you look at the cross-disability approaches. I have no clear thinking about it, but I can raise it as an issue and leave those thoughts with you. As you all understand that the blind person, if a person is visually impaired, the whole system of processing information and of understanding the world around, is dependent on non-visual elements. So the learning transacts through non-visual mediums, which could be auditory, touch, tactile and so on. On the contrary for a person who is hearing impaired, the entire process is entirely different because it is totally visually oriented. It is not oriented to other mediums but to visual mediums. Both are absolutely in opposite directions. One totally non-visual and the other totally visually oriented. Now if an abstract subject like mathematics, let me not go to the hi-fi subject mathematics. If we have to express sadness to a deaf child, I think it is very challenging. The deaf child may be able to understand what crying is, when you are sad, you cry. That is the manifestation. When you are sad your tears flow. That manifestation child understands. Sadness, this is very difficult to communicate this concept. Vice versa for a blind child it is easy to communicate to blind child what sadness is and what is shedding tears and how it is related to shedding tears. What is relation of tears to sadness? Therefore, a teacher, a rehab worker who is assigned the job of communicating simple to abstract concepts, to communicate them to learners, such diagonal, opposite learning needs. I do not know whether that is possible or not in an inclusive environment where there are so many students with diverse characteristics and personalities. These are the questions when we recommend cross-disability approaches and RCI has to really think about. Let me share with you the people who are deaf, who are blind, they perceive the reality. The World Federation of the Deaf and the World Blind Union. These organizations represent the deaf and blind people of about 165 countries of the world. Starting from United States, a resolution came in 1995 from the blind community and before that in 1992 from the deaf community, who said that up to primary level, we need special schools or at least exclusive teachers, having expertise in the area of blindness and deafness. This is the opinion of the people who are blind and who are deaf. The professionals may think differently and the administrators and the government have a totally different perception of the problem and perception of the solution also. So this is very different from the way people think. Another angle for you to ponder upon. I leave these thoughts with you when you suggest cross-disability approaches. I am only raising issues. The second issue I raise is very common. Everybody says cost effective. It is very economical to give services in a cross-disability approach or something like that. Can the question of guaranteeing the rights be measured by cost? No. No one in the world can do that. I give you a very crude example. Somebody has a brain tumor. It requires brain surgery which is a very specialized field in surgery and highly complex, complicated and costly. Would you tell a hospital, to suggest to a patient who has brain tumor, look this is complex, costly, so instead I treat you in your foot because afterall all nerves lead to brain. Because the foot surgery is very cheap. Would you call this response? Crazy, comic, divorced from reality, stupid. The same way when you say to be able to teach multi disabled children, deaf blind children, the teacher-pupil ratio is 2: 1. Which is arrived at after a long series of experimentation in the education of the deaf blind children. May be decades or centuries of experience suggests that this is what you need. So for a deaf blind child to enjoy his or her right of education, depends on the fact that they need very low teacher-pupil ratio. There could be no argument on that and say no, we can't do that because it is costly. The question of right is linked to the question of survival. Can you survive without good skills in life? No you can't survive without good skills. When you think of your children who are non-disabled, can you send them to schools which do not offer good education, where the teachers are non serious, not qualified. You don't risk with the future of your children. The same way the life is much more challenging in the job market when you go out and it is more harsh on people with disabilities than to the non-disabled. That is the fact of the matter. I know how to deliver goods at work but for other person to get convinced, I have to go extra mile. Please bear in mind these things when deciding the empowerment of people with disabilities. These are the thoughts which I have shared with you.

CHAIRPERSON

Thank you very much. You have narrated very good things. How the disabled movement started and how it grew globally. Now RCI has given this concept, how to adopt cross-disability approach. This is the need of the hour. We can make our beneficiaries aware about their duties also. Many a times we do not keep our beneficiaries informed, what is their role.

MRS. USHA DALVI

Communicative competence and literacy in communication disorders. With the passage of PwD Act, many disabilities have come up. Where do we account for. One major group is the communication disorder group. Communication disorders include both speech disorders and language disorders, speech disorder group may have articulation problem, pronunciation problem, voice problem, may be low, high, breathy, which is commonly known as communication disorders. Language has three major components, form, syntax or grammar, content—meaning of the sentence and also use. If I know how to write a sentence but if it is not appropriately spoken, my pragmatics is affected. Communication disorder group may have in isolation speech disorder, language disorder or combination of both. The causes of communication disorders are many but the major ones are, sensory loss which may result into individuals who have communication problems, hearing impaired, visually impaired, and also other major causes, cognitive deficits which you may find in children with mental retardation, aphasia, brain injury group, there are environmental crosses, which we poke about stuttering, and also pseudo mental retardation caused due to some psychological causes like neurotics. They may also have communication break down or communication problem. There is another major cause which is neurological disorder. Again we all know that there is a bigger group called cerebral palsy which has multiple concerns like cognitive, motor and other associated problems. That is one of the major group who has communication problem, aphasia, brain injury, neuro motor speech disorder due to Parkinson. Earlier they may be having normal speech but once they get neuro motor speech disorder, they have communication break down. Tumor due to neuro plastic growth, and recent inclusion in this group is HIV. Even these group of children do show some language and communication break down. The impact is speech and language disorder may occur in combination and it may result into unrecognizable speech which may be mild, break down in communication, with complete break down or partial and in many of them there is a poor communicative competence. This becomes very significant. When this communication competence is not appropriate and when it affects individual, social, and physical well being. Irrespective of mode of communication, that is, speech or alternate augmentative method, *i.e.* in hearing impaired we may be using sign language or in visually impaired they may be using Braille. That is augmentative and alternative communication. The communicative competence emphasizes on accuracy of idea transfer than correctness of form or delivery. The correct way of writing or correct way of saying, that is not important. But how that is conveyed becomes very important when we say whether the child has acquired communicative competence or not. It is also a complex process because it relies on knowledge, judgement and skills in four major domains, *i.e.* linguistic, operational, social and strategic. In linguistics it requires the individual to learn language spoken in their homes or social communities as well as the linguistic codes of their augmentative system, may be symbols, manual signs or other individualized signs used for communication purpose. They also need to have operational competence, *i.e.* they are required to learn the technical skills needed to operate their augmentative system, *e.g.* the visually impaired child has to learn Braille to communicate or learn, it may be academic or day to day communication. The systems are manual signs, low technology, low technology communication system which mainly uses boards or any other system and or electronics. These days you get even the dedicated devices which are used as communication systems. Social competence—it includes which relate to strategies, such as initiating conversation, continuing conversation, terminating conversation as well as those needed for functional acts, such as, choice making, requesting or rejecting. It also includes those that relate to inter-personal dynamics, such as knowing how to put partners at ease, actively participate in conversation, so on and so forth. Strategic competence which involves teaching adaptive or coping strategies to be used when communication breaks down. Normally what happens when we are communicating somebody has not understood my message, you say sorry, this is what I meant, excuse me, when I draw the attention but it happens in the children who have communication break down and those who don't have this strategic competence.

Hence they are not able to acquire the information. During the class also they may not understand what the teacher is saying and they don't know how to interact. Excuse me, can you repeat it again. Can you move, I cannot see the board. These are the strategic competence. These four strategies are very important to develop the strategic competence. Because many a times in special education we have seen, when we are teaching these children, we focus our attention in completing the curriculum. We don't even see whether the child is independent to use the skills whatever they have learnt. For that communicative competence becomes very important. With the philosophy of normalization and globalization, there was formation of a legislation for the handicapped and also with the U.N. Declaration of 1981 as the International Year of the Disabled, which was instrumental at least in our country for the development and implementation of PwD Act and also later on inclusive education. The emphasis is on quality of life and quality of life for professionals means that in the early childhood intervention there has to be a transition into adulthood developing independence in the individual. We have a figure of 6 per cent of population having communication disorders. It is a diverse group in terms of types, severity. To this group my topic connects to literacy also because competence, language and literacy all are inter-related. The statistics on literacy, NSSO 1991, they declared 42 per cent and in the morning they said it is 40 per cent. So there is not much variation between 1991 and 2003. With the inclusion we envisage that the figure will come down.

Strategy for different disabilities is quite different and we have to see whether it is possible or not in cross-disabilities. Literacy is a term which is commonly used for reading and writing. But it is not just reading and writing, it is a very powerful tool. It is a tool for communication, critical thinking and attainment of social and cultural power. Literacy learning is an interactive process and it has to be constructive, strategic, and meaning based. We have to think that some of them will have to go to inclusive setting up but what happens to others. In that condition we have to definitely think about individualized education programmes. For severe communication impact, literacy is at multiple levels and it is critical for developing self expression. It is also at the communicative level, skill improvement or developing skills for successful participation in the society of particular group. So when developing literacy skills, the programme for these groups, it is very important to consider alternative access to use the literacy material and assistive techniques. I am going to talk about four major groups without going into details about their limitations and difficulties. What barrier they face in development of communicative skills? The first group is multiple handicapped. Study indicates that about 80 per cent of this group, having minimum of two to three associated problems. It may be a motor disorder, cognitive deficits, visual impairment, and all these factors influence literacy learning. The barrier for this group is limited access to formal instruction and lack of exposure to the general curricula. Other barriers include physical barriers, attitudinal barriers. For the hearing impaired, the strategy adopted is which generally works for hearing impaired children. This strategy has its own inherent limitations. Second major barrier is low expectation from the individual. Acquisition of poor language. Again this group has difficulty not only at lexical and centricial level but also at higher level due to various factors like early language, environment, degree of loss. Access to learning material and inaccessibility to both language, may be we can consider sign, gesture, or augmentative system and the second language which is generally used as a medium of instruction in school. So there has to be a link which has to be established between written word, meaning, language used in one to one communication process for this group.

Cognitive impairment—this group generally has limited or reduced expectation or lack of exposure to literacy material. For the visual impairment group, the barrier is difficulty in identification due to inadequate tools and professionals. No proper assessment facilities for colour sensitivity, etc. are available. These children require additional adaptive systems.

For communication disorder group the challenges revolves around multi-linguism, assessment and intervention. India being a multi-lingual and multi-cultural country and we also know that in school, specially there are heterogenic patterns, which means there is a lot of difference, in some States there are two language policy. The child has to learn many languages. Sometimes the mother tongue may be different from the medium of instruction. There is inequality in the development of other language, the third language. Code switching in a multi tier media. Our children have to face it very often. It is being or even studies indicate that even normal children find it difficult in the early stages when they are admitted in a school because there is code switching. They know only one language in the class there is another language and sometimes they are expected to answer it in third language. This is what is meant by the codes switching. Given the scenario it is going to be a greater challenge, specially in the development of communicative competency and literacy skills. The programmes which we may focus or should focus should promote these skills of universal nature, that is whatever programmes we are framing should be applicable at least to a majority of the group. We all know that there is a dearth of specific language material. We the professionals face this problem every day because there is no test material to test the language skills. Here our focus should be on alternate assessment procedures. One should understand the cultural parameters being associated with the particular child being evaluated. Observe normal age peer in natural settings to determine culturally appropriate behaviour and communication behaviour. Observe the child in natural settings similar to those which would serve as normal recurrent and also teachers report. An important strategy would be involve parents and family members in assessment and modification of standardized testing. What I mean by standardized modification testing, sometimes they say the child has to respond within a minute, may be we can modify and give a little longer time to the child. Sometimes the child can perceive all the pictures. Such modifications can also be done. Intervention—

there has to be a pragmatic shift in the intervention strategies. I do not want to repeat as in the morning one speaker said that what is not applicable throw it out. Depending on the need of the child we have to see what is applicable there has to be a shift and a change in our approach and attitude as a professional. There has to be pragmatic shift which will promote the whole family involvement. Family involvement will facilitate development of self-determination, qualify of life, self-esteem and independence in the child and also it will be congenial relationship in the family among child, parents, peers and the siblings. There has to be collaborative consultation, contextual pragmatic approach, curriculum based approach, strategy based home language approach, and the present trend. There is an advancement in technology so augmentative and alternative communication, as we all know, the computer can function for these children as a multipurpose system. Because it can be used as a writing pad, can be used as a learning tool, it can be used as a work station for a child. Because it provides speech access. We all know that with the Windows XP there is a speech to text conversion available. Then with the physical or modified access child can also operate the computer, modified keyboard. Today there are so many computer softwares available to improve the literacy skills and also reading writing skills. Future direction is to develop language specific protocols, to develop training modules for professionals, parents care takers, grass roots level workers. Empowering the hearing impaired with rich language through two language paradigms, *i.e.* preferred language and the sign language, collaborative research with information technology for assistive aids.

CO-CHAIRPERSON

Thank you very much. We all could understand that communication definitely cuts across all disabilities. All the people we have irrespective of any disability, we have the communication problem and how to solve that she has given various things. Communication plays vital role cutting across all the disabilities.

Presentation by representative from Sense International

My presentation is on cross-disability approaches in rehabilitation. Since yesterday afternoon the whole concept of cross-disability approach has become quite a hot topic for discussion and I bet by tomorrow afternoon this is going to become a latest trend which catches up in the country and I am not going to be left behind this trend. Lot of brainstorming, discussions, thought provoking has gone in. Issues and topics have been thrown out to the participants in the inaugural session yesterday and the pioneers in the disability sector have been talking about their point of view regarding this approach. What is this cross-disability approach after all? It is an approach which comprehensively takes into account all different kinds of disabilities together and promotes collective planning. It is about making policy decisions collectively and gives equal weightage across all disabilities for the disabled people themselves. Co-operation and networking of non-governmental organizations working in various categories of disabilities. Specially in the context of RCI inviting all of us here as NGO representatives it is important to understand to promote this approach we need co-operation among ourselves and that has been emphasized a number of times since yesterday. What cross-disability approach has got to do with rehabilitation? What is rehabilitation after all? Since we are all practitioners in rehabilitation in many ways than one, what do we understand by rehabilitation. It is after all helping an individual to achieve its highest level of functions, independence and quality of life. That would respect to begin with, identity, confidence, creditability and most importantly the feeling of being wanted, belonged to and that is what Bhaskar Bhai would agree with me. But it is basically the rehabilitation to promote the sense of belongingness. The feeling of being wanted by this community. The feeling of being missed by people around us. That is the overriding principle of rehabilitation. Another caution to remember that rehabilitation does not reverse and undo the damage caused by a disease or trauma or whatever the cause for disability is but it helps the individual to restore the minimum health and general well being. We all have certain core beliefs. Beliefs that are very deep rooted within us. The belief that we feel very passionate about, that is what keeps us going inspite of all the challenges, unkept promises, to some extent insensitive bureaucracy or government. But still as individuals, as professionals we all have certain beliefs that are deep rooted within us and that keeps us going and makes us find solutions within our own programmes, within our little NGOs that we are trying to run successfully. What are those beliefs as far as rehabilitation is concerned? We all believe that rehabilitation must be comprehensive, if it is not comprehensive it is not reaching our overall goal of giving a good quality of life. Rehabilitation means mainstreaming. Rehabilitation can not be made in isolation. One disabled child or one disabled person within one NGO, with one project or programme. Effective rehabilitation leads to move all our own programmes and our own organization to the neighbourhood, to the community, to the State as the part of the national infrastructure. Rehabilitation, as I said earlier, builds self-reliance and independence. It is initiating, maintaining and keeping social relationship with the people around us. Building a healthy social, two way relationship. It also means satisfying the emotional needs Bhaskar Bhai has given us so many different examples. It also means improving overall quality of life. How do we do all this? What are we doing already about this? It could be providing education, inclusive education, special school education, depending on a target group. We want to give the best kind of medical care, correction, prevention and therapy. Vocational training, facilities for income generation, and mobilizing the community. That could mean creating awareness, organizing people, getting people involved in our programmes, that is all part of rehabilitation. Basically when we are talking of this new term of cross-disability approach, are we already doing some pieces of it? To a large extent all of us within our own organizations, within our own community, we are all promoting it. We have started developing it. May be we don't have a theory to prove it. May be we don't have statistics to prove it. We may not have very well documented back up process but individually, collectively as a programme, we have been promoting it and we are in the process of reaching out to overall cross-disability approach that we have been discussing and deliberating during this Convention. If we are talking of rehabilitation about our core beliefs things that we so passionately stand here, and these are the things that have taken long time to come up. These are not one day resolution that have come up. All of us can speak for hours on each of these areas. Yet since morning we are talking of challenges. We are talking of difficulties, we are talking of insensitivity, we are talking of lack of awareness. As Ms. Anuradha Mohit also said, a word of caution, listen to the disabled people's voice, in the name of cross-disability, in the name of inclusion, are we forgetting the essence of actual rehabilitation? Are we missing the point altogether? The point of caution that she raised and she left it open, it is probably my next slide would speak of. It is because of disabled friends and colleagues, we are still facing this situation very much. This situation in spite of all our concerted efforts and belief, disabled people are still saying it is the sense of pity, it could be a patronising attitude, but still a programme of an NGO are seen as giving charity. There are many prejudices, tragedy, discrimination, over protection, various other things about which the disabled friends are sceptical. The new approaches, the new fancy trends coming up, because basically what would they like. What have they faced till now, rejection in the society, resignation, giving up hope, anger, despair, helplessness, demoralized and less acceptance. Why, why do we need this cross-disability approach? My concern is that this cross-disability approach should again be focussed on the core values of which are confidence and belief in and not get side tracked by movements and trends. The cross-disability approach at the end of the day should include disabled people as people with different abilities. It should encourage more control over their lives, that means giving better access to decision-making. They should be participants to have more participatory role about their own policies, decisions, and programmes and not recipient of services, recipients of welfare. Cross-disability approach necessarily needs to lead to equal opportunities and not as a part of larger system because you have been included as a point of cross-disability approaches, projecting as a model service. It needs to lead to equal membership of the society for respect of the individual and equal rights. Ms. Anuradha Mohit has also spoken very very passionately as to how the rights of the persons with disabilities need to be protected, need to be promoted, spread out. That is a bit concern and cross-disability approach can be successful if we make sure that all these things are effectively monitored and implemented within our approach. We all have to work with the cross-disability approach because these are all challenges, these are all our core beliefs which cannot be achieved by one person, one organization or one forum or a consortium of organizations, across the country person to person, programme to programme, organization to organization, State government to State government, overall the national government in national forums. What could be some of the benefits of cross-disability approach? It leads to productivity, independence, full citizenship and total inclusion. Cross-disability approach being focussed on the disabled person himself or herself will automatically foster leadership. It will promote leadership. It will be lead by the people who believe what actually needs to be done. It will lead to full enforcement and implementation of disability related laws, programmes to enhance the life, programmes to reduce the poverty and unemployment, it will ensure the right to live and educate the government and public and policy makers. It is the power of numbers and numbers not being put together because we need to sign a memorandum or numbers because we believe in it. Number because we have a goal, we have a focus we are leading to and focus is based on basic emotive quality issues and not mere statistics, jargon or technical theories. How do we initiate this process? Again as I said this was a very new term for me and when I started surfing the net, I could not find enough literature on this. Things like what do we need to go back with. What are the tangible steps? Who will give us the list of things to do. Eventually we will learn from our experience but who is going to tell us, ok, now we have discussed about it, go back and do these things. You will learn from your own experience and you will develop your own cross-disability approach within your own region. Some of these kinds of out of the head ideas come. First thing uniformity in the terminology of the disability. Even now we have seen different presenters using different terms. One thing that could become consistent within the country is that the terminology would be uniform, it would be humane, it would be positive. Networking among the organizations in disability and for the disability. It is not for the professional, I know the jargon, I know the theory, what is best for you. You don't know how do you feel. You can never be in our position. We have to overcome these attitudes. It is becoming much more closer and closer environment. Emphasis on human resource development, again lot of time has been spent on this. If we have one focus we will have better quality, we will have better parameters for monitoring the quality. Cross-disability programmes, I would like to point out what Ms. Anuradha Mohit mentioned the children being denied services of cross-disability programme. Again getting side tracked because deaf-blind is my favourite topic. If we have a cross-disability approach, the idea is not to include a deaf-blind child in a classroom with eight children with mental retardation but the idea would be to develop a programme within the existing infrastructure using the available staff, with little bit of additional training and additional infrastructure. In that way it could be cost effective, could be more inclusive for the deaf-blind children, it could automatically lead to greater awareness about low incidence, severely disabled population. I would also like to share with you that there are two types of Diploma programmes in the country one is at Clarke School and Hellen Keller School at Mumbai and Sense International has developed the course curriculum and is doing initial funding for both the programmes. That is what is cross-disability. Clarke School has got the deaf children and they have added a deaf-blind component to it. That is a cross-disability approach working over there. Young and professionally qualified staff, I have an objection to the young but my Director has put it there. Young and smart. Probably that is what he meant. When I was going through the slide, I thought this might lead to exclusion. These are some of the physical, tangible, least kind of things to be done by people who are still wary about this approach. What do we need and do afterall about this whole approach or theory. This could be certain pointers what I can go back and start believing in implementing in my day-to-day schedule of work. Call up the other organization and tell them that I want to meet you. It begins just with one telephone call. Let us go back and follow up with each other. Let us begin the movement of cross-disability approach. Zero rejection policy. We have deaf children. We are sorry we don't work for the deaf children. Or this is a school for the mentally handicapped children, we can't take your child because he has cerebral palsy and we don't have infrastructure for cerebral palsy. Don't just inform parents that the child has a disability or impairment. Do tell them, I can't help you but I know someone who can help you. That is the crux of the zero rejection policy. Do make an effort to refer the child to an appropriate rehabilitation centre. It may not be your priority programme. But if you really believe in rehabilitation in those core values, we are talking about, let us help the parent of that child. Let us all work together.

CHAIRPERSON

Thank you. You have given very detailed view of the cross-disability approach. I was discussing with Dr. Mukherjee, why did you select this topic. He said this is the need of the hour. Giving you an example, I am a practicing pediatrician as well as running an organization. Many of our colleagues are unable to reconcile why there should be Diploma holders, how they can handle children with complex problems. They wanted to make Diploma two years, they are coming after intermediate, they can't write at length and you want to teach them philosophy, this subject, that subject, 16 papers I think they have made. I am still against that because he is a grass roots level worker. We have to reconcile as professionals who must have good hearts to accept these diploma holders, or the certificate holders. Though they are definitely supplementary to the qualified professional, for example, speech therapist our country needs, over 30,000, there are only 500, out of them many have gone abroad. Last year we started diploma in hearing, language and speech, many candidates came and we decided to take one candidate from each district. At least some service will be there. Just like a barefoot doctor, compounder you call him, a dispenser you call him. We had a meeting last month in Mumbai wherein it was decided that we must have quality in professionals. But we need a compounder also, we need a barefoot doctor also. Let us have an attitudinal change to develop master's programmes, to train the trainers. Let us not be totally against the grass roots level workers. Ours is an example where we treat all the disabled. All disabled under one roof, all specialization under one roof. Same premises utilized by different specialists at different times.

MR. J. P. GADKARI

I am the president of Parivaar, a National Federation of Parents Associations for the Mentally Retarded Persons. We started this organization in 1995 and in 1997 we changed the constitution of our federation to include persons with autism, cerebral palsy, mentally retarded and multiply handicapped. I being the member of the Drafting Committee of the National Trust, I knew that the Act is coming. So we took the opportunity to amend so that these four disabilities could be included. I am Secretary of the Karnataka Parents Association of the Mentally Retarded which is going to complete 25 years next year and I have been founder member of that. In 1979 when some of the parents including myself, we thought that unless the parents of the mentally retarded come together and try to do something for our children, nobody else is going to take the initiative. In 1979, I had just come to Bangalore from Delhi and I could not find any proper school in Delhi to put my four year old mentally retarded son in a special school. Since my wife belonged to Bangalore, somebody told me that there is a special school in Bangalore, I got myself transferred to Bangalore in order to see that my child gets special education. In 1979 when some of the parents got get together we thought of forming a parents association because that was the only way that we could raise our voice to get some facilities for children from the government. But when we started working we realized the very first thing that we can not work in isolation. We cannot work just for the disability of mental retardation. We will have to join hands with others so that something concrete could be achieved. That was the beginning of our approach to cross-disability. This is not a new concept for us. Cross-disability we thought unless we could come together nothing can be achieved. The result was that the Karnataka State Parents Association took lead in organizing All India conferences emphasizing that there should be a legislation on disability, you know the first legislation on disability was brought in 1995. Before that there was no comprehensive legislation. There were certain facilities available here and there but there was no all India approach. That was the result of our work, when we worked together with other disabled group, we succeeded in forming that. Another example of our efforts was that when we realized that the comprehensive legislation for the disability came, we realized that one section that is persons with Mental Retardation (MR) has got very little in that legislation. Along with others we raised our voice and the result was the National Trust Act was passed in 1999. It was passed on 15th of December, 1999. Something about the disabilities for which I am working. Among various disabilities, mental retardation and other developmental disabilities are generally the least visible. Therefore, the most neglected one. We were neglected, marginalized. Though mental retardation is now recognized as a disability in legal terms, it is still considered by many as some disease which can be cured by some medicines. Many a times it is also considered as a curse or the outcome of sins committed by the parents of disabled in their previous birth. This is despite the knowledge acquired during the last 50 years of research and development which determined the basic features and causes of disabilities. The medical science has made spectacular advances during the last two or three decades. As a result, much could be learnt about the condition of mental retardation and other developmental disabilities. Though no break through has been achieved to prevent mental retardation, the research in the field of genetics has given much hope that one day such a thing would be possible. Genetics is a science which is developing now. There are hopes that some break through some day will be made. When the parents come to us we tell them to accept the reality that mental retardation is irreversible position so don't run from pillar to post to find a medicine or some way to reverse the process. However, the parents of persons with these disabilities due to lack of knowledge and ignorance about the problems of mental retardation and due to superstition become the victim of rejection. They generally run from pillar to post to find a cure. They also treat this as a social stigma and try to keep the child away from the society. By and large the medical knowledge about mental retardation is available only at expert and specialized level. The ordinary medical practitioner or a family doctor is not of much help to them. The result is that the parents and their ward get isolated from the mainstream of the society. This is what is happening. Other disabled people are able to organize themselves, blind, orthopaedically handicapped, and so many others. They have formed their associations and launched their struggle but the mentally retarded could not do it. That is why the parents had to take lead and join hands with others to see that something comes out of this. The United Nations adopted a number of human rights resolutions, including the rights and privileges of persons with intellectual disabilities. Most among those is the 1971 declaration on the rights of the mentally retarded persons. Even the People with Disability (PwD) Act of 1995 ensured that persons with mental retardation and other developmental disabilities will enjoy the same rights as other citizens of the country. However, the ground realities speak of dismal scenario. There are a number of common issues on which we all can come together, work together and form a national movement. The cross-disability should not remain a subject with the RCI. It should become part of a strong national movement where all the disabled people can come around on one platform to deal with the common issues. What we have to do for building this national movement? First, to create an awareness regarding all the disabilities, that is too, among parents where these four disabilities are concerned. It is very necessary that the parents are mobilized. I am not saying that parents of other disabled people should not get mobilized but basically for these four disabilities, it is very necessary that awareness level increases. Then only the objective of bringing them on one platform could be achieved. To dispel the myths about the disabilities. To mobilize maximum number of people to support, co-operate and assist individually or in groups, part time or full time, in on-going activities concerning people with disabilities. To motivate people to give support in whichever way possible to them physically, emotionally, financially for persons with disabilities, their families, NGOs and centres working for their welfare. The long-term objective should be mobilization of the community in general, involving them in the task of providing facilities to the persons with disabilities to lead a life of dignity, honour and as normal citizens of the society. Mind you, that as far as mental retardation is concerned, it is always considered wrongly that they are not capable of doing any thing. We have proved through many experiments that many of them who are severely disabled, they are capable, they are trainable, they are educable and they can work as contributing citizens of the society. The other long-term objective should be to make the parents pro-active through their associations and organizations. Being the head of Parivaar I always tell parents the younger ones among them, that they must become active in their associations. Just putting your child in an institution and forgetting about it that that institution will take care about your child is not sufficient. The parents have to come forward and work in their associations and organizations. Learn from each others experience, know about the legislations, about various provisions in different legislations for the disabled and can unitedly strive to have the benefits and access to them. In order to achieve the short-term and long-term objectives, the following programme should be adopted:

1. Large scale awareness programmes for parents should be organized at all levels.
2. Lectures, seminars, workshops, audio-visual exhibitions should be organized to reach large section of people in urban and semi-urban areas.
3. Street plays, folk drama, nautankis should be organized to give expression to the problems of the disabled in rural areas.
4. Undertake widespread and sustained publicity campaigns. Now incidentally I have been a journalist for 35 years of my life and I know the attitude of the media. When I was working in Delhi as a correspondent of a newspaper, I know that whenever there was a problem of disability coming to us, we just used to show it the basket. That attitude has been fortunately changing now. Many newspapers are giving publicity. TV, electronic media, is also coming forward but it is not sufficient. It is our duty, the organizations like ours have to come have to develop active contacts with the media. Explain to them that what are problems, what are the issues and ask them to project them. Widespread and sustained campaigns through posters, banners and pamphlets. Make extensive use of print and electronic media to publish studies, examples of exceptional people with disabilities, success stories, personal experiences of parents, role models, etc. Question-answer sessions, interviews with professionals and talks should be organized on the electronic media. Bring about synergy between media and disability. Organize counselling and short duration educational courses. I think RCI should do that. Many times many parents come to us and ask us instead of diploma for one

year on MR, is there a short course which we can do. So I think I suggest it to RCI to organize short courses, educational courses for parents. Wherever possible such courses should be organized through correspondence. The target groups to achieve the objectives through planned programmes should be high school students, you know the students are very active if we can approach them, college students in particular, we have tried them in Bangalore. We found that they show immense interest to take and participate in these programmes, particularly from colleges and run special sessions for mental retardation and other developmental disabilities. Finally if success is to be achieved in bringing about widespread awareness among society, and mobilize the community to extend a helping hand to the disabled, it is necessary to strengthen the parents movement. I always emphasize on that. Parivaar has 170 parents associations spread all over the country as members of Parivaar and they are very active which has already taken roots in the country and they can effectively work as advocates for the cause of persons with mental retardation and developmental disabilities joining hands with other disability groups.

MRS. USHA GROVER

Don't you think we were talking about the concept "education for all", inclusive education, including human resource development, multi-category teachers, etc. Don't you think all these terminologies have direct bearing on the concept of cross-disability approach. So if yes, don't you think they are already promoting this concept. And if yes, don't you think all the courses which are being run by us given by RCI need to be reviewed because whatever courses are given to us, I don't think they synchronize with the concept of cross-disability approach. I will just supplement with an example. We are talking about inclusive education, integration, at the same time, as far as training is concerned, we have training in segregated disabilities. Why so? If we want to achieve this concept of cross-disability, we should have human resource in an integrated manner. Also we are talking about the schools for this category, that category, I am not saying we need not have specialists but they would be at higher level or wherever they are they have to continue. It needs to be reviewed if we believe in this philosophy. I think all the action plan needs to be planned accordingly which is not the case in the present scenario.

PROF. P. JEYACHANDRAN

The second point you have raised we have been debating on this for the last two years and we have done so many things. We have spent so much money but the inclusion has not taken place among the disabilities itself. So this is the position but we are trying our best and you will get two year curriculum.

CHAIRPERSON

We hope RCI will not stop here and this is a national movement, as Prof. Gadkari said, this will go on. This will be translated into reality. I thank Prof. Jeyachandran, my co-chairman.

VI

RESEARCH IN REHABILITATION

Chairperson: Dr. S. Hariharan

Friends, once again I welcome you. As has been said we want an interactive session. When I entered I was received by three people sitting. Now the hall is full. I am happy. Now I have Dr. Das with me as our rapporteur. The designated chairperson has not come, so he invited me to play the role of chairperson also we have distinguished speakers and I am not standing between you and the speakers because this is a very important session but I have doubts which I like to tell you that all of us know that the richest research in India may be because of the overload of the clients. We have been neglecting, this can happen in any area whether it is medical service area or it is the medical treatment area. Even, if the case history training a personnel and we are talking about we can have good data. In lot of the areas it has been mentioned in the foreground or the preface, various areas made some rough calculations that 3,63,000 personnel are required but we have only 21,000 so far. Even that requires assistive appliance, prosthetic, orthotic appliances. Dr. Banerjee is here. He is doing a very wonderful work with various appliances, we have appliances in Allahabad, so I think we will have a good interaction between senior and junior faculty. That junior faculty are supposed to do a lot of research for the future. So I personally feel that we have a very difficult task to come out and Dr. Tulsidas has already volunteered to take up the task of informing our celebration to the RCI. We have in the panel today, Dr. Jayram, Shri Rakesh Arora. Dr. Jayram is the Director of All India Institute of Speech & Hearing, Mysore. It is one of the pioneer centres in the area of speech and hearing disabilities in India and I recently visited the centre. They have a very good centre which can have lot of research areas. So I invite Dr. Jayram to give the presentation.

DR. M. JAYRAM

Thank you Dr. Hariharan and good afternoon to all of you who have come here. I am not speaking here as an expert for several reasons. One is I am not a specialist in all the disability areas. Second thing is that for whatever reasons there was wrong communication between me and the RCI. So, therefore, I am not well prepared. So what I would be doing is I would be speaking to you, the next result of this is you know I should confess, I am not very well prepared to present the paper and definitely there won't be any visuals. Therefore, my lecture is more formal. So, I would be speaking here as a person with some common sense and some experience in the area for the disability. The aim of all rehabilitation is to employ methods or measures to initiate the impact of disability in the person to achieve socio-economic integration of the person affected into the society and to give him better quality of life and to enable him to achieve self-actualization. So this rehabilitation not only includes training but also intervention at various levels, to modify the society, meet the need of the disabled, adaptation of the environment, protection of human rights. So the area of disability rehabilitation is relatively new, as far as I know for last 30-35 years people have focused on disability rehabilitation research now. So by no means we can say that we have put on the table a perfect system, which simply means that there is a tremendous scope for improvement. In fact we have been doing things for which the impetus and inputs have to come from a newer research in to the area, so we are required to generate more information through research. The need for research can be summarized in the following manner. So as I have said earlier disability management and rehabilitation is recent programme. Therefore, systems that we have developed and put in practice need a lot of improvement. There is scope for that and this input has to come from research and development in this area. The second justification is the size of the disabled population in this country is quite vast but the resources available are meager. Whether the resources are in terms of general finance or manpower available or aids and appliances, the availability is too meager so optimization of utility of these resources is of paramount importance and is of utmost priority. Therefore, research, which is meant for better management of the resources available and the third justification is generally accepted but the need of all the disabled persons are unique. No better evidence for this can be seen than in this country. People with disabilities in India live in diverse socio-economic, cultural and linguistic environment. There needs are dependent on a variety of factors including the family attitudes, the community attitudes, the socio-economic environment, language and even their genetic endowment. So though the professionals have recognized this particular scenario we have never tried to do our best. I think that the efforts that we have put in are not enough and a realization of goals that we have set in this direction. I think you need more meaning which can happen only with better information coming out of our research laboratories. So I said earlier that disability rehabilitation is relatively new area in India and any concept you have, any dimension of disability, rehabilitation, education, training or placement, educational placement, integration into the society, inclusive education, speech language, aids and appliances. You name anything there is a vast scope for improvement in all these areas so that we can talk about research in area of disability rehabilitation and be easy. Many of these things would not be known to you and I would not be spending my time on-going into all those things but in the next few minutes, I will be talking about three issues. You know research should be focused on things which are important. First one is the research into incidence and prevalence of disability in India. We have heard the people in the morning but all of them giving different figures and some saying that figure of 100 million is over estimation of extent problem that we have and some saying under estimation. There is no nation with precise figures. The percentage and figures of the disability in India the estimate of the size of disabled vary enormously as you have seen by the most comprehensive figures of disability census survey but we very well know that the census survey has limitations, most important being it excludes children below the age of four years. So 0-4 years are not considered in census survey and particularly since any disability but the actual figures of the size of disabled, the resources that they require, they have surveys that they require from the professionals and the society. What resources and extent of resources required, of what magnitude and for the optimal utilization of the available resources, there is absolute need for reliable estimates of incidence and prevalence of the problem. Also there is reasonable evidence to say that the incidence and prevalence of the disabled in India is on the increase from the past 15-20 years. There is also reasonable evidence to say that incidence and prevalence of disability and particularly the conditions causing them, vary depending upon there geographical locations within the country. Therefore, it is absolutely imperative that we have good estimate of this size of the population and therefore, I think that the need of hour is to conduct some chronological studies in this area for more accurate figures. Somebody was telling that the coming census survey, the results of which are expected in October, will come out with something around 3 per cent of which I feel, even if it is true, it is gross under estimation of disability in this country. So in advanced countries like United States, the figure for 2001-02 in the area of hearing impairment alone the different companies told, 11.8 million, and in 2001-02 Armenia has population of 240 million. So you can imagine if the percentage of hearing impaired is 12 million, the absolute number of all other disabled put together is much higher than that so when that country can have nearly 9 per cent of population disabled, I feel 3 per cent figure floated for India is gross under estimation. I said earlier the figure will help us to utilize our surveys and interlinking and network of organizations that we have. Yesterday evening we had Dr. Mukherjee saying that the Planning Commission has considered disability and rehabilitation as a failure due to several reasons. Some of the reasons that we put forward here is that Planning Commission thinks that disability rehabilitation is not needed basically in this country and second more importantly that there is no integrated approach to disability rehabilitation. Integrated approach has two connotations one is that specialist working with disabled, he or she is not taking into consideration the whole scenario, or totality of needs of any one given individual. Say, for example, somebody may be interested to do speech therapy forgetting about how handicapped can be reduced. What are the services that he requires in his job or in what way his quality of life can be improved. Things like that. The second thing is that the non-integrated service can also mean that there is very little integration between the various institutions and organizations which are providing these rehabilitation services. There is a bigger problem. People have talked about resource crunch for research in rehabilitation but just imagine, Central Government is spending so much money. Health Ministry and Ministry of Social Justice and Empowerment, there are various state organizations. Ministries in the States, *e.g.* in my State, Ministry of Social Welfare is spending a lot of money. Ministry of Women and Child Development is spending lot of money. There is a directorate of welfare that is spending a lot of money on disability and rehabilitation. Then there are many number of NGOs, local organizations spending lot of money on disability rehabilitation, but it is doubtful whether all these resources are reaching the persons whom we have targeted and this is true because there is no good integration or interlinking of various organizations giving services in the area of disability. I think the information and increase in it are aspects the organizations information related to the persons about the integration as these things will help us to plan the rehabilitation services for disabled and it should also help the government and other agencies to apportion these resources to different areas, to different aspects of rehabilitation. So I say that demographic studies in the area of disability are the areas of paramount importance. Second one is some how related to the first one. Research on organizational issues, the scientific studies of service delivery systems in the field of disability rehabilitation is relatively unexplored area in this country so when we say service delivery system, there are two aspects to that. One is that both are related to each other. There is need to develop theoretical perspective and clarify our inter-organizational linkages and net work that make up delivery systems for the disabled in India. This is related to what I said earlier. We can develop linkages with each other and optimize our resources for the common cause. The second thing is to generate information on treatment outcome and to link this to removing communication gaps which are between organization units. We have only talked of outcome of studies of all about rehabilitation measures but none really has tried to quantify that the services we are delivering are reaching the targeted population to utmost extent. They are benefiting from that. Whether we need to modify our measures, our procedures, our concepts and things like that and then see what is the role of organizations in streamlining this aspect. Such intense care is needed to map out relations between various aspects of service delivery system of the disabled. As I said earlier, there is not much emphasis on post treatment analysis of disabilities and as such effectiveness of our services or service delivery systems is in question. It is valid to think of any organization system as lying along a continuum of a product and service deliveries. However, the output of disability rehabilitation centre may be in the form of services like health care, education, guidance, advocacy, etc. The cost and quality of such services, speed and output parameters like acute patience or an informed client or improvement in quality of life etc. need to be quantified. This would throw information of effectiveness of our approaches and materials and methods employed. The need for research then is to extend the analysis to pin point like in a fundamental co-ordinating mechanism which are basic to all these things and to identify factors related to service delivery system. This would lead to development of coherent model organization systems. Our important goal for the next decade would be to produce an integrated design that optimizes productivity of services. Another plan may be to conduct large scale services for organizations but such an exercise may be very expensive. Other indirect ways are to conduct systematic and intensive surveys with key informants, establish citizen monitoring centres, consumer forums, extrapolates data and demands *vs* means for services, etc. Such evaluation should consider the acceptability, accessibility, awareness aspects and about services for persons with disabilities. The third area that I think is important is further research on what manpower resources are required. Again the integration is related to number of disabled. We all know that one of the factors affecting our rehabilitation programmes is the scarcity of manpower resources. So I have said earlier in the morning given estimate by RCI says that it is 124,000 professionals who are needed to take care of all the disabled people in four disability areas. Available manpower is in no position to attempt a fraction of what we want. So when we talk about professionals there are two levels of professionals, one type of professionals work in higher level organizations and laboratories also are training master trainers and things like that and other level of professionals is who provide service preferably at the door step of the disabled. Field of disability is unlike medicine because of life and death question associated with medicine field. Person with some kind of medical problem, they will go to any extent. They will go any place, provided they are assured to get good services but for the disabled population it is not like that. Person working in agricultural set up or person working in industry, if speech or hearing or other kind of problem, this is not going to be problem for him, he will not bother about our rehabilitation services but the cost of not rehabilitating such individuals would be huge for the country. Therefore, institutions like ours have to go to their door step and provide this kind of rehabilitation services. We have to think of how to or what level of manpower we are going to train. What is the level of training that we give and how do we utilize the services in a maximum permissible manner so identifying the personnel is very important. Before starting training, RCI has been training PHC doctors. We have been training school teachers, health workers and so far how many will sit with patience and provide rehabilitation services. That may require to see the problem of locomotor disabled, problem of visually impaired, the problem of hearing disabled, problem of speech and hearing impaired, problem of mentally retarded. They are entirely different, with some disabled categories. Rehabilitation has long-term effects. Therefore, we require a different kind and level of rehabilitation personnel, research is needed to identify the most suitable level or type of personnel, who can be trying to provide this service to disabled population and when we identify the person who have to be seen as to the goal, of our training, what purpose we are training him, are we training them to do long-term sustained speech language therapy at any level or any other level. I don't think that should be the goal. So further research is needed on all the aspects of training they get. So in this regard the training of one particular group of persons at the field level and I think mothers and care givers. See mother can easily spend 10-12 hours of the time with the disabled child at no cost or very low cost basis. The same level of training by a professional at whatever level is going to cost huge part of our resources and no professionals anywhere would be able to sit six to eight hours with any disabled child and provide facility required by a disabled child. Therefore, the mothers and care giver persons are to be utilized for this purpose. So I would call upon all the professionals to develop programmes and quality and type of training to be given to such mothers and care givers and how their potential can be best exploited and utilized. So I think with emphasis on these three issues I should stop and there are many other issues. There is lot of research that is needed in early identification and prevention. Prevention is better and cheaper than cure. The kind of material, low cost materials that they require it is known to all of us. There is no point in elaborating on that. Similarly you are familiar with problems that we have in finding right kind of low cost teaching materials and screening materials and diagnostic test materials. India is a vast country. We know that 80 per cent of our population lives in rural areas. We all come from different cultural backgrounds. There is very little similarity between any two regions and culture. So somebody was telling that you cannot travel for more than 8 km without coming across a dialect. To be precise there are 1,652 languages and dialects in this country. This is very valid figure I am giving. So the needs are diverse population for therapeutic resources, teaching materials, reading materials are entirely different plus we also have an issue, religion which influences our thinking. So lot of research is needed to develop the kind of material, there are different professionals, doctors need different type of resource materials, teachers need different type of resource material, mother needs other type, health workers are kind of professionals and skilled or non-skilled workers need different type of resource material. Some research is going on in those areas and I am sure that you all are aware of such developments. Therefore, I am not going to elaborate on that point. So as I said in the beginning, I have prepared as a person with common sense talking about research issues and disabilities and I think chronological studies and our resources development and working of our institutions and networking of institutions. These are some of the areas need to be looked into on a national scale. I would be happy to answer questions if there are any.

MR. RAKESH ARORA

Let me at the very outset share a few thoughts which are outside my presentation because there is some technical problem. I had my floppy which is not going to start. First the views that I am going to express are my personal views and they do not represent the views of Planning Commission. In fact these are the issues which Planning Commission will have to address at a later date because the issues that I am going to discuss are pertaining to disability. I am already going to be doing study with National Human Rights Commission. What are issues concerned with poverty and disability. I feel still Project Director DRC than Director, Planning Commission because emotionally I feel very close to this sector rather than feel closer to Planning Commission. Please do not quote me on this and third when anyone talks on research, one can do research in any area and I can quote an instance from a time when I was a Lecturer in afternoon session in college and everyone used to be very inattentive. One English teacher was always interested in taking afternoon sessions. So I said how do you manage to keep people involved in your talks. He said no, no English is a very different subject. You have to tell the people to start imagining stories, so whenever I reached in the class, I just told them to close their eyes and start imagining and most of them doze off and one of them was wide awake and looking around and he says, I asked him how come you are not thinking. He said the snoring of other people does not let me think. Coming to the issue, I am going to raise issues rather than answer questions as I have no answers to these questions. The topic being such that is poverty and disability. First thing that Dr. Jayram had indicated. Research can be very specific. It can be very general. As Director of S&T Mission for 4 to 5 years, we researched in 88 projects. You are all concerned with disabilities issues and I am sure most of you know more than 2-3 unless you have been directly involved with the project. Now that is the problem with specific research, it does not, it tends to first solve a very specific problem in a very different way. It does not catch the attention of each group which is concerned with disability. On the other hand there can be general research *e.g.* in specific research we developed solar battery charger. Here Dr. Jayram is aware of it and many of you are not. We developed plastic aspherical lenses for the visually impaired. We have developed an activity room through S&T Project in Mission Mode. Again people basically concerned with MR. Rest of the people first tend to forget. On the other hand when I was Director in Ministry of Social Justice & Empowerment, we tried doing a general research, like job identification for persons with disabilities. But that did not catch the attention of general people. But it did catch the attention of the Department of Personnel & Training, Department, of Urban Development and Employment. It did catch the attention of Education. First point that I am trying to make is if you have a specific research, a small group of people very deeply interested in the subject get to know about it. Get to know the details about it but does not get the Ministries, specially Ministries which are hub of policy-making, budget allocations, do not get interested. If we had to write to Planning Commission that look underserving. Under the Technology Mission Mode we have developed plastic a spherical lenses. They will say lot of research goes on, developing lot of things. If I would say give me budget allocation, they say no you look for a budget allocation from your Ministry. So my idea, my considered thought is that one should think in terms of general research if we want to wake up the policy planners, budget allocators. Where from Planning Commission, Ministries of Finance, Social Justice, Women & Child Development, Health Labour. Now then where do I choose a subject like poverty and disability. In my mind, one of the basic problem is every person with disability in this country, whether rich or poor is being economically independent. Other attributes the social status like ADL get very difficult. A person has to be economically independent to get others recognition. You would rarely see a person with disability not economically independent but yet is not important. Why because today with economic independence and without being productive there is very little recognition. Then there is also an argument that poverty and disability are closely related. Would anyone like to share the thoughts on poverty and disability are closely related. Do you think they are related or not. And the reason is very simple. Poor people tend to live in environment which tends to aggravate disability and people with disability find it difficult to get jobs as people are not willing to take them on jobs. There are both as they might not be trained well. The environment may not be barrier free. They may not have proper assistive devices. The tools and equipment which are available like the office table so are other bottlenecks on both demand side and supply side. In fact, in one of the articles that I have written in the disability Journal, I argued that it is both demand and factors which cause the problem of this vicious circle of poverty and disability. People are poor because they are disabled. They are disabled because they are poor. Therefore, to my mind if you want general attention, there is a need to first understand what is poverty. What is disability and to what extent are the people with disabilities poor. I don't think there has been a serious estimation. Dr. Jayram was saying that we have no precise data with regard to number of disabled people. Obviously less information on the number of people with disabilities below the poverty line. Problem is not only estimation, the problem is also conceptual. So you have to look at what is the concept of poverty within the country. Which in fact the Planning Commission follows and whether that same concept is applicable to people with disability. My strong argument is that you can not apply the same poverty line to people with disability. You have to add up on a few things which you are aware of. In a moment I will come to second is the problem of estimation. If we want to research on general areas one has to probably look at the estimation. The number of people with disability and as I said I am doing the project with National Human Rights Commission precisely on this issue. Then equally important to assess the requirement of people with disabilities. Now I will come back to the meaning of requirement and availability of services to people with disabilities. For example, a very simple area to research would be, does the person with disability provide sufficient provisions for doing away with poverty with people with disability. I have listed out direct provisions for fighting poverty that are contained in Persons with Disability (PwD) Act. There are indirect provisions also. For example, 3 per cent of all poverty related programmes should go to persons with disabilities. Incentive that is of Section 40 that says that there should be incentive to employers with 5 per cent persons with disabilities put in public and private sectors. This provision is very different from 3 per cent reservation. Three per cent reservation is mandatory. Every government department, or government funded department, must support 3 per cent of the vacancies which should go to the people with disabilities whereas one talks in terms of incentive for private sector. For example, the extra cost of employing the person with disability should be met by government. Laxity now that is an incentive so that Section 41 is different from Section 33 than Section 43 and provides land for establishment of factories or site modifications. Now there are direct provisions in PwD Act. Somebody wanting to do research should actually look into how implementable are these provisions. How much of them have been actually implemented and how many people have actually benefited from it. I don't think I can vouch with confidence that as far as Section 41 is concerned, nothing has been done. Section 33 something has been done. Section 40 is dubious section. Ministry of Rural Development has provided for money but money has not been utilized. Now that is where somebody wanting to do research should get into the reasons why funds available are not being utilized and to what extent will this provision reduce the poverty among persons with disabilities. That is the question you should be asking yourself. The question is how many people are going to be benefited and to what quantum both the number and quantity. You say we have provided a disability pension of Rs.50 or Rs.100 and I think that should be enough. But the most fundamental question is you must have heard about the poverty line. We talk of people above poverty line and people below poverty line. Planning Commission is always talking of family below poverty line but no research whatsoever has been done on trying to find out what is poverty line for persons with disabilities and my own contention is that same poverty line cannot be applied to persons with disabilities as is applied to general people and the reasons are very obvious. See I am talking about a concept. There is a very well defined poverty line as per Lakra Committee and as per NSSO round 56 they have found out this is the minimum basket of goods that anyone requires. This is expenditure pattern and according to this pattern 27 per cent people in the country are below the poverty line. There is a well documented information now. Whether there is efforts to move these people above the poverty line or not, I am not getting into that, what am I saying is today you have fairly well defined, may be debatable but fairly well defined and accepted. The question you are putting is very very valid. But accepted by whom, the people below the poverty line or accepted by the government. And who matters. The basic argument is that persons with disability are like any other consumer. He is also a consumer and like any other consumer a non-disabled consumer he requires a minimum basket of consumption beyond that he also requires help for assistive devices and may be an attendant. While estimating poverty among persons with disabilities we must take into consideration the minimum cost along with basket that you do for rest of the people at the health cost, the cost of assistive devices, the cost of barrier-free environment. For example, a visually impaired person requires a milk boiler which whistles because he will not know that milk has boiled. That is an extra cost. A person with Cerebral Palsy (CP) may require a different utensil. Or may be a little modification. These costs which are minimum to start living independently should be added on to the cost of the minimum basket which is used for rest of the population. The basic idea is we should research regionally, across sexes, across ages as to the poverty line for PwDs must include normal basket of goods that is used by other people and the cost of additional services. In fact I am doing a research with National Human Rights Commission for 3 States as to what is the cost of living for a person with disability and that should give the real poverty line. So a specific more precise estimate on additional cost of living for PwDs should be marked out with focus on working out separately poverty line for people with different disabilities. Obviously the cost will differ across different regions, urban, rural, age and sex.

Now the pension and financial support that you talk of. Don't fix it based on normal poverty line, fix it on normal poverty line. That is the argument. That is how you should work out. What you require to give them the support and that is the area of research. Similarly wages etc. don't talk of minimum wage which is used for normal people. Use the wages which reflects the minimum cost of living for PwDs. If you don't provide the cost then provide the services in programmes and schemes. That is the idea basically.

PROF. P. K. DAS

The remuneration of a handicapped person is normally fixed by an industrialist or entrepreneur is always less than a normal person with so much of training. It is the normal scenario in the society. You are just going to raise the salary plus the additional cost he has to bear for his disability.

MR. RAKESH ARORA

I got your point. I could not agree more with you. There is a dichotomy here. A person who is an industrialist fixes the wage according to productivity. And the general notion, even in Japan for example, the productivity of a person with disability is considered like lower. But my argument is that the extra cost, the extra wages, should be borne by the government. You don't expect the private sector to compensate or get into welfare. The State is a welfare State and must bear, what is attributable to the person for his productivity. What is the extra cost, that extra cost will be born by the government that is precisely my argument. Unless you have an idea what is the extra cost, how can you put an idea that what is the extra amount that should be given. Government can come back, I was a Director in Social Justice for 5 years, I could simply say we have a ADIP Scheme, we have a family pension scheme, you also have a non-employment scheme, so that compensates for the inconveniences.

SPEAKER

I just wanted to know for a general people to live on a very meagre meal, minimum money needed in India, how much it is. O.K. Rs. 400, I agree with you. Now adult mentally retarded child, what is the pension he gets. Rs.100, now tell me where is our research, there are the grass roots people they want to ask you. They want to ask that wherefrom a grass roots person will live, do we need research for this. I have full regards to, this is just a discussion.

RAKESH ARORA

I am totally in agreement with our friend that Rs.100 is very very meagre and the extra cost would be much more. In the government as you all are aware we are going to put an argument, you must have a quantifiable information. What is the extra cost. That is the precisely my idea that you must research on as to what is the extra cost. Suppose I think it is Rs.500, another person thinks it is Rs. 1,000, there is no scientific basis to arrive on that extra cost. So first thing is to do, we should be able to come out with a scientific extra cost that is needed. Then argue with government and may be get half of that. The government will always say that there is not enough budget. Therefore, while the extra cost is this much, we can give only this much. Why because for information of all of you, I do not know whether you are aware, there are still 27 per cent of the people who live below the poverty line. There is a scientific basis to say that. The Planning Commission says that during the Tenth Plan, we will move 10 per cent of this 27 per cent above the poverty line. You don't have similar information about PwDs. So where is the information. You give a quantifiable data and then you say during the Tenth Plan, there are 50 per cent people with disabilities among the poverty line, 25 per cent of them must move up.

SPEAKER FROM SURAJ MANDAL

All our efforts are going in vain because of lingering, denying and delaying by State government authorities to give sanction to appointment of person with disability and professionally qualified. How RCI will help us towards this.

RENU SINGH

I have a question for both of you. Mr. Arora what you are talking about research to find out what will be the minimal amount for a person with disability to sustain, is all in very good faith. But we still feel that the persons with disabilities are not being given the fair share of what other citizens have in terms of Rs.400 which is the minimum amount. Often we think of research issues which just go down into quantifiable data. I think every research question must have a logical conclusion to it and we can't do research for the sake of putting on agenda. People with disabilities must be given their fair share but unfortunately they do not get that in our country even today. Planning Commission, of course, has a very big responsibility to look into this affair.

RAKESH ARORA

I was expecting this question before I started my presentation and the simple answer is that on paper you can't prove that there is discrimination against PwDs. All the programmes being implemented by the government are beyond discrimination. There are programmes which support PwDs. So how can you say that they are not getting their due share in terms of normal poverty alleviation programmes. There is a 3 per cent reservation in all poverty alleviation programmes for PwDs. Rural development has been sitting over funds. If I am handling money, I would not give away money without meeting certain procedures and I could be biased and could give money to people without following procedures whom I want to favour. You can't go from one extreme to another extreme. Do you give a free hand to a Director and say here is Rs.20 crore and give to anybody you like without following the procedure. This is going to be misused. We are all human beings and any person sitting on that chair has his own personal interests much more than the official interests. So procedures are necessary so far as money is involved. Government is a non-entity in that sense. It must have systems and procedures which must be accepted by everybody. You can't say I am a better NGO. Don't worry about State recommendation. This is the kind of questions we used to get. Mrs. Gandhi tried her best to have apex NGOs groups which could recommend another NGO. But then the rivalry started. So procedures have to be there.

SPEAKER

In case someone slaps a disabled person and he files a suit in the court, then what should be the compensation required for a disabled person? In case of accident what should be the compensation or in case of a property dispute or property compensation, what should be the rate for the disabled person? In case NPTC requires a land in Ghaziabad and there are 10 disabled persons what will be the rate of the land.

SPEAKER

Now I am a pediatrician. When we talk about research not make it a speciality. In my opinion, prevention of handicapped children is missed opportunity. National health programme, nutrition programme, everything is claiming that they are reaching the unreached. Still low birth rate is 12 per cent and yearly diagnosis, yearly identification and yearly intervention has not popped up. So any research in this aspect should be given a good priority and in my area where I met with 60,000 population, the handicapped below 1 year is about one per cent and below four years is about 2-2.5 per cent. There are handicapped which start recognizing as child grows, particularly cerebral palsied, etc. at a early age and at the time of birth, six months onwards only we are able to establish the diagnosis. So if you happen to be in research planning, share research with those who are working with very young children.

MR. GOYAL

I am presenting here the finding of my social research done in the last 10 years in a district of Uttar Pradesh which is in the national capital region, newly developed and highly industrialized, known as Ghaziabad. The national perspective of welfare and development of people with disabilities in different aspects is yet to match the perception among people with disabilities and coherent human resource already sensitive to it. Their positive approach towards disabled and human resource be synchronized by involvement of family members of the disabled persons to share their articulated vision of alternative solution at a collective platform of a local intellectual group. Preparation of a fund of community resource already available in this sphere in the society which can be mobilized and people's interest with adequate bankability at the district level. The pattern of the growth of the voluntary organizations is the inception of the Societies Registration Act, 1860. In last 140 years we have analyzed and studied that 5,000 such organizations are registered under Societies Registration Act in the district of Ghaziabad. In the pre-independence time, the theme of the NGOs was charity perception, in the middle of the 20th century the theme was welfare, which was floated by Missionaries and backed up by all religious groups. After independence, specially in the last 25 years, the growth of the new NGOs with professional volunteerism and leadership took place. The current perception being problem related to the persons together with issues in development theme. The current pragmatic approach with development. The dimension is present day challenging development of our nation. To nationalize the action at grass roots level workers towards empowerment, rehabilitation can play a key role function in the empowerment movement. It is not impossible action but difficult and needs patience and attention. Reduction of inter-perceptional distance which is a grey area need intervention. It is possible through networking of coherent policies.

DR. MANSHISH

We are already conducting research on the spastic child under various physical activities at the centre as well as in the periphery, NGO or patient, how to make a bridge. We found new things. Upgrading the NGOs, therapists are using the same techniques, so we have to improve and upgrade them.

SPEAKER

I think the concept of research need to be understood. When we talk of generalized research, it means it should be of mass interest for mass welfare. We have to be more broad vision, thinking of the welfare of the disabled persons.

SPEAKER

Our long working has given us small experience that if you teach the poverty stricken people who have some abilities, talking of human resources, material resources and technological resources in those areas, when we try to take all those three things into consideration, the poverty stricken people have basket economy first, it is converted into sophisticated economy of making artificial aids. Now those artificial aids are made for people in the same area and they are taught skills which they are successfully able to use. It gives them a better economy because a number of other disciplines are involved in that and more people start getting money without much expenditure on the part of the government or on the part of the institution. That has given results, we had put in Rs. 2,000 per person, gradually the revolving fund went on increasing in various types of vocations as well as in giving of artificial aids. Now we have 40 people who have given back the money. Not only that we have Rs.1.20 lakhs which is extra which they have given back which we have to redistribute among the people who are poverty stricken. I think a technology of this kind, which is a static technology of making of artificial aids into dynamic technology of making aids, that may help poverty alleviation programmes for the government as well as ourselves.

PROF. DAS

Dr. Jayram has got lot of experience in research and he spoke on wide variety of areas in which research is needed and main areas were epidemiological studies, networking of institutions and organizations. Mr. Rakesh Arora spoke about research on poverty and funding and research is needed on how much fund is needed for below the poverty line and things like that.

CHAIRPERSON

I must congratulate both the presenters for stimulating ideas in this small group. I think the whole audience was attracted to Mr. Rakesh Arora's, below poverty line (BPL) and all of us are interested in that. Prevention of infant disabilities, we need lot of research in this area. Dr. Jayram gave very vivid presentation. Epidemiological studies should be included in research in disability. In our earlier meeting we had suggested orientation of all the NGOs and other organizations. RCI should orient organizations on research methodologies. We should develop a protocol with a definite aim. It can be an immediate objective or a distant objective or a general objective and how to satisfy that aim through various methods and materials. It calls for research. If you want to have economic research or fund research, what are the methods you can develop? What are the funds available? What are the resources available? Various methods. Once you have finalized the materials and methods, the next aspect is to implement the method of research. Various types of observations are possible and once you observe, develop, specify the results and may be monitor the results and analyse it. That is very important. The pediatrician was talking about early detection. She says only after six months of life of the child, we see the disability. Is it possible to detect it early at the child birth? Is it possible to detect that the child is going to have cerebral palsy? It is possible various technological advances have been made. Even diagnosis at the pregnancy stage is possible. So these procedures have to be implemented at the community level and if the process can be taken as a community based, community based cardiology, community based rehabilitation, etc. So we can have community based research. Dr. Jayram has done something in this area, specially with regard to the use of hearing aids, how to simplify the hearing aid. We can make recommendations. It is for the RCI to find funds. Funds have to be utilized for research components. We all are with RCI in promoting research and we hope in the next few years we will have data.

VII

BARRIER-FREE ENVIRONMENT

Chairperson: Dr. (Mrs.) Uma Tuli, Chief Commissioner (Disabilities)
Co-Chairperson: Dr. G. Karna

I am here more to learn, may be a little bit to share. If you chair a session, you are always in a beneficial situation because you can listen to people and you don't have to talk much. We have four eminent speakers for this session. Mr. Sanjeev Sachdeva, Ms. Anjali, Mr. Gautam Shah, and Mr. Hiramath. In fact, they are so well known in this field, they hardly need any introduction. If one knows how UN-ESCAP team brought pride to our country, it is because of these, two who have made us proud by their contribution and I am very happy to say that they are both in the apex body of our office team also. They are the one who are doing our access audit. We had these two and few more as resource persons to our five National Workshops and when you come to know what is the end result of those five National Workshops, you will realize what a wonderful contribution they have made. I am sure their presentations will speak for their contribution. Mr. Gautam Shah is the renowned architect from Ahmedabad. He is the brain behind the most important building, *i.e.* Indian Spinal Injuries Centre and we all know how barrier free it is. Mr. Hiramath has contributed in his own way. He is very innovative, very creative. The mobile toilets that we see at many places in Delhi are his creations. As a member of the Technology Mission, also, he has made several contributions and I am very happy they have come to this Convention.

MR. SANJEEV SANCHDEVA

The term barrier-free environment was unknown a decade ago. All efforts were made to integrate the disabled people into the mainstream society, the government and concerned agencies made their best efforts but the desired results could not be achieved. The reason being inaccessibility restricting the mobility of the disabled people. So the desired aim was not achieved. The most important, with the passage of the Disability Act, 1995 and dynamic Chief Commissioner, Dr. Uma Tuli, a new change can easily be seen. The barrier-free environment has become the focal point. It has become the main theme of all the major workshops. It has been introduced in all the major activities organized by the Government of India. At the moment it is picking up, the awareness is being built up, the momentum is gaining. The various agencies do feel and know the needs of people with disabilities but in the absence of diverse requirements of people with disabilities, though they want to do the things, they have not been able to do it as it should have been. Basically when we talk about the barrier-free environment, we think only of ramps which is a very incorrect picture. We must understand the needs and requirements of every disabled, visually impaired, hearing impaired, physically disabled or multiply disabled. I would like to briefly mention the diverse requirements of different disabled groups:

Visually impaired people—orientation and mobility are keywords. They look out for auditory clues, sound or textual changes and bright colour contrast are good for low vision people. But how do they identify that this is a room or a toilet? For the hearing impaired, communication, the better acoustics, better signage and more visual display, helps an hearing impaired person. For locomotor disabled people, again there are two categories like some are ambulatory, those who can walk with the help of walking frames, crutches. Some are non-ambulatory. They may be independent wheelchair users or assisted wheelchair users. Their requirements are different. They require non-slippery furnaces, they require ramps, corridors, width of the doors, counter heights, information centres, hand rails, etc. If we create separate things for separate disabilities or special needs for special people, that will not be the answer. The answer is a universal design, which will not only help people with disabilities but the vast section of the society. Universal design is the key word in the barrier-free environment. It should be inclusive and we should not ask for something separate. We will be automatically part of the society. When Dr. Uma Tuli joined, there was a national level campaign for barrier-free environment and five major workshops were held and you all must be aware that in each State five persons are trained to conduct access audit and to train others. All the 28 States have experts in this field. If you need further information, you may contact office of the Chief Commissioner (Disabilities).

MS. ANJALI

The barrier-free environment should be affordable and dignified for people with disabilities. There are barriers in public transport, buildings, and amenities which are available. There are many barriers and dangerous areas. There are large number of users of the built environment. There are users like families with young children, people who are ill, people with fracture, wheelchair users and people who use heavy luggage. These are the examples of barriers, there are stairs or steps and the wheelchair can not climb. This is a pavement which is not maintained and it is a barrier. This is a high control button of lift. Steps and curves in front of the escalators. Higher stand for the telephone booth. ATM counter, which is too high. There are different items, cooler, air conditioner, etc. which are barrier for the visually impaired. Toilet which has a curve. Curve in front of a shopping mall. While considering all these designs from the architectural point of view, parking space, approach area, circulation area, steps, stairs, doors, lifts, toilets, telephone booths signage, etc. have to be considered. There should be a designated parking space for people with disabilities, specially for wheelchair users and it should be near to the entrance, 30 metres from the entrance. This is the sketch of a parking area where a car is parked and there is a space from where the wheelchair can go into the building. This is an example of a parking space, there is a signage, and is nearer to the entrance. This is a parking area designated in the Metro Station in Shahdara where you will find ample space and place to go to the Station area. This is a parking place for the wheelchair with signage of 18" from the ground. There is a ramp which goes into the building. This is recommended and being implemented at the Metro Station. For every building there should be a ramp and width of the ramp should not be less than 1,200 mm. Approach ramps are of different designs constructed according to the space availability. Signage should be provided for each facility given. Ramp is not only useful for wheelchair users but also for those who carry heavy luggage. Steps should also be there besides the ramp.

Another example of Delhi Haat where they have provided a ramp along with single step. Stairs rails should have bright colours for the benefit of low vision people. This is a good example of steps, the handle should start 30 mm from the steps start. These are the examples of handle rails with a diameter of 40-45 mm. This is a good example from the Metro Station at Welcome Colony which has two handles one for adults and the other for children. The width of the corridors should not be less than 900 mm and minimum space for a wheelchair should be given and turning space should not be less than 1,500 mm. The lift space should not be less than 1,400 × 1,400 mm and the door should open wide enough to allow the wheelchair entry and the door closing mechanism should give enough time for the wheelchair. Buttons and switches should be within the easy reach of wheelchair users, *i.e.* 1,000 mm from the ground. Braille marking should be given for the benefit of the visually impaired persons. This is a very good example of a barrier-free lift. This is an audio announcement system in the lift. This is a bad example of a toilet with a small door where the wheelchair can't go inside. Kick plate is useful for the wheelchair user to open the door. Lever handle should be provided which is easy for the wheelchair users to open. Toilet should be minimum 1,700 × 1,450 mm, which is required for a wheelchair user to use the toilet. W.C. height should be equal to the height of the wheelchair sitting a person. Adjustable wash basin. Taj Hotel in Mumbai have fixed such type of wash basins. Floor surface should be non-slippery. There should be enough space for transfer from wheelchair to W.C. Flush button at a very convenient place which a wheelchair user can use with foot.

These have been taken from the Singapore Airport and these facilities are available at New Delhi International Airport. This is an example of moveable W.C. the height can be adjusted.

An example of urinal which can be used by disabled people who use crutches.

The public dealing counters should not be more than 800 mm high from the floor. There should be leg space under the counter. Public booths heights should not be more than 1,200 mm so that it can be used easily by the wheelchair users.

Tactile signage for visually impaired. Tactile map. Colour contrast for low vision persons.

MR. SANJEEV SACHDEVA

Friends, you see how the technology has helped disabled persons. The mobile phone has helped the hearing impaired. They can send SMS and talk to their friends. Now we understand that the land line will also follow the same thing and it would be a revolution for the hearing impaired. For visually impaired people we can develop some distant audio systems, beepers, distant sound systems are important. Delhi Metro will be having, we have suggested to them. New things can be done with the technological advancements. What role NGOs and other concerned can play.

First and foremost understanding the needs and requirements of different disabled persons. We can push forward the need for access through a coordinated effort. RCI can join by introducing a chapter on barrier-free environment in their curricula and all their workshops.

DR. UMA TULI

It is not easy to break barriers. Barriers, physical, attitudinal. We need access to education, we need access to employment, we need access to each other. These barriers have been broken basically because now there is an Act which is a very very effective Act. Sections 44 to 47 talk of non-discrimination which we are covering in this barrier free environment. Sanjeev and Anjali have told you a lot about how to break these barriers in public places but Mr. Hiramath is going to tell you more about accessible buses, accessible trains or planes.

MR. HIRAMATH

I will be showing you a slide presentation basically photographs taken from various barrier free places. This picture shows a typical metal ramp which is made by using the pre-fabricated material. This is somewhere in the US and wanted to show it because how quickly you can make a ramp for the disabled. This is available in a kit form and can be assembled, may be in a day or two the entire ramp can be ready for use. This is a small plate which is also available as a kit abroad and can serve as a barrier free place for the disabled. This is the picture of a small portable kit. Suddenly you may have to travel and you may or may not find a ramp. At that time you just have to remove these two cases, join them together, have your own ramp. This is another small concept. There is no place for a ramp to be made. This is called vertical elevator, which can be used to go up from the ground and enter a building. This is the picture of a vertical ramp which has been developed in India now where a wheelchair user can move from 0 to 600 mm height. This is another wonderful devise, made for individual use which shows a patient who has ambulatory problem. Just fixing a rod from ground to roof and having an arm here which can rotate, the person can be lifted and transferred to the wheelchair or any other thing. We have some grab bars here which are very wide and are used for showing and toilet use. We have some more pictures of grab bars. Regular and L shape grab bar. This is a barrier free toilet which can be placed near the bus stop or any where. This is a small tactile pass word which can be used by the visually impaired people and can guide them straight to the toilet. These are some of the simple devices which can be used for making the toilets barrier-free quickly. These are not permanent solutions but these are temporary solutions for the persons who may have an accident or are temporarily disabled. This is the picture of a mobile toilet where pre-fabricated set up can be made for wheelchair users. This is a combination ramp or a combination path way where there is a tactile ramp which is laid in centre of the ramp for the blind and then we have side rails. This is the toilet sheet of the mobile toilet. We have sinks with large arm operations to easily switch on and switch off the water. This is a typical railway station with tactile path way going to ticket counter and the coach. There is a small transfer mechanism for the wheelchair users. We have another mechanism here which is designed at Amar Jyoti. We have separate way for the bus users where there a provision for the wheelchair to move in to the platform and on to the bus, provided the doors are of 1,000 mm width minimum. We have a vertical lift which we have designed, earlier it was restricted to 3 feet but now we can go upto 10 feet where a wheelchair user can move from ground to top. This is a plan of a bus stop we are planning to have in Delhi. This is the design of a bus stop abroad. Mr. Sanjeev Sachdeva had suggested last time for such a design. Such a bus stop is being planned which is user friendly for any type of disabled person. The vehicle can not be a right candidate for redesign in full. What is needed is to combine the both bus stop and the vehicle complementary to each other and designing the public transport.

We have two methods for the blind to locate an area, one is through tactile and other through sound. For tactile we have something called blister tile which is about 1 inch × 5 mm which can be laid in a path. There is some kind of a sensory movement while stepping on them. Typically a visually impaired person moves in this way using his cane by tapping or moving in the air to find the right path or there is an obstruction or change in level etc. Junction tiles and linear tiles. Using the cane between these two, they can identify the path. There can be other differential material also other than the tiles. This is the simplest method used to making a tactile path. These are small buttons which have riveted on the tiles or this can be a dome shape or a concrete to give them a cue. This is the picture of a railway station. Most railway stations in India have already been built, the platforms are having a particular height and the particular specification is already incorporated. To make any kind of civil changes it would involve tremendous amount of logistics because no railway platform can be shut down for 24 hours a day. The solution was a thin tactile tile which can be pasted on the concrete without making much change in the level but giving a feel to the blind people, old people.

This is the picture of indications used in Braille at the crossings, signals, etc. We have speech and auditory inputs also which can be programmed. These are samples of some tactile maps which we are developing using low cost material. This is the embossed tactile map. These are some standardized symbols for doors, streets, curve cuts, steps, cross walks. Various symbols are being worked out with blind volunteers giving right feedback. This is a tactile map for a full street. This is another map of a building. This is a small map which was made in Bangalore for an exhibition in 2002. Another important thing to make the environment barrier free to visually impaired persons is to give them a feel how the objects look using figures. These are time clocks where they can put the finger and know the time. These are the auditory signals which can be placed at traffic signals, hazardous area or indicating toilets, bathrooms. This is another equipment which is being designed which will give

200 times different frequencies, sounds to indicate each premises. This is being standardized globally. These are small sound devices which guide the VI from one end to the other end of the road. This area is now for the hearing impaired. You can see a typical telephone which is known as DTY telephone. Whatever he is punching in comes out as a message. The other end hearing impaired person is also using this telephone. He can read the message and hear the message. Both persons have to have these equipment to talk to each other. This is a hearing aid using solar batteries. This is a vibro tactile clock. You keep this particular piece below your pillow and fix the particular time, for the hearing impaired person it will wake him up at the given time by vibrating the clock. These are different types of approaches now being used for the he0aring impaired, one is individual amplifier and behind the ear aids and amplifier body hearing aid. Two methods to communicate for hearing impaired. One is inducting loop and other is through speaker. Then we have direct speaker and through FM transmission where a person can receive it on hearing aid and hear it.

DR. UMA TULI

While Sanjeev took us earlier to Japan, Mr. Hiramath also took us to America and other places. May I request Mr. Gautam Shah to share his experiences please.

GAUTAM SHAH

Barrier-free environment is the subject. Earlier speakers have already demonstrated lot of technical details and other components. I would talk more from an Architect's point of view. As an Architect how do we proceed further. First of all to make a barrier free environment is the total team work which include architect, owner and administrator and they all must work together in order to achieve our objectives. We must set our objectives from the day one. Architects have to take the primary responsibility because he is a technical person. He must do analysis. He must know what are the technical specifications, details etc. Present day scenario what happens is people think barrier free environment is simply fixing ramps. There are many more elements which we have to incorporate. Our task begins the day we get a building to design. We have to do programming. People think put a ramp which is very costly. Then why don't we use lift. Then there is power problem. We have to assess the minimum requirement. If we start with these analysis from the day one, then this can be implemented in our design programme. We cannot look barrier free as a separate element. We look at the building material, flooring, marble, structural details, plumbing, construction details. Barrier-free must be part of our design process. If we start with that assumption from the day one, the task will be much simpler. Many of the architects are not exposed to barrier free concept. Now barrier-free is not related to only hospitals but all public buildings. Now we have to talk about the future. School of Architecture from the day one, the students should be exposed to barrier-free concepts, colours, texture, composition, graphics, proportion, etc. This is a must. By the end of the course after five years, they would be able to solve the problems of clients. For any of the projects we must set our objectives. One more element I want to inform you fire protection. Barrier-free is alright. But if there is any fire, what do we do about the visually impaired, wheelchair users, etc. We must train our staff in evacuation etc. Every care is taken to provide services to spinal injury patients. Effort should be made to provide barrier-free environment for all handicapped in all buildings. These guidelines should be enforced by both architects and the inspectors responsible for buildings. Aging is another kind of disability where we need all such facilities. An architect must know the standards required for making a building accessible to all types of disabled. The client must insist on the barrier-free design of the building. Architect should take proper care and proceed keeping in view all the requirements of barrier-free. After design, we must pay proper attention for construction. It is quite possible that the client may not be aware of all the guidelines. Therefore, architect must take the lead and proceed with the barrier-free design. These are the components of the barrier-free design, site development, parking, ramp, interior, exterior, entrance, doors, stairs, toilets, elevators, graphics, fire safety evacuation. Design implementation, architect's main role. We must make proper space allocation. Invariably what happens, the architect says I don't have enough space. It is not impossible. Where there is a will there is a way. We must allocate proper area so that proper space allocation and budgeting is done. Provide door of the required size. The biggest problem is if you go to any five star hotel, you do not find accessible toilet. Why? Because the door size is small. I don't see any reason when you spend crore of rupees you can't provide barrier-free toilets. Perhaps someone was not aware. This is where we have to orient them. We require wooden railings in the corridors, automatic doors at the entrance, which will make accessibility for the wheelchair users easier, non-slippery floors, another important thing is they should be of same level throughout. The difference of one or two inches should be avoided. There should also be fire doors, fire windows, to protect the environment. Elevators should be of adequate size. Ramps are very essential. Proper curve size should be given for free movement of wheelchair users. Parking requirement, parking should be allowed 2 per cent of the total for the handicapped. Proper sign marks must be indicated. Revolving doors are undesirable. We find that when people say 32 inch door, it should be net 32 inches which will allow easy movement of the wheelchair. Railing must extend 12 inches beyond the last step. If you happen to be at the Indian Spinal Injuries Centre, you may notice that we have complied with this regulation.

DR. UMA TULI

We have sent instructions to all the Schools of Architecture that the Course on Architecture should have a component on barrier-free environment. We have given instructions to all the banks, to all the public utility buildings. Our team is having regular access audit. Many buildings have become barrier-free. There are two types. Breaking barriers of all those existing buildings. It is extremely difficult than having accessible area in the new buildings. From the Ministry of Urban Affairs also, the directions have been given that no completion certificate shall be given till it is barrier-free.

MR. GAUTAM SHAH

Now coming to the question of toilets, besides meeting all the space requirement we must insist that all toilet doors open out. Many architects miss out on this important aspect. Toilets fittings must be at the appropriate heights. Normally there are two or three elevators. The door opening time should be maintained. This should also be incorporated in the lift design. Minimum dimension should be 54 inch × 54 inch for the wheelchair accessibility. Regarding signage it is also important that signage be given due recognition, exit sign, door identification sign, the height should be 54 × 66 inches, the number of identification symbols should be identified. The book on planning of the barrier-free architecture is prepared by the Office of the Chief Commissioner (Disabilities). Additional work is required to meet the fire safety norms keeping in mind the wheelchair user and blind. Such an effort can result in construction of safe, barrier-free building. We have provided all the barrier-free facilities at the Spinal Injuries Centre. There should not be any steps in front of the entrance. Many people create steps but then proper ramp should be provided. We have eliminated any steps whatsoever. Another problem we architects face in designing a building, there is nobody to give us guidelines. This is the Medical College building at Jallandhar where we have created barrier-free environment. What I would like to emphasize here is that there were lot of obstacles but keeping in mind that we must make barrier-free we have made sincere efforts and we are very happy we have succeeded.

PROGRAMME OFFICER

Whenever we go to any hill station, there is a problem of barrier-free access. Last time I was in Sikkim and I was trying to find out a place for stay of our Chairman, it was very difficult for me to find a place for him in a hotel. I would like to ask you how we can make the places accessible at hill stations.

GAUTAM SHAH

If no facility is available, then you have to break it and make it.

SANJEEV SACHDEVA

In a hilly terrain0 there is a problem of drainage, due to snowfall you can not have roof tops which are levelled and it is not that easy to provide access in a hilly terrain but with the help of bamboo trees, we can not have a ramp or a path of standard size. But the minimum we can have hand rails using local material, that can provide minimum access. But taking into consideration the overall terrain, we have to work on an universal design which is applicable to hilly areas.

DR. KARNA

I would like to express my high sense of appreciation and also thankfulness on behalf of RCI to the paper presenters for their scientific presentation, specially Mr. Sachdeva, Ms. Anjali, Mr. Hiramath, Mr. Gautam Shah. They have touched an area which is still unexplored in our country. There are number of government buildings which are not disabled friendly. This aspect has to be given top most priority. If we accept that the disabled persons are first and foremost the human beings, with the same basic needs as rest of the others, then we have to consider this issue in its entirety and government will have to give priority.

VIII

AWARENESS AND COMMUNITY MOBILIZATION

Chairperson: Mr. Ramaswamy
Co-Chairperson: Thakur Vijay Prasad

This is a very relevant topic "Awareness and Community Mobilization" without which, I am sure, we cannot do any justice to disabled. Our learned speakers in this session will enlighten us as to how to go about creating awareness and also mobilizing the community.

P.K. PINCHA

I owe deepest gratitude to the organizers Rehabilitation Council of India in general and to Major H.P. S. Ahluwalia, Chairman and its Secretary, Mr. J.P. Singh in particular for giving me this opportunity of interacting with you on a topic of crucial importance. I have to try to put together some stray thoughts and compress it into brief paper. This paper comprises six brief sections, section 1 introductory containing fundamentals of disability, section 2 refers to different stakeholders in respect of awareness creation and community mobilization, section 3 talks about major areas where awareness generation and community mobilization is indispensable, section 4 talks about relevant portion of standard rules on equalization of opportunities and full participation of persons with disabilities, section 5 refers to the barriers in the field awareness generation and community mobilization and section 6 is the conclusion. I feel deeply privileged to be associated with the deliberations of this session which will take a critical look at awareness generation and community mobilization in the context of disability. It goes without saying that awareness generation and community mobilization amongst all sections of society plays definite and distinct role in shaping the status of persons with disabilities, hereinafter, referred to as PwDs. Awareness generation and community mobilization are processes aimed at creating an inclusive and participatory society characterized by both equality and equity which would enable PwDs to assert and secure their rights and to lead a useful and contributing life as class one citizens with honour and dignity. The community mobilization is a direct fall out of effective awareness generation efforts and it manifests itself in a variety of ways, namely, enhance the understanding of critical issues of disability by the communities, increased participation of PwDs in matters that affect their life and above all in the emergence of organizations of PwDs as well as community based organizations. It would be in the fitness of things on my part to spell out certain fundamental concepts of disability that form part of all awareness generation and community mobilization programmes. They are as follows:

1. That one's disability need not necessarily be one's inability.
2. That disability is a development rather than a welfare issue and that disability is linked to poverty.
3. That disability is much more than a mere medical issue.
4. That PwDs can think, speak and act for themselves although surrogate participation in respect of persons with mental disabilities/children with disabilities must be provided for.
5. That there is a pronounced need to ensure that one's disability does not become one's handicap. The term disability summarizes a great number of functional limitations occurring in any population in any country in the world while the term handicapped is used for the

loss or limitation of opportunities to take part in the life of the community in equal level with others. In a sense it describes the encounter between the persons with disabilities and the environment.

Different Stakeholders

It would now be correct on our part to take a cursory look at the different stakeholders whose role both in acquiring and spreading awareness and undertaking sensitization programmes is exceedingly crucial. These stakeholders are as follows:

1. PwDs themselves.
2. Parents or guardians of PwDs.
3. Teachers/trainers/educators/professionals working in the disability sector.
4. NGOs and community based organizations working in the disability sector.
5. The mass media, electronic and fourth estate.
6. The civil society act as social activist, academia etc.
7. The state/government.

Some major areas of awareness generation and community mobilization:

1. Issues, situations, concerns, needs, and aspirations of PwDs.
2. Existing plans, policies, programmes, practices and schemes of the government meant for the benefit of persons with disabilities.
3. Programmes and services run, managed and maintained by the NGOs and the voluntary sector.
4. The legislation on disability including on PwDs, equal opportunities, Protection of Rights and Full Participation Act, 1995.
5. Right attitudes and fundamental concepts on disability.
6. Issues of more vulnerable groups among persons with

disabilities, such as women with disabilities, tribals with disabilities and people with disabilities living in rural areas and in urban slums.

7. Availability of concessions to persons with disabilities.
8. Utility and availability of assistive devices.

U.N. Standard Rules

The UN Standard Rules on the equalization of opportunities for PwDs, 1994 do comprehensively emphasize the urgency of awareness generation programmes. The said rules envisage that the State should take action to raise awareness in society about PwDs, their rights, their needs, their potential and their contribution. These rules interalia casts certain responsibilities on the State as follows:

1. In ensuring that responsible authorities put updated information on available programmes and services to PwDs in accessible forms to their families, professionals in the field and the general public.
2. In initiating and supporting information campaigns concerning PwDs and disability policies conveying the message that PwDs are the citizens with same rights and obligations and others. Thus justifying measures to remove obstacles to full participation.
3. In encouraging portrayal of PwDs by the mass media in a positive way.
4. In ensuring that public education programmes reflect in all their aspects the principles of full participation.
5. In inviting PwDs and their families and organizations to participate in public education programmes concerning disability matters.
6. In encouraging entrepreneurs in the private sector to include disability issues in all aspects of their activities.
7. In initiating and promoting programmes aimed at raising the level of PwDs concerning their rights and potential.

8. In ensuring that PwDs could also assist one another in awareness raising activities through their own organizations.
9. In making awareness raising a part of education of all children a component of teacher training courses and training of all professionals.

Barriers to Awareness Generation

1. Lack of political will evidenced among other things from absence of any statement on disability policy in the election manifestoes of major political parties.
2. Absence of proper awareness generation strategies.
3. Apathy on the part of a major section of bureaucracy to disability related issues.
4. Near indifference of the media resulting in inadequate issue based coverage on disability.
5. Inadequate information with NGOs working in the disability sector.
6. Relatively weaker linkages and networking amongst different NGOs and community based organizations working in the disability sector.
7. Existing attitudinal barriers.

Conclusion

In conclusion we will do better if we do not lose sight of the fact that both government and non-governmental agencies need to work in close conscious and coordinated collaboration after putting in proper place awareness generation and community mobilization strategies. It is also equally important that the mass media gives issue based rather than event based coverage to disability matters on a regular basis. Another area of focus could be to enlist active participation of the affected groups, the PwD in the present case, in conducting various studies or surveys so that such exercises acquire authenticity and legitimacy and that such persons are able to come together to share their problems and experiences in a bid to work out a better future for themselves.

K. KANNAN

We have a media group called Samatvam in Delhi which tries to promote coverage of disability and other social issues in media. What I would like to share with you from this platform is a study on management information systems and communication strategies in voluntary organizations working in the disability sector. We did this last year. We have been working very closely with the Rehabilitation Council of India to organize media workshops for media persons on disability issues as well as to strengthen communication skills of institutions working in this field. In fact last year we organized a communication skills workshops and at that time we shared the preliminary results of this survey which was going on and now present the full paper before you.

Knowledge today is recognized as the key resource for development. The world over the voluntary sector is moving towards better generation and sharing and application of knowledge. A process that is collectively termed as "knowledge management". Even in the disability sector the voluntary organizations are realizing the need to re-invent themselves and the professionals with them have already started in investing information management. Though the information management approach is important to reach out the stakeholders but also helps in advocacy. This survey which we did amongst 120 organizations looks at only two stakeholders, media and the NGOs. What is the perception *vis-à-vis* media and NGOs? What role can media play in stepping up coverage? To constantly generate and share and apply knowledge in their field, the voluntary organizations need to develop efficient information management system involving information and communication technologies. Samatvam, which was born in the year of International Year of Volunteers 2001, and MITHRA Technology Foundation undertook a study on information management systems with the organizations working in the disability sector in partnership with RCI last year. The aim of the study was to see the organizations working in the disability sector receive information, process and disseminate information. A questionnaire was sent to 120 organizations working in the field in different parts of the country and we received only 46 responses. Now taking a positive view of the fact that 46 people responded, we thought that at least these many organizations are at least realising the importance of information management. However, the response did show that there was a paradigm shift in the knowledge management that has started taking place and it is sure to catch with other voluntary organizations in other parts of the country as well. Almost all the organizations underscored the need for receiving and sharing information and building a collaborative relationship with the media. In fact many of them realized that the technology can be used to free the individuals from linear mode of transacting information and reinvent their work and create a knowledge base to address new challenges. On the importance of evolving collaborative relationships, these are some of the responses we have got. Each one of the respondent was a NGO. One of them says it is very important to plan future activities and sharing innovation. Media helps in disseminating information about facilities in rehabilitation processes. It is very important for creating awareness and disseminate information through media, both print and electronic, particularly the regional papers.

Samatvam has organized regional workshops at 11 places across the country and found that regional media is most forthcoming than the national media in terms of covering these issues. Media is the only source to reach out to rural, sub-rural areas in the country and the term media has to be broadened to include all media, not only print and electronic. The folk media is doing very good work in some parts of the country. We found that in West Bengal and in some parts of Madhya Pradesh and U.P. also the folk media is playing very good role. Some of the organizations feel that there is a need for correctly understanding the role of media and information users and their role is as provider of information on disability. If you look at the whole range of transacting information, it begins at some place and ultimately it reaches the people through the media. What we found is that information is usually nobody's baby. In the sense that nobody feels the responsibility to actually take the trouble to provide information either to media or other stakeholders. In fact one of the NGOs that responded to survey says that their role as information provider is very very critical. All the organizations have grouse against the media and unanimously they say that media does not give adequate coverage to disability issues. More coverage was required for extensive dissemination of information on availability of specific need based services in the community. We just found that an article which appeared was very general. The coverage in the electronic and print media is not sufficient as people are at a loss to know where to contact if they come across such problems. Another thing we found is the shift from charity to rights does not appear in the media to the extent that one feels it should. The media is not covering this sector, issue based coverage is not there. Either events or event the NGOs are to be blamed for this because the media people say that we are invited only when some function is going on. As regards the role of media, another response was media should also help in removing stigma and discrimination and also highlight the potentials of persons with disabilities. The voluntary organizations feel that media should provide special space, be it a page, special supplement, spots on TV and radio covering critical aspects like awareness of various governmental schemes, rules and regulations, amendments, if any, regarding implementation and non-implementation. Stories regarding non-implementation is we found very few people are tackling, giving example like there are journalist Sangeeta Thakur in Patna or Ms. Garimalla Subramaniam in Chennai who are covering it on issue based. Education, training and employment, problems and solutions in the field of disability, these are some of the issues that NGOs feel media should take up. Information on voluntary organizations, government agencies, rehabilitation centres working in the field of disability, denial of rights, success stories, early intervention, research occurring in this field. Most feel that professional guidance and training for voluntary organizations is a prerequisite. As communication strategy is dependent on this. People said that we can't hire Public Relations (PR) agencies. We said we are not talking about PR agencies. Any NGOs even with a single man show, the NGO should be a good communicator with media. There is a certain structure in which they respond to these issues. You have to understand the structure, whom to contact in a media organization, whether it is print or electronic. We also have to know which forms of media could be used where requirements of urban areas are quite different from rural areas. There is a whole range of development communication tools which have been used in the past and which are now coming up. All these things have to be used on need and specific basis. In terms of professional guidance in some of the responses we got, professional guidance is very important and the good work being done by voluntary organizations should be made known to others. They feel that only when they get some professional training, we would be able to communicate the good work being done by them. It will be very useful and result in quality services and evolve relationship with similar organizations. One of the organizations said that we have organized a series of management workshops conducted by professional consultants for their staff which has been very effective in improving communications and working out strategies for awareness and community mobilization. They felt that the professional training helps them to understand which media works where and what kind of strategies could be adopted. Professional guidance and training to evolve communication strategies is very important because there is very little awareness about the challenged individuals. Awareness in this field will enhance facilities for the disabled. Moreover such a training programme is not yet being done in the disability sector. Another reason that such a training is important because many organizations do not have specific persons earmarked for information management and communications.

While some do have Public Relation Officers or Public Relation Managers who keep in touch with media and other stakeholders, many of them have entrusted this job to a social worker who is not professionally equipped to deal with the issues related to information management. One response mentioned it is because of low priority given to this sector. Many organizations welcomes the outsiders, journalists and others to get the information on the work that the organization is doing. However, they keep in touch with the media only a few times in a year that too when they hold annual events or functions. There is a need for some regular mechanism of information sharing with media and other stakeholders. On the other side of the spectrum ask the media persons why they are not covering these issues. Given the fact that there is general apathy among media because of pre-occupation with politics and entertainment related issues. They did say that NGOs and other stakeholders do not come to us with these issues. They come to us highlighting their work or denial of rights or success stories these are not the priority areas for NGOs when they come to media. They come to media when they want to highlight their work or the work being done by their stakeholders in a particular community area. Media feels that NGOs have self-centered approach. We are trying to see the problem of other side as well to build a relationship. Even Nanipalakiwala was fond of saying that media is considered optional extravaganza. It is providing information on continuous basis. It is forming basis of the change you desire in the society. It is a knowledge based transaction, issue based transaction. As regards the stakeholders, parents, families, NGOs, we found that Newsletter is an important medium of exchange of information. Besides occasional bulletin with information sharing mechanism, even these newsletter are too full of themselves, they do not exchange information. They communicate more the work being done by an NGO or the government agency. Most of the organizations subscribe to journals and periodicals, all bring out the newsletter depending on their need. Periodicity of bringing out the newsletter also varies from organization to organization ranging from bi-monthly to annual issue. We also found that there is no single disability national magazine which pools information on disability world-wise. There are some good magazines like Success and Ability from Chennai, Family of Disabled. There are 10-15 magazine or newsletters but a niche disability magazine is yet to come. There is a need for having a information clearing house. That is why we launched a site Empathy India. NGOs say one way is to publish articles in newspapers, programmes and talks on TV and radio and advertisements also. A Workshop we did with RCI, we found that this advocacy has to be at three-tier level at the editors level, at the reporters level and the young journalists level. We are in touch with the Editors Guild, how we can work out informal guidelines on disability and other social issues. At the same time RCI through its media committee is trying to have a dialogue with the Indian Institute of Mass Communication to actually frame a course curriculum for the mass media students, both print and electronic media, in terms of disability needs to be covered. Keeping in view the availability of space, how much we can achieve. Another important finding is that many of the NGOs are technology savvy and they are using information and communication technology not only to project themselves but also for awareness and community mobilization. Many of them have been using net and e-mail for advocacy. There is enormous possibility in this area and it is not used in fullest. This is in view of the fact that they have realized the role of advocacy and media must redefine its role in lobbying and being a pressure group. Most organizations are trying to document the work that they are doing but that may not be of very high professional standard. Some feel that with little guidance they can do better documentation. They can be of much help to media persons and other stakeholders.

CHAIRPERSON

I am really glad that you have highlighted the major problem in creating awareness and community mobilization and how media is not playing necessary role and the responsibility towards the community. I wonder whether you have found yesterday's proceedings in today's papers. From this we can understand how media is treating us.

MR. ANIL JOSHI

I am indeed very happy to be with you to present a paper on inclusion in the mind-awareness generation and community mobilization with special reference to the mentally retarded. Primarily I am an electronic engineer working in the field of information technology for the past 21 years. Out of my personal pursuit, I studied mass communication. I worked for Tatas in computers only. Even today as a parent of a down syndrome child, I keep wondering what is my role in the society or in my organization Swekaar, which is a parents association. I have not found any role either as an IT professional where I can call myself as a rehabilitation consultant or rehabilitation engineer or rehabilitation IT techniques development person. We have been carrying out some work through our parents association in Nagpur. We talk of information technology usage and assistive technologies to be used for the disabled, I am sorry to say I got a beautiful presentation here which is modified version which I use to communicate issues to the masses. There is a thread woven into every fabric of Indian society. Down the centuries Indians have been known as givers, thanks to the spiritual heritage which every Indian has. Indeed after the primary material needs are addressed even otherwise, much like our western counterparts, we might plunge into domestic situation. The Indians naturally transcend to higher levels and giving comes as naturally as breathing. More often or not this giving also stems from the deep rooted deprivation that most Indians face during the earlier years of their lives. It is this common bond of suffering which manifests itself in various forms during crisis and in emergencies only to go in hybernation till the next disturbance. Ironically, the same circle of deprivation, it is not bounded apathy in its cyclic form also discourages the typical Indian for continuing charity for long. While the heart pushes him naturally to help the suffering of the under privileged, the already pinched wallet forces him to think otherwise. So, while the heart bleeds to see the blind beggars in the scorching heat at the traffic signal, the mind muzzles into silence, opens with a small gate which continues as a dull lake through his routine cycle of pain. The best form of charity that an average Indian can dream is to dip into his pockets, shell out whatever money he can whether at traffic signals or a fund raising function. The reasons behind this attitude being not difficult to follow the demand that depends on his survival of time leave any room for such affordable thoughts, sparing some time for the cause of the sufferers, the under privileged and the disabled. While the full time team of dedicated support groups often find themselves to see the magnitude of the problem to be addressed immediately, the common man is left for some free time that he may offer with creditable regularity. The empathy paradox. Seemingly a paradoxical situation arises wherein the wounded healers for ever embattled with the enormity of the suffering cries for opposite stance of the society, the society at large is at a loss to make its bleeding heart visible to the doers who are often accused of negative indulgence. Thus charity though it is highly motivated give it till it hurts expression does not change beyond offering money or some material relief. Another problem often faced by the non-sufferers while dealing with the disabled is lack of blueprint to lay a firm ground for interaction. Since they are not aware about the safe way of carrying out even normal conversations but the fear of treading on some delicate zones. They live in a constant fear of hurting the disabled. The result is avoidable situation of stony silence. A strong need was felt to break this rock face of outpouring apathy to let the outpour empathy, support and co-operation, flood the pierced minds of the sufferers in the families. My personal experience in this regard has more than corroborated this conviction. After blessed with a daughter with down syndrome, to be fortunate to be informed right after her birth, I took upon myself to collect as much information as possible, the literature, the books, support groups, the professionals, care givers. The efforts were constantly encouraged at national and international level. The results were advantages of early intervention. But to my shock and surprise the scenario on the domestic front on the disability horizon in general and mental retardation in particular left much to be desired. The information was scanty, professionals, these included some pediatricians as well were not updated on specific service delivery needs. Over and above all pervading passivity that appears to be present only in the field of disability social work. To make matters worse the parents, on the other hand, would withdraw in the cocoons of ignorance and despair, refusing to come to terms with the reality. The need for social change was felt. As a follow up to intense and sustained interaction with all state of people related with the disability over a period of ten years now, need was felt to convince them and society at large but doing something for the disabled, has to be part of day-to-day living as anything else. There is no need to set some time apart or to change one's routine to act for the disabled. This can be done without breaking the rhythm of their lives. That over and above money the disabled should be perceived as part of the mainstream as themselves and that the needs of the disabled be at the best uppermost. As per the statistics, some of you may not agree with this, approx. 6 to 8 per cent population is affected with some disability or the other. By a conservative estimate at least three families, next kin are involved in handling a disability which translates to roughly 12 persons, making it a very large population in varying degrees about some disability or the other. All that is needed is to sensitize this large chunk of society about the nature of disability, about problems as well as special needs of these persons. The obvious reason was to demonstrate that this was possible and that it was replicable too. With this in view, a broad spectrum of cultural and social organizations, corporate entities, private firms, NGOs, and individuals in and around Nagpur were approached.

The response was always heart warming. All the activities were carried out under the aegis of Sweekar, an oldest parents association of down syndrome, autistic, CP and MR children. Parents were motivated to come out of their cells, and get together in informal ways. The needs of various sub-groups were assessed and grouped accordingly. In order to facilitate identification with solution to specific set of problems resulting in an informal networking of parents. This was amply backed up by numerous home visits primarily to share information and to have better understanding of the family set up. In the year 1997, Sweekar hosted the national conference organized by NIMH. It was for the first time that parents, doctors and pediatricians shared the same platform. Ever since the disabled community continues to get whole hearted support from doctors. Involving the media, the media participation in all the events of Sweekar is being ensured by building up a strong rapport with the Nagpur journalists who regularly publicise issue based stories. As a good will gesture they have made a standing gesture to Sweekar for conducting press conferences in their premises without paying any charges. Involving engineers and architects. Similar waivers have been announced by Institute of Engineers, Nagpur Chapter for using the facilities for conducting awareness generation programmes. This was followed up in a Seminar for making Nagpur barrier-free, organized by Indian Institute of Architects, Nagpur in September, 2002. The Seminar involved various NGOs, railways, town planners, CPWD, and other decision-making authorities with a view to sensitizing them about the special needs of the disabled. Involving different strata. We conducted programmes for girls colleges, boys colleges, senior citizens, etc. Sensitizing the population at large. In order to motivate various sections of the society to take care of the mentally retarded by conducting routine activities. Some innovative steps taken included special membership of Twinkle Club. These are the largest children club in India with 24,000 members between the age group of 6 to 16 registered every year. The registration drive is a landmark achievement and much sought after by the hordes of sponsors who happily distribute free gifts and gift hampers to all the members. The Club is being run by the oldest English daily in Central India, the Dainik Vada. The Club has also won entry in the Limca Book of Records. The club organizes various types of programmes like magic shows, film shows, picnics and outings and competitions and annual fete on 26th January every year which is attended by thousands of people. The request for giving special membership to our special children irrespective of their actual age was made to the management which was readily agreed. The idea was to sensitize such a large gathering of impressionable minds about special children. Due publicity was given to this noble cause by the newspapers and banners were also put up all over the city. The special children now regularly attend all activities of the club. The club has also allowed one escort per child. In case an escort is not available, Sweekar has offered to provide an escort out of its pool of volunteers. This has enthused other children clubs also to provide similar facilities. Some of the Ladies Clubs have also offered to lend their support for this cause. With such cross-sectional support we are sure this is going to be a regular annual feature.

Sankalp is a social cultural organization set up by the elite business group in Nagpur with a view to promote social cultural activities. The highlight being Navaratri Dhamal of India. This event is regularly sponsored by the trade and industry resulting into scintillating minds. They were approached by Sweekar to allow special children in the grab of their facilities. They were requested to involve one child at selected food stalls. The idea was to make the crowd aware of them and to begin the process of acceptance. The request received whole hearted support from the decision makers. They invited the children to participate, made a prominent mention on the tickets and passes as well as inclusion in the media campaign. The message read "enable yourself to employ the mentally challenged". The icing of the cake was they donated Rs.21,000 to Sweekar out of the proceeds. For all these efforts Sweekar did not accept one rupee the result heightened societal awareness. Sweekar has also been getting warm support to all its requests from all the parties. To re-emphasize the motive of this paper all these efforts of awareness generation and community mobilization have been constantly though not consciously disassociated from fund raising activities. To conclude much more can be achieved by planned activities but with active government support. The idea behind sharing these experiences is to remove the doubts if any about the participation of classes and the masses in elevating the social acceptance of the disabled. All that is needed is an innovative approach, cheerful outlook and proper communication. The primary requirement is to shake off the feeling of being under dogs, dependent, the have nots. A creative idea and initiative is all that is needed to trigger off sentiments. After all the disabled are as much part of the society. The greater consciousness, as anybody else, as enshrined in the term "tatvasi".

MR. DHARMA RAO

After completing B.A. & M.A. in social work, I joined in the Leprosy Department as a Rehabilitation Officer. This awareness and community mobilization is my master's level course. In the initial six months I found that rehabilitation of leprosy patients is very difficult. Sometimes even the bank managers and philanthropic groups, leprosy patients are disabled, please help them, 3 per cent reservation is there, but they deny that leprosy does not come under disability. They are not disabled. Whenever I see other disabled people, physically challenged, these people are not bothered. They are giving pension Rs.100 per month. I was sending the leprosy children to Vijayanagaram. At the same time I referred the general disabled people also to Vijayanagaram. I tried to celebrate the world disabled day but I don't have budget. When I approached my office for budget they said no you have not budgeted for this, so you will not get budget. Journalists and other grass roots NGOs help me a lot. Rs.10,000 we have collected from the community and it is very difficult in the Kalahandi district to do it. I highlighted this in TV and local newspapers also. Social changes are much slower than the technological changes. Most citizens get confused and reject the new technology. Rehabilitation of the leprosy was very little initiative on the part of the government. Kalahandi district has high prevalence of leprosy cases. 7,000 leprosy cases were there. Persons with disability and children with disability are also 10,000. In order to mainstream the leprosy disabled into the general disability, we were able to prepare a blueprint of mass awareness without expenses. In our strategy local leaders, local NGOs, disabled people and social activists highlighted the issue in a big way. Leprosy disabled and general disabled are give vocational training together under one roof without any discrimination. No budget. Ask the local people to sponsor the programme. They agreed to the blueprint of the programme. Sponsors have supported the programme. Different sponsors provided different things. Like this the whole programme was conducted. The DM of the Dharamgarh was invited as the Chief Guest with all the sub-divisional and district officers to feel it more important. The organizing committee mobilized the local NGOs, DPEP, disabled persons, advocates, educationists, professionals, political leaders and social activists. The sub-collector inaugurated the rally on 3rd December in which 50 disabled and leprosy persons participated with their wheelchairs, tricycles. Local people provided slogans and badges to the rally participants. The awareness was carried throughout the town. Tricycle competition was conducted, to highlight the potentials of disabled persons in the high school where the athletic competition was going on for school students a cultural programme was performed for the disabled to exhibit their abilities. Three self-employed disabled people were selected and honoured with prize and shawls. A seminar was also organized on "Disability and Law". The PwD Act, 1995 was discussed. The programmes, schemes and channelising agencies was also discussed. All the local people and participants were highly impressed with the programme. World Disabled Day Committee (WDDC) has been formed with the local people which will be registered. Local NGO has started counselling programme for disabled people every Sunday. WDDC members were involved in the disability survey which was conducted by the government. We have also undertaken the programme to distribute aids and appliances to the disabled of three districts of Orissa. Thus we are helping the local administration.

THAKUR VIJAY PRASAD

I have been a humble worker in the Thakur Hari Prasad Institute for 13 years now. Awareness creation and community mobilization is the key for community based rehabilitation. It is very much required. We all know awareness has to be there at different levels and before we understand what awareness has to be created, levels of awareness have to be ascertained. We all understand it is essential and Mr. P.K. Pincha pointed out different areas of awareness creation and what are the barriers that are there in awareness creation. Now information is accessible, information management, knowledge management, anything going on we understand that. You can get to know everything in a democratic, civilized society like us. But who is to be doing what? This issue we must address to. What kind of awareness creation NGOs have to do? What kind of awareness creation a parent has to do? Or what kind of awareness government or RCI has to do? The job has to be defined very clearly. NGO they work in their own manner in their rehabilitation programmes, training programmes but many of them shy away from taking up the job of awareness creation. I think there should be clear cut guidelines provided by the Government of India, at the same time RCI must also develop something defining the role play of NGOs. The tools of creation, how to go about and what is needed to be done. Once we know our needs automatically development starts taking place. Once a person with disability comes to know that he can be trained, he could be rehabilitated, he has some schemes, concessions available with the Government of India and he has fundamental rights to dignity, automatically his mind starts working in that direction. Information is available through internet and you can know what awareness creation programmes are available at national and international level.

SPEAKER 1

The success stories of NGOs who have successfully come out with their own programmes in different disabilities should be highlighted. RCI and other organizations should project their work so that others can benefit from this.

SPEAKER 2

Social stigma regarding marriage, being a parent of a mentally retarded person, if they have a brother and sister.

SPEAKER 1

I throw back the question at you. Whose responsibility is it to sensitize the media about these issues. Is it the NGOs or the government? Government likes to publicise their policies, NGOs like to publish their work. Information is whose baby?

SPEAKER 2

I think we have a role. Specially in the field of mental disabilities, where Mr. Pincha mentioned earlier, the parents or the persons closest to the mentally retarded person. I think we have a role. We have to stand up and say that this is happening. Because that is a way of prevention also. Early detection to be more correct.

SPEAKER 3

Can I respond to the point which you have raised. The Indian mind is such, take such a private issue, marriage of a child is a private issue in our family. If it is taken to the mass media, there may be resentment among the community. But what we have tried to do in Nagpur, where similar cases have come up, formed a group of counsellors and parents who would also join a single father or mother of that family in trying to get these things communicated and there have been marriages of the siblings of MR brother or sister and the outcome has been fantastic. In fact, even the new member daughter in law or son in law has better understanding and dedication to the cause. Wherever the explanation is properly given, the new family which has been inducted it all depends upon your approach to the situation, put it positive. If I have to protect the interest of my organization or my family, then there may be some opposition but disability issues, myself being a marketing and communication man, at any place, I can say yes, when personal things are not involved, issue based issues can get tremendous response. Rather this is an area where according to me fund raising should not be a problem. This is an area where sensitizing should never be a problem. The problem is that most of the parents do not come out and share, do not express their views properly. That is what my findings are.

SPEAKER 1

I would like to make a couple of points here. It is in the context of one of the very important points raised in the audience with regard to publication or dissemination of success stories, *vis a vis* role of media and sensitization of media. Regarding media sensitization, I would like to ask who sensitizes the media on other issues, other than disability. Who sensitizes the media on economic issues, who sensitizes the media on political issues, who sensitizes media on other social issues, who sensitizes media on other disaster issues and why this question now that we should sensitize media on disability issues and media does not have to play any pro-active role. That is very wrong in the first place. Secondly, yes, governmental and non-governmental agencies have a definite and distinct role to play. This is not to suggest that they don't have a role to play but the point what I am trying to make is that media should not shy away from its responsibility and obligation to discharge its duty as the fourth estate and, I am talking about both electronic as well as print media. Success stories their publication is exceedingly important but what is of equal importance is the manner in which you project those success story. Sometimes how you say something matters more, perhaps than what you say. I will give you an example from my own personal experience. Nothing is original than the product of your own experience. I was being interviewed by one of the newspapers. The reporter asked me, what do I feel is the root cause of militancy in North East. I am happy that you asked me this question and consider me as part of the society as others are. I replied to that but you know what appeared in the newspapers? I was projected as having said, what a blind man will know about terrorism. Look what distortion crept in, not that he did intentionally and the ego they have, if you request them before you publish please show it to us, they feel bad. Everyone has ego, we have ego, other people in other walks of life do have ego. I am not trying to put any blame on media, there is a section of media, there are very good people in the media, what I am trying to say is that all the disciplines of public activity has got to play a pro-active role in disseminating and spreading awareness and mobilizing community.

SPEAKER 4

In majority of the cases where they are aware of the problem, only one part or so go for early identification. If we can give more information to the parents, families, then the social stigma need to be broken and we can get many people in the rehabilitation fold.

SPEAKER 5

Suggestions have been coming that we should go more to the community and explain what the disabilities are, and particularly in the case of mental retardation very few people are aware that mental retardation is different from mental illness and that is why the outcast of children, that they are mentally ill they should be looked at differently. We in Sweekar had taken up a programme where we went to various schools, invited principals, fixed up dates and conducted lecture and question answer session with children of 8th and 9th classes, who were in the puberty stage and their thoughts become permanent. We went and explained to them that mental illness is different, mental retardation is different and the response has been very good. Such programmes should be held every where. Community as such will become more knowledgeable that mental sickness and mental retardation are different things.

SPEAKER 6

Mental retardation is different from mental illness but mental retardation is not mental illness gives a wrong signal because mental illness also comes under disabilities. The government has recognized this and it is recognized all over the world. We should not talk about different disability groups, comparing them.

SPEAKER 7

There has been a slogan mentally retarded are not mentally ill. There is stigma in the community about mentally ill. Since ours is a cross disability group, we should not try to create a slogan or something among different disabilities.

SPEAKER 8

To remove this specific problem in the 1996, we started an organization in Assam, we are dealing with both mental retardation and mental illness. Both are comparable to each other because one fact that has universally come out, upto 40 per cent of people with mental retardation may have inappropriate behaviour pattern.

SPEAKER 9

My humble suggestion is that if we start awareness generation right from the primary school include it in course material, write to the NCERT, the apex body to take disability as a subject and examination of that subject so that at least children are aware right from the beginning and their opinion and attitudes are formed favourable. They would move hand in hand and would accept the disabled people as a part of society and rightly and gradually we will move on to other stake holders.

SPEAKER 10

I agree with you. The U.N Standard Rules on Equalization of Opportunities do provide for this and they have recommended that all the member States should ensure that community mobilization is incorporated in the syllabus. It is the question of implementation.

SPEAKER 11

Mr. Pincha has been in the field for a very long time. If we have to concentrate at every level and see what would affect which media would be good for which level, how contextual, because we are a very very diverse nation. Things which affect one State do not affect the other, mentally. If these things were to be kept in mind, we are talking of sort of making policy decisions on awareness and mobilization or may be thinking of issues, it can help us more.

SPEAKER 12

We are running a school for the last six years for MR and HI children. We can interact with other NGOs and mobilize the community. But what will our child do when he grows up. Ultimately the community says what he will do after education, we are hiding him now, but what would happen later on. Vocational training is going on in isolation for candle making, etc., but can it make a MR child independent and self-sustained. A uniform solution should be found to this problem.

SPEAKER 13

How uniformity can come in this? If you are in a village in Rajasthan and you talk about chalk making, it will be of no use. This has to be need based.

CO-CHAIRPERSON

We, the chairperson and co-chairperson appreciate the enthusiasm that has come from all of you. We are in the evolution stage. Everybody is doing in their own way. What is the role of government, what is the role of NGOs, what is the role of parents associations and community at large, its evolution. Awareness, as I said, necessity is there. Gradually we are going towards the right direction. We have a very pro-active RCI, the government is very much sensitized. RCI is creating awareness in its own way through Public Health Centre (PHC) doctors training, even other medical personnel are also going to be trained. Well that is the catchment area where the persons with disabilities could be identified. Early intervention can take place, preventive aspects could be looked into, as Madam pointed out, the need for sensitizing the children from the primary school level. So at different levels government has to do, NGOs, parents association, community everybody has to do. Multi-sectoral convergence and coordination is required for awareness creation. I thank RCI for having given this opportunity to co-chair this session and I feel privileged.

CHAIRPERSON

I would like to thank everybody and the presentations made appears to be sermons but here fourth paper, including Mr. Dharma Rao, all the experiences they have been going through, it is just not imaginary. That way it was helpful. I can add from my own personal experience. We have been talking about media, electronic, newspapers, etc. But all of you have forgotten one media. We have got telegram, telephone, and what we are following, what we are spreading through our organization is only through word of mouth. We are in a pilgrimage town where we have 50,000 floating population. We have kept our messages at strategic places and they keep streaming into our organization not to sympathize with people but meaning of service and spread to other people. It is catching like a wild fire. But this can happen only when we show the real value of work. People should be impressed about that. We are not taking any government funds but we are surviving because of the community involvement.

IX

EDUCATIONAL SERVICES FOR PERSONS WITH DISABILITIES
Including Children with Special Needs

Chairperson: Mr. S.C. Tripathi
Co-Chairperson: Dr. M.N.G. Mani

DR. R. RANGASAYEE

I am very sure that in the area of hearing impairment the scene is not very encouraging. Enrolment ratio is only 35 per cent in children with hearing impairment and it is true in other disability areas as well. It is absolutely dismal. If you go through the literature, it says much less. As somebody in the morning said only 2.5 per cent have received help. In order to educate all persons with disabilities in the community there is no single facility that can really meet the requirement. I have listed about seven types of facilities that are required. Children who can directly enter into education, children with resource support service they may be able to cope up, there are children who specially need special education provision, children who need day school with boarding facility, and there are children who need home based intervention, children who need open education provision. Today the situation is that lot of them are not enrolled in schools at all. These are children who will necessarily need open schooling method. Non-formal or adult literacy programmes are needed. By and large these are the types of patterns. The group of people who are identified go through medical, surgical, rehabilitation provisions and then enter into preparatory phase and then go into general education facility or into special education facility. Programmes in different Ministries are strategically different with each other. What is common in this is the word education, the goal of education is common. But the process is not common. The structure, the system, the style of functioning, staffing pattern, skills of the staff are unique to given Ministry, in this case given system. To think that all are equal is not right. The parents have direct impact on the educational achievement. Individualised Educational Plan (IEP) should continue to remind as a priority activity to be monitored in whichever system, whatever option. Want, ignorance, idleness, scholar are issues that need to be addressed in the families of the persons with disabilities as poverty and disability are closely related. Empowering local bodies towards managing the needs of people with disabilities is a viable goal. I want to bring to your kind notice what AYJNIHH has done in Mumbai. At a place near Mumbai, the town panchayat has agreed to give Rs.10 per property per year towards disability rehabilitation. They have resolved it and they are doing it. They have made all the schools barrier-free. They have started their own community based rehabilitation centre and they are in the process of vocationally providing support to many. All that I wish to inform is that there are 22,000 properties in the township and Rs.2.25 lakhs is the total money collected every year. That is the good model programme. Last year they won the best barrier-free town panchayat award but they are also very well on the road of educating children with hearing impairment.

Prevention of diseases causing disability needs to be considered seriously and also kept in mind while planning. The number game we saw in the morning. We need so many lakhs, where are we. It is like dreaming. Dreaming about what? Is it an achievable goal? Do we have a strategy to achieve this? I am of the opinion the approach being taken is more based on wisdom. Let me give the example of having 10 children at home and having some rice. If you have 250 gms. of rice with you and if you have to feed 10 children, will you feed four of them and make six of them starve. Will you look for an alternative? What is happening in this country today is absolute lack of strategy. Strategy to reach the children who need these services. Manpower development should evolve around the strategy that will address the issue and the strategy of not manpower training alone, strategy which is as accepted by the funding sources. Its socio-economic implications have to be considered when you are planning for it. Without it it is like putting the horse before the cart. Block Development Officers (B.D.Os) need to be involved. In this country, NGOs have great enthusiasm but the point here still remains that NGO is a voluntary organization. Voluntary organization be it in education or special education, they will come where they want to come. They will work in the area where they want to work. And they will cater only to the people whom they want to cater. Because it is volunteerism. Therefore, if you look at the Aids and Appliances Scheme, lot of money is going through Ministry of Social Justice and Empowerment (SJ&E), good work is going on, distribution of aids and appliances is going on, but even today less than half the country is not covered. 250 districts have not been served at all. Even where it has been served, it is only 5 per cent who have received services. Tell me, how do we handle it? When will an NGO come there. And when the children who need the aids and appliances will get it. Medical, surgical rehabilitation can certainly enable many children to avail schooling, therefore private voluntary organizations have to be considered. I am of the opinion that contracts for 100 children, like UNESCO has suggested area based approach, there are 100 children who need to be educated, I float a tender and you quote. Whoever quotes less can get, achieve the target and avail the funds. This is one area which needs to be experimentally tried. Early identification, intervention including ECG need greater thrust. We have a project also to identify the children below the age of 5 years with hearing impairment. Once early intervention is given, they can enter into mainstream within 3 years. Then the general education system can take over. But otherwise what is happening in the general education system, these children were getting 20 per cent in 5th grade. If that is the norm, what norm do we set for children with disabilities when they are put in general education. I am of the opinion that lessons learnt from one disability area availing that in other disability, may not lead to, I think the data bases have to be looked into. Fund flow, growth rate, predicted growth, sustainability, these are few areas that need to be looked into. In fact one of the great concerns is the kind of people who enter to be trained as special educators, that is a great botheration for all the training centres and if that has to happen we are of the opinion that insurance like countries where such things have happened, insurance has played a great role. Flow of money is very important. Economics of education of persons need to be addressed and Education Commission to look into various aspects have to be considered.

MS. ANURADHA

First we will go into introduction about sense of hearing what is it? It is something that gives us multitude of experiences. It is a primary channel for acquiring skills of verbal communication, a skill very much needed by human beings. Feedback mechanism for monitoring verbal communication skills is also to the hearing mechanism. Therefore, you can imagine that without hearing sense what disadvantage such persons would face. W.H.O. in 1980 said hearing impairment is any loss of hearing or impairment of psychological, physiological or anatomical structure or function. It says that hearing impairment is a deviation or change for the worse in structure or function usually outside the range of normal. You can classify hearing impairment into conductive, sensory, neural or mixed base type. This is basically depending on which part of the ear is affected. Similarly, you can also have degrees from mild hearing impairment to profound hearing impairment. We see that hearing impairment is a very heterogeneous group. Some impairments are treatable and some are not treatable. Most severe long-term effects will be present if hearing impairment is by birth or if it was acquired in childhood, or acquired before language was developed. Hearing impairment deprives the child of the sensory experience which is very vital to the acquisition of verbal communication skills. The effects of hearing impairments or verbal communications skills depend on many things. The type, the degree of hearing impairment, the age of onset, the type of onset whether it was gradual or whether it was sudden, at what age the child was identified, at what age and what type of intervention did the child get, what is the support that the child gets from the environment. There has to be a good multi-dimensional approach for good rehabilitation. The first provision the hearing impaired child would need is amplification, care of giving him necessary auditory experience which is required for him to develop verbal language. The second would be education, which can be achieved either through special schooling or inclusive education.

Let us focus on technologies which a child with hearing impairment can use in the inclusive set up. First thing is barrier-free environment. The hearing impairment child would need an environment which would be more conducive to listening and communication. Therefore, poor acoustics which are often found in regular schools most often make listening very difficult for such a child. The problems are weakening of energy with increased distance, loss of energy due to scattering, echoes and reverberation. Due to this, in addition to child having problem in understanding will also have difficulty in paying attention. So we can control the signal to noise ratio. This difference between the signal and noise should be positive. The signal should be higher than the noise. This can be done by controlling the noise by acoustically treating the classroom, or by having the classroom at place which is not very noisy. Or you can control the signal itself, the distance between the person who is speaking and the child who is listening. Reducing the distance between the child and the teacher will go greatly towards improving the signal. Then the control of amplification through personal devices, through cochlear implants, through group amplification devices, and assistive devices. Basically hearing aid is a device which amplifies sound energy. It converts sound into electrical energy, then amplifies it and then converts it into electrical energy and back to sound energy. Based on different kinds of signal processes, you have different kinds of hearing aids. The most commonly used hearing aids in India are analog hearing aids, more so the body level hearing aids. Body level hearing aids are also given through the ADIP Scheme, which make them all the more popular in India. Incidentally with the ADIP Scheme hearing aids you also get the solar battery charger which are rechargeable and which greatly reduce the cost for parents for the battery. The problem with the analog hearing aids is that they not only amplify the signal, the speech but also the unwanted part. Then how do you achieve the good acoustic environment. You can make out how much signal the child is getting by using a simple instrument like sound level meter, which you can place where the child is and take the output of the hearing aid and see what is the level of output. That level should be above the child's level of hearing. We can know from the audiologist how much level will be required by the child. If it is hard to achieve that level, then the child can be brought closer to the teacher or if possible the teacher could speak more loudly. Digital hearing aids are a step ahead. They reduce noise, they suppress noise. But they are also very expensive. Therefore, not very commonly used by many children. Cochlear implant has received lot of popularity because it has been very successful. Cochlear implant totally bypasses the inner ear which is defective in these children and directly stimulates the auditory nerve endings in the cochlear, thereby giving better sound reception to the child. But these are also expensive. There has to be post-implantation. Also the children have to be selected on the basis of strict assessment. What are the assistive listening devices. They supplement the hearing aids. Some of them are for specific listening difficulty and some of them bring the attention of the person to the specific environmental sounds such as alarm clocks, or signal alerting devices, which converts sound energy into some other energy which the person can perceive, like vibrations or visual signals. The main goal is to provide a wide frequency range of amplification system, to maintain a constant signal noise ratio, that is, signal higher than the noise and to allow the listener to hear the speaker who is speaking himself or herself so that the auditory feedback can be there. Loop induction system has also been very popular. In this, there is a microphone which is connected to amplifier and then there is an electro magnetic field created around the loop which gives the hearing impaired person the required position. Although we have these different technological devices, the effective use can only be ensured if the environment is co-operative. Simple equipment like Overhead Projectors and power point presentations can be used to make the teaching much more accessible to the child. Then there is more advanced technology which converts speech into text and it can help the hearing impaired to get the text on the screen. Also tele-captioning devices and multi-lingual SMS are the latest technologies which have been very useful. The choice of the device should be made according to the life style of the listener and communication requirements and the audiologist can select the device based on the assessment made by him and can recommend the same. The school authorities should keep in constant touch with the audiologist so that the evaluations are done regularly. Also the inclusive set up should have a resource teacher, who can advise regarding the child's progress. Therefore, the role of technology and its contribution in inclusive education cannot be undermined. However, the best of technology can be a waste in the hands of the inexperienced user.

MRS. S.S. JAYALAKSHMI

I wanted to share my experience with you and I don't think I will be taking much time. I want to share an experience which I had this morning while coming in a taxi. The taxi driver's son was with him when I asked him what is his name, he informed me that he cannot hear. He informed that he is not accepted in the school. I informed him that I was going to a meeting where experts are coming to discuss all these things. I was thinking how long it will take for creating awareness. We are doing awareness programmes continuously and mine is a institution and training centre where I integrate mentally retarded children with children in regular school and I have training of care givers given by National Trust. I am Chairperson of the Local Level Committee also and conducted RCI Bridge Courses and organizing workshops etc. I was wondering when are we going to reach all these people, especially children who are not in organized sectors like schools. May be I get an answer by tomorrow. At the moment, I have undertaken research to go in rural areas and find out how many children are there and what can we do about their education. We have the institution called Vidya Vikasini, Vidya means education and Vikasini means expansion. I started my school in 1981 with one child who was different from others. That was the time when NCERT was thinking about mainstreaming. I had my fears and inhibitions about social stigma and parents rejection. But gradually we succeeded in integration and also vocational training. Currently, including children with disabilities right from the play school and some of them got their vocational training and education through State Board and Open School and we are fortunate to have such a set up of parents. Advantage for me is that we have normal school teachers whose help I can take like music, dance, etc. My teachers are talking lot of inclusive education, it is already happening in our institution. So our normal teachers also know what to do with these children with special needs. Sometimes to start with, the parents had their problems whether the children will mix with other mentally retarded children, or not. Then started teachers training programme, integrated education, both pre-service and in-service. I have rural projects of awareness programmes, implementation of National Trust Act, and National Open School Examination to the special olympics children go for competitions with children with normal intelligence and they bag awards. They participate in our special school programme and very recently we had an interview in The Hindu, they wanted to talk to the parents, and parents asked about acceptance. Parents said we did not accept at all and some of them broke down. Now we are very happy because the children say that they go to Vidya Vikasini Higher Secondary School. We have vocational training. We have about 75 teachers and 10 special teachers. We have already received the State Award and the National Award from the government.

DR. R. RANGANATHAN

I want to share my experience. I was a student of Ramakrishna Vidyalaya way back in 1982-83. My teachers were making sincere efforts to introduce Integrated Education for Disabled (IED) in 1980s for the disabled in collaboration with CBM and the State Government I was also one of the teachers in that group. After 1991 when I entered Andhra University as Assistant Professor, all the serious thoughts about B.Ed. level and M.Ed. level training we are giving would go. And the present education system like special schools can deliver the goods. And what is the solution for it? We thought first let our trainee's who are doing B.Ed. and M.Ed., (Hearing Language and Speech HLS) should get the job. So with that idea we started moving with the government, first we got approval from the State Government to get the job. We are giving training on the one side and the students are getting admission in schools. These are the two extreme things. First of all we want to take up this problem. In our university we have minimum of 2 or 3 MLAs, one MP. The teachers are very co-operative, the students are very good. We used this opportunity to get our teachers appointed in special schools and we got the Government Organisation (GO). Then we diverted our minds to start integrated schools and special schools. At least one school in each district in each category. Five schools in 1990 now it has grown to 26. Apart from special schools we have integrated programmes to enrol the disabled students. That was the humble beginning in 1992. At that time we started one school in each district. We expanded this entire education programme to mandal level. Nearly 120 schools we have established through government. We gave training to teachers under inclusive education to 50 teachers from each district. Teachers those who are working in ordinary schools, these teachers can go back to ordinary schools and enroll the disabled children and give them education. This is the concept because we have been talking of inclusive education for the last 5 years. By implementation of inclusive education programme, with the NGOs, we can cover the education for all. Because if this education of the disabled children comes under the Education Department, especially in the States, only then we can achieve the education for all. One special school 100 students, one inclusive school 10 students, if you include this inclusive education programme in the general education programme, and if we train 50 teachers in a district those who are working with normal children, it will be a great impact. We talked to our government, through our Vice-Chancellor, and then we got the GO, every district we should train at least 50 teachers from each district. There will be a State Education Officer and the Coordinator will be there. These people are not qualified. 45 days training programme of teachers has been started. It is a humble beginning. So we thought let the government start the programme and the government started the programme. If the programme goes through government it will be successful or it will be partially successful. Now Bhoj University has started the B.Ed. programme but the problem is where the students will go, after the training. Because there is extra ordinary opposition for them. Once RCI approval is there, it is not necessary that the State Government will give the jobs. This is another problem which we can overcome in the next two or three years. We have to take up this issue with the State Government. We have very good environment, our Vice-Chancellor is good, organisations are excellent. Already 1,500 teachers have been trained under inclusive education. If we continue this programme, then Education for All will be a reality.

MR. DEEPAK SAHAI

I am deaf. I saw presentations on education of children with disabilities. How to use hearing aids? Some deaf people cannot use hearing aids, they are not benefited from hearing aids. Those with mild and severe hearing loss can be benefited. In the past there was no sign language available to people but Dr. Mani and his team has published some dictionary. I have travelled all over India and found the teachers have no communication with their students. So how can the deaf children be given education. We are emphasizing use of hearing aids and not emphasizing use of sign language for education of hearing impaired children. Parents are under pressure very much and as the child grows older and older, and quite often hearing goes lower and lower they remain deaf. They are unemployed and the situation is very pathetic. Other methodologies of vocational training etc. should also be used.

DR. RANGASAYEE

You would be knowing the activities which AYJNIHH has initiated for training of teachers for deaf children for sign language. As you are aware in the area of hearing impairment, there is one group of children who go into mainstream education and then get into open employment and then get mainstreamed into society. There is another group of people who do not understand sign language who remain in different world of their own. The children who are not able to or willing to, use a hearing aid as per their choice, will have the option to learn through sign language. We have an Indian sign language cell in our institute through which now we have training for hearing impaired persons who will be sign language teachers in general schools and special schools, wherever they are. As you are aware we have also prepared "A" and "B" level sign languages courses with us. Level A is self-instructional material, that is available on Video and CD form at a cost of Rs. 400. They can join level "B" which Ramakrishna Mission will be conducting. We also have Hindi, if you learn Hindi there is incentive available.

If we can provide incentive to people to learn sign language. This is another process we are looking at. On the other side, we have early intervention programmes where the children can go and learn. We have one month sign language training for vocational instructors. It is primarily focused on ITI vocational instructors. Any organization interested can write to us, details are available on our web site also AYJNIHH.org.

MR. TILAK VARMA

Placement of persons who have been trained under various programmes should be assured by the government because they have no where to go after training. The trainees spent lot of money for learning IT but he is not rehabilitated.

MR. PADMAKAR SHUKLA

In all the integrated schools, special teachers may not be available. RCI and other authorities should sensitize, trained teachers who are working in normal schools for these programmes so that they can work with the handicapped children, who are integrated in the regular school. They may be given some incentive for this.

MR. ANIL JOSHI

I am parent of a down syndrome child of 10 years, who is attending normal school. My question is specifically to Ms. Jayalakshmi. It is a creditable achievement to integrate 45 children in normal school at various places. What about scholastic achievement? Does the State Government offer any concessions as far as writing of exams is concerned. As a teacher what is your overall assessment about the reading, writing and arithmetic skills?

MS. JAYALAKSHMI

Yes, the scholastic achievement is there. First we give part integration and then full integration, according to that they are sent to classes. The child will be good in mathematics but not in English, so he will be sent to the class in other subjects and in which he/she is slow, he would come back to the resource teachers, they will be able to coach them. They will go up to the standard according to their capacity. After that they will be sent either to State syllabus which has less load otherwise they will be sent to National Open School. Once we see that the reading, writing skills do not develop as we expect in two or three years, then we will send them to pre-vocation and then vocation. We give them placement through our centres in and around Coimbatore. 89 children or so and all the topics will not be there. Scholastic achievement of every could will be unique and different, one will be with normal intelligence, the child could pass B.A. (Pass) and other children could go up to 12 standard. Some of them take National Open exam.

MR. KAPADIA

My question is to Ms. Anuradha. She told about FM hearing aid. I would like to know what is its performance and where it is available and at what price?

MS. ANURADHA

The results of FM hearing are very good. Because the microphone which the teacher uses catches the sounds from nearby and ignores the sounds from distant places. So the voice of teacher is amplified and heard by the student clearly as the other noise is reduced. In normal schools, it may be difficult for children to sit closer to the teacher. So the FM system has advantage even if the child is 500 feet away he can still hear the voice of teacher. But its cost is very high. For a single transmitter its cost is Rs.1.25 lakh.

PROF. P. JEYACHANDRAN

Regarding the programme on integrated training I would like to ask. You know the DPEP programme, in the district where I am incharge, we have integrated 2,161 children with disability. But for integration they were locked in the house or roaming on the streets. Regarding the academic achievement now we have sent an evaluation report, disabled children's attendance is 100 per cent. No drop-outs. Comparing to normal children the attendance is 100 per cent and there is drop-out in the normal children. There are various reasons for that. The visually impaired children excel the normal children in language but the children with hearing impairment or visual they have excelled in mathematical ability. These are some of the hard findings from that experience. We are also sceptical how we can integrate and some one asked for training, yes, RCI has developed some training programmes, 45 days training. Programmes are available and regarding Andhra Pradesh when we were about to start the DPEP programme, I was involved in that. Before we started the children were integrated in the mainstream school with many disabilities.

MR. RAMAN SANKAR

This is strong reaction to Prof. Ranganathan what he concluded in his presentation. He said that we will achieve education for all if we follow the approach mentioned by him. I really have my own doubts. Because if we promote inclusive education programmes without adding the component of a special teacher in specific disabilities categories, we might achieve enrolment and I really wonder whether we will be able retain these children in regular schools. No matter how much training we can give to the regular teacher but no where in the world the entire responsibility of educating the disabled child is being taken over entirely by regular teachers. He made a statement we are training lot of special teachers, where will these teachers go. We have to prevail upon the government and insist that in every inclusive education programme, at a cluster level, may be for 15 children or 20 children, there has to be a special teacher in each category of disability. This is where our special teachers whom we are training should go.

DR. M.N.G. MANI

I will just sum up what has been said by my four colleagues. Dr. Rangasayee made a very strong message that we should expand the services. We can call it any thing. Just change of terminologies is not going to expand the services. We have to increase the services for children with disabilities. There are so many models so many strategies. Are we expanding the services? I was just going through a newspaper article the other day, when a person writes, he has to use politically accepted technically correct terminologies. This means that in future you should not call a short person, a short person. In future you should call a short person, vertically challenged. Similarly he says you should call a fat person, horizontally challenged. I was asking my self how he will call a person who is short and fat, may be globally challenged? So that is why, by just changing terminologies, inclusion, special education, integration, visually impaired, are we really increasing services for persons with disabilities? There are so many models why can't we take up those models and expand the services. That is the message given by Dr. Rangsayee. So I think we have to follow our own philosophy of India. Unity in diversity. There are so many models. Out objective is to provide better education to our children with disabilities. Second speaker made a very strong appeal about the application of technology. It is true that if we don't acknowledge technology in the field of special education we will be outdated. I would like to give a small statistics. Beginning of this century the development ratio between developed nations and the developing nations was 1: 4 the end of the last century the difference was not 1 : 10, 1 : 20, etc. that was because of the technology, application of technology. So the technology can be used in the disability service in many ways. In reducing the handicapping conditions, technology can be used for enhancing the learning, technology can be used for expanding the services in the professional training and also for education of persons with disabilities. So we cannot wait, we have to use technology in the field of special education. At the same time we have to see whether we are using the existing technology to the optimum extent. This is the message given by the second speaker. The third speaker gave a very strong message that the parents should be partners in the learning process, parents should be partners in policy making. So without involvement of the parents, we will not be able to provide quality services. That is the message given by the fourth speaker. The last speaker told that so many models are available and we have to make these teachers to work but at the end he made a very strong statement, we are not getting away with the special teachers, we have to have special teachers supplemented by the efforts of general classroom teachers. Though we have to work towards effective inclusion for persons with disabilities. But the last statement he made has lot of relevance. That is NGOs can develop models but for expansion, unless the government steps in expansion will not be a reality. So now what we are looking for. We have been discussing about wonderful models of education, rehabilitation. All are existing in the country, what we are looking for is expansion. For expansion we need the political will, we need the support of the government, now let us hear to the chairperson of the session who is the Secretary of Ministry of Human Resource Development, who is the policy maker as far as expansion is concerned. Let us try to get answer from our hon'ble chairperson.

CHAIRPERSON

Thank you Dr. Mani for your very nice and thought provoking summing up and I must confess I am not expert on this subject and I am here more to learn than to tell you about what is happening but it is through the process of interaction with experts like you and the experts of RCI we have been working on some policy measures and let me once again thank the organizers of this conference for giving me the opportunity to hear your views, to hear from you, to learn from you and to use this very valuable input into our working processes which will go into preparation of the policy and implementation. As you are all aware the 86th Amendment of the Constitution makes the elementary education a fundamental right of every child including those with special education needs. Therefore, it is now the constitutional responsibility to give education to all children in most appropriate environment. People talk about DPEP because this provision relates to children between age group of 8-14. People talk about DPEP because that was the first large scale programme almost across the country taking care of crores of children where an attempt was made on inclusive education and according to information given to me the special education needs of the children forms an important part of DPEP programme where 6.2 lakh children were enrolled in regular schools. This was possible because thc programme was implemented in a phased manner. Enough focus was on proper identification of programmes for teachers training and evolving strategies for adequate resource support. For any programme endeavouring to meet the needs of these special children it is necessary that the teachers are trained and necessary resource support is provided. For this, convergence was established in DPEP with RCI to impart training to teachers. So far 4,000 teachers have been provided this training and more and more teachers are getting gradually empowered. Recent evaluation study in IED in DPEP shows that training not only equips the teacher to use effective pedagogical strategies but also promotes acceptance and positive attitudes towards children with special needs. Then another lesson learnt in DPEP was that education to such children should be provided in a most appropriate environment. It means that no child can be rejected. Sarva Shiksha Abhiyan offers multi optional model to the children with special needs in which attempt is being made to educate every child with disability in a setting what is most suited to his/her learning needs and is in consonance with the Persons with Disabilities Act, 1995. Now this is the theoretical constitutional position but I agree that still, the real practical position is that we have really a very long way to go. There are many severely disabled children who can not benefit from the regular school. Therefore SSA is converging with the Ministry of Social Justice & Empowerment, Ministry of Health, Ministry Rural Development and NGO's to ensure that a comprehensive education programme is developed. Now it is important as everyone mentioned here. Initially, SSA when we say it has now become a fundamental right for every child to access education and the child in the age group of 6-14 years, we are talking about child population of 19 crores. Now in this 19 crores children who have this constitutional right to access education, our estimates, different estimates are given to me of how many could be children with different kinds of disability. A rough estimate, some people say is 3 per cent, some say around 5 per cent and disability of major kind, of different thing, with minor disability who can be taken into regular school provided the teachers, parents are sensitized, provided they are identified at an early stage, provided the remedial teaching, coaching and teachers with sensitivities, teachers with training are immediately put into place, they can be taken. Perhaps a number of those who will be needing special schools will be a smaller number. In the SSA framework what we are doing is that we are providing Rs. 1,200 per child per year for developing all these strategies. In some case requirement may be less, in some other case it may be more, Rs. 1,200 is the average. Now I am not saying that the special schools would be there but for the large body of children who can be identified at an early stage, they can be taken care in the SSA programme. We are suggesting that these Rs. 1,200 are properly utilized. Now in most of the case they come back to me and say they don't know how to utilize. So there is a lack of information. There is lack of communication between State agencies, the education agencies whether at district level or village level and the NGO's and the specialized agencies working in this area. We have given details about various institutions which are recognized by RCI. About 200 institutions are all over the country but that number is also a small number compared to requirement of the country and if you see the requirements of the children again take it as whatever percentage you think is reasonable for the 19 crore children. So what, therefore, we need is that most of the teachers and the parents of these children should also be sensitize and educated and for this reason we had meetings with RCI. We have IGNOU programmes for teachers, programmes for parents. Programmes of teachers will be of several levels. There will be programmes for teachers who are already B.Ed. so that a 3 or 4 months or 6 months special B.Ed. programme can be run for them so that they can be sensitized to the level desired, and specially empowered and trained to deal with the problems of children with special needs. Now it may not be possible for teachers to equally adapt in tackling the problem of children with special needs, with different kinds, in different areas, different kind of specialization and service specialization may also be required but this is one programme we have requested National Council of Teachers Education to put in place. This programme we have also requested NCTE that in all new B. Ed. and BTC Diploma programmes, a capsule, a module on how to take care of requirements of children with special disabilities, what are the kinds of disabilities, which are not very acute and severe, how they can be tackled in inclusive education process by these teachers. They should learn when they are in the stage of B. Ed. and the Diploma which is an essential qualification for elementary school teachers. There are 40 lakh elementary school teachers and 15 lakh secondary teachers so above 55 lakh teachers. So the teachers we have today and if we had sensitized them, much of our problem at the initial stage could have been identified and as the remedial mode the practices would have been started but the problem arises that most of the teachers in their teaching or training they did not have this background or training. So at least from now onwards who is going to become a teacher in his training programme of teacher of B.Ed. for one year or more than 2 years this should be included as a compulsory part of training programme besides these teachers in the Sarva Shiksha

Abhiyaan all teachers receive 30 days training. We are suggesting that in these 30 days training whatever can be included one week, ten days, I agree is not enough but all teachers must be sensitized and this will again give a backlog that these 35-40 lakh teachers have had no understanding or training of this kind of situation. In a couple of years of time all must be sensitized to this problem and wherever in whichever area they join, disability is more prominent, more common thing, more about that disability, then we are also suggesting that since this is not one time thing, one time thing is to take care of backlog, this will be a part of B.Ed. and in programmes along with curriculum of B.Ed. and Diploma programmes it should be a part of curriculum for in-service regular training programme for which in every district there is DIET. In all we have 15-16 professionals but teachers, teacher educators, we are suggesting that in every DIET one or two of them should have a special degree so that they can teach the teachers and to that extent they should have a special degree. Then we are suggesting that every upper primary school and mind you there would be 3 lakh upper primary schools. Every upper primary school will have 3 teachers. I think they have 3 teachers and some of them who do not have should also have 3 teachers. They will get additional teachers in a year or two so out of 3 teachers one should be trained in the manner that 6 month training programme which is on distance education or one of them should be there. Now if in 3 lakh junior high schools, one teacher is trained, then 3 lakh teachers will be trained. I am not saying that it will happen overnight but this is our objective, this is our goal and objectives are for this plan. This means, therefore, is little less than 4 years left. So in less than 4 years time we should make provision for proper training of about 3 lakh teachers who are in all 6.4 lakh villages, thousands of towns. If they get some training, I am quite sure the situation will change quite dramatically but it needs community support. We have scheme for community awareness also in which we give training programme regarding school management, etc. to the community leaders. Now there also we are suggesting there should be an input to identify such children, how to sensitize people towards needs of these people, how to organize so that they are, institutions are more friendly, more hospitable to such children and their general climate is built in which such children are taken care of. They are associated with rest of the society. They are as much part of the society as the community, as everyone else they can contribute as much help as anyone else. As has been pointed out by our friend that DPEP experience shows that these children given proper environment, given the sensitivity that is required and some special focus on them, they can out beat other children. So these are the various things we are trying to put in place. Since all of you are leaders in this area, I would request you to kindly let us know how best this programme can be carried out and we are open to suggestions. We have been interacting with RCI, interacting with Social Justice Department, closely and frequently on these issues but I confess that this is the area where we are not experts, we are starting from a very poor base. We have a long way to go and given the support, co-operation of everyone, there is no reason why we cannot do that after all given the will power and the technology as we see, Stephen Hawkings who has all disabilities except that his mind works but he is greatest philosopher, scientist of the last century and even this century, so in this country also we have many brilliant people we must do our best to provide an environment convenient to them. With these words, thank you for giving me the opportunity and I hope that a constant dialogue will be maintained between those who have worked in this area. I have to confess that experience is very poor. Therefore, the lady who was making presentation over her score, I said that we need so many more scores like this, people with real life experience who are working in this area who can tell us how to go about it, also RCI is statutory organization working in this field, we keep taking guidance from them and we associate them in all our programmes.

SPEAKER

We would like to thank our chairperson, co-chairperson, and speakers for their valuable contributions. Now I would like thank Dr. J.P. Singh, Member Secretary, RCI to kindly present mementoes.

I think Mr. Tripathi, Secretary, Ministry of HRD deserve a great applause. What he has spelt out is going to make a quantum change into the education system and all of us who are here should give big applause to the Secretary.

X

VOCATIONAL EDUCATION AND REHABILITATION

Chairperson: Dr. Thakur V. Hari Prasad
Co-Chairperson: Dr. A.K. Mukherjee

Let me first of all record the legacy which I started as Chairman of Rehabilitation Council of India making it a vibrant body in the country and building up the linkages and for first time introducing the national programmes. I am happy that RCI is continuing this legacy. This is one of the good experiment and also explorative endeavour. The people around are very much interested in this area and apart from that their passion and professional involvement is very important. Such a big conglomeration has arrived. I really appreciate and record my happiness for the initiative taken by RCI, the chairperson, the secretary, the team, and Dr. Mukherjee. I would like to say few points, panchtantra we call it. Time shows we have definitely moved forward during this 40-50 years. Let us not forget the excellent initiative played by volunteerism. Today the PwD Act is the result of the positive approach of the voluntary organizations. The PwD Act was passed by voice vote without any discussion on the same day by both Houses of Parliament. This became possible by taking into confidence all political parties, including Shri Vajpayeeji who was the Leader of the opposition at that time. PwD Act has come. More than that, we had the RCI Act because without RCI Act, PwD Act has no meaning. Because standardizing by a statute has special importance. The government itself was resisting. They never wanted it to be a statute. On the other hand it is misnomer. National Institutes, RCI and NGOs are complementary to each other. They have to co-exist. This is the reason when I became the Chairman of RCI, I brought to notice that these three organizations must work together. Otherwise, if you start working apart then our system of management and achieving our goals will remain a pipe dream. Unless the RCI is given the mandate of conducting all India examination it can not be strengthened. It should not be got further delayed. So examination board has got to be part of RCI. I hope this zeal which I initiated shall come through. All of us have to support. Otherwise there is no end for it. So we want equalization of services and equalization of opportunities. These are the main principles of PwD Act. How do we achieve improving the quality of life of persons with disabilities? This can happen when there is a trained manpower. When we say education for all, up to 14 years of age, minus handicapped. Health for all they said, in fact have accepted prevention, intervention, rehabilitation as mandate of Social Summit. All the Committees of Nations have agreed in toto. So why this is not a mandate in operationalisation, functionalisation. It cannot remain a mere charity of giving small grants amending the rules every ten days. We want to be part of education. Unless special education is mainstreamed in general education with its wisdom, we know how to take care of it. Enabling process, this is very essential. I am very happy today because vocationalisation is one of the very important area as the ultimate goal is how to integrate people with disability for independent living. I am sorry to tell you out of 6,45,000 villages 2,00,000 villages are not reachable. This is the pathetic situation of our Indian sub-continent. Yesterday I had discussion with the Planning Commission. So this is very crucial to know how to reach the unreached areas. Urbanisation of course is there. RCI must be strengthened, unless you strengthen RCI there can not be quality education. Without quality manpower, there cannot be improvement in quality of services. I am very happy so many people have come on their own.

I must tell what is this adopting the foreign words, CBR. CPR, there is a resolution, I don't know why RCI does not follow. Without participation there is no base. Because they are already integrated. Hundreds of them are employed in agriculture today. Ours is a agro based economy. Industrialization has yet to take place. Information technology is just coming in. But agriculture is going to be our main base for the next 50 years. So naturally our employment opportunities are more in that. Without participation where is the rehabilitation? These things may be addressed by you yourself. Let noble thoughts come from all sides. You people have come from all parts of the country with a main desire to learn something, to know something so that you can adopt it and adaptation is not duplication. This is another form of assimilation.

PROF. A.K. SACHETI

As you are aware I am going to talk to you on a topic which is not very new to all of us now because of the unemployment problem in the country. The universities, colleges, institutions are trying to switch to vocational courses and there is a concern in the country about the unemployment and Government of India is also thinking that something should be done in this direction. During my brief presentation I will be talking to you about what is the thinking of Government of India so far as technical vocational education is concerned. My topic is Rehabilitation of Persons with Disabilities through Vocational Education and Training. While talking about this particular topic, I will talk about the work done by my institute, Pandit Sunder Lal Sharma Institute of Vocational Education. This Institute is a constituent unit of NCERT established by Government of India, Ministry of HRD on 5th July, 1993. It is supposed to be a national apex institution in the field of vocational education and it is located at Bhopal. Since last 10 years this institution is catering to the work done by the Department of Vocational Education, NCERT further and the area of operation is the entire country. As far as the target group for which this institute is working both formal and non-formal, even informal courses are developed and offered. This institute works in six major areas in which employment opportunities are there as our Chairperson already said agriculture is where 60 per cent of people make their living. So we have one area with large number of vocational courses that is the agriculture. The second area where we have vocational courses is business and commerce. Third is services sector, engineering and technology. Health and para-medical area. We have home science and humanities. I have divided my talk into four sub-parts. The first part will be dealing with the role and functions of PSSCIVE, the second part is about the courses developed by PSSCIVE, third part relates to disability, we have done some work in the field of mental retardation. Fourth part contains some points for consideration of RCI.

First role is to assist the Ministry of HRD in preparing policies and other things in the field of vocational education. Establishment of a comprehensive management system in the country. In all States we are trying to establish a management system for vocational education and training. Undertake, guide and co-ordinate curriculum development work, that is our strength. In this area we have done wonderful work. This I am saying from my side because we feel that excellent work has been done in the field of curriculum development in all six area. We have teacher preparation, staff development and other roles which we are doing for different States. We also study and monitor vocational education programmes through out the country. We also try to promote excellence in vocational education in delivery of vocational education through formal, non-formal and informal methods. We have started work in disability area also and now we have staff on roll, permanent faculty in disability area in the institute. We ensure uniformity of patents in the country.

Important work done by the institute, *i.e.* development of courses. We have courses for neo-literates because after adult education people started asking how can we increase our income. So we thought let us prepare some vocational programmes even for neo-literates. Then we have pre-vocational programmes. These pre-vocational programmes are meant for students joining the class IXth and Xth. These pre-vocational programmes are taken up by schools. Then we have vocational courses because yesterday one of the speakers said that we have work experience from class I to VIII. We have pre-vocational education and then vocational education at XI and XII.

This is excellent work we have done in the country. Why I am saying excellent because as Thakur Hari Prasad said that in the area of agriculture where 60-70 per cent people work, we have identified occupations in agriculture. We have a programme based on competencies. We have identified competency for each occupation. A milker, who undertakes milking, we have a particular programme for that particular person, Tea Taster, etc. This we have done in the area of crop production, horticulture, sericulture, inland fishing, marine fishing, food processing, agriculture engineering and building construction, electrical engineering, accountancy, tourism and travel. One of the finest things about these courses is that entry level we have defined. For the courses that are at the L level, entry level is primary education, for next 6 to 9, and 10 to 12. These are the entry qualifications existing in the society. We have prepared these modules which are ready with us. In all these areas there are 600 modules. All these courses which are available with us can be modified to be suitable for disability area. Work can be done. We have modules which require minor modifications suited to different disability areas.

We have identified some tasks in different areas. A publication has also been brought out on this. There are about 29 modules which are there. We have started work in mental retardation and modules can be taken up specially for mild and moderate mentally retarded persons.

We have also incorporated guidelines on how to implement these modules. These guidelines have been developed which have an objective, task, group is 18 + and the selection of module based on the requirement of the rural area, what are the resource, or economic activities. Selection of site where training can be organized. Duration of training ranges from 2 months to 4 months depending upon the module. Selection of instructors from the rural area. Training strategy, what should be the size of the group, we have to involve one or two organizations. Assessment is based on how much he has learnt and how accurate he performs activities. Monitoring and evaluation is left to RCI and other concerned institutions.

Organisation of Awareness Programme: Only 3 per cent of NGOs are working in vocational education because awareness is not there or funds constraints are there. Therefore, RCI has to take up awareness programme with the NGOs.

Development of Data Base for NGOs: We do not know how many NGOs are interested in taking up work in disabilities under vocational education and training. Some kind of data base should be prepared. Selection of NGOs for implementing different programme. PSSCIVE and RCI involvement in orienting NGOs. Development of a detailed project report. Government of India is likely to come out with a scheme on technical vocational education and training and may be it is launched in July and August and funding will be available for NGOs for imparting training to disabled people also. One of the requirements of the scheme will be to prepare a detailed project report and PSSCIVE can help in selection of NGOs. If we come to know where there are large number of physically and mentally retarded persons, where the programme will be more effective, that will help in taking up vocational and educational programmes in rural areas. Parents involvement in vocational training programme, specially for MR persons. We have suggested orientation course for vocational instructors so that they will know how to handle disabled people. The vocational training is to be imparted to VRWs, MRWs, and coordinators of NGOs.

DR. BHATTACHARYA, NIHH

While planning out a strategy, we have to know the magnitude of the issue. Here the 2.28 million is the projected figure of the Tenth Plan, 2.04 is the Ninth Plan. Tata Statistical Year Book—2002. This is the population of hearing impaired only. If we include other categories it will come to 7 million. Keeping in view the magnitude, what facilities we have with us. Number of vocational training centres by the NGOs, the pre-vocational programmes are included in this, 190, number of training centres of MSJE—116, VRC – 17, all of these are situated in the State capitals. Many of them run extension services and one of them is exclusively for women with disabilities. Number of collaborative vocational training centres of NIHH—30, we need to expand it in a big way. We provide financial assistance to NGOs and help them in developing the project proposals. Many of the NGOs are present here who may think that I have sent a proposal, my proposal was not accepted. It may happen. The viability of the trade and the total cost of the project is of paramount importance. If we are convinced that this particular trade will be viable in particular region, we go out of our way and help those NGOs. I will appeal to all NGOs to please write to us. We will send you the format of the project proposal and if you apply we will be happy to collaborate with you. These are the exclusive institutions working for persons with disabilities. Instead of isolating them, we always look for concessions and facilities for the disabled, we forget to count them as part of us. They are also out of 100 crores. They are also human beings and citizens of India. We must try to integrate them in main institutions, departments of Government of India. Number of industrial training institutes—2,263, number of training institutes by private institutions—2,708. In these institutes some 9 lakh trainees are trained. Out of that even if we take 3 per cent it comes to 75,000 persons with disabilities. We train only 15,000. In addition to this, there is a big network of KVIC which have 478 institutes. It has reached to the remote rural areas. There also we should try to explore this. Nehru Yuvaka Kendra has got a network throughout the country. Training facilities are there. So we can say 1.75 million persons with disabilities have vocational training opportunities. In ITIs, 3 per cent seats are reserved for persons with disabilities. Selection of trade is of vital importance. Somewhere we go wrong we end up with vocational training only without looking beyond the horizon that it is linked to market. We need to establish a linkage between the training and employment centre. Therefore we have to conduct a market study. It is not very difficult to start a training programme, it is doubly difficult to make it sustainable. Regional trades, you all know India has its beauty in diversity. This is also applicable to our handicrafts and cottage industries sector. With the changing needs of the society, these trades need to be revitalized and updated with the current trend. Socio-economic and educational background of the candidates is another important factor in the selection of trade. There is a big chunk of people who cannot be ignored. We must make some provision for them also. It does not require any formal qualification to get vocational training and subsequently get employment. This is the missing link we have come across between the vocational training and employment. Curriculum does not include adequate theoretical input. Again this is more true in case of hearing impaired and the mentally retarded but due to lack of communication skills on the part of instructor, it becomes difficult to communicate theoretical information to the students. Training becomes practical based and it does not get recognized certification for open employment. It also restricts self-employment opportunities. Vocational training does not include the entrepreneur development skills to be given to trainees. There right from marketing, cost of production, how to establish marketing network, profit and loss, all these concepts should form the part of the curriculum. Sheltered employment though it is not directly related to persons with hearing impairment, it is related to persons with multiple disabilities, with hearing impairment. There are people who are aged. They have potential to work to some extent in a sheltered employment who are not able to cope up in the open employment environment. For them we have to think of the option of sheltered employment. Manpower development—RCI has developed a Certificate Course for the

Instructors of Hearing Impaired. Initially due to this problem, hearing impaired could not be mainstreamed. I am happy to mention here that NIHH has already taken up this course and initiated the programme at two places. Thirty persons have been trained in this one month programme. Introduction of the Certificate Course by the NIHH. There is no dearth of schemes and provisions at all. Ample opportunities are already available in our existing infrastructure. Central Social Welfare Board conducts a number of studies related to market studies, related to trade selection, related to hearing impaired in a particular region *vis-à-vis* to their self employment. Ministry of Rural Development has put up a tie with the Directorate of Technical Education to train in all government polytechnics about 600. NHFDC has come up. Why don't we jump upon it and exploit as much as possible. I am told even in NHFDC due to lack of viable projects they are not able to give loans. I will request RCI to have a tie with SSI to develop a programme on entrepreneurship development programme. Already they have such a one month programme for the normal population. If we can modify that and make it suitable for persons with disabilities, it will go a long way. District industries centres are another source for trade development. Swaranjayanti Swarojgar Yojana (SSY) in which 3 per cent of total allocation is earmarked for the persons with disabilities. It is a huge amount already available. Let us utilize that. With the changing of globalization and technology, now all public sectors and all leading private sector want to train their manpower according to their specific needs. As a part of that they have a provision of pre-recruitment training. This advantage could be exploited for the benefit of persons with disabilities. On the job training is another aspect. Insurance scheme during pregnancy if the child is born with a disability. The insurance company pays for the education and rehabilitation of the disabled child. This scheme is not much publicised. I would request all of you to take this message. Recently we have launched a website called www.jobsforthedeaf.com. It enables the employers to notify their vacancies and the disabled to apply for such jobs. Even the professionals can enroll for better prospects.

MR. P. ESWAR MURTY

Ours is a small educational organization catering to the educational needs of children and adults. The categories of students include disabled also. The disability is due to accident rather than by birth. It is worth nothing that Government of India has passed the Persons with Disabilities Act to create barrier-free environment for persons with disabilities to mainstream them. The basic requirement of children, adults and aged are obviously different and self explanatory. Since this is the age of information and communication, a computer centre with Internet connection would be the need of the hour. Trainees and tutors for disabled also would require special training to manage their situation effectively. A coordination centre would be required to sustain the programme in a long run. This coordination centre would be a starting point a beginning could be made by various agencies of Central and State Governments. Various courses can be offered in different fields. Computer courses hardware and networking and data communication, application software process, multi-media course, accounting package course, etc. Computers for higher sections of disabled, co-ordination section of English and Hindi course. Disabled person hostel. Society in harmony. Every building should have at least one entrance accessible to handicapped. We have tried to highlight the feelings of NGOs towards implementation of governmental schemes to help the disabled.

CHAIRPERSON'S CONCLUDING REMARKS

One thing has emerged convergence. Tenth plan has accepted the policy of convergence. Every department has to understand each other what they are doing. So that has yet to take place. Primary level is itself the starting point. I am very happy a very good thing has happened. A few days back a good announcement made by my good friend Prof. Dikshit, Vice-Chancellor, IGNOU. Actually that was the action plan of RCI, I had initiated when I was Chairman of RCI. Centre for Disability Studies with international connectivity. I am extremely happy Prof. Dikshit, helped RCI in taking up B.Ed. at Bhoj University. RCI should join hands to develop the partnership because this is a very important segment and can become a research component. I am very happy, British Government has joined hands with IGNOU. So this is another information you should know that. Ask for it, it will be available there. I am very happy to tell you that a person deeply interested in the area of disability, whenever chance comes please be in touch with IGNOU and try to know the developments that are taking place there. Let us realise the basic universal truth. Any training without any job market link up is of no consequence. This is a developing country still 45 per cent people live below the poverty line. Nobody has got wish to learn so many things just for fun. Some job linkage must be there.

OPEN DISCUSSION

MR. RAMAN SHANKAR

I would like to draw your kind attention to the vocational training centres in many parts of the country. I have observed that these vocational training centres have become income generation centres for those who run, individuals or the institutions, and exploitation centres for the disabled. What is happening is that disabled in search of shelter and two square meals a day are flocking the vocational training centres. They move from one centre to another whereas the vocational training centre they go hunting grants from the government, they have become production centres but they pay very very small sum stipend to the trainees. There are centres where disabled persons are staying for years together on a stipend of Rs.100 or 200 rupees per month. They have no place to go because there are no jobs available but what they need is a shelter and two square meals a day which is why they are living in these institutions, moving from one to another and spending their entire life. The government has to consider whether they should keep supporting such centres and we have to see that these centres are worth existing.

DR. TULSI

I have come to one basic truth and I think everyone unconsciously realizes that is still in India which is such a big country so much of unemployment, pollution, illiteracy and everything. Basic point I would like to stress for all the NGOs to join hands to do an awareness campaign for disability. That is the first point not only among us but among the general population also. We should do some programme together taking care of people like Thakur Sahib and RCI. I have started a programme in Uttar Pradesh which is known as Pulse PMR. I have a model for that. If RCI proposes we can have a meeting and I can suggest a plan, pulse disability programme for India which covers a phase of five years in which we cover all kinds of disability to reach the grass roots level. Same programme, same words, same ways of doing things. It is not that some NGO doing something somewhere. One programme which is designed by RCI we all speak the same language. Gas connections, we all have cooking gas cylinders in our house, if we can use that gas cylinders to create awareness among the masses, every body in the rural areas is now having gas cylinders, we can have print out on that. Or we can use postal department. Taking care of simple things I have developed a model so if anybody is interested we can do that.

MRS. DESAI

As mentioned by Mr. Bhattacharya the finance schemes from the National Handicapped Finance Development Corporation are not coming up because of lack of viable projects, we have a suggestion. The mentally challenged need sheltered workshops for their vocational training. Some kind of change in the method of delivery of finance scheme, *i.e.* private business entrepreneurs can engage disabled people in their regular business, and they can be treated as sheltered workshops because disabled people input in production is given there, and finance can be released at concessional rates directly to the private entrepreneur, that little difference the money will go to private enterprise, jobs can be created for the disabled people. The interest should be provided by the business houses. This way employment will be created, sheltered workshops will be established, and finance will be delivered to the larger section of the disabled people.

MR. J.P. GADKARI

Our organization represents 117 parent organizations and other voluntary organizations spread all over the country. I would restrict my comments to the vocational training centres but pertaining to the grant in aid. When I saw a graph where it was shown that 196 NGOs vocational training centres are being run. How we will survive because we know many examples of our parent association or voluntary organizations running these vocational training workshops, who just have to run from pillar to post for getting their grant in aid. They have to visit and plead in the corridors of Shastri Bhawan still they get nothing and they have to go back with empty hands. The second thing which I would like to point out is recently for good reasons Ministry has appointed Satyam Advisory Committee for collecting opinions from the NGOs from all over the country. The Satyam Committee has been visiting many centres and collecting the information so that they can advise the government how to handle the grant in government. In the meantime, what the Ministry has done has issued new guidelines which are being made applicable from 1.4.2003. When one studies these guidelines one finds that there is an attempt from the backdoor to cut the grants at various levels from these NGOs which are giving services for the vocational training to disabled persons. There are some glaring things over there. They have abolished certain posts like supervisor for vocational training. From where these NGOs are going to find funds. A mentally retarded person has to leave the vocational training centre after three years. For example, I am a parent, I know that my son or many other persons with mental retardation it is not possible for them to pick up any trade within a limited period of three years. But the Ministry says you send him out and make way for others. Similarly the ratio about the instructors in vocational training centres is made 1: 30. You know that when the mental retardation is severe, it has to be one to one. Also the maximum number you can put is one to ten. But these are the things which are there. In 2000 the Ministry made an effort to phase out the grant in aid and our organization fought against it, won the battle when the Ministry had to withdraw that.

CHAIRPERSON

If you all agree we can pass a resolution also that let them not implement it, keep it in abeyance. Because the very purpose of the Satyam Committee will be defeated. It is a very retrograde step. If everybody is agreeable we would take this opportunity to pass a resolution, let them not implement the new scheme which is retrograde, most de-beneficial and undemocratic also. We will take it as a unanimous decision and convey the voice of these people to keep it in abeyance. Let us await the Satyam Committee.

SPEAKER

We should take the example of Gujarat where the Government has taken up CBR projects in 39 blocks of the State. It is to be implemented in the whole State within the next few months. I have been able to find out 3,307 persons with disability in 102 villages of Jamnagar block. Our observation says that there are certain persons with disability who need training at their own places as they cannot be brought to the organization for vocational training. They need particular type of training in particular type of trade where they can earn something. We are jointly trying to organize camps for short-term duration for these type of people with disabilities. They will be earning a lot in their respective areas. Music has been a very good source of employment for persons with visual impairment. You all will be happy to know that during the course of last three years we have been able to place more than 600 people with visual impairment in primary schools managed by district panchayat and parishads. We have passed a resolution to the effect that 7 per cent of the posts of teachers will be reserved for music and drawing teachers, out of which 4 per cent are specifically reserved for music teachers, persons with visual impairment to be given priority. Other States can also follow the model of Gujarat and get the visually impaired people gainful employment. The post of warden by the MSJE has been completely abolished. Now remuneration amounting to Rs. 1,000 is to be given to any staff member.

PROF. BHASKAR MEHTA

Let us make an earnest request to the government that multiply disabled people be given vocational training. Let them earn something at their own doors. I have seen some multiple disabled serving very well in USA. Why India can't be USA in this regard?

MR. SHUKUL

National Trust has started a course for care givers programme. The training people can take but the job market is concerned we are working in the below poverty line, unless there is some data base or networking of the users and the trained persons who are looking for jobs, the training goal is not achieved. If you are working below poverty line the people who are trained they need jobs. Some norms may also be fixed for the purpose that will be better.

CHAIRPERSON

We need to have a separate Conference on National Trust because the very purpose of what will happen to our child after our demise, that is the answer we wanted. That was the purpose for going in a National Trust. Now I leave it suddenly the change overnight whatever it is that is why we have got our own reservations but somebody should take initiative to have a national conscious because it is too late the purpose of fighting, crusading for so many years now that has become of no consequence. I have no hesitation to make this point whether some people get hurt or something. We have dard ka rishta. I am also father having 43 years old son. I have seen suffering. I have not taken single paise on these things. Crores of rupees from my own family have spent. We brought the Act. This is for RCI to strengthen the statute. The statute has also weakened. That should not happen. We have to strengthen RCI otherwise there is no future. Gadkari or somebody should take the initiative.

LADY SPEAKER

I would like to share the vocational rehabilitation model that we are following. We train them in printing, bakery, etc and place them in open employment. The second one is we have a rural project at Rajahmundry. We are trying to identify mentally handicapped persons who can not travel to other places for employment, we are also trying to identify trades and place them once they achieve the required skills. This is a very good model and we have been able to place more than 100 mentally handicapped people in villages. RCI should take up to bring all the organizations who are following the vocational rehabilitation model so that they can be disseminated to others to follow the role models.

MR. VARMA

For the last three days we have been emphasizing the role of IT in educating the disabled. Institutions are being encouraged to work in this sector. But after completing the training when the student goes out for job, he is left alone. What will he do, nobody thinks about his rehabilitation. Government pays attention only to the training institutions and not on the students who pass out the training. Institutions are given grant from time-to-time but no help is provided to the students. Corporate sector should also be encouraged to employ disabled persons.

MR. GEORGE KUTTY

I am fully in agreement with Thakur Sahib that professional training should be linked to jobs. In the Persons with Disabilities Act Section 32 says about identification of jobs for disabled persons. How many States have done it? I think Central Government has made some study and it is available. Earlier in the late 70s, employment and training scheme of the government. What I suggest in this regard is that every State Government should make a thorough study of the jobs identified that can be done by disabled people of all categories and insist on employment and training scheme in various institutions within the State. The disabled people will get training suitable to them as per their disability and environment as well as training in jobs which have some hope for them. Why they are not doing this because of the labour laws are not in favour of disabled employees and also those who are running any sheltered workshop or whatever employment unit for the disabled people. I wish to be enlightened on the Satyam Committee. I do not know whether we have any role to play because the existing norms of grant in aid were finalized in 1998 after discussing in a Committee wherein NGOs were represented. But afterwards Ministry has been making some changes and last year in April some sort of guidelines for social welfare departments officials were issued which created lot of problem in our inspection. Many of our colleagues are not properly recommended and we are not getting grants. If anything is to be done it should be done by consulting NGOs who are actually involved in this field.

CHAIRPERSON

The Ministry has appointed a three member Committee to look into the problems of NGOs. They are collecting information how best they can make this grant in aid scheme more successful not only in terms of qualitative service delivery but also in terms of integrating with other national programmes. You can meet them in Delhi, they have office. You represent a very important federation.

DR. HANUMANTHA RAO

This question is regarding all NGOs running training programmes. All diploma courses are made two years. So far the Ministry has not assured the two years grant and people coming to these courses are intermediate. I request this august body and I request you to take a consensus from them to request the Chairman, RCI to keep the decision of making diploma courses two years in abeyance. I feel it would be better to continue for some more time. Higher level manpower B.Ed. and other courses we are already developing. This programme will be totally destabilized.

CHAIRPERSON

The point made by Dr. Hanumantha Rao is well understood. We have been running RCI programmes, all diploma courses of one year programme, run by various institutions recognized by RCI, and it is a statutory approach. Now they have come out with an idea may be lot of exercise must have been put, from one year programme to two years to extend it. Here one important point is suddenly if you make it from June we are starting the course, the guidelines, there will be difficulty in getting the candidates also, which will be reduced to 50 per cent also. Many good things are happening, special schools are running. No, no I don't want to criticise RCI but the point made by Dr. Hanumantha Rao is for you to decide. His suggestion is better holding down for a year because two years may become a little difficult.

DR. J.P. SINGH

This is not a place to make a resolution. For any training programme it takes two years to develop. It is not a running horse we are stopping. We worked for two years to three years. We can have a technical committee and go on discussing on that. So this session is for vocational training programme. It cannot be like a resolution just passing. We have to stick to the session which relates to vocational training. We can have separate technical session.

MS. MANJULA KALYAN

A mentally retarded person should be allowed to have a joint account, particularly in my organization we have adult girls with no parents and where do they go with that money. They get 1,200 to 1,800 rupees and when I go to all the banks they refuse to open an account. I think we have to think about it. I wish has any other organization started putting that money for that person I would like to know.

LADY SPEAKER

My question is addressed to Dr. Sacheti. NCERT has developed curriculum and modules but they have not been implemented. While developing curriculum did they consult or incorporate disability into it or when they are going to do it, what is the time frame? How far the programmes they have developed have been implemented? How many people have benefited from them?

DR. A.K. MUKHERJEE

I thank you very much for this lively discussion.

XI

OPEN FORUM

Chairperson: Major H.P.S. Ahluwalia
Co-Chairperson: Dr. A.K. Mukherjee

We would like to have your suggestions and questions related to RCI and concerning every body. Please do not ask personal questions. You can write to me and I will reply within 24 hours.

SPEAKER

Is it possible for RCI to conduct a programme uniformly known as disability programme on the lines of pulse polio programme for creating awareness all around India.

CHAIRPERSON (Translation from Hindi)

He said that the programme should be uniform. We have constituted Zonal Committees and we have taken a decision that the Zonal Committees will prepare a calendar of activities for one year and the programmes will be uniform for all the Zonal Committees so that we know that similar programmes are being conducted in all the zones. We would request all of you to conduct the similar programmes be it seminar, workshop. Bigger programmes are there. But it will not be good if we do not prepare short programmes aimed at grass roots level. We will have to see your model if it is suitable for grass roots level.

MR. PRAKASH MANKORI

We have been given to understand that RCI is celebrating a decade of its existence in the month of June. I being one of the Western Zonal Advisory Committee member. There are certain programmes like sensitization of rehabilitation professionals, doctors, advisors, CBR workers and teachers. These programmes are to be organized throughout the country on this decade. My organization in Jamnagar will be having a sensitization programme for rehabilitation professionals of seven districts of parts of Saurashtra and Kuchh. Each and every organization can participate in this campaign and make the RCI a public institution. The campaign can be launched by all concerned and awareness can be created by organizing such type of sensitization programmes. I would like the Chairperson to highlight what type of programmes they are going to organize on this occasion.

CHAIRPERSON (Translation from Hindi)

We have just taken a decision that we should organize some programmes in June when we complete our tenth year. Programmes at the grass roots level. Because the time is very short, I would request you to get in touch with our Zonal Committees and also write to me about your programmes. We will continue these programmes for one month. We will have celebration for one month. The decade will be celebrated for one month. The persons with disabilities at the grass roots level should also know that RCI is organizing such programmes for them. In every State there should be some programme. We will celebrate from 22nd to 30th June. Is it alright? Ok.

MR. P.K. DAS

This is a good idea that RCI has formed Zonal Committees. I know that one Zone has been formed for Eastern region. I do not know the activities of the Zone because we do not have clear idea about the Zonal Committees how and what they can do. With whom they will be working. How they will prepare their programmes or just take up the programmes. Please clear the functions of the Zonal Committees as many of us may not be aware about activities of Zonal Committees.

CHAIRPERSON (Translation from Hindi)

East Zonal Committee is in Patna under Mr. Manoj Kumar. They have organized seminars and sensitization programmes. Because they have some problem in Patna, the activities are affected. I was discussing with him either we further decentralize it. Our idea for setting up Zonal Committees was to organize programmes in each member State and State representatives are members of the Zonal Committees.

MR. MANOJ KUMAR (Translation from Hindi)

The main objective of the RCI is training programmes and we have tried to meet this objective of human resource development. Monitoring the programmes, to oversee the examination system, to send Central Level Observers, etc. We have organized sensitization and orientation programmes so that people with disabilities are informed about different schemes and programmes for them. We have organized programmes in all the member States. We have MLAs sensitization in Jharkhand, Orissa and West Bengal. We also organized sensitization programme for media, bureaucrats, heads of institutions in public sector in Bihar and Jharkhand. We have also organized programmes at the grass roots level for elected representatives of Gram Panchayat in West Bengal, Orissa, Bihar and Jharkhand. We have also done a programme for primary school teachers as a model. A programme to have the programme in all the districts has been prepared. West Bengal Disability Commissioner has been very active and he has sent details of the programme. We have prepared an action plan for all the States and we will organize programmes equally in all the States as approved by RCI.

MR. K. ANAND RAO

The guidelines and rules and regulations of the Ministry of Social Justice & Empowerment.

MR. ARUN RAO

I am father of a deaf child. My question is about employment of disabled people as our ultimate aim is to make these disabled people self-reliant in the society. The PwD Act has made a provision that concessions will be given to companies who employ disabled people. After seven years of the Act, this has not been spelled out in any way.

DR. A.K. MUHERJEE

I think you are asking about the PwD Act and how much it has been implemented in relation to employment. The Act is quite clear and all the benefits that go to the handicapped are also quite clear. The objective was to have a government view on this but no government representative is present here. We have discussed this issue at length. We know that the need is so high and very little has been done. We are not here to debate that why it has not been done. Here we have to debate how we can improve the situation. We have discussed this at length at gross inadequacy of employment in this area.

CHAIRPERSON

Let me tell you that the percentage of reservation, yesterday, there was an advisor from FICCI, I spoke to him also. I said that all the industries here, it is pathetic situation. 0.9 per cent is the rate of employment if you take the statistics of 200 leading industries.

Now there has to be sensitization or some forum to tell them that the private sector including the government and the multi-national, 3 per cent reservation should be undertaken. We feel that this is not going to make much difference because you will be moving from pillar to post. You have the National Handicapped Finance Corporation. There is the Ministry of Rural Development. We were toying with the idea with the Rural Development that is called self-help group. At panchayat level, we have seen in some cases it was successful, 3-4 persons with disabilities joined together with one or two able people and they have a micro finance scheme up to Rs. 3 lakhs and the rate of interest is 4 per cent for male and 3 per cent for female. There are some kind of bindings that NGO should be there, money should be there, etc. But lot of people are taking benefit of that. I know a place where they have opened a loom factory and they obtained a loan of Rs. 15,000 each. They borrowed about Rs. 80,000 and within 8 months they have returned the money. So with the panchayats, each State has panchayat people, rural development people, block level people, these kinds of ideas have to be thought of if you want to generate. Otherwise for a normal person also he is also not hundred per cent employed. In the case of disabled there is great advantage of National Handicapped Finance Corporation and 3 per cent is not a very heavy amount. There are lot of organizations who can help you. Even the Zonal Committees will help you.

SPEAKER

I would like to ask you Sir, whether RCI has developed any human resource development programme for mental illness? If not, will we have anything in the future.

DR. A.K. MUKHERJEE

The mental illness has just been included in the RCI Act and as you know there is a mental authority in India set up way back in early 80s by the Ministry of Health. There has been rapid expansion in the mental illness programme by the Government of India with directions from the Supreme Court and it is in fact going on. Though the mental illness has been incorporated in the RCI, the programme has not yet been made. We have to have a dialogue with the Ministry of Health. That is the scenario of the mental illness. Supreme Court is itself monitoring the programme from time to time. I happen to be the member of the team which has to submit the report to the Supreme Court on hospitals in the country.

MR. J.P. GADKARI

Let me congratulate RCI for doing this Convention. In my opinion this should have been the responsibility of the organizations working for the disabled but RCI has done it and given us the lead. You have mentioned about the Zonal Committees which is a good step again. But there is no information about the Zonal Committees anywhere. In my area the confusion is whether the Zonal Committee is at Coimbatore and contact them or I have to contact Hyderabad. There was a plan to have a convention in Bangalore and later on it was transpired the letter went wrongly from RCI to the Zonal Committee situated in Coimbatore and they informed that this is not within their jurisdiction and I have to approach Hyderabad. That confusion will be removed once full information is there. When you form the Zonal Committees, please include the representatives of the Parents Associations. We have 117 member units spread all over the country and we parents have stake. Therefore, our representatives should be included in all the ZACs. Our problems can be taken up by that Zonal Committee.

CHAIRPERSON

We have included the ZACs in our Newsletter. You have to tell us what programmes we have to take up. As you have said that you do not receive information, as you have now registered, we will bring out our newsletter every two months. If you have any material you can send it. You will receive RCI Newsletter containing all the details.

MR. UMA SHANKAR PRASAD (Translated from Hindi)

Our organization is working since 1995. We have formed 150 self-help groups. A survey has been done in Poorvi Champaran and 12,000 disabled have been identified. We have talked to D.M. but no positive steps have been taken. Apart from RCI, a number of foreign societies are also associated with us. I would request all of you who are present here to inform each other about their plans. Correspondence should be done in Hindi so that we do not have problem in knowing about plans and programmes of RCI. I am very happy with the programmes of RCI and will implement them. I will collect details from D.M. and send to you along with our plans.

SPEAKER (Translated from Hindi)

Uttranchal Government has not appointed the Commissioner (Disabilities), nor constituted the Coordination Committee or Executive Committee. We also requested you when you visited Dehra Dun at RAPHAEL. We would request you to take up this with the State Government.

SPEAKER

Disability Commissioners should be compulsorily invited to national conferences.

CHAIRPERSON

Commissioner's meeting is held separately. We are empowering you. Summit of the Mind means that we all should discuss and decide what we can do for the disabled. We also involve the State Governments in our programmes. I met the Governor of Uttranchal and their Secretary also. Our main purpose is to look after the disabled that is why we have gathered here to discuss our problems and find solutions.

SPEAKER

As per the provision contained in the Section 19 of the RCI Act, professionally qualified personnel are being registered with RCI. Same way those who have undergone the Bridge Courses are also likely to be registered or are under the process of registration. What about those who have played pioneering role in founding, and delivering services to persons with disabilities in specific areas. Can't we have any provision to register these pioneers who have dedicated their lives for 30 years, 40 years, 45 years. Provision may be made to register these persons.

CHAIRPERSON

But when we started the Bridge Course all the categories were covered. Why they did not complete the Bridge Course. We have already covered about 14,000.

SPEAKER

I am blind by birth. I am a teacher in a normal college. Even then for the last 20 years I am rendering services in the area of rehabilitation of visually impaired. So the persons like us and even senior to us, who have not undergone any training, even then they are working. So for their registration provision should be made.

CHAIRPERSON

O.K. we will make a provision. Let us see what happens.

SPEAKER

I had a mentally retarded son. Therefore I started an institution in 1983. Our teachers have done the Bridge Course. Today there are 72 mentally retarded children in our society. We have doing the courses of BPA and RCI PHC doctors course. We are associated with RCI.

LADY SPEAKER

I have a suggestion. I do not know whether RCI can help in it. We are talking about Research & Development here. A number of organizations working at the grass roots are also present here, who have made research and innovations. But there are difficulties in obtaining patent and copy right. Can RCI help in this. Secondly, if there are such things which can be useful to others, to give information about them to other NGOs, can RCI help in this also. Another thing is, a number of methodologies and case studies have been presented, if a compilation can be made of all these case studies and distributed to all, it will avoid duplication.

CHAIRPERSON

All the proceedings of the Convention are being documented. These will be published and sent to all whose addresses are available with us. If you need any extra copies, you can order for that. Please send your suggestion in writing with regard to patent and copy right.

DR. CHANDRASEKHAR

Very little work has been done for rehabilitation in Himachal Pradesh. Only one organization from Himachal Pradesh has participated in this Convention. We have gained lot of knowledge from this Convention. I would invite you to organize a State level or any other programme in Himachal so that disabled people living in the hills who can not travel to cities, can also be informed about the schemes and programmes of the government for them.

CHAIRPERSON

I have lot of love and affection for the hills. Last year we had organized a Media Workshop and Zonal Committee meeting in

Himachal Pradesh. However, if you organize any programme, I will certainly come. But the problems should be removed.

SPEAKER

I thank you for your kind patience and your encouraging attitude towards us. Information should be sent to all the institutions working at the grass roots level so that they can take benefit of different schemes. I come from Uttranchal, Pauri Garhwal which is a very backward area. Disability statistics should also be made available so that we can provide service to them according to need. I would request you to help us in this regard.

CHAIRPERSON

I am very unhappy with Uttar Pradesh because our PHC programme has not yet been started. There is a backlog of 3,000. We have difficulties in some States. I have met their Secretaries also. Now we have to think how to sensitize them. You should associate yourself with the Zonal Committee.

MAJOR GROVER

We give aids and appliances free of cost to the poor people. We have imported artificial limbs. I am also user of an artificial limb for the last 32 years. I want to put up a proposal to RCI that any artificial aids required by physically handicapped or any other disability, are we going in for some Research & Development where we can have latest technology available with us developed in the country or imported and it is available to everybody. Today we are using calipers also which are so heavy, the person has to put an effort to walk. But if we can give him some better quality with lighter weight and more powerful, that will be required for all the disabled people. Are we going to do some research or having a separate wing for research or do it in our own way.

CHAIRPERSON

This does not fall within the purview of RCI. But nevertheless this point had been under consideration. Earlier there was heavy duty on imported appliances. But now the customs duty has been removed from the appliances and the prices of these aids have come down substantially. Research and Development is under the Ministry of Social Justice and Empowerment and ALIMCO. But this point we will put to the government but certainly there has to be continuous research. The point is whether the poor disabled can afford such high prices. We have to low cost high quality appliances. I will tell Mrs. Sandhu to include high quality under ADIP Scheme or the price of ADIP Scheme should be increased. The decision will be intimated to you through Newsletter.

DR. CHANDRA

I am Dr. Chandra practising Pediatrician for more than four decades. Now we are providing diagnosis and intervention. I find that early detection, intervention and prevention is not given due importance and thrust. I request RCI to institute a multi centric research project on this subject because working on research in early intervention is very gratifying and encouraging. Multi centric studies taking Tamil Nadu and other 12-13 centres should come together. Plan a uniform strategy, implementation, evaluation and present the research to other people so that they can understand the importance of intervention.

DR. A.K. MUKHERJEE

I think she has raised a very important issue. Prevention, early identification and minimal intervention in early childhood. RCI has to act within its mandate, RCI Act 1992 and revised later on. It can not function in any other way. The programme for prevention, early identification and intervention in the childhood phase, there is already a programme by the Indian Council of

Medical Research. Your suggestion is very good and a project is already going on in various parts of the country. I think that is the reason that we have not incorporated this particular area in this particular meeting. But since Chairman represents just RCI alone but represents a voice of the disabled for the disabled. Obviously he will agree with me that any particular suggestion not in the service delivery form, but in the form of research, it can be added. PwD Act says research has to be highlighted and research again in manpower development. Actually we can do it in a way that RCI can come in the picture. I have done this kind of exercise for positive manipulation and it could be thought on those lines for human resource development and not in service delivery and request the doctors to get in touch with ICMR and get the information.

DR. MARITA ANGAM

We see lot of school children with learning disabilities who get zero in the examination but they can answer the same question orally. These children are thrown out of school. My question is we are putting lot of effort, doing lot of sensitization, putting intervention and want to start research in this area. What is the position of learning disability as far as PwD Act and RCI Act is concerned.

DR. A.K. MUKHERJEE

You have raised a very important issue about the learning disabilities, whether they are disabled or not. The PwD Act has defined very clearly what are the disabled. But of late for the learning disabled group, RCI has been thinking about it and how to give advantage to this group, nothing concrete has yet come. I think it deserves consideration and I appeal to RCI to look into this more seriously. RCI Act does not incorporate this particular point but I think there is a room for it.

MR. DEB

We are suffering from the lack of professionals in the area of rehabilitation of the disabled. Three years back one organization organized three batches of Bridge Course in the field of MR only. Other fields of visual impairment, hearing impairment and locomotor impairment were not covered. What is your action plan with regard to North Eastern Zone.

CHAIRPERSON

We are trying to give lot of importance to the seven States and we are trying to raise the standard and communication because of inaccessibility. Ketki can you throw some light on this.

MS. KETKI

Your question is specifically for lack of training opportunities in other training fields.

MS. LEELA VARDHAN

For the last two days focus was given on that NGOs should be encouraged to run services and government should act as facilitator. I am told that government has financial constraints and the NGOs have to become self-reliant gradually. Is it possible for the government to prepare a guideline for gradation system on the basis of the services provided by the organization and provide financial assistance accordingly. Then they will be justified to support the services and distribute the funds uniformly. I think on the other hand institution will also strive for upgradation.

CHAIRPERSON

Somehow a year back or so they had started to reduce the funding of NGOs and due to reasons beyond my knowledge. Then we lobbied around and said that it is not possible and NGOs can't raise funds, as you are not in foreign country people come forward and give fund. This process has been stopped. In anybody is affected please let us know. The government has taken a decision not to reduce anything. If you have any problem let me know.

MR. TARUN

I take this opportunity to thank the organizers. I was hoping, since this is a cross-disability convention, someone to come forward with a direct helpline for the disabled. Idea is already accepted by the Ministry of Social Justice & Empowerment being implemented through Child Welfare Foundation, the helpline number all over India is 1098. If RCI could take up such cause because ultimately we all work for the welfare of the handicapped. Can we not put up a proposal to Ministry of Social Justice and Empowerment seeing the success of Child Welfare Foundation, Ministry has taken it as a full-fledged project. If we have a that kind of network and a cross-disability network, at every district or at 30-40 places to begin with, and the reports of these centres could be sent to the Ministry or RCI or to the Chief Commissioner.

CHAIRPERSON

It is part of our recommendations. It is well taken.

SPEAKER

Whether the rate of compensation of the land belonging to a disabled is acquired by a government agency should be the same as for the normal person or he should be given a preferential treatment. If a disabled person becomes doubly disabled due to accident on road, how his compensation is decided by an insurance company, what is the logic behind this. I will request all my friends that research is needed for this. As far as Revenue and Finance Ministry is concerned, certain rebate should be given to the disabled for land holding so that they can adopt at least five disabled as guardian who are poor.

CHAIRPERSON

This is a policy matter involving Ministry of Finance and Ministry of Social Justice and Empowerment. We will forward this to the Ministry. Society must also consider this point. With this we close this session.

PART II

PAPERS

1

HUMAN RESOURCE DEVELOPMENT (HRD): GRASS ROOTS AND HIGHER LEVEL

J.S. Grewal

INTRODUCTION

The RCI Act emphasizes that "RCl should collaborate with, various service providers to develop appropriate human resource to help persons with disabilities". It is in the context of this stipulation that the theory and practice of HRD should be dealt with.

Human Resource Development (HRD) in the context of disabled population is to be based upon 'balanced human resource policy'. A case for HRD in this regard has to be built on both ethical, economic, social, cultural and ecological (environmental) grounds. HRD cannot be an isolated affair. It has to form part of or be integrated with other sectors of development. It is 'for the sake of individuals and societies themselves that efforts should be made to expand and improve the education of youth and adults.

The concern of the RCI and NGOs is the population of disabled persons. Though the exact numbers of these persons are not available, yet it is estimated that their number varies somewhere between 6 and 10 per cent.

BASES OF HRD

Jacques Hallak (IIEP, UNESCO, 1990) in his book titled "Investing in Future" has identified the bases of HRD as namely; (i) The Ethical and Human Dimensions; (ii) Improvement of Health and Nutrition; (iii) Technological Development; (iv) Socio-Cultural Change; (v) Inequalities in HRD; (vi) Economic Development; (vii) Ecological Development. These factors, which constitute the HRD, are elaborated below:

Ethical and Human Dimensions: We must go beyond the economic and psychometric views of Education. One must deal with its fundamental ethical and human dimensions. Education is a human right. It leads to individual creativity, improved participation in the economic, social and cultural roles in society and hence a more effective contribution to human development.

Improvement of Health and Nutrition: Education contributes towards improvement of health and nutrition of children and parents. Nutrition reduces mortality rate and increases life expectancy. Malnutrition reduces one's resistance to disease and physical and mental development. World Bank studies of 29 developing countries have shown that 'each year of schooling means, on the average, 9 per 1000 fewer infant and child deaths'. Longitudinal studies also confirm the effect of literacy on life expectancy. At MPBOU, Bhopal two studies are currently in progress to know the extent to which the nutritional status of children is affected by their being disabled. Two Ph.D scholars are conducting field studies of heights, weights and socio-economic variables of children with different disabilities.

Economic Development: There is general agreement on the close relationship between HRD and economic growth. Comparative studies have observed that 'four years of primary education increased productivity of individuals by 8.7 per cent across countries'. It is further observed by researchers that when earnings were taken as a measure of productivity in developing countries, primary schooling averaged around 27 per cent economic returns and secondary education around 15-17 per cent more earnings. Literacy and innumeracy levels of individuals account for differences in the ways of secondary school completers. Education plays a crucial role in the technological change for which the people must be trained and used effectively both at grass roots levels and higher levels.

Technological Development: According to some researchers, schooling promotes 'modern attitudes' and 'rationality', but we must be cautious in the use of normative terms for subjective phenomena. A country's pursuit in the development and use of new technologies has implications in terms of employment and skill requirements. Both these aspects are important as HRD activity.

Socio-Cultural Change: Secondary school instruction in Arts and Science subjects proved to be most 'effective' in producing attitudes considered to be most modern. The number of years of schooling correlates with savings and consumer choices.

It is reported that 50 per cent of women in Africa, 40 per cent in Asia and 30 per cent in Latin America and the Caribbean are married by the age of 20. Childbearing which is common among adolescents in developing countries has to be curtailed because reduction in fertility rates is a necessary condition for development. A survey of 14 countries shows that women without education have more children. Education of women is a key factor for population control, family planning, health and hygiene, nutrition and educational motivation of children.

Inequalities in HRD: Education is a major institution which contributes to democracy and hence equality. Inequalities of opportunities are caused by geographical, socio-economic and gender factors. They relate closely towards the distribution of income, cultural goods and political powers. Education plays a transformation role by reaching the socially deprived groups. It facilitates upward occupational mobility and, more varied human capital. It reduces social disparities and reaches widely the spectrum of development.

Ecological Development: In developing countries inadequate water supplies, floods and food shortages are caused by over exploitation of land and soil. Very, fast urbanization causes manpower shifting to cities resulting in imbalanced development. Public awareness of environmental problems and issues is to be done through use of mass media, exhibitions and excursions of students to places of environmental interest.

Education for environmental literacy may be imparted by incorporating environmental education across the curriculum into various subject contents and out-of- school activities. Introducing environmental dimensions into science education issues and scientific knowledge. 'Caretakers of Environment', a publication brought out by an international NGO, is an excellent example of forward-looking education that keeps people abreast with the changing environmental problems and their possible solutions.

HRD AT GRASS ROOTS LEVEL

The HRD at the grass roots level in my opinion means training people with basic educational qualifications are being trained in various skills. In certain countries of the world, Basic Education (mostly upto class VII or VIII) is considered sufficient to acquire employable skills, The present formal education system is based on a 4 -tier model, with 8 years of elementary education (primary school examination after class V and middle school examination after class VIII); 2 years of secondary consisting of classes IX, X; 2 years of higher secondary consisting of class XI and XII; and finally duration of 3 years for the degree courses. For the purpose of HRD, basic technical and vocational education should be available at the end of terms in classes VIII, X and XII. The National Curriculum Framework for School Education (NCFSE) has suggested work education for the secondary school stage. However, in certain developing countries of Africa (*e.g.*, Uganda), primary education is treated as terminal stage because there is a low transfer rate of pupils to secondary stage. They have introduced at the primary stage certain Integrated Production Skills (IPS) subjects, namely: (i) Agriculture (including Home Economics); (ii) Basic-Primary Technology and Art; (iii) Business and Entrepreneurship Education.

As many disabled children will not move further higher on educational ladder, they could be provided training in subjects like IPS for promoting the concept of HRD. In our situation, the drop-out rate is also a problem. Therefore, it will be better to infuse the skill training through the subjects of upper primary level.

It is often pointed out that agriculture is the main source of livelihood in our country. Agriculture is treated as a vocation subject in Uganda and is included as a subject right from class P1 onwards in a modest way and its content increases progressively upwards. HRD vocational activities might begin with production skills. It is believed that secondary education plays crucial role in HRD because it provides entry to tertiary level, academic and professional courses.

Though vocational training is now being taken on by a wide range of institutions in our country to meet the demands of developing and modernisation of industries and the labour market, yet the training is not intensive enough and these trainings are not properly oriented to meet the training needs of disabled population.

HRD AT HIGHER LEVEL

There is 1111precedented growth or post-secondary institutions at tertiary level which are catering to the HRD needs of the country, in fact many other countries as well. Separate Universities have been established in many states for the co-ordinated development of agricultural, technical and medical education States like Chhattisgarh have passed legislation to establish private Universities for organising innovative programmes. This very State has established medical institutions to conduct specially designed medical courses of 3-Year duration to meet the HRD needs of the tribal areas. The products of traditional Medical Colleges did not like to stay and work in the tribal areas.

There are important unresolved questions and issues. There is a wide gap and mismatch between demand and supply of higher level agricultural, technical and medical education. There is unbridled expansion of technical education. Professional institutions have been opened on large scale private sector in the recent years. The cost of education at the higher level is also very high and there is little attention paid to quality aspect. If we draw a map of priorities of HRD at higher levels, the following factors appear to be emerging:

(i) *Selective Expansion*: Increase the participation of beneficiaries; change output mix, that is, fields of study correcting and improve quality.
(ii) *Promoting Equality*: Expand short-term courses; improve efficiency; and mobilize private financing.
(iii) *Improving Quality*: Develop applied sciences develop (and provide) alternative distance education and short-term courses.
(iv) *Correcting Imbalances*: Regional representations have been ensured through policy planning and implementation. Coverage of courses has been expanded.

If we examine the above listed factors, we find that many things have happened in respect of HRD in our country. The programmes have been expanded, diversified and private funding is also available, on large scale, though at very high cost. Numerous short-term courses of diverse fields are also available. The only thing that has not happened is non-implementation of quality-management concept.

INTEGRATED APPROACH TO HRD

Jacques Hallak (1990) has arrived at a number of conclusions on HRD:

(i) Education and human resource policy become driving forces of development only if they are according to the general development policy of a country.

(ii) It takes long time to consolidate HRD and the achievements of one period strongly influences the future developments in the following period. Sustained efforts and mobilisation of resources are necessary to achieve targets.

(iii) Though poverty is not a favourable factor for HRD, but it is not sufficient excuse to stop progress in HRD either.

(iv) Primary education of poor quality impedes HRD at all levels. It discourages demand for schools, lowers efficiency and contributes to wastage of resources.

(v) Job opportunities of school leavers and graduate correlate closely with the quality of their instruction.

(vi) Success of Asian countries, particularly in engineering and applied Arts is secondary and tertiary education. On the contrary African and Latin American countries laid emphasis on disciplines of law Humanities and Social Sciences. It is not to suggest that certain disciplines are more important for HRD. The plea is for more balanced distribution of courses and related job structure.

The Readers may refer to. ***Investing in the Future*** by Jacques Hallak (1990), LLEP, Pergamon Press, 1990.

2

AWARENESS AND COMMUNITY MOBILISATION

J.P. Gadkari

Among various disabilities, mental retardation and other developmental disabilities are generally the least visible and therefore, the most neglected ones. Though mental retardation is now a recognized disability in legal terms, it is still considered by many as a mental disease which could be cured by some medicine or the other. Many a times, it is also considered as a curse or the outcome of the sins committed by the parents or the persons with these disabilities in their "*previous*" birth. This is despite the knowledge acquired during the last 50 years of research and development which determined some of the basic features and causes of this debilitating disability.

The medical science has made spectacular advances during the last two, three decades. As a result, much could be learnt about the condition of mental retardation and other developmental disabilities. Though no breakthrough has been achieved so far to prevent or reverse the condition of mental retardation, the research in the field of genetics has given much hope that one day such a thing may become possible.

However, the parents of persons with these disabilities due to lack of knowledge, ignorance about the problems of mental retardation and influence of superstitions become the victims of dejection and despondency. They generally run from pillar to post to find a cure. They also treat this as a social stigma and try to keep the child away from the society. By and large, the medical knowledge about the problem of mental retardation being only at expert/specialized level, the ordinary medical practioner or a family doctor is not of much help to them. The result is that the parents and their wards get isolated form the mainstream of the society.

It·is now a universally accepted fact, that though mental retardation remains an irreversible condition, the persons with mental retardation are educable, trainable and could be transformed into contributing citizens of the society. Much has been done in developing special courses to educate the children with these conditions. Many novel methods have been found and adopted to train them in day-to-day skills to overcome the deficiencies; to train them in vocational skills by finding out their capabilities so that they can live as independently as possible.

It is a sad commentary that persons with mental retardation and other developmental disabilities have not been found capable of learning a vocation and find themselves suitable employment or occupation even though their disability has been legally recognized. Under the Persons with Disabilities Act, 1995, it is only the persons with other disabilities, except mental retardation and other developmental disabilities, are considered fit for employment and 3 per cent reservation in Government jobs have been provided for them.

In our country the percentage of mental retardation and other developmental disabilities is estimated to be over 4 per cent. This works out to nearly 4 crores of people with these disabilities. It could be safely assumed that atleast one-third of this population which is mildly affected, could have been considered for employment or for suitable occupation.

The United Nations have adopted number of Human Rights Declarations including the legal and constitutional rights of people with intellectual disability. The most important among them is the 1971 'Declaration on the Rights of Mentally Retarded Persons.'

Even the Persons with Disabilities Act, 1995 ensures that persons with mental retardation and other developmental disabilities will enjoy the same rights as other citizens of the country. However, the ground realities speak of a dismal scenario.

The immediate short-term objectives to reverse the situation could be as follows:

1. To create an awareness regarding the disability, especially among parents.
2. To dispel myths about the disability.
3. To mobilize maximum number of people, to support, co-operate and assist, individually or in groups, part-time or full-time, in ongoing activities concerning the welfare of persons with disabilities.
4. To motivate people to give support in whichever way possible to them, physically emotionally, financially, for persons with disabilities, their families and NGOs and centers working for their welfare.

The long-term objective should be mobilization of the community in general and involving them in the task of providing facilities to the persons with these disabilities to lead a life of dignity, honour and as contributing citizens of society.

The other long-term objective should be to make the parents proactive through their associations and organizations so that they learn from each others experience, know about the legislations, about various provisions in different legislations for the disabled and can unitedly strive to have the benefit and access of them.

In order to achieve the objectives of the short-term and long-term plans the following programmes could be adopted:

1. Large scale awareness programmes for the parents should be organized at all levels.
2. Lectures, seminars, workshop and audio-visual exhibitions should be organized to reach large sections of people in urban and semi-urban areas.

3. Street plays, folk dramas, nautankis, etc., should be organized to give expression to the problems of the disabled in the rural areas.
4. Undertake widespread and sustained publicity campaigns through posters, banners, pamphlets etc.
5. Make extensive use of the print and electronic media to publish studies. Examples of exceptional people with disabilities, success stories, personal experiences of parents, role models etc. Question-answer sessions, interviews with professionals and talks etc. should be organized on the electronic media.
6. Bring about synergy between media and disability.
7. Organise extensive counselling and short duration educational courses for parents. Wherever possible, such courses should be organized through correspondence.

The target groups to achieve the objectives through planned programmes should be the high school students and teachers, particularly from those schools which run special sections for children with mental retardation and other developmental disabilities. Similar efforts should be made to involve college students and lecturers, activists from women groups, artists and professionals from different fields.

Finally, if success is to be achieved in bringing about widespread awareness in the society and mobilize the community to extend a helping hand to the disabled, it is necessary to strengthen the parents' movement, which has already taken its roots in the country, so that they could effectively work as advocates for the cause of persons with mental retardation and developmental disabilities.

3

LOW VISION CARE IN ORDINARY SCHOOLS

L. Shanmugam

INTRODUCTION

There is a great need to develop appropriate services for children with residual vision. Many need surgery or refractive services to improve their vision, others need low vision care. Most the services for Low vision are inter-related with other disabled children. The techniques utilized for Low vision is also useful to blind, hearing impaired, mentally retarded and learning disabled children.

LOW VISION

The WHO working definition of Low vision (WHO, 1992) is as follows "*A person with Low vision is one who has impairment of visual functioning even after treatment, and/or standard refractive correction, and has a visual acuity of less than 6/18 to light perception or a visual field of less than 10° from the point of fixation, but who uses, or is potentially able to use, vision for the planning and/or execution of a task*". The WHO working definition has been adopted since WHO consultation in 1992. This working definition is solely used for reporting purposes and should be used eligibility of services.

Thus the recommended definition for low vision in Indian context should be *"Low vision are those who suffer visual acuity between 20/200 to 70/200 (snellen) or 6/18 to 6/60 in the better eye after the best possible correction*".

IMPORTANT FACTORS FOR LOW VISION CARE

(*a*) *Psycho-social Support*: A children with low vision needs to understand his/her own abilities and communicate these to the environment. Self-esteem needs to be built-up as much as possible.

(*b*) *Integration*: Visual training programmes need to be integrated as much as possible in regular activities, at school, at home, at work.

(*c*) *Family Involvement*: Apart from the teachers and CBR workers involvement of family members is vital. They can stimulate a lot of the training needed, it they understand why and how.

(*d*) *Low Vision Devices*: Production, distribution, cost and durability of optical and non-optical low vision devices.

(*e*) *Eye Checkup*: Yearly/regular eye check and follow-ups where needed.

(*f*) *Rehabilitation Inputs*: Continued input from education rehabilitation personnel where needed.

(*g*) *Systematic Assessment*: It is very important to find out what each children with low vision can do with his/her vision, and to teach people how to make the best use of it.

Low vision care	*Blind*	*Hearing impaired*	*Mentally retarded*
Psycho-social support	Need	Need	Need
Integration	Possible	Possible	Possible
Family involvement	Vital	Vital	Vital
Low vision devices	Limited use	Not useful	Not useful
Eye check-up	Need	if need	if need
Rehabilitation input	Essential	Essential	Essential
Systematic assessment	Very important	Important	Important

VISION SCREENING

Vision screening is a process of estimating the visual efficiency of a child with Low Vision. Visual efficiency differs with individual. It is absolutely necessary to test every individual who is with visual problems.

The procedure of vision screening consists of five stages:

- Distance visual acuity
- Near vision acuity
- Visual field
- Contrast
- Co lour vision

The methods of vision screening, staff involved and facilities needed are noted below:

Methods	*Staff involved*	*Facilities needed*
Vision screening in existing IED/special school children	Resource teachers, Muti-skilled rehabilitation workers refractionist/Low vision specialists	Vision screening materials, screening forms referral forms
Community vision screening camps	School teachers health workers community volunteers	–do–
Low vision mobile clinic/Eye care programmes	Ophthalmic personnel and low vision special educator	Mobile van and vision refractometer

ASSESSMENT OF FUNCTIONAL VISION

Visual functioning assessment of a functional vision of the child is not a straightforward procedure. It involves careful observations of visual behaviour of the child under different conditions. The observations should be shared with parents, other family members, regular teachers and even peers. Before the assessment, the resource teacher will concentrate the following:

1. Determine current visual functioning level of each child.
2. Determine the visual stimulation and instruction needed.
3. Help child to use his/her limited vision to the highest potential.
4. Plan courses with specific content, O&M training, or adaptive training in use devices.
5. Using visual stimulating materials most appropriate to the child.
6. Determine nature of the primary reading medium.

Functional assessment is an on going process. Every time the resource teachers has to prepare a new set of items so as to increase visual efficiency by providing various activities in numerous situations. The following chart shows the areas on which the Resource Teachers has to assess the various skills in visual functioning.

A. *Optical functioning*	B. *Perceptual functioning*
1. Visual Awareness	1. Visual Discrimination
2. Visual Attention	2. Figure Ground
3. Visual Fixation	3. Visual Memory
4. Visual Focus	4. Visual Closure
5. Visual Fusion	5. Spatial Relations
6. Visual Tracking	6. Mobility
7. Visual Scanning	7. Visual Motor—Coordination

The functional assessment and training should go hand in hand. Some teachers are keeping a catalogue for activities which promote visual functioning so as to give training to the individual in a sequential manner. Refer the functional assessment form for optical and perceptual functioning. The book 2 on "Assessment of Low Vision in Developing Countries"—by Dr. Jill Keefee gives the visual skills used for functional vision.

ASSESSMENT KIT

Self-made assessment kit for assessing the Low Vision children is very essential to resource teachers. It includes the following materials:

1. E-Chart (Snellen Chart)
2. E-Cutout
3. 6 metre tape
4. Jill Keefee's E card for near vision
5. Pinhole mask
6. 3D and 2D material /objects for contrast test
7. 3D and 2D materials/objects for colour vision test
8. Functional vision assessment materials real objects, 3D models/shapes, 3D pictures/drawings /shapes.

Teaching and Training

There are three major activities will cover the teaching and training of Low Vision children. Most of the activities are applicable to other disabled children.

I. Curricular Activities

A. *For print readers*:
   - Print books
   - Large print books
   - Enlargement of picture books

B. *For large print and Braille readers*:
   - Large print materials 0 lessonwise
   - Colourful picture books available in the market
   - Large print book diagrams
   - Large print general essays, grammar, letters, vocabularies, proverbs, maps and graphs
   - Print books—(tables) underline the headings/marking the words with the help of fluorescent pen
   - Picture album from the old books
   - Cassettes.

Curricular activities – 60% Co-curricular activities – 95%
Plus curricular activities – 80%

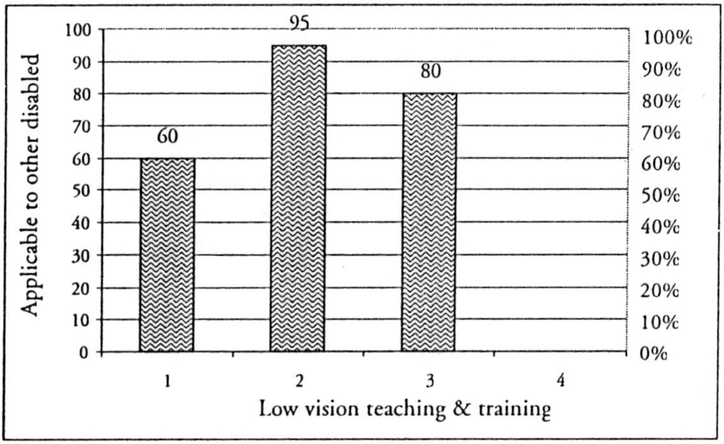

C. *For Braille readers*:
- Album (in areas of shape, size, colour, letters, words, symbols, pictures, diagrams, 2D drawings)
- Flash cards
- Tactual aids with different colours
- Braille books and cassettes

II. Co-curricular Activities

- Physical education
- Craft
- Art
- Music
- Movement (Drama, Dance, etc.)
- Science (Laboratory work)

III. Plus Curricular Activities

- Sensory skills

- Training to use special devices
- Orientation and mobility
- Daily living skills.

LOW VISION DEVICES AND FACILITIES

I. Optical Devices

The optical devices need to be prescribed by a person trained in low vision, either an ophthalmic or a low vision specialist.

- A strong magnifier
- Glasses with special prescriptions
- Tinted lenses
- Visual field expanders
- Pocket scope
- Electronic magnification

II. Non-optical Devices

These are some of the non-optical devices that might be useful:

- White board
- Writing paper
- Signature card
- Dark piece of paper/scale
- Typo scope
- Black ink pen
- Audio recorder and cassettes
- Adjustable reading stand
- Fluorescent highlighter
- Table lambs
- Large print books
- Bold—line paper
- Album
- Textbooks
- Chalk board/Black slate
- Computer

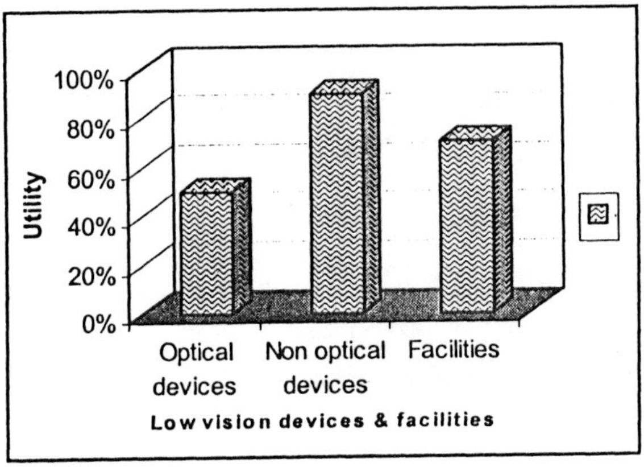

III. Facilities

- Good lighting

OTHER IMPORTANT ASPECTS ON LOW VISION SERVICES

A. Parents

- Organize a general workshop or counsel parents about how to help their low vision children
- Encourage parents to visit at any time

B. Routine Eye Examination and Counselling

- Re-examined atleast once in a year: Children with unstable / deteriorating eye condition should be seen more frequently
- Schedule for examination
- Control amount of physical activities of some low vision children
- Develop understanding and realistic attitudes about own eye defect
- Counselling to level of child's understanding

C. Record Keeping

- Medical record
- Educational progress record

D. Case Conferences

- Coordination and communication efforts of involved persons
- Consistency of goals, objectives and approaches to visual behaviour

E. Visual Aids

- Given proper training in its use
- No all devices best for all purposes, at all distances for all Low vision persons

F. Legibility of Print

- Maximum contrast: most visibility
- Paper with dull, non-glare finish
- Spacing between letters, words and lines
- Thickness of individual letters
- Avoid ornate and elaborate letters
- Avoid cramped margins
- Lay out of illustrations
- Unduly long lines

G. Classroom Adjustments

- The Low vision students, should be properly seated in respect of eye conditions and diseases
- Usually the Low vision children will be seated in the first row, of the classroom preferably at the centre position
- Generally Low vision students should be seated near the windows or doors, to get better light

- Some Low vision students with photophobia illumination of light especially albinism should be seated at the centre of the classroom.

LOW VISION CENTRES

There is a need of establishing Low vision service centres in different places with the provision of providing Low vision aids, imparting training in the use of such aids and referring the Low vision clients to various programmes of education, vocational training and employment.

Services to Low Vision and Other Disability

Sl. No.	*Low vision services*	*Totally blind*	*Hearing impaired*	*Mentally Retarded*
1.	Special educator for Low vision	They are serving with totally blind also	They need special training	They need special training
2.	Identification	No difficulty	Need guidelines	Need guidelines
3.	Vision screening	Able to screen the functional vision	No difficulty	No difficulty
4.	Functional assessment	No difficulty	Need guidelines	Need guidelines
5.	Pre-training	No difficulty	Need short-term training	Need short-term training
6.	Teaching and remedial teaching	Possible	Need special training	Need special training
7.	Teaching and learning materials	Useful to some extent	More useful	More useful
8.	Special devices and equipment	Not much useful except tape recorder and recorded cassettes	Not much useful	Not much useful
9.	Low vision centres	Utilising for education and rehabilitation	Utilising for vision assessment	Utilising for vision assessment

Concluding Remarks

Low vision services and training need to be part of each eye care, education and rehabilitation programme for the disabled. The method of teaching for daily living skills, orientation and mobility, concept development is also applies to other disabled children. The teaching and learning materials are also useful to other disability. The uniform evaluation procedure is also applicable for other disabled children.

4

REHABILITATION NOTES: POVERTY AND DISABILITY

Rakesh Arora

INTRODUCTION

There appears to be at least two road and distinct paradigm shifts in the philosophy, approaches and practices in rehabilitation of persons with disabilities (PwDs). In the beginning and in the mid-eighties, the purely medical model of rehabilitation of PwDs was abandoned in favour of a CBR model, with focus on social integration and community support of PwDs, in undertaking activities of daily living. The mid-nineties and the early part of the millennium however, appear to be witnessing a completely new approach—one of providing equal opportunities and empowerment. The philosophy of PwDs as equal partners and productive citizens rather than those living on welfare and charity has been ushered in. The theme for the World Day of Disabled Persons (1996) was 'poverty and disability'. This was a global expression of concern about the deplorable conditions that disabled persons live in, and the need to provide them equal access to services, especially employment. It was noticed that they are acutely affected by a shortage of basic necessities like water, food and housing, apart from bad or non-existent public transportation, health care, employment or other income opportunities. Even when these services are at close proximity, the PwDs find it difficult to access them due to various inhibiting factors like handicapping physical environment, lack of assistive devices, tools that cannot be used by the PwDs etc. The most critical element of empowerment that is universally accepted is economic rehabilitation. Economic emancipation is therefore taking a central stage in the contemporary thinking on disability issues. Accordingly, disability is also considered as a development issue by planners and policy makers in an increasing number of countries across the world. It has therefore, become imperative and even fashionable in both international and national fora, to be discussing the correlation and the causality between poverty and disability. Disability and development are closely linked in a cycle of cause and effect. Multilateral agencies like the UNDP in the project, 'Support to Children with Disabilities' and in the Asian Development Bank-Regional Technical Assistance (ADB-RETA), being or undertaken in India, consider including studies on disability and poverty as an important 'and integral part of the projects. The government of India has also given significant weightage to the issue. The People With Disabilities (PwD) Act has provided for reservation of 3 per cent of the vacancies in government and government supported institutions. Benefits to the extent of at least 3 per cent of all poverty alleviation programmes are meant for PwDs. The PwD Act also states that the appropriate government and local bodies shall provide incentives for employers, both in the public and private sectors to ensure that at least 5 per cent of their work force is composed of PwDs. The Swaranjayanti Gram Swarozgar Yojana accords a special focus on the vulnerable groups among the rural poor. Identification of jobs suitable for PwDs, vocational training, modification of tools and equipment, incorporating barrier-free features in training, are all aimed at fulfilling the objective of promoting employment opportunities to PwDs and alleviation of poverty.

VICIOUS CIRCLE OF POVERTY AND DISABILITY

There is a strong and definite, vicious cycle of poverty and disability.

The propensity for the poor to be disabled and for disabled people to be poor, is very strong. People living in poverty tend to become disabled because of aggravating factors such as malnutrition and squalid housing, hazardous occupations and so on. Measures for disability prevention, including health care measures such as immunisation, maternal and child care, nutrition, screening for early identification of disability, and so on, are largely not accessible for poor and illiterate persons. Environmental sanitation and hygiene which are equally important for disability; prevention are also poor in areas occupied by the poor especially in urban slums and shanty towns. Conversely, people with disabilities tend to become poorer because they lack access to income, jobs, basic medical services and rehabilitation. The constraint on the demand side is that governmental and private sectors are hesitant to employ people with disabilities because of myths about low productivity and efficiently. The low level of demand is further compounded by lack of information and awareness about the employment potential of people with disabilities. On the supply side, are limitations related to lack of facilities for vocational training, education, skills development and the limited number of vocational trades available for PwDs. This is further compounded by lack of confidence, awareness, and information among PwDs about possible areas of employment.

CRITICAL ISSUES

Most studies attempt to resolve all issues related to income generation simultaneously. While holistic approach 15 most desirable, the problem must be broken down into its various components—long-term, short-term, demand side, supply side and so on, otherwise the result would only be a superficial analysis and a wish list, rather than pragmatic solutions to each component of the problem. The author contends that region-specific, disability-specific and issue specific evaluation of the problem is necessary. For example, the factors determining the supply of vocational training for persons with mobility problems in a hilly region, would differ from those in the plains.

There are other factors that need to be analysed at the conceptual, theoretical and practical levels, before one can even begin to address the issues at hand. Firstly, definition of concepts such as disability, poverty and cost of living, for example, in the context of PwDs need to be more precise. In the example of poverty, can we estimate poverty among PwDs by applying the poverty line in the same way as the rest of the population, or do we need a different 131 poverty line to more accurately estimate the poverty and cost of living among PwDs?

The author contends that the poverty line is higher for PwDs as compared to the rest of the population. As a result, using the conventional poverty line is likely to give a much lower estimate of the number of PwDs living below the poverty line. While it is beyond the scope of this paper to estimate the exact poverty line for PwDs, an attempt is made to suggest some items that could be considered to derive a realistic poverty line for them, giving only an indicative cost range for the additional minimum facilities to be added in the poverty line.

POVERTY LINE FOR PwDs

It is well known that PwDs require certain facilities to even live independently, and this would be much more, if they are to be given a wage or are self-employed. The poverty line for PwDs should include the cost of facilities that enable PwDs to live independently and to undertake activities of daily living, or the imputed wage of person(s) assisting PwDs to carry out those activities. There is accordingly a need to have a number of add-ons to the general poverty line to get the true minimum cost of living for PwDs. The cost of these additional facilities should preferably be provided by the government, free of cost to PwDs. This can be an important and definite step towards providing equal opportunities to PwDs.

It is contended that cost of living for PwDs includes cost of living for the non-disabled, plus, cost of assistive devices, cost of converting living areas into non-handicapping environments, cost of modification in gadgets, tools, equipment, appliances etc. to make them useable by. In PwDs, and cost of attendant, even if it is a family member, the imputed cost or opportunity cost of his/her input.

Most of the PwDs require various types of aids and appliances for functional independence, mobility and activities of daily living. The type of assistive devices required by a PwD depends on the type and degree of disability and the living environment of the PwD. The cost of the assistive device is an additional cost without which the PwD may not be able to, to carry out activities of daily living. This is an additional minimum cost for the PwD. The government already implements a scheme of assistance for disabled persons for purchase/fitting of aids and appliances, with the main objective of assisting the needy disabled persons; in procuring durable, sophisticated, and scientifically manufactured modern, standard aids, and appliances. Assistive devices costing between Rs. 50 and Rs. 6,000 are provided under the scheme free of cost to the eligible PwDs (income is a primary criterion for determining eligibility). Hence, as far as assistive devices are concerned, the necessary step for providing equal opportunities has already been taken by the government. However, its coverage and reach, especially at the grass roots level, needs to be strengthened.

In order to permit easy mobility and for activities of daily living, there is a need to modify the houses that PwDs stay in (here we are focusing on PwDs basically as consumers). The modifications needed, again would depend on the type and degree of disability. For example, an orthopaedically handicapped person on a wheelchair requires doors, including that of the toilet, to be minimum 90 cm, with horizontal and vertical grab bars, especially in toilet. A visually impaired person may require embossed markings on different parts of the house, including on the floor, to carry out activities of daily living. It is estimated that it can cost about 5 per cent to 7 per cent of the building costs to incorporate barrier-free features. The author opines that even if locally available materials and skills are used for adding these features in a house of a PwD, the additional cost that may be incurred is about Rs. 300 to Rs. 500. Since this is a one-time expenditure, the cost needs to be annualised and included in the minimum, cost of living, along with the costs of maintaining these features.

To permit PwDs to live independently and carry out activities like cooking, cleaning, personal hygiene etc., the gadgets use need suitable modifications: For example, a visually impaired person may need a milk boiler (which whistles when milk boils) rather than an ordinary container. A person with cerebral palsy may require a flexible handle in a spoon, a handle for holding a plate for eating, a special chair to sit and so on. Here again, the requirements may differ from person to person, but an element of additional cost needs to be built in. A minimum expenditure of Rs. 100 to Rs. 200 could be provided for this and included in the poverty line.

In many cases, houses may not have been modified, and suitable assistive devices and gadgets may not be available. In such cases, the assistance of family members or professionals may be required for the PwD to carry out activities of daily living. Here, there is the need to cost the payment made to professionals along with the opportunity costs to the family or community. In most instances, the family members care for PwDs, along with their other duties, hence only apart of their wages could be imputed to be included in the cost of living of PwDs. It could estimated to be about Rs. 500 to Rs 1000 per month.

As stated earlier, these are only rough indicators and are by no means precise and accurate. The endeavour is to highlight the components of additional costs for PwDs rather than provide an accurate estimate of these costs. Much more empirical research is needed to estimate the actual costs, which could possibly be worked out separately for different disabilities, regions, and for urban and rural areas separately. Hence, the additional minimum cost that needs to be incurred by a PwD is either the sum of cost of assistance devices, barrier-free features and modifications in gadgets, equipment; or the imputed/actual cost to the family member/ community member/professional rendering these services. The costs of some of these services provided by Government (*e.g.* assistance devices, modification in equipment), need not be added to the poverty line as the individual PwDs do not have to bear the additional cost.

RECOMMENDATIONS

1. A specific, more precise estimate on additional cost of living for PwDs should be worked out International bodies, Governments at different levels, independent bodies, it of professionals and NGOs should provide technical and financial support for such research. These studies should also focus on working out separately the poverty line for persons' use, with different disabilities, from different regions and for urban and rural areas.
2. To bring the PwDs on par with the rest of the population, schemes, programmes and projects should be initiated and the existing ones strengthened to provide the different in a facilities highlighted above, so as to promote equal opportunities to PwDs. The endeavour should be to provide facilities like non-handicapping environment, suitably modified gadgets and tools, requisite assistive devices 'to reduce' the dependence on family and community members for carrying on activities of daily living
3. To break the vicious circle of poverty and disability, access facilities need to be provided throughout the nation at the eariiest. An attempt may be made to provide, in phases, a universal design, for both buildings and the transport sector.
4. Pension and financial support to PwDs should be fixed, keeping in view the additional tents costs that they have to incur, compared to the rest of the population.

5. The wages/remuneration to PwDs may be worked out in terms of a realistic minimum cost of living rather than pegging it on the basis of the poverty line for the rest of the population.

ACKNOWLEDGEMENT

The author expresses his gratitude to the officials at the UNDP and those undertaking the ADB-RETA study for the focus on the area, and for discussions on critical issues relating to poverty and disability.

5

ROLE OF TECHNOLOGY IN INCLUSIVE EDUCATION AND REHABILITATION OF CHILDREN WITH HEARING IMPAIRMENT

Aparna Nandurkar & Anuradha Bantwal

The sense of hearing is vital in establishing a link with the world around us. It not only enables a multitude of experiences from the environment around us, but it also is the primary channel for acquiring a skill that is unique to human beings—*verbal communication.* The hearing modality also serves as a feedback mechanism for monitoring the verbal skills that an individual has. Naturally, if the sense of hearing is affected or impaired, we will be at a great disadvantage in these respects.

WHO, 1980 defines impairment as any loss or abnormality of psychological, physiological or anatomical structure or function. *ASHA*, 1981 defines hearing impairment as a deviation or change for the worse in either auditory structure or auditory function, usually outside the range of normal.

Hearing impairment can be classified in different ways. Classifications by *type* of hearing impairment and *degree* of hearing impairment are the most commonly used for clinical purposes. These are shown in Tables 1 and 2.

It can be seen from Tables 1 and 2, that the term hearing impairment encompasses a *heterogeneous* group. Depending on the

Table 1

Type of Hearing Impairment	*Part of the Ear Affected*
Conductive	Outer and/or middle ear
Sensorineural	Inner ear
Mixed	Outer and/or middle ear and inner ear

Table 2

Type of Hearing Impairment	*Hearing Threshold in dBHL*
Normal sensitivity	– 10 to 25
Mild hearing loss	26 to 40
Moderate hearing loss	41 to 55
Moderately severe hearing loss	56 to 70
Severe hearing loss	71 to 90
Profound hearing loss	91 and above

location and type of damage to the ear, some types of hearing impairment are amenable to *medical or surgical* treatment while some are of a permanent or irreversible nature. The impact of irreversible hearing impairment on an individual is far reaching and permeates all the spheres of his/her functioning. The *long-term effects* of hearing impairment are more severe when it is present at birth (congenital) or is acquired in early childhood. This is because the presence of hearing impairment deprives the child of the sensory experiences vital to the acquisition of verbal communication skills. The effects of the hearing impairment on development and use of verbal communication skills depends on:

- Type of impairment
- Degree of impairment—the greater the degree, more severe are the effects
- Age of onset of the impairment—before or after acquisition of language
- Type of onset—gradual or sudden
- Age of identification
- Age and type of intervention
- Support received from the environment—family, school and society

The intervention for a young child with permanent hearing impairment necessitates a *multi-dimensional* approach for the overall habilitation of the child. The important components of a habilitation programme that are relevant to this discussion are:

- *Provision of amplification*—As the primary concern in such children is the development of verbal communication skills the focus has to be on provision of the necessary auditory experiences through appropriate amplification. This can be provided to the child by means of special devices that increase the energy of the sounds to a level at which the child hears; thus enabling the child to hear the sounds and speech around him/her.
- *Education*—This can be provided through special school facilities or inclusive education. *Special school* environments provide the child with assistance in developing requisite skills but they are unable to provide opportunities for interaction with hearing peers within the school environment. Secondly, such schools are not available in sufficient numbers across the country. On the other hand, the option of *inclusive education* seems to be more accessible and cost-effective since it means that the child with hearing impairment can go to the nearest available school with his hearing peers. However the child with hearing impairment has some special needs that the inclusive set-up should provide for in order for the placement to be successful.

A *barrier-free environment*—an environment conducive to listening—is a basic need and right of any child with hearing impairment. However, classroom environments in regular schools often have *poor acoustics*, making listening an increasingly difficult task for the child with hearing impairment, thus undermining the learning process. Acoustical problems in classrooms include weakening of the speech energy with increasing *distance*; loss of energy from *scattering*; *echoes* and reverberation and problems due to excessive *noise*. The more the acoustical problems in the classroom, the more difficult it becomes for the child to attend to tasks or communicate.

Certain measures targeted at improving *signal-to-noise ratio* (S/N ratio—this is the difference in dB between the intensities of the signal and the noise) can help in minimizing the acoustical problems in school classrooms. These measures can be classified as:

1. *Noise control measures*: These can include *acoustically treating* walls, floors and ceilings of classrooms to suppress noise from outside and within the room. As far as possible schools should be located far from sources of high levels of noise such as traffic etc.
2. *Signal control measures*: For good listening the intensity of the signal (the meaningful sound) should be higher than the intensity of the noise in the room, *i.e.* the S/N ratio should be favourable. The signal level reduces by 6dB with every doubling of distance from the source. Signal level can be improved by reducing the speaker-listener *distance*. In the classroom, this can be achieved through preferential seating (as near as possible to the teacher). The *speaker characteristics* also contribute towards the acoustic environment. The teacher must speak clearly and audibly.

Although these simple measures can improve S/N ratio to some extent, effective signal control can only be achieved through the *use of amplification*. Various types of amplification devices are commercially available. Grossly, they can be classified as *personal/individual* and *group* amplification systems. Group devices are used in special schools. In the inclusive set-up where there might be as less as a single special child in a regular classroom, individual amplification systems and *assistive listening devices* are of significance. Individual amplification systems include personal hearing aids, loop induction systems and FM systems. Another device that is becoming increasingly popular due to better success in rehabilitation is the cochlear implant.

In the very basic sense, a hearing aid is an electro-acoustic device that amplifies sound. It consists of a *microphone* that picks up sounds and converts them into electrical energy. An *amplifier* increases the strength of this electrical signal and sends it to a *receiver* that converts the amplified electrical energy into sound and directs it to the ear of the user.

Personal hearing aids are of different types.

(*a*) Based on the manner in which the *signal is processed*, they can be classified as analog, digital and programmable hearing aids. *Analog hearing aids* process acoustic information in the form of an electrical analog, literally an analogy of the sound wave. On the other hand, *digital hearing aids* use the latest digital processing technology in which the acoustic information is recoded into a numerical digital code. This form of coding permits the acoustic information to be modified in ways that cannot be achieved by conventional analog circuits. *Programmable hearing aids* process the signal by analog but use digital memory storage to provide options and to control how the signal is processed. Advanced systems of programmable hearing aids permit a wide range of characteristics to be programmed and re-programmed (with the help of an external computer system) by the audiologist while the user is wearing the aid.

(*b*) Depending on the placement on the user, personal hearing aids can be classified into body-worn aids, post-auricular aids and in-the-ear aids. The *body-worn or pocket type* of aid is the most commonly used by school-going children in our country even today. Depending on the income range, these aids are distributed free of cost or at concessional rates through the *ADIP* scheme of the

Ministry of Social Justice and Empowerment. Children are provided with binaural (two) hearing aids. The ADIP scheme also has the provision to provide a solar battery charger and two rechargeable batteries with the hearing aid. This works out very cost effective for the user and the parent does not have to worry about purchasing batteries. Body-worn aids are rugged and *inexpensive* to purchase and maintain. The *post-auricular or behind-the-ear* hearing aids provide better amplification due to the advantage of being at the level of the ear. They are also inconspicuous and therefore cosmetically appealing. They are more expensive than the body-worn hearing aids. The *in-the-ear type* of hearing aid is not suitable for young children as the size and shape of the ear changes with age. Also, these aids are not designed to provide high amounts of amplification required by children with permanent impairments.

The effectiveness of a good hearing aid is fully realized only when the aid is worn with well fitting custom made earmoulds. Earmoulds are made from an impression of the user's ear. In children new earmoulds have to be made whenever the size or shape of the ear changes resulting in poorly fitting moulds.

The analog hearing aid picks up and amplifies all sounds that impinge on it, including *unwanted noise*. Therefore, a good acoustic environment is still a primary requisite for deriving good benefit for classroom listening. A sound-measuring device called the "Surveyor" can be used in the classroom to measure the level of the amplified signal reaching the child's ear at a distance of 6 feet from the teacher. The teacher has to attach the receiver of the hearing aid to the instrument and the instrument reads the value of the level of the sound. This level should be high enough for the child to hear the speech from the location of the teacher during class. If the level is not

> high enough, the distance between the teacher and child can be reduced or the teacher could speak more loudly if possible. Such simple devices offer a quick way to know whether the child in the classroom is hearing what is being taught. Digital hearing aids provide good S/N ratio even in noisy surroundings as they incorporate *noise suppression* technology; thus enabling good listening even in a classroom with poor acoustics.

Some individuals with hearing impairment have very little residual hearing and receive little or no benefit from hearing aids. For this relatively small group of profoundly hearing impaired individuals, hope has been provide by a prosthetic device called the *cochlear implant.* The cochlear implant functions by bypassing the defective inner ear to directly provide *electrical* stimulation to the nerve fibers, thus enabling the sensation of hearing. It has external and internal components. A *microphone* placed on the ear picks up the sounds in the environment and converts it into electrical energy. The *speech processor* analyzes and codes this information and sends it to a *transmitter coil* placed on the head of the user. A *receiver coil* that is surgically implanted under the skin receives this information and then transmits it to the *electrodes* placed in the cochlear of the inner ear. These directly stimulate the nerve fibers. The cochlear implant does not restore normal hearing. Candidates for the implant must satisfy strict *screening* criteria. After implantation as well the individual requires to undergo a rigorous *rehabilitation* programme. The results with implanted children have been very encouraging with respect to ease of listening and speech and language development. Although such children get a *better listening* experience than hearing aid users, environmental noise in the classroom affects them too. Therefore improving *acoustic conditions* in the classroom and decreasing teacher-student distance can further improve S/N ratio for these children.

In recent years technology has provided a range of devices

and systems designed for individual users to *supplement* the capabilities and benefits provided by the personal hearing aid. These devices are identified as *assistive listening devices* (ALDs) and listening systems. Some are designed to surmount specific listening difficulties that arise from distance, noise and reverberation effects. Others are intended to draw attention to events occurring in the environment or to provide means of receiving information other than through sound transmission. Devices such as the vibrator alarm clock which indicates alarm through vibration and various alerting devices are vital for promoting the independence of a person with hearing impairment.

The main goals of ALDs are to provide wide frequency range amplification with *fidelity*, maintain at the listener's ear a constant *optimal S/N ratio* and eliminate distortion from reverberation, and allow the listener to hear not only the speaker but also *him/herself* and others. To achieve these goals, these systems function in the following way:

(*a*) *Receive* the acoustic signal with minimal acoustic masking or distortion.

(*b*) *Replicate* the acoustic pattern as an electrical analog or copy.

(*c*) *Amplify* the patterned signal well above the background noise level.

(*d*) *Convert* the signal into a form that allows it to travel to a receiver sensitive to that medium.

(*e*) *Reconvert* the signal to an electrical analog that can be amplified, shaped, and controlled to meet the listener's needs.

(*f*) *Convert* the amplified electrical signal back into sound for delivery to the ear.

The most widely used special amplification system in all types of educational settings is the *FM system*. The system is comparable to a miniature radio station. The teacher broadcasts to a child or a group of children on a specific FM radio frequency; the children tune into the teacher's station on their wearable radio receivers. The teacher wears a lightweight *microphone* hung on the chest that picks up speech in close proximity to the mouth, ensuring a constant high S/N ratio. The microphone is connected via a cord to a small *transmitter* that may be clipped anywhere on the clothing. The signal is converted to an electrical analog, amplified and then patterned on to an FM radio signal that is broadcast into the environment. The child wears a lightweight *FM radio receiver* tuned to the frequency of the teacher's transmitter. This picks up the signal, converts into an equivalent electrical pattern, amplifies it and shapes it according to the child's needs. FM systems provide greatest *mobility* and *flexibility* to the listener in any situation indoors or outdoors at ranges from 3 to 500 feet.

Another widely used amplification system is the *loop induction system*. This system was also developed with the goal of providing *mobility* to a child in a classroom while providing favourable *S/N ratio*. The system consists of a *microphone* connected by a wire to an *amplifier*. A long wire extends from the amplifier. This wire may be looped around any area of space. The area may be as small as the head and shoulder of a person (neck loop) or an armchair in front of the TV or it might be much larger. The wire, under its insulation is wound around a *magnetic core*. This core sets up a magnetic field around it. When current flows through the wire coiled around the core magnet, the pattern of its magnetic field changes, mimicking the pattern changes of the electrical current. These changes can be picked up by a personal hearing aid that has a *telephone circuit*.

The use of the personal amplification systems and listening devices such as those discussed here make the auditory environment more *accessible* to a child with hearing impairment in the inclusive set up. However, effective use of these systems can be ensured only through adequate support and co-operation from the personnel in the inclusive set up. The *teachers* and other adults who are in contact with the child must all be familiar with the operation of the system and the appropriate settings for the child using it. The teacher should also realize that despite using the different amplification systems there will be limitations to the child's hearing abilities and therefore, he/she will require more inputs compared to the hearing children.

Besides amplification devices there are other technological aids that can be adapted for use with persons having hearing impairment. Even a device like an *overhead projector* or power point presentations can be of great help to the child with hearing impairment with respect to making the material accessible to the child for learning. One technology of converting speech to text is the *C print technology*. This is a note taking system. In this a transcriber types whatever the teacher is saying, on a special laptop that has reduced key strokes. This is displayed as text on a screen which the person with hearing impairment can read. The student gets an experience of the real time lecture with all the information. A print out of the lecture can also be taken. *Tele-captioning* devices can also be used very successfully with persons having hearing impairment. Real time tele-captioning is also available with some service providers. *Multi- lingual SMS* facility is another technology that holds promise for persons with hearing impairment as many of them are not educated in English. It facilitates communication with other hearing impaired persons as well. In this the subscriber sends an SMS of the chosen language, typed in English, to a service provider. This text is dynamically converted into the text of the language of choice and sent back to the subscriber who then forwards the message wherever he/she wants. It is already in use and can be used with phone handsets that have picture messaging facilities. *Tele rehabilitation* is another area which has wide application in India. A family or child living in a remote place can access rehabilitation facilities without having to come to the centre.

Assistive devices should be chosen according the individual's needs which include his/her lifestyle and listening requirements. Advice regarding the most suitable device for a child can be sought from an *audiologist*. The audiologist will use the data from assessments of the child to decide which type of amplification and assistive devices are most suited to the child. She or he can also recommend the settings for the device and how it should be used in day-to-day activities by the person with hearing impairment. The school authorities must remain in touch with the audiologist and ensure that the child is referred regularly for all the necessary follow-up evaluations. Schools should also avail the services of a special resource teacher to ensure that the child is given any special help that is required for his/her progress.

Thus, the role of technology and its contribution towards inclusive education and rehabilitation of children with hearing impairment cannot be undermined. But remember *the best of technology can be a waste at the hands of an uninformed and inexperienced user.*

REFERENCES

1. Berg, F.S. (1993), "*Acoustics and Sound Systems in Schools*", Singular Publishing Gp. Inc.: San Diego, California.
2. Katz, J. (1994), "*Handbook of Clinical Audiology*", 4th edn., Williams and Wilkins: Baltimore, Maryland.
3. Sanders, D.A. (1993), "*Management of Hearing Handicap Infants to Elderly*", 3rd edn., Prentice Hall, Englewood Cliffs, New Jersey.

6

VOCATIONAL EDUCATION AND REHABILITATION

Ms. Annie Shyam

The Persons with Disability Act on full participation and equality of people with disabilities draw attention to the fact that social and physical barriers are formidable to persons with disabilities. This makes their opportunities for education, vocational training and employment very minimal. Further reducing the vision of integration into society.

We have all recognized the role of vocational education but most often get struck at the same level of vocational training with the same skills being repeated.

An important prerequisite for anyone to have opportunities in life is education. Vocational Education increases the opportunity for Persons with Disability not as an end in itself, but towards the goal of appropriate employment.

At the Spastics Society of Tamil Nadu an affirmative action to ensure access to quality vocational education and training was started (including women with disability. The model that SPASTN devised is called 'ABLE ART', which is a job oriented training programme which is both a training centre and production workshop for young adults with multiple disability. The axis of our project is the individual. It:

- Empowers young adults with disability to become

financially independent. Identifies, improves and sustains vocational skills in persons with disability.
- Facilitates opportunities for self-employment.
- Brings about social integration.
- Cultivates motivation, reliability and acceptance of constructive criticism.

The training areas are: 1. Food Production, 2. Printing, 3. Desk Top Publishing, 4. Tailoring, 5. Office Management, and 6. Weaving.

Each of the trainers are technical experts with a good knowledge of the "philosophy and principles of special education on the different disabilities". They cater to the training needs following the respective pre-set curriculum and syllabus with an evaluation and monitoring system. Sensitization of potential employers in disability issues is an essential and on-going process. This together with practical placements begins to give the trainees the first experience of independence, and self-esteem.

The SPASTN model is Empowerment through Employment and ultimately social integration.

7

ROLE OF NGO'S IN REHABILITATION PROGRAMME

A Case Study of Sunday School, Project of Friend's Society, A Non-Governmental Organization, Baroda (Gujarat)

Ankur Saxena

INTRODUCTION

The Evolution of NGO's

As globalization and international trade impact, societies, NGO's have become increasingly influential in world affairs. They are consulted by governments as well as international organizations like the United Nations which have created associative status for them. There are now ten- thousands of NGO's in the world operating in the most countries. These organizations are not directly affiliated with any national government but often have a significant impact on the social, economic and political activity of the country or region involved.

The development of NGOs can be placed within the context of historical evolutionary development so as to clarify their current position. Korten (1987) describes this development of NGOs in three phases or generations, beginning with a focus on relief and welfare, then moving towards local self-reliance and finally to sustainable systems development (Table 1).

Table 1: Three Generations of Non-Government Organizational Development

Generation	*First*	*Second*	*Third*
Defining features	Relief and welfare	Small-scale self-reliant local development	Sustainable systems development
Problem definition	Shortages of goods and services	Local inertia	Institution and policy constraints
Time frame	Immediate	Project life	Indefinite, long-term
Spatial scope	Individual or family	Neighbourhood or village	Region or nation
Chief actors	NGO	NGO + beneficiary organizations	All public and private institutions that define the relevant system
Development orientation	Starving children	Community self-help initiatives	Interdependent systems
Management orientation	Logistics management	Project management	Strategic management

Source: Korten,1987, Marielle Snel, *Indian Journal of Social Work*, Vol. 62 Issue 4, Oct. 2001

With the outset of independence, India rose from an oblivion and set afoot in an era of development pipeline. The ideology which marked the beginning of the development process in this country was the "Socialistic Pattern of Society". As the parliamentary form of government consolidated itself the State became the major source of support for the existence of NGO sector and their ameliorating ability for the plights of the poor. Despite the fact the NGO sector have been supported materially and non-materially, the nature of funding are definitely posing major challenges before the state.

India has a glorious tradition of organizing voluntary work for social good. NGOs, are thus, no more regarded marginal actors they were perceived to be through the 1970s and much of the 1980s. In the changed situation, they are rather considered to be the key players who can have a substantial impact on development.

In line with the growing critiques of the State and market mechanisms, NGOs are considered as the "third sector" possessing a vast potential for change and development by virtue of their comparative advantages.

CASE STUDY OF SUNDAY SCHOOL PROJECT OF FRIENDS SOCIETY

History

Friends Society is a Non-government Organization actively functioning since August 1969. The society is registered under Public Trusts Act 1950 (Regn. No. Baroda/F-109). Friends Society stands for the mobilization and rehabilitation of voluntary efforts of persons, especially the differently abled persons for conducting need based community service projects and developing their personality and rehabilitating them.

Projects of Friends Society

- Cheer-up
- Sunday School
- Blood Donation Programme
- Child Health Care Centre
- Youth Club
- Public Reading Room and Library
- Balwadi
- Income Generation Programme
- Programme for Educated Housewives
- Programme for University Youth
- Senior Citizen Programme
- Mother Health Care Centre

Sunday School

It is Non-institutionalized differently abled school for children of the Baroda city. The main objective of this school is provision of supplementary education, medical rehabilitation, mobility acceleration and social integration of its beneficiaries. This school started in 1978. At present there are about 60 differently abled children attending the Sunday School the age group of these differently abled children are from 6 to 12 years and the classification of the children is as follows:

Classification of Different Abled Children at Sunday School

Sl. No.	*Number of Children*	*Category*
1.	40	Physically Handicapped
2.	03	Mentally Retarded and Physically Handicapped
3.	17	Mentally Retarded
Total	60	

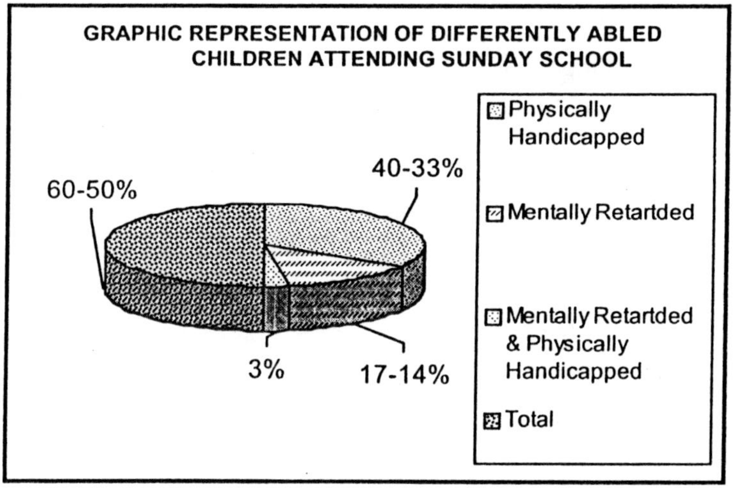

Activities/Programmes Undertaken for Rehabilitation

- Medical rehabilitation is done through physiotherapy, check ups by orthopaedic surgeons and paediatricians.
- Counselling sessions for family members of the children with guidance in correct handling and child rearing practices.
- Educational activities includes exposure to banks, railway station, yoga camps etc.
- Art therapy like drawing painting, clay modelling, mehandi work, origami is carried out to improve the fine motor co-ordination of the children.
- Monthly parents meeting regarding rehabilitation and development status of their child.

FAMILY AND DISABILITY

A family's functioning results from the interaction of their beliefs, their resources, and the unique manner in which they respond to mundane and critical events in their lives. Some of the areas in which families manifest diverse views include parenting styles, beliefs about causes and consequences of disability, concerns about seeking help and relationships with medical or social service personnel.

Understanding a family's beliefs and concerns about disability, health care, and involvement in bureaucratic systems is vital in order to involve the family in an assessment of its strengths and weaknesses and in developing appropriate interventions. If the family is not included when the therapeutic regime is established, they may have little reason to support and administer one more set of activities imposed by people who may not be viewed as having their best interests at heart (Alston & Turner, 1994).

ISSUES IN WORKING WITH FAMILIES

- Recognize and value the family's cultural and ethnic background.
- Identify and respect religious beliefs and customs.
- Realize that the family's views of the causes and consequences of disability can affect their willingness to participate in prescribed activities and programmes.
- Develop an extensive and current base of resources to provide support for the person with the disability and the family.

OTHER SPECIAL ACTIVITIES CARRIED OUT FOR SUNDAY SCHOOL CHILDREN FOR THEIR REHABILITATION

- Activities for daily living (ADL).
- Instrumental activities for daily living.
- Reading writing and arithmetic skill development.

- Extra curricular activities like support, culture, vocational, and social activities.
- Independent living skill development.
- Community integration.

1. **Habit training**—This emphasises per personal cleanliness and toilet habits, care of property (such as crayon, paste, toys, dress, etc.), food habits, health habits, etc.
2. **Social experiences**—Presentation and discussion of good relationship involving father, mother, sibling, school-mates, neighbours, visitors and others.
3. **Sense training**—This includes recognition of names when called, matching shapes, colours and size, sound, picture completion, puzzles, observation of natural phenomena (sky, cloud, trees, sun, moon, rain etc.), recognition of objects by sound, smell, touch, taste, colour and so on. All these are taught in the form of games with special apparatus.
4. **Speech training**—Speech is a social passport. As most of them have speech difficulty, emphasis should be laid on clear enunciation, correlation of baby talk, broken language, lisping, stammering and other speech defects.
5. **Muscular co-ordination**—This includes rhythmic exercises, dancing, marching, outdoor games, exercises like walking on balanced rail, playing on swings, seesaw etc.
6. **Nature study**—Acquaintance with common pets, flowers, trees, seasonal weather changes. It should be based on objective training by talking them to zoo, botanical garden etc.
7. **Pre-reading activities**—Orientation and kinaesthetic visual development, language growth, visual discrimination, auditory discrimination, promotion of thinking power. All these activities conducted in the form of varieties of games with special apparatus, can be used

as the foundation for training in vocabulary and background of experience.

8. **Participation in social and civic activities**—This is most fundamental in the education of normal children also, but more so in the case of the mentally deficient, because public opinion about their future is so fatalistic that they are barred from talking interest in social life and are least encouraged to participate in its.
9. **Music, percussion band, arts and crafts, etc.**—The mentally defective are not without potentialities. They have some specific ability in music or arts and crafts which, if developed can make them self-supporting. It is the function of the psychological services of the school to find out their latent potentialities and direct the teachers accordingly. They also serve as emotional stabilizers; children derive emotional satisfaction from them.
10. **Reading, writing and arithmetic**—Progress in these subjects is very very slow, but if taught in an attractive and interesting way with concrete objects, they do show some progress. However, these subjects should be taught only to the extent that they may be useful in their practical life.

ROLE OF NGO IN REHABILITATION PROGRAMMES

In rehabilitation of mental retardation in India majority of population live in villages. Due to poor literacy and lackness of awareness they are unknown about the schemes of Government for them and their mentally retarded children so in this situation it is important that NGO play their role significantly and NGO can play following role:

- NGO you should know about all the available scheme of the Government of India.
- NGO should be aware of all the acts and legislations for ensuring the right of disabled people.
- NGO should integrate the disabled people in the society

by the acting as a bridge between Government and mentally retarded children.

- NGO can strengthen the hands of the Government by coordinating with various Government departments to ensure that disabled people in their area are given all the benefits at Government programmes.
- NGO can help to create good awareness about the right of the disabled.
- NGO can help to prevent the discrimination in society against the disabled people.
- NGO can mobilize the disabled people to get assistance from programme available for the disabled people.

REFERENCES

Biswas Manju 1980 : "*Mentally Retarded and Normal Children*", Sterling Publication, New Delhi, p. 11.

Government of India, 1988 : "*Mental Retardation—A Manual for Guidance Counsellor*", published by NIMH, Secundrabad, pp. 1-3.

Government of India : "*Mental Retardation (Handbook)*", published by National Trust, New Delhi, p. 6.

Government of India : "*What We Can Do to Insure the Sure the Right of Disabled People*", published by National Trust, New Delhi, pp. 6-7.

Government of India : "*What We Can Do to Insure the Sure the Right of Disabled People*", published by National Trust, New Delhi, p. 14.

Government of India 1966 : "*Mental Retardation in India—A Report of the First All India Conference on Mental Retardation*", Indraprasth Publication, New Delhi, p. 19.

Government of India 1966 : "*Mental Retardation in India—A Report of the First All India Conference on Mental Retardation*", Indraprasth Publication, New Delhi, p. 78.

Government of India 1966 : "*Mental Retardation in India—A Report of the First All India Conference on Mental Retardation*", Indraprasth Publication, New Delhi, pp. 151-153.

Government of India 1988 : "*Mental Retardation—A Manual for Psychologist*", published by NIMH, Secundrabad, pp. 13-16.

Government of India, 2000 : "*How to Identify the Person with Autism, Cerebral Palsy Mental Retardation and Multiple Disabilities*", published by National Trust, New Delhi, pp. 1-6.

Gupta and Yadav 2002 : "*Management of Mental Retardation*", Spandan (Journal), Vol. 13, New Delhi, pp. 64-97.

Kadushin A. & Martin A.J. : Child Welfare Services (4th Edition), Macmillan Publication, 1988 (U.S.A.).

Kapoor A.K. & Sng D. : Rural Development Through NGO's (1997), Ravat Publications, New Delhi.

Mohsini B.R. & Gandhi P.K. : The Phy Handicapped and Government (1985), Seema Publications, Delhi.

Quinn P. Understanding Disability, A Lifespan Approach (1998), Sage Publications, New Delhi.

Rao L. Govinda 2002 : "*March Challenge in Mental Retardation—Quality Concern*", KARAVALAMBAN (official news letter) published by NIMH, Secundrabad, pp. 1-3.

Sen Anima 1990 : "*Mental Handicapped Among Rural Children*", Sterling Publication, New Delhi, pp. 78-81.

Wardia A.K. 1996 : "*The Handicapped Children*", Royal Publication, Bombay, pp. 30-33.

8

MANPOWER DEVELOPMENT FOR DISABILITY REHABILITATION
Need for Research

Dr. K. S. Prema

Rehabilitation of individuals with disability in India dates back to many decades. In the ancient period, depending on the social and cultural beliefs that prevailed in the community, the individuals with disability were either neglected or protected. However, in the recent times, a strong need has been felt by the society at large to implement rehabilitation measures as a strategy to make them self-reliant and productive, which would in-turn improve country's resources. In order to carry out this Herculean task so that the requirements of individuals with disability can be met, it is necessary to develop adequate manpower with a scientific approach.

Development of scientific manpower involves investment in higher education and training. With the advancement of science, technology and health care, there is an increased need for specialized training and education in almost all the disciplines, rehabilitation science posing the maximum challenge. The Health Survey and Planning Committee (1961) recognized the need for manpower resource development in most of the areas, Speech Pathology and Audiology, being one among them.

The present paper attempts to discuss the current trends in manpower generation in the speech and hearing discipline. A brief review of small-scale research studies in manpower development is also made with implications for scientific approach to manpower development.

A. TRENDS IN MANPOWER GENERATION IN SPEECH AND HEARING

Historically, manpower generation in speech and hearing has its roots in deaf education, that gradually shaped initially into diploma in Audiology and Speech Therapy (Jagadeesh, 1993), followed by post-graduation in speech and hearing for non-speech and hearing graduates and finally the graduation culminating into other higher degree courses in two major cities of India (Rathna, 1993). Currently, there are various courses available at different levels directly or indirectly related to the discipline of speech and hearing such as,

- Diploma in Communication Disorders
- Diploma in Hearing aid servicing and Earmould technology
- B.Sc (Speech and Hearing)
- M.Sc (Speech and Hearing)
- Ph.D (Speech and Hearing)
- PG Diploma in Special Education (Hearing Impairment) –to be initiated
- B.Ed (deaf)
- D.Ed (deaf)
- B.M.R (MR)
- B.R.Sc (Rehabilitation sciences)
- M.R.Sc (Rehabilitation sciences)

Within the discipline of speech and hearing, many specialized courses are included at the graduate and post-graduate curriculum, thus enhancing the scope of the discipline. The flow chart indicates a few specialized branches.

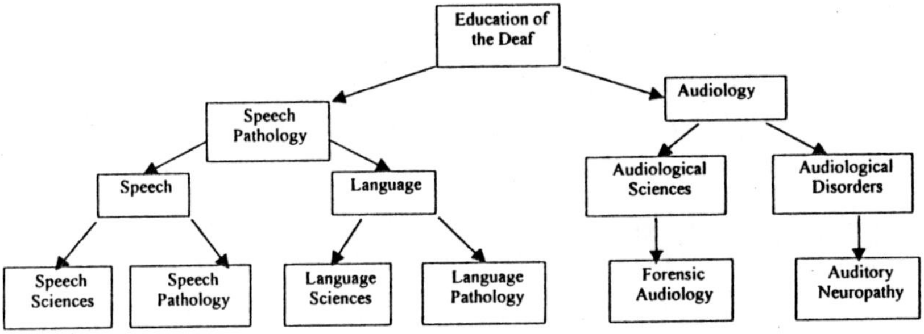

.....and many more specialized branches in each of the above.

B. MANPOWER IN SPEECH AND HEARING *vs.* POPULATION WITH DISABILITY

Manpower Generation

To date, there are abo ut 16 institutions (See Appendix 1 for addresses) offering degree in Speech and Hearing at different levels. To the best of the knowledge of the author, an approximate number of 300 candidates graduate at different levels in the Speech and Hearing discipline (Earlier the number was too small. With the emergence of more number of institutions in the past 5-6 years, the number is slightly increased). This is a very meagre number compared to the enormity of population with Speech and Hearing discipline.

Extent of Disability in India

The NSSO survey (1991) estimate indicates that around 1.9 per cent (16.15 million) persons have physical/sensory disability including speech and hearing disabilities apart from others. The report also mentioned that the prevalence is more in rural areas than in urban cities. There is a general agreement among the professionals that the NSSO estimate would not have covered the entire range of conditions (not yet identified as disability by PwD) who require rehabilitation measures, suggesting that the estimated figures are far below the reality.

Considering the disproportion between the manpower need and manpower generation, it is high time we plan alternate strategies and schemes with sound scientific base to set the pace for the new millennium.

C. LOSS OF MANPOWER DUE TO BRAIN DRAIN

It is a well-known fact that although there is an intensive need in our own country for para-medical professionals including Speech and Hearing, majority of our graduates and post-graduates seek appointment for reasons best known to everybody (Fig. 1). An estimate of students graduated from AIISH but staying abroad is around 22 per cent, which is high enough to caution everybody considering the very low percentage of manpower generation in speech and hearing to the existing high prevalence figures. The disproportion between manpower requirement and manpower availability (although trained in India) is increasing beyond imagination. An estimate of expenditure incurred by a government-training institute with sufficient infrastructure for training a speech and hearing professional is reported to be around Rs. 3 lakh/student (Savithri, 2003).

Despite huge investment, is there a gainful return to our country? This is an issue to be viewed in serious terms.

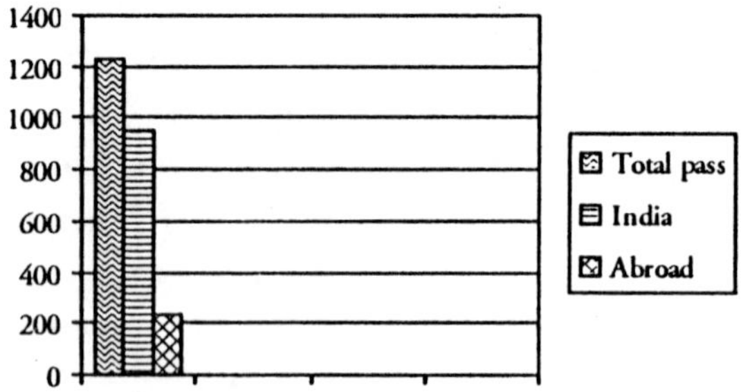

Figure 1: Brain-Drain from AIISH

D. RELEVANCE OF SKILL TRAINING IN CURRICULA FOR MANPOWER DEVELOPMENT

Programmes for manpower development emerge because of practical needs. Majority of these programmes, at one stage or the other either become dilute or become too rigid, thus paving way for unrealistic career training. Two important issues need to be examined in this perspective.

1. A gross look at the courses and the practical skill imparted for graduates and post-graduates of speech and hearing suggests that the candidates are not exposed to fields and hence, lack hands-on experience with the practical difficulties generally faced in semi-urban and rural situations while dealing with the population with disability. With the objective of improvising on this perspective, an internship of one year is, however, made compulsory for speech and hearing graduates. Paradoxically, from the candidates point of view, it is a blessing-in-disguise as most of the students would easily fetch 16 years of education and find it a smooth sweep to western countries, thus paving way to increased brain-drain. Again, report of one of the projects recently completed (Savithri, 2003) suggests that there is no match between the type of training imparted and the nature of work being done by the candidates. Irrespective of their Bachelor's, Master's or Doctoral training, it is found that majority is employed in clinical set-up (both within India and abroad. Clinical work—37 per cent); In Research Activity, only—3 per cent; Teaching—7 per cent; Administration—1.3 per cent; Not working—5 per cent; Not known—47per cent. When a candidate does not utilize the skill acquired, cost effectivity of the huge investment in training becomes highly questionable. This issue needs to be scrutinized.

2. Within the discipline of Speech Pathology and Audiology, there is a major distinction that needs to be considered in training programmes. While the practice of Speech-Language Pathology is less expensive materially but requires much more manpower being ***man-hour intensive*** (Personal communication with Dr. Karanth, her letter to RCI dated 18-1-2002), the practice of Audiology requires considerable initial investment but is far less manpower dependent—a fact that has not been considered in our manpower development policy. "By compulsorily clubbing both areas of training at all levels and listing staff and infrastructure requirements to meet needs of both disciplines without taking this divide into consideration, we are setting needlessly high standards for our training institutions. This cannot but be a hindrance in taking the discipline forward in the quickest possible time."

Research Needs in Manpower Generation

1. Urgent need for Central Rehabilitation Registry so that manpower development could be approached through sound scientific foothold.
2. Unit cost of training rehabilitation professionals should be worked out for both government and private institutions in order to economize on the huge investment by the country.
3. The benefits to the country in terms of returns by the trained professionals through clinical services/research/ manpower support in training programmes should be worked out. The concerned council should insist that precise documentation of work be maintained and submitted by the professionals to the concerned authorities for the needful. Such data could be subjected to fruitful analysis to establish scientific database for manpower development.

4. Training programmes should be tailored to suit the needs of our community instead of mimicking the course curricula of western countries.
5. Manpower generation programmes should keep cost effectivity as one of the crucial factors. Consequently, instead of imparting training for 4-6 years at graduate level and post-graduate levels, who, barely take-up any clinical or community service in rural areas after obtaining degrees (where the need is maximum), empowerment of ancillary professionals such as teachers, nurses, grass roots level workers should be planned. Keeping the nature of work to be performed by each of the above group, differential training should be given to meet the requirement of varied clinical population. For example, matrimonial bureaus and marital counsellors should be sensitized towards the genetic causes of various disability so that they can facilitate prevention of disability per se.
6. *Empowerment of mothers/caregivers* of children with disability should be prioritized as the service provided by a mother to her child is beyond comparison to that provided by a professional—both in terms of time and dedication. While a mother/caregiver, when trained would involve with her child for a maximum of 12 hours a day (leaving the sleeping hours a child) at low-cost/ no-cost basis, a professional would certainly demand a few hundreds of rupees for the same amount of time that he/she would spend with the child, thus making the service not accessible by majority of needy people. It is apt for RCI to envisage programmes to empower this special group in order to beat the mismatch between the professionals and the clinical population, which would also be highly cost-effective for our developing country.

To summarize,

"All educational programmes for which resources are required should be subject to the test of relevance of skill and training they impart." (Rao,1966)

Human Resource Development should be gainful. Investment should be critically evaluated.

Higher the level of specialization, greater is the investment involved. Hence, it is necessary to investigate whether their duties are commensurate with their levels of training.

Empowerment of different categories of people should be targeted.

APPENDIX 1

- All India Institute of Speech and Hearing (AIISH), Manasgangothri, Mysore
- Ali Yavar Jung National Institute for Hearing Handicapped (AYJNIHH), Kishenchand Marg, Bandra (W), Mumbai
- College of Audiology and Speech Therapy, TN Medical College Nair Hospital, A.L.Nair Road, Mumbai
- Dr. SRC Institute of Speech & Hearing, Hennur Road, Bangalore
- MVS College of Speech & Hearing, Vidya Nagar, Panjimoger, Mangalore
- College of Allied Health Sciences, Manipal 576 119, Karnataka
- College of Speech & Hearing, Sri Ramachandra Medical College & Research Institute, Porur, Chennai
- Department of ENT—RUAS, AIIMS, Ansari Nagar, New Delhi
- Department of ENT, PGIMER, Sector 12, Chandigarh
- AYJNIHH Regional Centre, NIOH Campus, Bon Hoogly, B.T. Road, Calcutta
- AYJNIHH, SRC, NIMH Campus, Manovikas Nagar P.O, Bowenapally, Secunderabad
- Sweekar Rehabilitation Institute, Upkar Circle, Picket, Secunderabad
- Indian Institute of Health Education & Research, Health Institute Road, Near Central Jail, Beur, Patna
- ICCONS, TC 6/1969, Prasanth Nagar, Ulloor, Medical College, P.O, Trivandrum
- NISH, 17/1883 Palace Road, Poojapura, Trivandrum
- JSS College of Speech & Hearing, JSS Medical College Campus, Bannimantapa, Mysore

9

TELE-REHABILITATION

R. Rangasayee

The aim of this presentation is to draw the attention of this august gathering to the emerging facility of Tele-rehabilitation and to create an environment for collective effort, in this area for the benefit of the target population in India and elsewhere.

BACKGROUND

Developments linked to Electronics, Information Technology and Market Economy have vastly influenced the life of people with disabilities, too.

India has been a fore runner in mending the emerging technologies and professional practices to meet the needs of persons suffering from Speech and Hearing handicap. These efforts have also been time and again quoted and lauded allover the World. Such efforts include camp approach, effective use of analog body level hearing aid, mass hearing screening through Radio and Television, innovative developments in low cost/no cost hearing screening practices, development of solar charger for use with body level hearing aid, indigenous hand held hearing screener which could also be used for screening infants, use of modified CROS hearing aids which brought National Technology Award to its inventor Shri A.K. Sinha of NIHH Regional Centre in Kolkata and developments of Language tests and Articulation tests through use of unique methodology to meet the multilingual needs.

DEFINITION

Tele-rehabilitation is an emerging technology that needs to be addressed by all of us as professionals and the areas of its application have to be explored. Tele-rehabilitation programme seeks to use Video Camera, video phone, Computers, Internet and Telephone to improve the quality of life of disabled persons. This technology can be used to provide a range of rehabilitation services to beneficiaries who live a distance away from rehabilitation experts.

We are in the age of speed. Tele technology has emerged in this era to meet our demand to reach beneficiaries with speed, accuracy and effectiveness in terms of rehabilitation of persons with disabilities.

SCOPE

Application of tele-rehabilitation can include screening, diagnosis, therapy/intervention, supervision, training of trainers and research. Emerging areas in tele-rehabilitation programme include the following: tele-assessment, tele-speech therapy, tele-coaching, tele-therapeutic play, tele-clinic visit, tele -group therapy, tele- home care and tele- monitoring.

TELE UTILITY IN INDIA

In India there are over 9,425,05 Internet users as on March, 2000. 4,89,60,414 number of telephone lines as on 31-10-2002. 18,84,311 number of Mobile phone users as on 31-10-2002. The use of such connectivity grows exponentially. Therefore the information technology facilities are bound to grow. When the first e-mail connection was established, it did not make any meaning; but when the second person got connection, value was added to both. As the number of users increase, the value addition grows exponentially. Thus the emphasis on making adequate use of this technology for reaching the persons with disability, is well justified.

HEARING HANDICAPPED IN INDIA

There are 4.482 million persons with hearing impairment in India as per National Sample Survey Organization (NSSO) 1991 survey. Approximately 25,000 children are born with hearing impairment every year. Our capacity is grossly inadequate and not more than 20 per cent of the needy have been reached. The Institute based rehabilitation, the Camp Approach, as well as Community Based Rehabilitation can further be strengthened through tele-rehabilitation procedures.

WORK DONE ELSEWHERE

In Developed Economy, efforts have been initiated particularly in helping persons with Hearing Handicap, Learning Disability, Autism, Dysphagia and Stuttering. A web based science teaching programme for the deaf has been successfully studied by Charles Bandara (American Annals of the Deaf No.3, 2002). Gery Punch (Oct 2002) in Audiology Today has also underlined the need to use this technology.

ACTION PLAN FOR INDIA

If we can ponder over on the immediate application, the following areas are worth exploring without any advanced technology or software needs.

(i) **Telephone:** Use of telephone/mobile phone for the purposes of awareness, guidance and counselling

(ii) **Video Camera and Video Phone:** Video Camera can be used in Store and Access mode. For *e.g.* Disability Certification is a major on going activity in the country.

As Professionals, we all know that there are selected groups of persons with disability including hearing handicapped who have visible observable handicap even in the eyes of a lay person. Such conditions can be identified wherein a less trained person can store the necessary behaviour/ physical appearance on a digital Camera and later access it to the experts sitting at Headquarters through Internet, for the purposes of certification.

(iii) **Use of Internet and e-mail services:** The website and e-mail are already being used by many of the individuals and institutions in the country. For *e.g.* the Website *www.ayjnihh.org* and www.iobsfordeaf.com are 2 sites that provide referrals and guidance. *www.ayjnihh.org* also has Chat and e-mail facility. We do have a number of clients seeking guidance through this facility on a regular basis.

(iv) **Commercialisation:** The process of commercialization needs to be defined and described.

RESEARCH NEEDS

Newer areas that can be foreseen include hearing testing through the website, conducting ABR and Electro acoustic analysis of hearing aid through a suitable web based technology and interface. Perhaps if we have the peripheral terminals which include probes / electrodes and a monitoring head, the main processing unit should be made available through the web which would save cost on infrastructure, maintenance, in addition to bringing down the cost of the facility. On similar lines, in the field of Biochemistry, the application of chip technology is expected to make the entire gamut of biochemical tests just at the cost of 2 U.S. dollars. The wave pattern in the ABR may not be I to V or VII but it may be different when an interface is used to enable use through the website.

CONCLUSION

Tele-rehabilitation has great potential to increase the reach of an individual expert world over. If you are good, people from allover the world will consult you by paying your fees through credit card. You may not really even need a clinic. You can just have a tele-clinic, sitting in your own room and still be a consultant and a therapist to hundreds and thousands, allover the world. If one would endeavour SWOT analysis, there is more of strength and opportunities than weakness and threats in the application of tele-rehabilitation to an individual, to an agency as well as to an Institution. We are in the process of developing a tele-rehabilitation package under Indo-US Project.

NIHH is open to collaborate with Institutions in strengthening the approaches in reaching the unreached persons in this country and to improve the quality of services to people with hearing handicap.

10

IMPLEMENTATION STRATEGY OF VOCATIONAL TRAINING FOR THE DISABLED

M. Radha Ruckmani

INTRODUCTION

The term Vocational Rehabilitation normally has been understood as part of continuous and coordinated process of Rehabilitation, which involves—

- Vocational guidance
- Vocational training

Selective placement the end result of 'rehabilitation' is not only securing employment suitable to the capacity of the person and making best use of his/her residual ability and skill but also helping the disabled to retain the employment.

VOCATIONAL TRAINING NEED TODAY

1. Changes of education policy
2. Provide systematic training
3. Provide opportunities
4. Orient instructors
5. Establish technical instructors
6. Strengthen the existing training centres

7. Modify the general trend
8. Training related industrial work

VOCATIONAL GUIDANCE

Vocational guidance is the process of assisting an individual in solving the problem of choice of career options based on his aptitude, interest *vis-a-vis* employment opportunities. The process includes

- Interview
- Examination of his records including scholastic, medical records
- Ascertainment of the interest, abilities, characteristic through various tests
- Family background
- Analysis of his physical capacity and occupational requirement

BASIC PRINCIPLES

- Principles, measurers and methods applied in training
- Training should continue
- Same condition as non-disabled persons
- Special training arrangement
- Training is wasted unless it leads to placement

TECHNIQUES AND METHODS

- Training should be conducted in and efficient business
- Systematic analysis of the operation, skills and knowledge
- Safety factors are necessary
- The level of skills to be attained.
- Prefer the production work
- Give practical exercise
- Arrangement should be satisfactory
- Adequate supervision

SUITABLE TRAINER

- Specially trained and multiskilled
- Experienced field work
- Knowledge in disability

SELECTION OF OCCUPATION

- Trade should be economically suitable
- Rural areas—agricultural training
- Limited training—factories and companies.

MATCHING THE TRAINER WITH JOB

Here are some basic principles in placing the disabled:

1. The disabled person must be also to meet the physical requirements of the job with any modification that may be necessary and practicable.
2. His aim should be to place the disabled person in work where he or she can utilize residual abilities (*i.e.*, intelligence, educational attainments, qualifications skills, etc.,) to the fullest.
3. The disabled person must not be a hazard to him/herself.
4. The disabled person must not jeopardize the safety of others.
5. Placement should be the logical conclusion to any vocational rehabilitation programme.
6. The situation of the job, working conditions and environment, are as important as the job itself.
7. Segregation of the disabled in their work should be avoided if at all possible.
8. Placing in employment should be on the grounds of suitability for the job, not sympathy.
9. Medical practice usually requires that medical information should be regarded as confidential the employer being

told only in lay terms of any limitations or employment capacity and any risks to be avoided.

CONCLUSION

- Educational institutions should take up systematic vocational guidance.
- Prevocational training should provide wide range of experience and assist to acquire good work, habits and attitudes that are critical for job success.
- Every school should have a social worker to help the school leavers to find satisfactory jobs and follow-ups.

Higher education should assist to develop a core of specific knowledge and skills. The existing vocational training centres should and courses related to information technology, in view of the changes in the present industrial scenery and in the structural changes in the world of employment.

11

RESEARCH NEEDS IN REHABILITATION WITH SPECIAL REFERENCE TO SPEECH, LANGUAGE AND HEARING DISORDERS

Dr. Y.V. Geetha

Rehabilitation aims at using various measures at reducing the impact of the disability for an individual, enabling him or her to achieve independence, social integration, a better quality of life and self-actualization. It includes not only training of persons with disability but also interventions in the general systems of society, adaptations of the environment and protection of human rights.

Speech and hearing disability poses a greater threat to the individuals afflicted in terms of acquiring communication skills, which is basic to their educational and occupational attainments in life. Rehabilitation of these individuals is a challenge to the professionals involved, as it requires long-term, intensive management by a team of qualified professionals.

There are no nation-wide surveys to identify different types and extents of speech and hearing handicapped in our country. As per some small-scale studies the estimates range around 5-6 per cent of the population, which is an enormous figure considering the population of the country. Rehabilitation of these individuals is facilitated if the problems are identified and intervened very early. Knowing the magnitude of disability prevalence is essential for the

Government in planning its resource allocation for the purpose of rehabilitation.

There are various bottlenecks in the service delivery for the disabled individuals. These are basically in terms of availability of standardized screening, assessment and training materials to suit different age, disorder and language speaking populations, availability of adequate number of qualified professionals in the multi-disciplinary team, appropriate educational and vocational training and placement. Thus, large scale and more focussed research on all these issues are very crucial to streamline the rehabilitation programmes for the disabled population at large.

BOTTLENECKS IN SERVICE DELIVERY

1. **Non-availability of incidence and prevalence figures for various disabilities:** There are a few sporadic studies, restricted to smaller geographic locations, on the incidence and prevalence of disabilities in our country. It is important to know the incidence and prevalence figures for various disability groups and sub-groups which will enable the Government to mobilize resources and plan for the management in a global manner instead of using a piecemeal approach.
2. **Inadequate early identification and preventive measures:** Prevention is better and cheaper than cure. Early identification of the problem is a crucial first step in reducing the impact of the disability in most cases through successful preventive strategies at the primary, secondary and tertiary levels.
3. **Dearth of appropriate, standardized, low cost screening/ assessment procedures:** There is a dearth of materials available for screening or assessment of various disabilities and unless it is done systematically, objectively and uniformly across the set ups the intervention planning will not be adequate to meet the challenges involved.

4. **Dearth of appropriate, standardized, field tested, low cost training materials:** It is essential to provide early, intensive disability management programmes to the handicapped individuals by the professionals and caregivers. This requires development of appropriate and specialized training materials. In India, with its wide cultural and linguistic diversity this poses a greater challenge to address these factors in developing tools for training these individuals, with specific reference to speech, hearing and language disorders. These individuals require intensive, one-to-one treatment planning, which increases the demands for development of low cost aids to be affordable by the vast majority of people.
5. **Scarcity of trained professional/para-professional/non-professional workers:** The number of trained professionals available at present is highly inadequate to meet the challenges of rehabilitating the huge population of the disabled. Various levels of rehabilitation workers including special educators, teachers, Anganvadi workers, parents and other grass roots workers need to be trained to meet the demands. Services provided by theses individuals vary to a great extent depending on the duration of training, curriculum contents, minimum qualifications and experience required to learn the skills in imparting training. Short-term intensive training programmes, refresher courses and adequate monitoring systems are required to maintain the efficacy of these programmes.
6. **Inadequate educational opportunities:** The recent policy of the Government to promote inclusive education for the disabled children as against the segregated or institutionalized care for them has increased the demands on the normal school teachers. Adequate adaptations in the curriculum content, instructional practices, learning environment, evaluation procedures, time management etc. are required to be made.

7. **Inadequate vocational training and placement:** The handicapped individuals are required to be trained in various vocational skills depending on their residual capacities, interests and motivation. Proper placements in shelter workshops and suitable jobs are to be planned with periodic monitoring and guidance for the rehabilitation to be complete and effective. These vocational training and placement needs of the disabled are at present highly inadequate.
8. **Inadequate knowledge about treatment outcome:** There is not much emphasis on the post treatment evaluation of the disabilities and as a result the effectiveness of treatment rendered is not available for many of the disabilities. This is especially true with the speech and language disorders like phonological, voice or fluency problems.

These bottlenecks in rehabilitation of the handicapped can be adequately addressed to by undertaking comprehensive research programmes focusing on all these issues. In particular, research programmes addressing the following aspects need to be undertaken on a priority basis.

RESEARCH REQUIREMENTS

1. **Incidence and prevalence:** There is an urgent need to undertake nation-wide large scale surveys and screening programmes to arrive at incidence and prevalence figures for various disabilities in order to:
   - Identify various disabilities
   - Identify nature and causative factors
   - Estimate extent/degree of handicap caused
   - Classify disabilities and their sub-groups (Develop uniform approaches like ICD 10/DSM IV)
2. **Early identification and prevention:** Research study is required to implement early identification and preventive

measures in the management of disabilities. This should be focussed to:

- Study the identification procedures for various disabilities—Develop uniform, low cost, large scale approaches
- Develop appropriate preventive measures at primary, secondary and tertiary levels for various disabilities
- Monitor identification and preventive measures through sample surveys

3. **Screening/Assessment materials**: There is a need for developing appropriate, standardized, low cost screening/assessment procedures for early identification of disabilities and field testing the utility of these procedures with regard to:
   - Different disabilities
   - Different language groups
   - Different age groups
   - Different professionals/workers
4. **Development of training materials**: It is also very essential to develop appropriate, standardized, field tested, low cost training materials for:
   - Different disabilities
   - Different language groups
   - Different age groups
   - Different professionals/workers
   - Different racial, ethnic and culture groups
5. **Training of para-professional/non-professional workers**: Manpower development is an important aspect of rehabilitation programmes for the disabled. There are acute shortcomings in this, as training the professionals in the field requires lot of time and funding. Parents, teachers and other health care workers will have to be imparted training and guidance to promote intensive management plan for the disabled. Research is required to:

- Study the man power training programmes for disabilities
- Formulate course curriculum and practicum content
- Analyze the adequacy of duration of the programmes
- Developing cost effective programmes and their monitoring

6. **Educational management**: Handicapped children are often not provided adequate, appropriate need-based education. These children are also entitled to Governments "education for all" policy. The available special schools are too inadequate to cater to the disabled population so also for all varieties of disabilities (for *e.g.* autism). Although the new inclusive education policy for the disabled is theoretically very good, it poses great challenge for the concerned teachers, parents and children. Sound research based information for the educational management of children with various disabilities is the need of the hour. It is important to study the following educational adaptations for various disabilities:
   - Normal *versus* special schools
   - Training requirements for teachers
   - Curriculum content
   - Evaluation procedures
   - Modification of peer/group involvement
   - Identifying and removing physical/environmental and social barriers
7. **Vocational training and placement**: As the disabled children are not educated or educated inadequately, employment opportunities for them are very restricted. Because of this they are often left with no options but to be dependent, although most of them are capable of fending for themselves. There are many vocations in which some of the handicapped individuals fare better than their normal peers. Research can throw light on some of the

specific issues in the vocational training and placement of disabled individuals like:

- Identifying vocations to suit different disabilities
- Studying the vocational training requirements
- Placement opportunities in sheltered workshops, public and private sector agencies.
- On-job training /monitoring schemes

8. **Treatment outcome research**: It is very essential to undertake research to study and develop appropriate procedures or techniques in the management of disabilities. Some of the disorders (for instance, stuttering) are treated on a symptomatic approach and by a variety of techniques by various professionals without much benefit. There is a need to streamline the management options for the disabled with more focussed research on identifying the following aspects of treatment:
   - Identify factors contributing to recovery/progress
   - Management options for various disabilities
   - Treatment out come with regard to:
     — Various techniques/procedures adopted
     — Optimum duration of treatment
     — Professionals involved
     — Maintenance of recovery/progress

CONCLUSIONS

There is an urgent need to initiate vast scale research strategies in the disability management issues. This will provide the essential database to face the challenges of rehabilitation with a more holistic approach in terms of allocation of funds, resource mobilization with regard to utilizing the public and private sectors along with the State and Central Government organizations, formulation of policies for the welfare of the disabled and the like. In this context the author would like to mention the research projects undertaken by her along with others (see References 1-5 below) in addressing some of these issues. However, data and information obtained from many such studies and projects should be pooled and compiled to create the database required.

REFERENCES

1. Karanth.P, Manjula, R. Geetha Y.V. & Prema K.S. (1999). "*With a Little Bit of Help*"—A manual and 634 cards for language training. An UNICEF Project on Production of Language Training Materials in ten major Indian Languages: Books for Change Publishers, Bangalore.
2. Geetha, Y.V., Pratibha, K., Ashok, R. and Shetty, R. (2000). Classification of Childhood Disfluencies Using Neural Networks, *Journal of Fluency Disorders*, Vol. 25, No.2, 99 -117.
3. Geetha Y. V. and Prema K.S. (2000). Classification of Developmental Language Disabilities (DLDs) using Artificial Neural Network: Paper presented at the First International Conference on Language, Neurology and Cognition, 20 Dec. 2000 held at Trivandrum.
4. Geetha, Y.V. (2001). "Intervention Programme for Children with Cerebral Palsy and Mental Retardation—A Multi-Disciplinary Approach"—An Epidemiological Study. Principal investigator of project funded by the KRPLLD, CDS, Trivandrum—an unpublished report.
5. Geetha, Y.V. and Jayaram, M. (2002). Associated Problems as a Basis for Sub-grouping Disfluent Children, an All India Institute of Speech and Hearing Research Fund Project (in progress).

12

COMPUTER ASSISTED TEACHING LEARNING MATERIALS FOR IEDC IN DPEP

A Case Study

Dr. K.N. Pavithran

A large segment of the hearing impaired population undergo mainstream education in our State. In a verbal society like ours where language is the prime mode of communication mainstreaming is the logical option for any hearing impaired child. Mainstreaming fosters better interactions with the hearing world and can reduce social isolation and personal unhappiness. It offers wider curriculum possibilities than is possible in special schools.

However, mainstreaming of hearing impaired children requires extra support for its success. Visual aids have been used extensively as teaching aids for training hearing impaired children. They take the form of picture cards, toys, drawings, real objects etc. However, they have their limitations. The introduction of computers is opening new vistas hitherto thought to be unfeasible and impracticable. The immense graphic capability and animation facility of computers can produce visual realization of any real situations. The proper application of this strategy can make a sea change in the methodologies of teaching hearing impaired children.

National Institute of Speech and Hearing (NISH) undertook a project to develop Computer Assisted Teaching Learning Materials for the District Primary Education Programme (DPEP). The project was to develop computer assisted teaching learning materials for class I-IV. The script was developed with the assistance of DPEP teachers and the software implementation was done by the software engineers and graphic artist of NISH. T9he TLM included visuals and animations wherever possible and lot of innovative teaching methods could be introduced as the development progressed.

The computer assisted TLM for standard land has been completed. The TLM for 40 lessons is available in 4 CDs which are used by 72 Block Resource Centres of DPEP. The TLM is extremely popular among teachers and students of DPEP and the feedback is very encouraging.

Though the computer assisted TLM was developed particularly for the integrated education of hearing impaired students it turned out to be a useful teaching aid for any student. There is abundant scope for its use in inclusive education.

13

VOCATIONAL TRAINING PROGRAMME FOR THE PERSONS WITH HEARING IMPAIRMENT

R. Bhattacharya

Globalisation and technological advancement have changed the requirement of manpower profile both qualitatively and quantitatively. While it has led to emergence of new avenues in job market, the labour intensive industries are forced to reduce its manpower. This has resulted in greater competition among the job seekers. The skill development programmes are well geared to meet the needs of the employment market. Therefore, it is needed to equip the persons with disabilities with the skills having high employment potentials enabling them to compete with the rest on equal terms. Gone are the days, when the persons with disabilities were provided with employment opportunities out of sheer compassion and sympathy. Now, they must prove their abilities to secure jobs. However, the persons with disabilities should be afforded equal opportunities with non-disabled. Therefore, the emphasis should be placed on the abilities not on disabilities of the persons. The right to work is basic to all human being. It not only provides individual with a source of livelihood but also imbues sense of personal worth in them.

The vocational training programmes for the persons with disabilities need to play a key role in skill development. The range of vocational training be widened and linked to requirement of the employment market. The issue of economic rehabilitation cannot be dealt in isolation. It is necessary to adopt a multi-sectoral approach in ensuring economic independence to the persons with disabilities.

Keeping the trend of open economy in view, the vocational training programmes for the persons with disabilities should be seen as a gateway to successful self-employment ventures. Moreover, emphasis should be laid on integration of the persons with disabilities in mainstream technical training programmes. Necessary technical know-how and infrastructural facilities should be made available to impart training to the persons with disabilities depending on their specific needs.

The issue of vocational training should encompass the magnitude of the target population, statutory provisions, available infrastructure, selection of trades, linkage between training and employment and/or self-employment, manpower development and multi-sectoral approach.

TARGET POPULATION

In India, the number of persons with hearing impairment in employment age group (15-59 years) was around 2.04 million during Ninth Plan Period (1997-2002). During the Tenth Plan Period (2002-07) the projected figure would be 2.28 million. (*Source* : Tata Statistical Year Book 2002-03).

The majority of the population lives in the rural area whereas most of the facility available are in the urban areas. There is acute need to create vocational training facilities for rural hearing impaired.

VOCATIONAL TRAINING OPPORTUNITIES

It has been observed that the vocational training facilities as well as options available for the persons with hearing impairment are grossly inadequate. The rehabilitation process needs to be equipped with proper vocational assessment, counselling, training and employment facilities.

At present there are 306 Vocational Rehabilitation and Training Centres for the disabled in India. This figure includes both government and voluntary organizations. Only 3,000 persons with hearing impairment are provided with vocational training in these centres per year.

In addition there are 17 Vocational Rehabilitation Centres for the Physically Handicapped (VRCPH) established by Directorate General of Employment and Training, Ministry of Labour, Government of India. Out of 17 VRCPH, one is exclusively for the Women with Disabilities. All the VRCPH are located in State Capitals. Many of them have set up Rural Extension Centres.

Realising the need to create vocational training opportunities for persons with hearing impaired in rural areas, Ali Yavar Jung National Institute for the Hearing Handicapped (AYJNIHH), an autonomous organisation of Government of India, Ministry of Social Justice & Empowerment, introduced the Scheme of Collaborative Vocational Training Programme for the Hearing Handicapped. The prime objective of the scheme is to encourage the Non-Government Organisations to undertake vocational training activity for the hearing impaired, particularly in rural areas. AYJNIHH provides initial financial assistance and continued technical input in the areas of Instructors Training, Identification and Selection of Trades and Development of Course Curriculum. As on date there are 30 such collaborated training centres across the country.

In addition there are 2,263 government I.T.I.s and 2,708 private I.T.I.s in India catering to approximately 900,000 trainees in mainstream. However, the representation of the trainees with: hearing impairment in I.T.I.s is negligible. This is mainly due to lack of trained manpower in the vocational training sectors to impart training to the deaf.

STATUTORY PROVISIONS

The enactment of Persons with Disabilities (Equal Opportunities,

Protection of Rights and Full Participation) Act, 1995 has widened the scope of Technical (Vocational) Training opportunities for the persons with disabilities including the persons with hearing impairment through its provision of 3 per cent reservation of seats in educational and technical training centres under Section 39 of the Act. However, the same could not be implemented in its real essence, as there is dearth of technical support system and trained manpower to impart training to the deaf. Thus, the provision of reservation of 3 per cent seats are filled by other categories of disabled depriving the persons with hearing impairment of their share of 1 per cent too. As a result of the above, hearing impaired trainees are not able to qualify in the regular examination conducted by National Council of Vocational Training (NCVT). This becomes an obstacle for seeking open employment.

Section 40 of the Persons with Disabilities Act, 1995, envisages that not less than 3 per cent of the total allocation be reserved for the persons with disabilities in all poverty alleviation schemes. Rural employment programmes under Swarna Jayanti Swarojgar Yojana Schemes envisaged by Ministry of Rural Development should be disabled friendly and be made accessible to the persons with disabilities. Necessary relaxation and modification both in the eligibility criteria and infrastructure be made to suit to the needs of the *persons with disabilities.*

Section 38(1) of the Persons with Disabilities Act, 1995, emphasises formulation of schemes to ensure employment of the persons with disabilities and such schemes may provide for:

(a) The training and welfare of persons with disabilities;
(b) The relaxation of upper age limit;
(c) Regulating the employment;
(d) Health and safety measures and creation of non-handicapping environment in places where persons with disabilities are employed;
(e) The manner in which and the persons by whom the cost of operating the schemes is to be defrayed; and

(f) Constituting the authority responsible for the administration of the scheme.

Section 33 of the Persons with Disabilities Act, 1995, provides reservation of not less than 3 per cent of vacancies for the persons with disabilities in government sector and Public Sector Undertakings. Out of which 1 per cent each for Hearing Handicapped, Orthopaedically Handicapped and Visually Handicapped.

It is not enough to make statutory provisions only, the essence lies in the implementation of the provisions made under the Persons with Disabilities Act. Creation of all round awareness support infrastructure and attitudinal changes is essential to achieve the desired result.

SELECTION OF TRADE

While considering the issue of vocational training for the persons with hearing impairment, selection of trade is plays a crucial role. It is not very difficult to start vocational training programme for the hearing impaired. But to make it sustainable, cost effective and market oriented is a gigantic task.

Due to lack of expertise in the areas of job market analysis, Vocational Assessment of persons with hearing impairment, Trade Development and Designing Training package, the trades at various Vocational Rehabilitation/Training centres for the persons with disabilities are traditional in nature and do not have sufficient employment/self-employment potentials. With the emergence of precision engineering and Information Technology, the job market is changing constantly. However, the training organizations are yet to gear up their "activities conforming to these changing needs". The obsolete, trades to be substituted with suitable and viable trades having high employment potentials.

India is known for its unity in diversity. This is also true when it comes to regional excellence in trade development. Depending on the socio-cultural background, availability of a raw material, familial occupations and skilled craftsmanship different parts of our country have made an imprint in world market. Today, particular region of the country is known for its excellence in particular cottage industry/trade. We should be able to identify the regional trades and update the skills with the changing trends in the market.

Socio-economic and educational background of the hearing impaired should be taken into consideration while selecting the trade. The illiterate and less literate needs to be placed appropriately in vocational training and subsequent gainful employment.

Looking at the manpower requirement in agricultural sector and abundance availability of natural resources, efforts be made to identify suitable agro-based rural trades for vocational training purposes.

MISSING LINK BETWEEN VOCATIONAL TRAINING AND EMPLOYMENT

It has been observed that the employment options, vocational training facilities and trained vocational instructors available for the persons with hearing impairment are grossly inadequate. The employability of the persons with hearing impairment essentially relates to diversity in the job market, abilities of the trainer and trainees. These diversities include range of employment options, emerging trend in job markets and varying levels of skills needed and available among the vocational instructors. In addition to this the trainees, namely persons with hearing impairment vary based on their level of literacy, gender, urban-rural milieu, age of onset and nature and extent of deafness etc.

Lack of market oriented vocational training programme is one of the major obstacles in promoting vocational rehabilitation and open employment of the persons with hearing impairment.

The problem of uneducated and less educated persons with hearing impairment hinders the use of verbal language for communication. Therefore, their training is mainly based on practical demonstration. The practical based training without theoretical input makes it difficult to be recognised at par with the mainstream training programme. In turn, it restricts employment opportunities in the open employment market.

VOCATIONAL TRAINING *VIS-A-VIS* SELF-EMPLOYMENT

The present trend in the world economy, has resulted in emergence of new avenues while discarding the traditional labour intensive industrial process. Many industrial giants have come up, creating lot of scope for small-scale industries to emerge as their ancillary units.

However, the initiatives towards self-employment did not take off as desired due to number of reasons. The one of the main reasons for inclination towards wage employment is assured time bound income without any risk. Lack of entrepreneurship skills also compels for wage employment.

The vocational training programmes are geared only towards development of technical skills required to perform the particular job. The component of entrepreneurship development programme does not form apart of the curriculum.

During early seventies, Government of India through State Governments created a nation-wide infrastructure at the district level called District Industries Centres to encourage the youths for self-employment. Establishment of Khadi and Village Industries Commission is also considered to be a land mark in the field of self-employment. Ministry of Industries, Government of India created another infrastructure at the State level called Small Industries Service Institute with the objective assist small scale entrepreneurs in running their ventures and conduct Entrepreneurship Development Programmes for the youths willing to take up self-employment venture.

Entrepreneurship Development Programme should be a component of all vocational training programmes.

VOCATIONAL TRAINING *VIS-A-VIS* SHELTERED EMPLOYMENT

The concept of sheltered employment came in vogue keeping in view the multiply handicapped who is unable to cope with open employment environment. It was thought appropriate to create an opportunity for the severe multiply handicapped to prove their abilities, even it is in a protected environment.

The sheltered employment may be the only option for the multiply handicapped with hearing impairment. Such employment opportunities could be created in Training-cum-Production Centres run by the persons with disabilities.

MANPOWER DEVELOPMENT IN VOCATIONAL TRAINING SECTOR

The enactment of Persons with Disabilities (Equal Opportunities, Protection of Rights and Full participation) Act, 1995 has widened the Scope of Technical (Vocational) Training opportunities for the persons with disabilities including the persons with hearing impairment through its provision of reservation of seats in educational and technical training centres. However; the same could not be implemented in its real essence, as there is dearth of and technical support system and trained manpower to impart training to the deaf. As a result, the provision of reservation of 3 per cent seats is filled by other categories of disabled.

The rate of employment of the hearing impaired is far less than that of the orthopaedically handicapped. The provision of reservation of jobs for the hearing handicapped under the PwD Act, 1995 could not be implemented due to non-availability of qualified candidates. The main reason behind it is lack of mainstream vocational training opportunities for the deaf. Lack of communication skills on the part of the instructors of the I.T.I.s restricts the admission of the hearing impaired trainees in mainstream technical training programmes. As a result, the deaf are deprived of the recognised vocational training opportunities, thereby, affecting steady flow of trained/skilled hearing impaired in the employment market. It is important that the hearing impaired should undergo vocational training programme in an integrated environment to enhance their employability. It is essential that trained instructors with the adequate skills to communicate with the deaf effectively are made available for making any vocational training programme successful.

Realising this need, the Rehabilitation Council of India developed a short course entitled "Certificate Course for Vocational Instructors of the Hearing Impaired" so that the instructors are exposed to educational, audiological, psychological, sociological and emotional aspects of the adult deaf and equipping them with the skills to communicate with the deaf effectively.

AYJNIHH has conducted the first "Certificate Course for Vocational Instructors of the Hearing Impaired" in Mumbai in the month of January, 2003 and intends to conduct this on regular basis throughout the country.

NETWORKING WITH EXISTING INFRASTRUCTURE

Considering the magnitude of target population and their geographical distribution, it is not viable to create separate infrastructure for vocational training for the hearing impaired. On the other hand, there is vast infrastructure for vocational training and self-employment already available under various programmes of Government of India and State Governments. It is worthwhile to establish a network with such organisations for utilising the resources for skill development of hearing impaired.

To start with, a network with the organisation like Small Industries Service Institute, District Industries Centre, Community Polytechnic, Khadi Village and Industries Commission, Directorate of Technical Education, Swarna Jayanti Swarojgar Yojana, Nehru Yuva Kendra, Central/State Social Welfare Board, Vocational Training Centre.

Non-Government Organisations and National Handicapped Finance & Development Corporation is worth considering for enhancing vocational training opportunities and subsequent self-employment prospects.

SUGGESTIONS AND RECOMMENDATIONS

1. Barrier-free environment for the PwD should be made pre-requisite for all to enable education, training, travel, working environment, housing etc., Department of Education and Training, Rural Development Department, Urban Development Department and Public Works Department are required to take lead role in the matter.
2. The range of Vocational training be widened and linked to requirement of the employment market. Most of the Vocational Training Centres are stuck with the obsolete trades. It is necessary to introduce new/modern trades having high employment prospects. While doing so, the industries should be consulted in conducting the market research and developing the course curriculum. The vocational training courses should also be aimed at widening self-employment prospects. In this case, Directorate of Technical Education, Directorate of Employment and Training, Corporate Sectors and Ministry of Labour and Industries need to work in close collaboration. The National Institutes have played a key role in this sector.
3. Development of Entrepreneurship Skills should be an integral part of the Vocational Training Programmes to enhance self-employment prospects. The expertise available with Small Industries Service Institutes (SISI) and District Industries Centres (DIC) can be utilized in this regard.
4. The Rural Employment programmes under Swarna

Jayanti Swarojgar Yojana (SJSY) Schemes envisaged by the Ministry of Rural Development have to be accessed to the PwD. Necessary relaxations and modifications both in the eligibility criteria and infrastructure be made to suit to the needs of the PwD, need to be researched.

5. Closer scrutiny of the recruitment of Government Offices and Public Sector Undertakings in relation to the observance of the policy of reservation of jobs for PwD have opened up for the PwD. The NGOs receiving grants from Public money should also come under this purview.
6. To enhance the employment prospects for the PwD in Private Sectors. The Persons with Disabilities Act,1995 made the provisions of incentives to be given to the employers for employing atleast 5 per cent of the employees with disabilities. The incentives like Tax rebates, Excise Concession, Tax Holidays, preferential allotment of land, Soft loans, Easy payment terms etc. could be thought of. The State Commissionorate for the Persons with Disabilities may take up the matter with Department of Finance and Department of Commerce and Industries. However, the Best Employers Awards need to be popularised.
7. The Ministry of Social Justice and Empowerment provides financial assistance to the NGO under its Scheme of assistance to NGOs towards vocational training and other vocational services. The National Institutes for Disabilities can offer consultancy services to the NGOs in developing project proposals and provide technical guidance in conducting the training courses, if needed.
8. To ensure admission of the PwD to the extent of 3 per cent in Technical Training Institutes under Craftsmen Training Scheme, it is necessary to train the Instructors so as to enable them to train the persons with hearing impairment. The Rehabilitation Council of India has

developed the Course Curriculum for Training of Instructors for the hearing impaired. NIHH have already launched such course. The Directorate of Technical Education need to sponsor the Instructors from I.T.I.s in phases so that all the Instructors of I.T.I.s are trained to impart training to the deaf.

9. The enhance self-employment opportunities for PwD in rural areas, the initiations of NHFDC and Nationalized Banks can be availed.
10. The Micro Finance Scheme of NHFDC holds greater promise. NGOs should come forward and implement the same for the PwDs.
11. The loan amount under Differential Rate of Interest (D.R.I.) scheme be increased and implemented in its real spirit by the Nationalized Banks.
12. Sheltered workshops, Cottage Industries (Home Bound) for severely disabled persons can be supported under the existing schemes.
13. The local bodies need to give preference to the PwD in allotment of Shops, Kiosks and space for Self-Employment.
14. The Ministry of Human Resource Development has identified 50 Polytechnic Institutes across the country to undertake Community Polytechnic Schemes for the PwD. This is an unique opportunity for the PwD to take advantage of this scheme and avail the facility to undergo mainstream technical training programmes leading to employment in the organized sectors or successful self-employment ventures being in their own community.

CONCLUDING REMARKS

Government of India has created a nation-wide infrastructure by way of establishing 107 District Disability Rehabilitation Centres,

Vocational Rehabilitation Centres, Special Employment Exchanges for the Physically Handicapped and other service centres under NPRPD (National Programme for Rehabilitation of the Persons with Disabilities). The need of the hour is to implement the schemes of Government of India and State Governments in real spirit to open up new vistas for the persons with disabilities.

14

BARRIER-FREE ENVIRONMENT

Anjalee Agarwal & Sanjeev Sachdeva

Every individual including People with Disabilities (PwDs)

- Have the equal right to live with dignity and grace.
- Are citizens, community members, students and employees.
- Have the same capacity to be productive citizens, given equal opportunities.

Opening doors for people with disabilities to mainstream programmes makes for a society, which is inclusive of everyone and not just a few.

Recently, there has been a major change in thinking and practice of inclusion of PwDs. It is acknowledged that disabled persons shall be given equal educational and job opportunities and full participation in all social and cultural activities. The PwD Act provides for incorporation of barrier-free features in built infrastructure—both inside buildings and outside and in the transport sector. The promotion of barrier-free environment leads to inclusion of PwDs in the mainstream society.

The types of disability determine the various measures to be adopted to create an accessible; environment for persons with disabilities. They may be:

(a) People with reduced mobility like senior citizens, families with young children, pregnant women, people with temporary ailments, wheelchair users etc.
(b) Low sighted and vision impaired persons.
(c) Hearing impaired persons.
(d) People with intellectual disabilities.

The minimum dimensions for space in the built environment should therefore take into consideration the needs and conditions listed above. The following criteria should be considered:

1. Varying sizes of persons, the range of reach and vision in both standing and sitting positions.
2. Provision of adequate space for people with locomotor disabilities (wheelchair users: walking frames crutches etc.)
3. Orientation and mobility clues for people with vision impairment.
4. Audio-visual information and other communication techniques.

The following elements need to be considered when creating a barrier-free environment:

(i) Parking
(ii) Entrances to buildings
(iii) Doors and thresholds
(iv) Ramps
(v) Staircases and steps
(vi) Lifts
(vii) Circulation and space within buildings
(viii) Toilets
(ix) Floor finishes
(x) Handrails or grab-bars
(xi) Information boards and signage's

(xii) Lighting and illumination
(xiii) Public telephones.

ACCESS BENEFITS ALL

People with reduce mobility (senior citizens, families with young children, pregnant women, people with temporary ailments, people with heavy luggage etc) and also people with disabilities.

15

INFORMATION AND COMMUNICATION TECHNOLOGY FOR VISUALLY IMPAIRED PERSONS

Ashwini Kumar Agarwal

How Visually Impaired Persons Utilise Information and Communication Technology to Access Information?

To understand accessibility of visually impaired persons to Information and Communication Technology it is important to understand there is little or no need for modification in hardware. What is needed is special software called screen reading software with speech engine. The specialised software, which with synthetic sound provides an alternative to monitor to gather information. The screen reading software is flexible as it provides all control to the visually impaired user to manoeuvre the information on monitor as per his requirement. With the software one can read character by character, word by word, sentence by sentence, line by line, paragraph by paragraph or the whole document in one go. It provides flexibility to gather information regarding font size, font style, colour and other relevant information if desired by the visually impaired user.

With the help of screen reading software, visually impaired persons can handle e-mail and giving their reply independently. Similarly blind persons can serf the net with complete independence. With the help of scanner as the hardware and

Optical Character Recognition software most of the books in English language can be accessed through the use of computers.

With screen reading software blind persons get complete independence in reading and writing needs of theirs. Writing papers, articles and preparing power point presentations has become feasible. Visually impaired persons can manage spreadsheets and databases with the help of specialised software.

With specialised hardware in the form of embossers and the Braille transcription software makes it possible to convert text in computers into Braille with considerable ease. The electronic Braille display is yet another technology empowerment for visually impaired persons. The focus area of the screen is displayed through refreshable Braille dots.

Serious efforts are on to develop screen reading software in Indian languages to enhance the accessibility of the technology in our languages too.

Role of Information and Communication Technology in Education of Visually Impaired Persons

Information and Communication Technology has made a revolutionary impact on the education of visually impaired persons. Accessing information at school level and university level through the use of computers has put visually impaired child at parity with his sighted counter part. Most of the schoolbooks are being made available as electronic text. Availability of books in Braille script has considerably increased. Bringing out desirable modifications in the desired Braille text has become quick and accurate. Accessing catalogue by the visually impaired students themselves has empowered them to get desired books and material for thëir information.

Introduction of computers into the curriculum of visually impaired children at primary level itself has enhanced their cognitive and psychomotor capacities. The technology has provided necessary stimulation.

The need for e-text library is being strongly felt for visually impaired persons. NAB, Delhi is working on the project and is aiming it to be made accessible to large number of visually impaired persons in the country.

Role of Information Technology in Empowering Visually Impaired Persons

People with visual impairment with the skill to use Information and Communication Technology to enhance their capacity find themselves with greater opportunities. The technology has opened new avenues of employment like software developers, medical trascriptionists, call centre managers, computer operators and tour planners. Similarly computers have helped to empower visually impaired persons not only to sustain the existing avenues but to find themselves to do more effectively and with greater efficiency. Visually impaired administrators use the information technology to refer to their correspondence, maintain their critical data, quickly communicate through internet, maintain their personal records and access any referral material on their own. Visually challenged persons in the profession of teaching have found the technology empowering as they have used it to read more and more books. They are gathering and organising their information more systematically. They are in a position to guide their students in the use of technology. Visually challenged persons in clerical posts have become greater participators in office automation. As larger number of people are getting training in the use of screen reading software and other enabling technology they are suggesting new utilisations.

The Information and Communication Technology has made lifts with audio signals friendlier to blind persons. Similarly Automatic Teller Machines in Banks with audio signals have become accessible to blind persons. The developments have empowered people with low or no vision. These facilities are available at very limited places and have to be made more and more prevalent. Efforts need to be made to ensure that modern products are incorporated with full accessibility features right at their manufacturing spot.

Role of Information and Communication Technology in Entertainment of Visually Impaired Persons

Entertainment has a very important role in the life of the individual irrespective of the fact that the person is of any cadre and from any walk of life. The information technology has played an important role in providing entertainment in the form of games, challenges and leisure activities.

With the advent of screen reading software's playing chess by a visually impaired person with the computer through the use of information technology has become feasible. Considerable recreational opportunities including light reading is possible for people with visual impairment. Entertainment with the use of digital music output is accessible to blind person also and they utilise it optimally for their leisure activities.

Digital Technology being Utilised for Visually Impaired Persons to Provide Daisy Talking Books on Compact Disc

Besides the use of computers as reading and writing tool as well as tools for empowering visually impaired persons in managing their job requirements the digital technology is playing very important role in making the world friendly to people with visual impairment. The availability of talking thermometer, talking wrist watches, talking automatic teller machines in bank and similar other equipment's are the direct gifts of digital technology.

Yet another area where the digital divine is bringing revolutionary change in the facilities for visually challenged persons is the introduction of Daisy talking books. Till date the talking books were available on audiocassette tapes, which had certain limitations like a cassette could hold 60 minutes of recording and the accessibility was serial. This posed a major limitation to blind persons to refer material from time to time. With the advent of digital technology the talking books have been transferred compact discs, which can hold 50 hours of recording. It also allows accessing text section-wise, page-wise and chapter-wise. The provision of book mark makes reading more comfortable with easy referencing facility.

Our Experience in Imparting Training in IT to Visually Impaired Persons in Information and Communication Technology

It has been our experience that the training in the use of Information and Communication Technology to visually impaired persons should be started as early as possible. Earlier we start the better is the acceptability. Main components of the training include:

(a) Familiarisation with the components of the computer.
(b) Awareness about operating system.
(c) Control of screen reading software.
(d) Enhancement of comprehension capacity of synthetic voice.
(e) Empowerment in the use of application software packages.

We stress if the trainer is a sighted person he should remove the mouse and then train visually impaired persons in the use of information technology. This is in view of the fact that using mouse to execute desired controls in the window based environment is visual based, therefore, it is very important that visually impaired persons are extensively trained to use the alternative controls right from initial stages. Our experience with visually impaired persons as faculty for training the use of information technology to blind persons has been very positive.

The Information and Communication Technology usually fascinates each individual including people with visual impairment. It is important to share with the trainers that training visually impaired persons would require hundred per cent of their commitment towards its learning. The training can never be taken as alight activity and needs to be pursued seriously.

The training includes making use of word processors,

spreadsheets and data base management. As the information technology makes printed world accessible to blind persons, therefore, the training in the use of scanners and OCR' s is of paramount importance.

One of the most important components of the training is the control over screen reading software. Maximum stress should be laid in training to empower blind persons to make use of help files and empower them with skills to have complete control of the screen reading software. This would empower them to overcome any difficulty, which might come in their higher level jobs with computers.

After Training Utilisation of the Skills is very Important

Every training has three important aspects which include right induction, right training and right post-training utilisation. The training in the use of computers imparted to visually impaired persons at NAB-Delhi gives considerable importance to post-training utilisation. The strategies include:

(a) Facilitating acquisition of hardware and software control by blind persons by giving them necessary consultancy and training through regular exposure.
(b) Providing interest free soft loans to trainees.
(c) Close follow-up with the employers for optimal utilisation of the training.
(d) Providing consultancy to employers for necessary facilities.
(e) Holding follow-up meetings with ex-trainees and updating their skills from time to time.

The training in the use of Information and Communication Technology to visually challenged persons is a much specialised activity and needs continues updating.

Conclusion: Challenging Future Ahead

Digital technology is making in roads in all the spheres of human life. These include production of goods, providing services and consultancy. Its role is extending to bridge the gap of distances and building bridges of constructive co-operation.

Empowering visually challenged persons with the help of Information and Communication Technology is continuously gaining importance and needs greater attention of educationist, human resource manager and policy makers. This would ensure that we are in a position to create equal opportunities, provide protection of rights and allow full participation to visually challenged persons in the main stream society.

16

VOLUNTEERS PROMOTING EDUCATION OF DISABLED PERSONS

Ashwini Kumar Agarwal

Abstract

The paper focuses on the contributions of volunteers of National Association for the Blind to provide quality education to visually impaired persons. Besides stating the background and objectives of NAB, the author explains the voluntary services procured by NAB, the need for the voluntary services and methodology adopted to promote as well as coordinate it. The paper stresses the importance of voluntary services and its timely availability. The paper brings out advantages to NAB through voluntary support. The need and importance of feedback as well as follow-up has been stressed in the paper to continue to gain from voluntary services. Special emphasis is on involvement to establish belongingness among volunteers visiting NAB. The need for increasing participation and establishment of report to build connectivity. The paper concludes with recognising that volunteers have given the best gift to NAB in the form of their services.

Outline

1. Background of National Association for the Blind.
2. Who is a Volunteer in NAB.

3. Why does NAB need volunteers?
4. How to identify NAB's need for voluntary services?
5. From where does NAB get volunteers?
6. When does NAB need voluntary services?
7. When can volunteers extend their service?
8. Matching services through NAB data bank of Volunteers.
9. Matching of needs and interests.
10. How to prepare schedule to match the two?
11. Why NAB gets feedback from volunteers?
12. Why NAB does follow-ups with volunteers?
13. How does NAB establish rapport with volunteers?
14. What are the ways of voluntary participation?
15. How does NAB promote volunteerism?
16. How does NAB train and empower volunteers?

Background of NAB

National Association for the Blind is the largest voluntary organisation working for the education and rehabilitation of persons with low or no vision in the country. We have a network of voluntary services along the length and breadth of the country. With our 19 State Branches and 65 District Branches, we are promoting voluntary services in an organised manner. This year we are celebrating Golden Jubilee year of our existence and in this long span, the voluntary work is marked with a number of achievements.

Volunteers have been playing an important role in the progress of National Association for the Blind. There is an urgent need to further promote the voluntary support with a view to make it a propelling force in line with our objectives. We need to identify areas of deficit and enlist them so that we know our need gaps. This will help in laying down the options for them and getting the commitment with clear goals. There is an enormous potential in our country studded with best brains in the world. People want to do well but only a few know how to do it. A little guidance can do wonders.

Who is a Volunteer in NAB?

Volunteer service has been a part of virtually every civilisation and society. Defined as a non-profit, non-wage and non-career action that individuals carry out for the well-being of their neighbours, community or society at large, it takes many forms from traditional customs of mutual self-help to community responses in times of crisis and effort for relief, conflict resolution and the eradication of poverty. The concept includes local and national volunteer efforts, as well as bilateral and international programmes, which operate across borders. Volunteers have contributed significantly to the welfare and progress of industrialised and developing countries and within national and United Nations programmes of humanitarian assistance, technical co-operation and promotion of human rights, democratisation and peace. Voluntary service features prominently in the activities of associations, trade unions and civic organizations.

In National Association for the Blind a person extending his services in accordance with the objectives of NAB without charging or getting remuneration is a Volunteer. We have office bearers in the Management like the President, Vice-President, General Secretary, Joint Secretaries, Members of the Governing Council, Teachers, experts, readers, technicians, young students of schools/ colleges, professionals and other service providers as volunteers. These people extend their valuable services for various lateral benefits other than monetary gains.

To become a volunteer one needs to fill a form meant for volunteers. All those who are interested in extending or are motivated to extend their voluntary services fill the form. Those volunteers who are interested in the management of the Association have to acquire membership by filling membership form and submitting the membership fee. The elections for posts in governing body are held every third year. The Association encourages voluntary services and continuously work towards optimal utilisation of the resource.

Why does NAB need Volunteers?

NAB needs volunteers to promote our objectives on account of several factors

(a) **Generation of Quality value services with low cost:** Channelisation of voluntary support is cost effective and enhances the capacity of the organisation to deliver better services with less funds.

(b) **Generation of financial resources:** Financial support is the backbone of an organisation and volunteers play a very important role in promoting financial support since NAB has volunteers coming from work in all walks of life, it helps to build the image once they are convinced.

(c) **Generation of Peoples Movement towards exclusivity :** Building inclusive society with no barriers for people with disability is the final objective of NAB in which volunteers are contributing significantly.

(d) **Furthering of Integration of disabled persons into the mainstream society:** Students and teachers coming to NAB as volunteers have been able to understand the importance of integrated education and have given impetus to promote it effectively.

(e) **For Networking:** Volunteers play a very important role in carrying our message to other organisations and in its networking. Other organisations like Youth Reach and volunteers have introduced supports like Empress Club to us which have been very instrumental in building strengths of NAB. This kind of networking has empowered us to enhance our rate of growth to quite an extent.

(f) **Building Synergies:** Presence of a volunteer in classes has a very positive impact on individual attention to the child as well as direct sensitisation of the volunteer. This inclusion promotes multiple benefits.

(g) **Sensitisation:** Through volunteers we have been able to change the mindset of different persons in the society. The volunteers when are convinced about the abilities of blind persons, spread the word about the ability of blind persons in their social circle. They understand that little guidance and co-operation can play a vital role in ensuring fulfilling life for people with disability. This kind of word of mouth promotion helps a lot to reach a wider audience and sensitise them.

(h) **Utilising latent Professional skills to meet needs of areas of deficit:** It has been observed that volunteers have been able to discover themselves anew after their involvement with us since their latent potentials have found opportunities to come on the surface. Similarly, a number of professional skills which are needed for the students, if are possessed by the volunteers have been acquired as voluntary support which otherwise would be very expensive. Professionals like doctors visit us to provide necessary clinical advise, financial experts advise in our financial management, technicians provide their skills to maintain our equipment efficiently, administrators provide us necessary procedural guidance. Artists have also come to extend their services to teach vocal music or playing instruments or dramatics or painting and physical educators provide physical training to NAB children.

How to identify our own needs for voluntary services ?

We believe each unit and the organisation either grows or degenerates. We all choose to grow rather than degenerate. To grow we need to add new energies. We strongly believe that nothing is perfect and there is always scope of improvement, so we better look for those. We could add new energies through voluntary support. With limited fund and the good cause in our hand we can add new energies through voluntary support.

Our entire team continuously thinks about improving our

services. The need for human resource is identified at various sections and points of need. The team members work out various ways through which more and more people can be involved. First, the desirable skills required are identified and then, the people who can be involved to impart the necessary skills.

Our needs are continuously reported to the co-ordinator and put up on the notice board. We all at NAB are in a process to encourage all those we meet in society to visit our organisation. The atmosphere itself is regenerating and encouraging. Enjoying work is a value addition. We share our experiences with our volunteers. With a belief that our failures are our learnings and our achievements are our motivators, we intend to make NAB a learning organisation. There is a direct relationship between degree of involvement and degree of learning. Each individual has skill and knowledge to share to build synergies. The gift of constant questioning and looking for possible solutions to choose the best option in the human beings to be utilised optimally.

We all realise that the nature has gifted us but with limited memory, limited intelligence and limited time. If we memorise good, there will be no scope for bad memories. If we continuously use our intelligence for constructive purposes we will be left with none to use for destructive purposes. If we continuously plan and utilise our time for development we shall be left with no time to worry for apprehensions.

Our team strongly believes that each individual is selfish and to be selfish is a virtue if directed rightly. Each individual needs recognition and acknowledgement and the feeling of being wanted wherever he/she is. We make each volunteer feel wanted, as there is a lot to do. Each individual can find a place for him/her with us.

Where do We get Volunteers?

NAB generates voluntary support through its employees, donors, other organisations, visitors, schools, colleges, corporate world and neighbourhood.

Employees of NAB are aware of the objectives of the organisation along with our need for voluntary services. We interact with people wherever we go and give open invitation to extend their voluntary services. Each one of us plays a catalytic role in promoting voluntarism in our Association.

NAB donors are invited regularly to make them participate in our activities. Our donors have always guided volunteers to us. Once they are convinced with our objectives and are committed to promote them they guide people to us. Rotary Clubs, various ladies clubs, trusts and donor group members visit us for donations and become voluntary service providers too.

Other organisations like Youth Reach and Empress Club are aware of our need for voluntary services who have an objective to spread voluntary services. They play a very important role in guiding volunteers to us. We also keep informing the organisations of our needs and requirement with respect to specialised services. Similarly these organisations inform us about the specialists they have who can extend voluntary services. These organisations have co-ordinators for the purpose to ensure smooth growth of voluntarism. These organisations help us in organising events effectively and efficiently.

Schools are also playing very important role in providing voluntary services to NAB. Students of Springdales, Hamdard Public School, Lakshman Public School, Ramjas School and Sardar Patel have supported their voluntary services. These services include developing tactile diagrams, collecting educational toys and sharing them with our children, recording books, acting as writers for the examination of our children.

Colleges and Educational Institutes of higher studies have been guiding their students to extend voluntary services to us. Students from Jesus & Mary College, Kamla Nehru College and IIT, Delhi has extended voluntary services. Students from DA V College participated in a street play with our children. College students helped in spreading awareness about our activities in their College festivals. Rotry Clubs have made voluntary contributions in terms of money as well as services.

Visitors to our organisation often are motivated to provide voluntary services. Many of them start visiting us regularly. They understand our requirements and work towards whatever they can contribute in terms of services. People from All India Radio, Doordarshan and other television channels have visited us and have become volunteers.

Media people have enrolled themselves as volunteers and extended their support in different manner.

We often approach *the corporate world* for their support. In this exercise we often have to listen to a 'no' also. The officials while expressing their inability for monitory help offer to extend their voluntary services. It works very well. Their connection and attachment plays very important role in our growth.

The social circle of the volunteers is also helpful in increasing the number of volunteer support once the word of confidence in our activities is passed on by an existing volunteer.

People from neighbourhood visit us who are motivated to extend their voluntary services. Volunteers from neighbourhood are of immense importance since they can be called upon for their support in odd hours of the day.

When do We need Voluntary Support?

The identified need of human resource support is as per scheduled time of need. Once the need for voluntary support is identified, it is of immense importance to lay down the timings as to when all it is desirable. The time when we need the support is identified and indicated on the notice board. Similarly the days when we need support are also indicated.

When and how can Volunteers Support?

It is very important to know when can an individual extend voluntary support. Whenever an individual is motivated to extend voluntary support, he is requested to fill a simple form. The form seeks information about identity, recommending person, source of information about NAB, areas of interest, skills possessed and the probable time the person can provide. This information is collected into NAB's data which helps us to further build a data bank of motivated persons. Through this information we come to know about their interests and the time they can share with us to start with. The volunteers are then made aware of our requirements and the vision we have for our organisation.

Matching Services Through NAB Data Bank of Volunteers

Once we get information about volunteers' interests, time that they extend to offer along with address, telephone, e-mail, referring person and skills, we offer them possible responsibilities that they can take up. The options are open for the volunteers to choose from various activities. Further we have to help the individual to adjust to the needs of our organisation. We have to give him time to observe the working where the person is going to participate.

Matching of Needs and Interests

In the world, more often than not people get themselves employed on jobs which are not of their interest. As the employment is fetching them the necessary money, they continue with it. Voluntary services provide an individual to do something of his interest, where the person is not compelled to work and at the same time derives enjoyment and satisfaction. They want to take up challenging tasks and enjoy creativity and our organisation provides them such opportunities. These are in accordance with our objectives with self-motivation. The needs are immense and provider of these services are also in abundance. But the need is to match the two. If we are successful in doing that it provides us a win- win situation.

How to prepare a schedule to match the two? Once the needs and interests are matched, the next step is scheduling the two to match each other. It is the most difficult proposition. Often people who are busy want to do more. It has been observed that who want to work more are always happy as they keep enjoying their work as well as love to take up new challenges. Those who do not want to work are always unhappy and keep complaining about the system.

There are certain limitations also at times. The volunteers very often want to extend their services on Saturdays and Sundays since they are off work on these days. But it is not certain that the work they would like to do is available on Sunday. But definitely with some extended efforts we find volunteers whose time match our schedules. In the cases where the two do not match we compromise in the matching of needs and provide them with next best alternative, which they could do at their home or on a Sunday, as they desire.

Volunteers are also introduced to the staff with whom they shall be working. They are initially allowed and advised to be observers to understand the scope of work as well as the challenges it offers. Subsequently when they take up the assignment they are constantly encouraged by a feedback that there presence and consistency is of immense importance to us.

Why we get feedback from volunteers? Volunteers are encouraged to provide feedback with respect to their assignments, environment, co-operation from staff, co-operation from children and over all improvement of the system. This information helps us to encourage our team to do better. We can understand our strengths and weaknesses. We can work to strengthen our strengths and weaken our weaknesses and thus puts the system on the path of growth. Simultaneously our understanding about the volunteers improves.

Why We do Follow-ups with Volunteers?

Follow-ups with volunteers help us to understand the role volunteers can play to build the organisation and also understand what makes them consistent as well as happy. In case we have not been able to come up to their expectations, we look for ways as to how we can do that. We work towards doing the same in line with the objectives of the organisation. If there are genuine problems, these are communicated to the volunteer. Follow-ups have helped us to build a team of volunteers, which is our strength and is playing very important role in our success.

How do We Establish a Feeling of Belongingness in the Volunteers?

Feeling of being wanted or the sense of belongingness among humans is of paramount importance. This is achieved in our organisation through involvement of volunteers with the motivating staff. By taking meals together, planning together, inviting for functions, participating in workshops, the volunteers become an integral part of the system. They tend to identify themselves with the organisation. They are given due importance during functions and are thanked for their good work. They are also invited to give prizes to students to connect them further with the students. Their work is appreciated in our newsletter.

What are the Various ways of Voluntary Participation?

Volunteers in NAB are involved in

- Recording of talking books.
- Co-operating with the teachers to give one to one attention to students.
- Teaching rhymes and English communication skills to students.
- Editing of textbooks on computers.
- Managing talking book library.
- Guiding in managerial skills to NAB staff.
- Promoting voluntary eye donation.
- Promoting voluntary medical services by doctors.
- Voluntary support to train teachers with respect to low vision, communication skills, computer skills, personality

development, art of living skills, management skills, organising skills, and marketing skills.

- Voluntary support in reading, writing, editing, communication skills, personality opment skills, presentation skills, music, painting, home science, language skills, daily living skills to students.
- Volunteers act as scribe in the examination of students.
- Help in repairing equipment and maintenance of equipment.
- Voluntary support from schools, developing teaching material, tactile diagrams, going for picnic, teaching English songs, collecting funds, spreading awareness.
- Training of volunteers by the senior volunteers by sharing their experiences.
- Co-ordinating voluntary services by volunteers.
- Volunteers are involved in organising mela, organising picnics, games, annual functions, outside trips, escorting, visit to artillery units, museums, competitive activities and preparing for competitive examinations.
- Professional volunteers in field of medicine, computers, engineering, marketing, education provide their expertise as voluntary services.
- Volunteers encourage parents to become volunteers.
- Volunteers encourage our students to take up sports and provide them necessary coaching.
- Volunteers play vital role in organising training's, workshops and conferences.
- Volunteers were involved in development of presentation skills of blind person's workshop with British Council Library.
- Volunteers have promoted home management training for our children.
- Volunteers have helped in forming parent pressure groups.
- Volunteers have been visionaries in creating services for the visually impaired.

- Volunteers have been trained to become special educators.
- Volunteers have worked to create barrier-free environment in shopping centre, post offices, hospitals, public places, worship places, banquette halls, parties, functions, etc.
- Volunteers with experience act as parent counsellors.
- Volunteers promoting positive image in media.
- Volunteers making technology friendly for disabled.
- Volunteers making advocacy groups for the rights of disabled persons.
- Volunteers play positive role in developing self-esteem of disabled persons.
- Volunteers ensure full integration.
- Volunteers sensitising Police, administrators, custom officials, media personnel and public servants.
- Volunteers developed pamphlets, photographs, posters, and paintings to promote positive image of our children.
- Volunteers bring their children to integrate with our children at a very young age.
- These children participate in birthday parties with our children, organise melas and fares.
- Volunteers help to reduce discriminating attitudes.
- Volunteers help in enhancing the participation of disabled persons in the political life.
- Volunteers help blind persons to exercise the right to vote and participate in political activities.

How do We Promote Volunteerism?

Volunteerism can be promoted through recognition, belongingness, wantedness, appreciation, networking and through involvement. Efforts are constantly made to recognise the good work and highlight it. The organisations playing vital role in promoting voluntary services are informed about the developments and are given due importance in our programmes.

How do We Train and Empower Volunteers?

Empowering volunteers is one of our main objectives. We provide induction training by introducing our organisation and making them observers of our activities. They are told about the various assignments that can be taken up by them depending upon the skills they have and the extent of challenge they intend to take up. There involvement into our activities empower them with the knowledge of our working. They are made active member of various committees to suggest solutions and help in their implementation. They are provided with the necessary information to improve the system as a whole. Our problems and limitations are discussed with full transparency in the larger interest of the society.

Conclusion

Voluntary services are the most wonderful gift to our organisation that a large number of our well-wishers are extending to us. The International year of Voluntary Services has imparted a new thrust to our efforts. We at NAB are continuously working to improve our services and create more and more opportunities to promote voluntarism.

17

REHABILITATION IN NEW MILLENIUM: CHALLENGES AND OPPORTUNITIES

Bhushan Punani

Friends, we are at a historic juncture today. Disability, persons with disabilities and rehabilitation are no more the term, which concern only rehabilitation professionals and organizations working for any aspect of rehabilitation, education or development. The United Nations is at the verge adopting Convention on Human Rights of the Disabled; the World Bank has established the disability division; the Asian Development Bank is likely to include disability in its Poverty Alleviation Programme; Biwako Framework aims at comprehensive rehabilitation of persons with disabilities. At the national level, our country is ceased with the idea of amending its PwD Act to make it more effective; Ministry of Social Justice & Empowerment has taken a variety of initiatives for reaching the PwDs in the rural areas; many State Governments have also taken state-wide initiatives on reaching the unreached; many NGOs have introduced innovative programmes on comprehensive rehabilitation.

Let us begin with an optimistic note that the disability development services are bound to stay and grow. The major concerns however are what services, for whom, to what extent, quality of services and extent of coverage. The service delivery should no more be a passive activity of covering a few hundred PwDs under a few traditional programmes. On the contrary, it should emerge as a people driven movement of reaching each and every person with disability with a package of individual need based comprehensive services with the active participation and involvement of individuals, family, community and other stakeholders.

EXPECTATIONS FROM SUMMIT

To me, Summit of Minds is a step in the right direction. Let us not take is another opportunity of meeting our colleagues and developing inter-personal relations or learning new techniques of mobilizing resources and soliciting grants. Let us consider it a golden opportunity of sharing our thoughts, experience and understanding with the objective of evolving a comprehensive package of innovative, result oriented and realistic services aimed ensuring comprehensive development of the persons with disabilities.

Let us not rewind the clock by always focusing on failure of existing programmes, blaming the system for its ineffective delivery of services, lack of opportunities, non-implementation of the PwD Act, limited financial, human and material resources and apathy of concerned officials and service providers. Let us think of vast opportunities within the community, tremendous resources within the system, great potentials of stakeholders themselves and wealth of knowledge and experience of professional workers and voluntary workers in the field. A large proportion of existing infrastructure, establishment, resources and knowledge remain either underutilized or wrongly utilized. To me, teaching chalk making to the blind; admitting a person with calipers in the residential schools when she could easily walk to a neighbourhood school, teaching sign language to persons with mild or moderate hearing loss, admitting slow learners in the special schools for the mentally retarded are some of the example in this respect.

TOWARDS A NEW MILLENNIUM

The new millennium should usher in a new era not only for 10 per cent persons with disabilities who have already received some intervention or some services but also for those remaining 90 per cent who have not even been identified or covered under any services. Similarly, the quality of service delivery needs to be improved significantly to render the existing and envisaged programmes realistic and result oriented. The new millennium would require qualitative as well as quantitative improvements in the services. According to me, the new millennium should afford a variety of challenges and opportunities to the persons with disabilities:

1. **Support to Envisaged Disability Convention**: The United Nations is on the verge of evolving and adopting the "*Convention on the Fundamental Rights of Persons with Disabilities*". The guiding principle for this Convention is that human rights are universal and according to their nature thus include all human beings, among them persons with disabilities. All people, disabled and non-disabled, are born equal and have the same inalienable rights to life and development, education and work, and the right to self-determination, independent living, self-representation, inclusion and access to active participation as equal citizens in all aspects of society and community life. India must express solidarity will the international organizations, which are at present struggling to get the convention, adopted by the United Nations.
2. **Adoption of Biwako Framework:** The present document sets out a draft regional framework for action that provides regional policy recommendations for action by Governments in the region and concerned stakeholders to achieve an inclusive, barrier-free and rights-based society for persons with disabilities in the new decade, 2003-2012. The regional framework for action identifies seven areas for priority action in the new decade. Each priority area contains critical issues, targets and the action required. In fact, most of areas identified in the framework

are in consonance with the policy being pursued in India. Our country should take lead in adopting the framework as a policy document for its implementation within envisaged time frame.

3. **An Independent Ministry**: The implementation of Persons with Disability Act and adoption of international declarations certainly requires that our country must have an independent Ministry for the achieving targets of enhancing coverage, improving quality and ensuring access to stakeholders to a variety of services. Similarly, there should be an independent Departments of Disability Affairs in each and every State. Some State Governments have already taken initiatives in this regard and others need to follow.
4. **Pro-rata Allocation of Budget:** While the nodal Ministry will co-ordinate activities for the persons with disabilities, all the concerned Ministries as well State Departments must make pro-rata allocation of their regular budgets for promotion of respective services for persons with disabilities.
5. **Amendments to the PwD Act:** The draft amendment bill has remained pending for a number of years. As per the dictum of law, justice delayed is justice denied. It is essential to expedite adoption of amendments so that the amended PwD Act is able to fulfill aspiration of persons with disabilities in a more effective manner.
6. **Inclusive Approach**: Only way to enhance coverage and to provide a variety of services to PwDs is to adopt and implement inclusive approach as envisaged under the PwD Act and under a variety of international declarations to which India is a signatory. Even after the Supreme Court has upheld the provisions as regard reservation in admission of PwDs to all educational institutes receiving grants from the Government, many Universities and educational institutes are not willing to grant admissions.

7. **Comprehensive Services:** The days of running one room, one person, single category of disability for specific services are gone. Such "match box" organizations are no more viable and effective. To become effective, economically viable and sustainable, the organizations must emerge as professionally managed entities with comprehensive service delivery. Such organization should provide services to all categories of disability with all type of services, both in rural and urban areas with multi-pronged approach. The nature of service delivery must encompass prevention and cure of disability, early intervention, appropriate education, support services, income generation and other developmental services. Such organizations would be required to maintain high standards of accountability, complete transparency and visibility. Such organizations must encourage participation of PwD, their family members and service providers in the management and at policy formulation level.
8. **Networking among NGOs:** The NGOs at the local as well as national level should pool their resources, share information and exchange expertise to avoid duplication of services and to ensure efficient and effective use of resources and services. The networking may not remain confined only to disability development organization, it should extend other such organization which are associated any part of service delivery and provision of services to stakeholders.
9. **Parents Associations and DPOs:** As a large number of persons with disabilities have already acquired professional skills, academic qualifications and managerial skills, more organizations of the disabled people and parents associations should be encouraged. Such organizations would be able to ensure participation of PwD and their parents in the administration and monitoring of organizations. The respective State Governments and

concerned Ministries should encourage organizations as services providers, intermediate organization and as mentors of the programmes.

10. **Shift in Focus from Individual to Family:** Most rehabilitation programmes focus and plan intervention centered on individual. In fact, the right segment for planning and promoting appropriate rehabilitation should be the family to begin and community in the long run. Such participation of these segments would ensure sustainability of the programme, promotion social communication and creation of public awareness.
11. **Participation of Corporate Sector:** The concept of social accountability of corporate sector must be exploited to seek participation of sector in promotion of need-based services. As now services for the persons with disabilities have been covered under the provision of Section 35 AC of the Income Tax Act, it would be possible for the recognized organizations to extend exemption on all donations. Such exemption may emerge as a strong tool for mobilization contributions from the corporate sector and individual donors. The corporate sector as demonstrated by Confederation of Indian Industries has a great potential for extending open employment opportunities to PwDs. It also has a great potential of promoting use of technology for comprehensive rehabilitation of the PwDs.
12. **Use of Information Technology:** It is emerging as a great avenue for improvement in quality of life and for income generation for each and everyone. In this world of dynamic growth, the PwDs should not lag behind. In fact, new technology can compensate certain sensory losses to a great extent. For example, use of "Jaws for Windows" for the visually impaired; "visibility" for the low vision; internet for the persons with restricted mobility; computer aided sign language for the hearing impaired; and special

telephone instruments for the deaf-blind. It is the new millennium, it should be ensured that the technology is appropriate, affordable, available and accessible.

13. **Barrier-Free Environment:** Access to all persons with disabilities to built environment, transport and other facilities is an area of great concern. Sporadic attempts that have already been made must become a national movement. It would, however, require sensitization and involvement of architects, builders, town planners, local authorities, concerned State Departments and Ministries. The new millennium should see an Authority especially devoted to this task.
14. **Data Base:** While the National Sample Survey Organization is at the moment busy carrying a sample survey on demographic details of disability, the findings of the same should be widely publicized. An appropriate authority should be established at the national level for maintaining and monitoring demographic pattern on regular basis.
15. **Removal of Disparity as regard Compensation to Staff:** In the same organization, the workers of the PwD are being compensated differently depending upon the source of grant. To most staff members, covered under the grant in aid, the regular payments are made under the guise of "honorarium". I hope the new millennium will upgrade the devoted professional workers from the status of honorarium receivers to salaried persons. How sad! Even today, a qualified full time professional person is paid consolidated honorarium without any terminal benefits.
16. **Effective Implementation of PwD Act:** There is no denying of the fact that the various provisions of the Act have already drawn attention of the Apex Court and legal authorities. A few judgments of the Supreme Court, of the High Court and Chief Commissioners as well as Commissioners of Disabilities have resulted into some

specific provisions of the Act getting implemented. Still there is an immediate need of strengthening implementation of various provisions by Act. The major stumbling blocks at the moment are lack of awareness about the Act, apathy of concerned officials and limited powers of the enforcement machinery. The NGOs, Parents Organizations and other stakeholders must establish legal cells for providing appropriate guidance to PwDs and initiate legal advocacy in this regard. Inauguration of Legal Cell for the PwDs by the Honourable President of India on 28th March at Ahmedabad is a step in the right direction.

17. **Standardization of Training Curricula for PwD:** So far, the RCI has standardized a large number of courses for the service providers and rehabilitation professionals. Now it should focus its attention to standardization of course for the training and rehabilitation of persons with disabilities themselves. Such standardization would ensure improvement in quality of training, better standards of equipment, and minimum standards of intervention, appropriate evaluation of performance and monitoring of progress of the PwDs.

18. **Kangaroo Day:** Last but most important, each concerned Department and disability development organization should celebrate Kangaroo Day at least once in five years. On this day, all the concepts which are outdated, all programmes which are irrelevant and ineffective; all machinery and equipment which are non-functional, beyond repairs and are no more used in the industry; and all vocational training activities which never result into income generation or employment must be thrown out of window. Unless all these outmoded, outdated and irrelevant system and equipment are disposed off, there would be not scope improving quality of our services and making our efforts result oriented. Similarly all service

providers, rehabilitation personnel or professionals who have not improved their skills and providing services that are no more relevant must be compelled to undertake appropriate training to enhance their skills and capabilities.

CONCLUSION

The New Millennium must ensure a shift from charity to human rights of PwDs. They should have access to all the services on early intervention, education, vocational training, micro credit, gainful occupation, employment and social security as a matter of right like any other individual. While focus on quantity is essential, the quality of services should also not be ignored. Another shift, which is essential, is to upgrade the programmes from single service for single disability to truly comprehensive programmes covering all the disabilities and all areas of service delivery including prevention and income generation. Another dimension is use of appropriate technology for expanding scope, nature and quality of services. At the same, the service providers need to modernize their services, organize refresher training of staff and adopt innovations in their programmes. The target for the millennium should be reaching and every person with disability with a package of need based appropriate result oriented services.

18

INTERNAL ENVIRONMENT: A CHALLENGE IN THE NEW MILLENNIUM

C. Tulsi Das

Thousands of years back, from the beginning of human civilization to the present scientific computer age, human being has always tried to change the environment. In the beginning, first he tried to understand the nature and to adjust himself as per the demands of the environment. Then he had some mischief in his mind, started playing with it and started molding the environment for his selfish gains. Now, he wants to dominate, create and formulate a very new artificial environment wherever he wants.

This power game between human being and environment definitely resulted in so called scientific advancements. For example—conquering the moon and other planets, cloning of human being and detection of genome, are some of the examples that can be considered as landmarks of scientific achievements. But a dangerous twist in this process of dominating over the nature also resulted in the destruction of human nature, breakage of human values, code of conducts and development of aggressive instincts in human being leading to wars, atomic explosions and many other new diseases which were not known before. Human being while trying to understand or win over the external environment never felt that a simultaneous shift or change in himself is also required to face the challenges of outside developments. He the human felt that changing the others is much more easier than changing himself.

If 17th century is known as age of enlightenment, 18th century as age of reasoning, 19th century as age of progress and 20th century as age of anxiety then this 21st century is definitely is the age of confusions.

In my opinion, this confusion is emerging and becoming more and more prominent because of the fact, that our attention is completely based on changing others and not on changing ourselves, which has been well documented and well shown in some of the ancient Indian scriptures and thoughts. For example—if we look at the photograph of Lord Vishnu in the picture of "VISHNUSHAYANAM", we will find that Lord Vishnu is sleeping on a thousand headed serpent whereas Goddess Luxmi is pressing his feet and the environment around them is full of typhoon and looks very dangerous but still we find Lord Vishnu in a very relaxed, peaceful and harmonious state

This particular picture of our ancient scriptures has impressed me a lot and now after twenty years of work I have started feeling that Rehabilitation professional on personal level and family level also needs equal attention as much as we expect from him in the rehabilitation of the handicapped.

It is not just the money or financial status of rehabilitation professionals which needs more attention rather to be more specific, he has to undergo or get some counselling and guidance in some personal coping skills which can give rise to calm, peaceful and relaxed feeling in himself while working in the areas of cross-disability. This area needs to be more researched but my feelings is that we should work more on this issue on changing the internal environment of ourselves rather than completely modifying the external environment of the handicapped.

This concept has been well understood by corporate people and big business houses around the world, who are trying their best to bring changes in their own internal environment through different types of stress management programmes, meditative and yogic practices. This has resulted not only in job satisfaction; family coherence but also there is an increase in work out put.

If we look back into our ancient religious scriptures then we will find that they are full of mythical stories and characters who tried to change themselves from inside to bring a positive effect in their on going work. For example—if we look at the story of epic MAHABHARATA in which one of the brothers of Pandavas, the great archer ARJUNA feels depressed and humiliated when he sees his own relatives, near and dear on the other side of field the war with whom he has to fight the war. He puts his bow and arrow down before his chariot driver Lord Krishna and says that he can't fight the war. At that moment, *Lord Krishna* gives him a sermon on KARM YOGA and also shows him the whole universe in him. This brings a new insight and coping skills in Arjuna to fight the war with utmost bravery. This sermon of Lord Krishna symbolizes the fact that there is not only a universe outside which, has to be controlled, changed and altered by the human being but also there is a universe within ourselves, which has to be controlled, altered or changed through KARM YOGA.

So, it is a high time that we Psychologists, Rehabilitation professionals, Social scientists and Special Educators should also utilize these concepts in our own philosophical thoughts and work culture as they make a person less anxious and tension free. If we don't follow this ancient thought in our rehabilitation programmes in the new millennium then I personally feel that we are in the process to face frustrations, conflicts, psychological problems and job turnovers in our day to day life.

Here, I would like to point out some of the ancient methods, which are suitable in our culture to alter the internal state of the human being:

- From our Vedas and Upanishads—chanting of sounds, role of Guru
- From Bhagavad-Gita—Concept of Karma Yoga
- From Ramayana—Simple stories to motivate children towards values
- From Patanjali Yogasutra—Various do and don't of daily

living, food and nutrition, postural exercise and various methods to increase the attention, contemplation and concentration.

- From Ayurveda—Methods to promote longevity.
- From Jainism—Promotion of vegetarianism.
- From Buddhism—Vipasana and middle path of living.
- From Suffism—Methods to develop inner self.
- There are also some cults and movements like Sikhism, Jainism, Tibetan scriptures which have suggested an effective way of living, and promotion of Mental Health.

Thank to social scientists of present day, that they are now accepting the terminology of "Spiritual Health" with Mental Health and Behavioural Health. The recent Conference of Indian Association of Clinical Psychologists is one of the examples in this direction.

My point of view through this theoretic empirical paper, is not to turn the wheel back to spiritual or stone age and to forget about scientific laws of experimentations, but I would like to emphasis that a high success rate the work of rehabilitation professionals can be achieved, if one is trained to control or modify his internal make up without getting frustrated, depressed or getting aggressive. Definitely, this is something humanistic approach of thinking, which may not counter terrorism in the outside world, but definitely it will counter terrorism of the internal world of human being.

19

THE ROLE OF NGO'S IN REHABILITATION PROGRAMMES

Dr. D.K. Singh

Today we have assembled here to talk about the role of NGOs in cross-disability rehabilitation.

NGOs are India's greatest asset and are involved in promoting health, education and social welfare development. Lives needs and expectations of people with disabilities in India like the rest of the world are changing and therefore the policy of welfare state must also change to the new situation.

I graduated from P.W. Medical College, Patna in 1952 and was selected for higher studies in the USA. My father who was a Government Medical Officer at Pirpainti, Bhagalpur in Bihar wanted me to stay back and work for the upliftment and all round development of the under privileged poor, tribal and disabled villagers as I was born and brought up here and owed a high commitment for them. There was no electricity, no roads, and other necessary amenities in the village but I obeyed my father and started private medical practice at Pirpainti in 1953.

I began visiting patients in different villages on horse-back. I was surprised to see the poverty and suffering of the disabled. One day in 1954 while I was waiting for a boat to cross a river, I saw a leper begging. His fingers and toes were eaten up by deep ulcers. His name was Sk. Chedi. I told him to get treated for his wounds. He was reluctant. He said he had nobody to look after, with no money and felt it was a course of God. I assured him free treatment and told him to come to my clinic. He came to me and stayed at my hospital for 3 months. His wounds dried up and he was able to walk freely, I gave him a new set of clothes, Pyjama etc. and helped him in starting his old job of fishing. Other lepers saw how his wounds healed and they developed faith in treatment. One by one I kept treating them and about 250 lepers were treated and rehabilitated between 1954 and 1974. Their entire expenses were borne by me.

I started organizing free eye camps from 1974 each year in winter. This impetus arose in me when I saw almost physically fit men and women between the ages of 40 to 70 years completely disabled due to blindness mostly due to cataract of both eyes. These patients ware unable to move around and found it difficult to even go out to urinate or defecate. They were abused by their own children and few would lend a helping hand. This suffering was disgraceful. After proper investigations, diagnosis and surgery they were provided with spectacles and they could see. The brightness in their eyes and a smile on their faces makes us understand what eye sight means. An average of 150 patients per year were treated. All the expenses till 1984 were borne by me.

In 1978, I took up another good cause when I saw little children limping around. I imported 1000 doses of OPV from Russia and immunized the children of this are.

In 1965 as sole delegate from India to the World Asthma Conference in East Town, England, we discussed about disability in physically fit Bronchial Asthma Patients with severe airway obstruction. In the US we saw big size nebuligers in which the patients would put their heads in side and breath for 2-5 minutes. This would keep them fit for next 2 days.

I would Recommend that

1. Disabled people with locomotor, Visual, Speech, Hearing or Mental impairment should be included in decision-making bodies of the Government.

2. Representation of women should increase from present 3 per cent in Executive bodies of the Government of NGOs.
3. Industry related skills *e.g.* Art, Crafts making of stationary items, TV & Radio repair, Computer handling & repairs should be taught and handled by disabled people.
4. Low cost aids and appliances and service for their repairs and maintenance should be made available.
5. Hostel facilities should be given to such disabled working people especially women.
6. Government should allocate more funds for the disabled sector.
7. Many NGOs are facing problems as they remain starved of funds and resources working with RCI in mutual interest and purposive co-operation will aged to better service conditions, proper use of resources improved training of staff and more effective and efficient service.
8. The struggle for survival of NGOs is fierce and the thought of having co-operation, co-ordination and joint vision is becoming an unattainable dream.

20

REHABILITATING PERSONS WITH DISABILITY THROUGH VOCATIONAL EDUCATION AND TRAINING

Initiatives of PSS Central Institute of Vocational Education

Dr. A.K. Sacheti

INTRODUCTION

Education plays an important role in the holistic development of a person. Vocational Education and Training (VET) provides knowledge and skills related to the occupations in various economic and industrial sectors. The provision of VET has a special relevance for facilitating application of science, technology and economics on one hand and preparation of different target groups for gainful employment on the other.

In India, there are about 100 million people with different disabilities including visual, hearing, locomotor and mental impairment. Of these, 30 million are children in the age cohort of 5-14 years who require special education. But, others require vocational education and training for their rehabilitation and economic empowerment.

ROLE OF PSSCIVE IN VET

The PSS Central Institute of Vocational Education (PSSCIVE), a constituent of NCERT is playing key role in the Vocational

Education Programme. The important role and functions of the Institute are:

1. To advise and assist the Ministry of Human Resource Development (MHRD), Government of India, State Governments and Union Territory Administrations on in implementation of vocational education (VE) and work education (WE) programmes.
2. To promote, supervise and guide the establishment of a comprehensive management system for vocational education at different level *i.e.* national, state, district and institutional.
3. To undertake, guide and co-ordinate curriculum development, training, dissemination of information, extension, research, monitoring and evaluation and to offer consultancy to State Governments in the area of VE, both formal and non-formal.
4. To study and monitor the vocational educational requirements of the country as a whole with regard to preparing manpower for development.
5. To promote excellence at all levels of various types of vocational education programmes, *i.e.* formal, non-formal and informal, throughout the country.
6. To ensure uniformity of patterns in the context of national system of vocational education and to maintain quality and standards, including those of teaching professionals at all levels.

The Institute is developing vocational courses for different target groups in the area of Agriculture, Business and Commerce, Engineering and Technology, Health and Para-medical, Home Science, and Humanities and Education. The number of vocational courses developed by the Institute are given in Table 1. The PSSCIVE has published a variety of instructional materials including textbooks, practical manuals and teachers guides.

In addition to the above, the PSSCIVE has developed vocational modules for occupations suitable to different target groups in Dairying, Horticulture, Sericulture, Building Construction, Agriculture Engineering, Electrical Engineering, Inland Fisheries, Marine Fisheries and Fish Processing, Accountancy, Travel and Tourism, Poultry Production and Agro-processing. The modules have been categorized into four levels - 'L' (Class I to V), 'O' (Class VI-IX), 'A' (Class X) and 'H' (Class XII) based on the hierarchy of knowledge and skills.

Table 1: Area-wise Vocational Courses Developed by PSSCIVE

Area	*Courses for Neo-literate*	*Pre-vocational Courses (Classes IX-X)*	*Vocational Courses (Classes XI-XII)*
Agriculture	04	15	32
Business & Commerce	—	06	14
Engineering & Technology	11	15	20
Health & Paramedical	—	—	08
Home Science	06	21	11
Humanities, Science & Education	—	03	06

The number of modules developed for various economic sectors is given in Table 2.

VOCATIONAL MODULES FOR PERSONS WITH MENTAL RETARDATION

The PSSCIVE has done a pioneering work in developing vocational modules for persons with mental retardation in rural areas. The Institute has developed the following modules in Agriculture and Engineering:

Agriculture

1. Ploughman
2. Silkworm Rearing Assistant

Table 2: Number of Modules Level-wise of Different Economic Sector

	Level 'L' (*Class I-V*)	*Level 'O'* (*Class VI-IX*)	*Level 'A'* (*Class X*)	*Level 'H'* (*Class XII*)	*Total*
Crop Production	7	13	28	12	60
Horticulture	10	9	15	19	53
Sericulture	8	9	16	15	48
Inland Fisheries	2	4	14	5	25
Dairying	14	9	39	18	80
Marine Fisheries	15	13	25	13	66
Agro Processing	11	18	21	14	64
Agril. Engg.	6	13	24	34	77
Building Construction	12	14	6	8	40
Electrical Engg.	2	6	11	6	25
Accountancy	—	13	16	—	29
Travel & Tourism	—	11	15	9	35
TOTAL	87	132	230	153	602

3. Farm Attendant (Sericulture)
4. Field Worker (Horticulture)
5. Nurseryman (Ornamental)
6. Cattle Attendant
7. Milking Attendant
8. Layer House Attendant
9. Cage House Attendant
10. Poultry Feed Mill Attendant
11. Broiler House Attendant
12. Basket Maker
13. Fish Packager
14. Fisherman-cum-Net Mender
15. Fish Farm Helper
16. Rack/Pen/Cage Making Helper
17. Fish Processing Helper
18. Fish Filleting Helper
19. Net Maker and Mender
20. Fish Curing Helper
21. Helper for Fish Meal Preparation

Title of Occupation: Farm Attendant (Sericulture)

Course Content

Duration : 2 Months

S. No.	*Task*	*Syllabus*	*Work readiness skills*	*Duration in (Hrs.)*	
				Training with aid	*Training on the job*
1.	Ploughing	– Acquaintance with the plough – Identification of parts – Hitching the plough on Bullocks with assistance – Handling the plough properly – Balancing the rope while ploughing – Maintaining the depth of furrow – Maintaining the line of furrow	– Eye-hand coordination – Bilateral hand coordination – Gross motor activity – Bilateral foot coordination	30	60
2.	Planting sapling	– Recognising the plant distance – Preparing the pits – Treating the saplings with hot water and Bordeaux mixture – Planting the saplings in the pits	– Eye-hand coordination – Hand-foot coordination – Gross and fine motor activity	30	60
3.	Irrigating the field	– Applying water using different methods of irrigation *e.g.* furrow method – raining excess water	– Bilateral foot coordination – Bilateral hand coordination – Gross and fine motor activity	10	20
4.	Application of fertiliser	– Identification of fertiliser – Applying fertiliser through broadcast method – Washing hands and containers used	– Manipulation and transfer (lift and place) – Bilateral hand coordination – Identification and discrimination	10	20
				80 16 days	160 32 days

Engineering

22. Automobile Attendant
23. Animal Transport Helper
24. Tractor Helper
25. Briquetting Plant Helper
26. Mason Attendant
27. Plumber Attendant
28. Brick Layer Helper
29. Carpenter Attendant

Each module has a list of tasks to be performed, syllabus, work readiness skills, duration, place of training and placement. A exemplar vocational module is given below:

Place of Training : Mulberry Garden

Placement : Sericulture Farm/Mulberry Raising Farm

Guidelines for offering of vocational modules, which includes objectives, target group, selection of module, syllabus, selection of training site, selection of instructors, duration of training, training strategy, assessment and monitoring and evaluation have been developed for NGOs.

It has been suggested that an orientation course for the instructors of vocational institutions/organisations and a certificate course for Village Level Workers/Mental Retardation Workers/ Coordinators of Non-Government Organisation who would work as vocational trainers for persons with mental retardation should be organised to apprise them of the various teaching-learning processes and technical aspects related to the modules. While there is a general acceptance in the society, that there is a need to implement a comprehensive vocational education and training programme for physically and mentally challenged persons, but concrete steps in this direction are lacking. It is, therefore, suggested that the following points may be considered by the Rehabilitation Council of India, New Delhi for offering vocational modules through NGOs having experience in implementing special education programmes in local situations, especially in rural areas.

1. Organisation of awareness programmes for informing NGOs about the availability of short and long duration vocational courses developed by PSSCIVE.

2. Development of database of NGOs willing to offer vocational courses.
3. Selection of NGOs for implementing VET programmes.
4. Involvement of PSSCIVE in orienting NGOs for preparation of Detailed Project Report (DPR) required for getting funds under the proposed TVE&T Scheme by MHRD.
5. Detailed survey of physically and mentally challenged persons in rural areas.
6. Organisation of awareness programmes in rural areas amongst parents about the importance of VET in rehabilitating challenged persons.
7. Arranging orientation courses for instructors of vocational institutions/ organisations working in rural areas and willing to train trainers.
8. Arranging certificate courses for VLWs/MRWs/ Coordinators of NGOs.

21

SELF HELP MOVEMENT OF PERSONS WITH DISABILITIES

Dr. G. Muniratnam

INTRODUCTION

Rashtriya Seva Samithi (formerly known as Rayalaseema Seva Samithi) established in the year 1981, operates in the States of Andhra Pradesh, Orissa and Tamil Nadu. RASS over the period of existence has successfully implemented more than 40 projects/ programmes in 3,540 villages for the benefit of 2.31 million people. Some of its important programmes are:

* Women and child development.
* Agriculture and community development
* Programmes for the handicapped and destitute

The services of RASS have been recognized by many organisations and people, in the form of several national awards. RASS was conferred with National awards by the Government of India for its outstanding contribution in the field of Child Development and disabled a during the years 1984, 1989 and 1994 respectively. In addition to this National prestigious award *i.e.* Jamnalal Bajaj Award was also conferred. These reorganisation are sources of great strength and support to RASS to design and implement long-term perspective development activities.

The increasing realization that people with disabilities have the same human needs as non-disabled people living in the wider community. People with disabilities need to develop their skills and personality as part of achieving their full potential. By realizing the fact, RASS started a separate wing within itself and named it SAHAYA (Help). It is indeed the culmination of decade long work with the people and search for better deal to the disabled at Tirupati, Chittoor, Ananthapur, Cuddapah and Proddatur.

SAHAYA

SAHAYA the word means to Help. Here Sahaya is to help the disable persons. Sahaya is having different programmes like - community based rehabilitation, Day care centers for children with mental retardation at Ananthapur, Cuddapah, Chittoor, Tirupati and Proddatur Residential school at SAHAYA Village (15 km away from Tirupati). Training Institute for Diploma in Special Education (Mental Retardation) and AWO/CBR project for the physically handicapped children. The target area covers in and around Tirupati of Chit to or districts of Andhra Pradesh.

SAHAYA CBR PROJECT

SAHAYA CBR project of RASS initiated in 1991 as a project with partnership with of Action-Aid, India. The Community Based Rehabilitation (CBR) approach has a special appeal to RASS, because the community involvement, which it envisages, is very much in line with autonomous village units in which village committees have to plan and execute programmes for their own welfare.

The project area consisted of 253 areas in and around Tirupati, with a total population of 2,31,629. The area has total disabled population of 1258. This was identified through door to door survey.

The main aim of CBR programme is to identify the disables in the community and rehabilitate them through the community.

Functions

1. Identification and Early Intervention
2. Prevention Aspects
3. Medical, Education and Economic Rehabilitation
4. Home Bound Intervention

With the view of achieving these objects the project implants its services through four specific sectors.

Group Organisation

The Group Organisation sector has expanded considerably widening its activities and strengthening its gross roots level links. Report with the Communities has increased to such an extent that Sahaya is being unanimously identified as Community Based Rehabilitation Programme.

Activities of Group Organisation Sector

1. Awareness Meetings
2. Health Education
3. Local Support Group Meetings
4. Financial Management Training
5. Exposure Visits for Parents and Community Members
6. Referral Services
7. Workshops for Anganwadi Teachers
8. Workshops for Parents and Village Leaders

Medical and Health Rehabilitation

The health and medical rehabilitation programme addressed the need for preventive, promotive and rehabilitative aspects of health care for the disabled. Different camps conducted in the areas created a lot of awareness to the community to control the onset of disability.

The Camps conducted by Medical and Health Sector

1. Medical Camps are Multidisciplinary in nature. They are:
   (a) General Health Camps
   (b) ENT
   (c) Eye Screening
   (d) Psychiatric Assessment
   (e) Polio Prevention
   (f) Encephalitis
2. Workshops on
   (a) Counselling parents
   (b) Occupational Therapy
   (c) Physio-Therapy
3. Provided aids and appliances to the need persons like:
   (a) Crutches
   (b) Wheelchairs
   (c) Hearing Aids
   (d) Cycles

Special Education

The main aim of the special education sector was to provide home bound training to almost all the persons with disabilities and their parents in the areas. Different programmes were conducted for different type of disables.

For Children with Mental Retardation

(a) Assessment was conducted
(b) Followed by setting of goals and objectives for the child according to their age, sex, need.
(c) Training in ADL's (Activities of Daily Living)
(d) Sports
(e) Yoga
(f) Sports, Games

(g) Tour programmes were arranged for the children for expensive.

Vocational Training and Income Generation

The adult disabled persons were trained in vocational skills according to their ability. They are trained in the community centres as well as their home. The adult disabled trained in different Income Generation Programmes like:

(a) Lamination
(b) Envelop making
(c) Chalk-piece making
(d) Agarbathi making
(e) Woollen handicrafts (doll making)
(f) Tailoring
(g) Candle making
(h) Computer training
(i) Type writing
(j) Selling of Water bags
(k) Leaf Plate making

In the self-help programme, the parents of PwD and Adult PwDs (People with Disability) are involved. They form in to a groups and subscribe a fixed amount in the group, which helps them to improve their savings and get loan to start a business or what they prefer to do. They repay the amount in instalment with an interest. In 1998, the pattern of approach from sector changed to mandals by dividing the total project area of 253 areas into 4 Mandals.

The community participation has increased, they co-operated in all the activities of the project. The Mandal Committee involved in planning and implementation of the programmes. They contributes land to construct building of their own.

Likewise RASS has given enormous help to the disabled to stand on their own feet with its 12 years experience with CBR

Programme, RASS achieved 100 per cent results in forming 'Self-Help Groups' for disabled, by the disabled and of the disabled.

At phased stage of CBR Programme RASS has provided Rs.40 lakhs to the Mandal Committees for the sustainability of the programme, with this financial support, self-help group working effectively.

Outer area of CBR Programme, where disabled persons need institutional care, RASS is constructing 'SAHAYA VILLAGE' with in 20 acres of land near Reenigimte, Clitroo district.

Sahaya Village is constructed for the poor, destitute and orphan children with disabilities. It offers services for destitute women and old age person also. For this purpose, RASS constructed buildings, where 200 children can accommodate, 10 bedded fully equipped hospital and well equipped Physio-therapy centre and integrated school. For the persons with disabilities self sustainability RASS started Vocational Training Units like Binding, Soft Toy making etc. At present 70 children with Physically Handicapped and 65 children with mental retardation are residing. RASS is providing free boarding and lodging facilities for these children.

Day Care Centres (Vikas Vihars) of RASS at Chittoor. Cuddapah Proddatur. Anantapur and Tirupati

RASS is providing Individualized Educational Programme to the children with Mental Retardation through its day care centres. All these centres create more awareness among communities regarding prevention, causes, referrals, management, care and importance of special education and involvement of family and community in rehabilitation programme of children with mental retardation. Day Care Centres providing necessary training to the children, with involvement of parents as well as community to integrate them in the mainstream of society. We are grateful to the Ministry of Social Justice and Empowerment for extending financial support. In the Chittoor and Anantapur Centres 5 candidates from each centre passed 7th class in open schools examinations. Like wise RASS is working for the benefit of the disabled, wherever there is support from Government and community. RASS is guiding number of grass roots voluntary organisations.

Training Institute for Diploma in Special Education (MR)

Along with the above programmes, RASS is running Training Institute for Diploma in Special Education (Mental Retardation) since 1993. So far RASS Training Institute produced 158 qualitative special educators. At present 10th batch have completed its final examinations and awaiting for results. We are inviting application for 11th batch with revised curricula and now along with this course, Training Institute conducted short-term training programmes like 6 Bridge Courses for in-service candidates and Craft Teachers, CRE Programmes for Special Educators, VIKALANGA BANDHU Programme for village volunteers/Community members to start self-help groups, Foundation Course on Children with Disabilities for Teachers. The Ministry of Social Justice and Empowerment is providing financial assistance for this programme.

RASS, Training Institute is inviting applications for Special B.Ed., in collaboration with MPBOU [Madhya Pradesh Bhoj (Open) University], Bhopal for the academic year 2003-2004. As non-Governmental Organisation, RASS is playing its role in sharing the statutory responsibilities of RCI and increased human resources in the field with its guidance.

Composite Camps

RASS is organising composite Rehabilitation camps for disable in collaboration with the National Institute for the Mentally Handicapped (NIMH) in Chittoor District. So far it has conducted camps in 5 Mandals of Chittoor District and got good response. In future RASS is planning to extend these camps throughout the Chittoor District in Andhra Pradesh.

22

THE ROLE OF NGO'S IN REHABILITATION PROGRAMME

Indumathi Rao

In India, the rapid growth of population in general and persons with disability in particular has created a huge demand for basic rehabilitation services. Most of the world's disability population is believed to be living in India. A majority of them lives in rural areas and are below poverty line.

Though government is putting enormous efforts for rehabilitation there still exists large gaps between need and actual availability of rehabilitation services. Thus in current scenario, Non-Governmental Organizations/Voluntary Organizations are emerging as alternative strategy of development of rehabilitation services. There are about 60 million disabled people in India. According to the Directory of Institutions compiled by the National Information on Disability and Rehabilitation of India, there are more than 2,000 NGOs working in the area of disability. Most of these organizations are engaged in service delivery-providing education, distributing aids and appliances and imparting vocational rehabilitation. (NCEDP-website)

The magnitude of the problem of disability is vast and its impact is very severe on the individual, families, and the community. There are several accepted political goals such as Universalisation of Elementary Education, Mass Literacy programmes, Poverty eradication programmes, Health for needy people, and other developmental programmes. These are aimed at improving the quality of life of under-privileged groups which included people with disabilities. India has participated in almost all international conventions on disability and has been a signatory to all the important declarations made by UN agencies. It is important to develop rehabilitation plans for persons with disabilities aiming at a wide coverage and good quality services in a sustainable manner by optimal utilization of existing resources available. This is possible by convergence and synergy between government, stakeholders, and NGO's.

Table 1: State-wise NGOs Working in Different Disability Sector

Sl. No.	*State*	*VI*	*HI*	*MR*	*PH*	*CD*	*MD*	*MI*	*Total*
1.	Andhra Pradesh	6	5	28	10	27	1	1	78
2.	Arunachal Pradesh	1	1	1	1	2	2	1	9
3.	Assam	1	1	3	1	1	1	1	9
4.	Bihar	1	3	2	4	1	1	1	13
5.	Chandigarh	1	1	1	1	1	1	1	7
6.	Delhi	10	2	10	6	8	1	1	38
7.	Goa	1	1	1	1	1	1	1	7
8.	Gujarat	5	2	4	1	3	1	1	17
9.	Haryana	5	2	1	1	3	1	1	14
10.	Jammu & Kashmir	1	1	1	1	1	1	1	7
11.	Karnataka	10	11	6	2	21	1	1	52
12.	Kerala	3	4	23	7	17	1	1	56
13.	Madhya Pradesh	1	1	1	2	2	1	1	9
14.	Maharashtra	4	13	8	8	1	1	1	36
15.	Manipur	1	1	1	1	2	1	1	8
16.	Meghalaya	1	1	2	1	1	1	1	8
17.	Mizoram	1	1	1	1	1	3	1	9
18.	Nagaland	1	1	1	1	1	1	1	7
19.	Orissa	2	1	2	4	9	1	1	20
20.	Punjab	1	1	2	1	3	1	1	10
21.	Rajasthan	1	2	3	1	2	1	1	11
22.	Tamil Nadu	8	6	11	8	7	3	1	44
23.	Tripura	1	1	1	1	1	1	1	7
24.	Uttar Pradesh	8	10	6	13	19	1	1	58
25.	Uttaranchal	1	2	1	2	1	1	1	9
26.	West Bengal	4	7	8	13	6	1	1	40
	Total	**80**	**82**	**129**	**93**	**142**	**31**	**26**	**583**

VI—Visual Impairment; HI—Hearing Impairment; MR—Mental Retardation; PH—Physical Handicap; CD—Cross Disability; MD—Multiple Disability; MI—Mental Illness. This database is based on the NGOs list given in the "Handbook for Parents of Children with Disabilities" by the Planning Commission, Government of India, 2002. (All zeros have been converted to one by default)

It has been half a decade since the people with disabilities (equal opportunities, protection of rights and full participation) Act, 1995, passed. However, the goal of Rehabilitation services for all differently abled persons has yet to take its root.

It is an accepted fact that people with disabilities constitute nearly 4-5 per cent of our population and it is estimated that people with moderate to severe disabilities constitute 2-4 per cent. Having mentioned this, it is necessary to state that there is no authentic data on prevalence disabilities.

Civil Societies in India

In India volunteerism is an integral part of the social fabric. The socio-cultural landscape in India has promoted/ing volunteerism, civil societies, and community based organizations. The sizes of these organizations have a wide range both in terms of geographic area, sectoral reach etc. The priorities and strategies are based on the individual organization's capabilities and vision.

In disability sector a majority of the organizations in the post-independence era were initiated by families with children with disability. In the 70's we find a large number of organizations registered as trust/societies. It is important to understand the nature of these organizations in terms of their geographical operation and reach. It is intrinsically important to analyse the role of NGO's in the rehabilitation sector as they are emerging as the major contributors in the Disability sector. It is interesting to note the NGO's of the 70's, focussed on providing services such as special schools, residential schools, and vocational training centres, moved on in 80's to the areas such as Human resource development, Community based rehabilitation, Integrated education etc. In the

Table 2: Prevalence of Disability in India Based on 2001 Census Data

Code	State	Total Population		Disabled Rural Population			Disabled Urban Population		
		General	*Disabled*	*Persons*	*Male*	*Female*	*Persons*	*Male*	*Female*
1	Jammu and Kashmir	10069917	254769	191385	99324	92061	63384	34781	28604
2	Himachal Pradesh	6077248	153754	138704	69683	69021	15050	8374	6676
3	Punjab	24289296	614519	405906	215066	190840	208613	112907	95706
4	Chandigarh	900914	22793	2331	1438	893	20463	11420	9042
5	Uttaranchal	8479562	214533	159626	79528	80098	54907	29677	25230
6	Haryana	21082989	533400	378712	202846	175866	154688	83744	70944
7	Delhi	13782976	348709	24369	13490	10879	324340	178053	146287
8	Rajasthan	56473122	1428770	1094672	566580	528092	334098	176776	157322
9	Uttar Pradesh	166052859	4201137	3327968	1748148	1579820	873170	464749	408420
10	Bihar	82878796	2096834	1877250	974320	902929	219584	117475	102109
11	Sikkim	540493	13674	12156	6461	5695	1518	831	688
12	Arunachal Pradesh	1091117	27605	21971	11475	10496	5634	3046	2588
13	Nagaland	1988636	50312	41386	21420	19966	8926	4934	3992
14	Manipur	2388634	60432	46001	23363	22638	14431	7183	7248
15	Mizoram	891058	22544	11385	5913	5472	11158	5719	5439
16	Tripura	3191168	80737	66996	34390	32606	13740	7004	6736
17	Meghalaya	2306069	58344	46892	23777	23115	11451	5769	5682
18	Assam	26638407	673952	588200	303174	285026	85752	45657	40095
19	West Bengal	80221171	2029596	1460688	749033	711655	568908	300606	268302
20	Jharkhand	26909428	680809	529345	269709	259636	151463	80981	70482
21	Orissa	36706920	928685	789628	397510	392118	139057	73382	65675
22	Chhatisgarh	20795956	526138	420502	209762	210740	105636	54685	50951

(*Contd.*)

(Contd.)

Code	State	Total Population		Disabled Rural Population			Disabled Urban Population		
		General	Disabled	Persons	Male	Female	Persons	Male	Female
23	Madhya Pradesh	60385118	1527743	1120348	581274	539074	407396	214585	192811
24	Gujarat	50596992	1280104	801950	412122	389827	478154	254382	223772
25	Daman and Diu	158059	3999	2549	1608	940	1450	731	719
26	Dadra and Nagar Haveli	220451	5577	4301	2325	1976	1277	755	521
27	Maharashtra	96752247	2447832	1410033	719614	690419	1037799	553843	483956
28	Andhra Pradesh	75727541	1915907	1397166	704660	692506	518741	263996	254745
29	Karnataka	52733958	1334169	880797	445750	435046	453372	233715	219657
30	Goa	1343998	34003	17081	8593	8488	16922	8754	8169
31	Lakshadweep	60595	1533	851	435	416	682	352	330
32	Kerala	31838619	805517	596359	289705	306654	209159	101652	107506
33	Tamil Nadu	62110839	1571404	882193	442977	439216	689211	348120	341092
34	Pondicherry	973829	24638	8238	4139	4099	16400	8175	8225
35	Andaman & Nicobar	356265	9014	6068	3260	2809	2945	1623	1322
	Total	1027015247	25983486	18764005	9642872	9121133	7219480	3798438	3421042

90's there is a distinct trend in NGO sector wherein added focus is on human resource development, professionalization, Advocacy, Networking and increased role in reaching the unreached in the rural India through application of some of the global approaches such as CBR, Inclusive education, Portgae etc. Convergence and synergy with other NGO's working in development sector and meaningful partnership with the government is also seen in many states. It is interesting to note that a majority of NGO's, around 77 per cent, are contributing in the education sector (Table 3). Less than 1 per cent are involved in early childhood intervention programmes. Around 3 per cent are running vocational training and placement centres. Less than 1 per cent are involved in advocacy and networking services. Around 17 per cent are involved in Human resource development activities. Less than 1 per cent are focusing on gender issues in disability sector exclusively.

Table 3: NGO's in Education Sector

ECCD	*Education*	*Vocational training and placement*	*Advocacy and networking*	*Gender focus*	*Human resource development*
1%	77%	3%	1%	1%	17%

Source: Analysis of 700 NGO's initiatives in India-2000, CBR NETWORK (South Asia). NGO's who are providing more than one services are reflected under different categories of services.

The above data clearly indicates that NGO's need to develop services based on the local needs. Local needs may vary from one region to another. Therefore, there is an urgent need for micro planning to identify local needs. Approaches, which are driven by the schemes and grants available from the government and international organizations, need to be replaced on the local needs and priorities. This is possible only when there is decentralization of powers from central and State Governments to district level bodies such as Panchayati Raj System. This also needs training of the local bodies in identification of local needs and priorities, CBR,

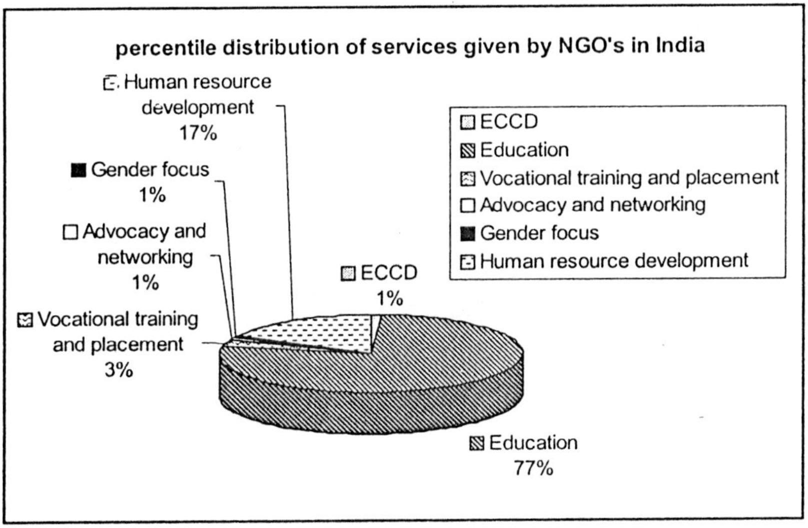

Inclusive education strategies and similar community based cost effective approaches.

Update of Technology — Need for a Cross-Disability Shift

NGOs are moving from single disability approach to cross-disability (Table 1). Such shift is occurring at two levels:

(a) Integration of one more disability to the existing services.
(b) Inclusive approaches, which meets all special needs irrespective of the type of disability, contributing to the specific special needs.

As of now we have four national institutes each one focusing on different disabilities such as mental handicap (NIMH), Visual disabilities (NIVH), Hearing impairments (NIHH), and locomotor disabilities (NIOH).Even though these institutes have a wing in which other institutes run their activities to cover the specific geographical region they work independently of each other. NCERT is providing guidelines for inclusive education based on cross-disability approach.

The cross-disability approach is a major challenge for the next decade: There is a need for research, high quality training of cross-disability personnel, policies, plans and funding guidelines for both government and international aid agencies. There is a need to develop a cross-disability research and development units in all the national institutes to develop materials, skill development, planning and management strategies for cross-disability projects such as CBR, Inclusive education, employment placement centres, vocational training and so on. This demands meaningful convergence and synergy of the national level apex institute. As it is today we do not have much experience in the inclusive approaches though a major step has been taken by NGO's in integrating services.

In India colunteerism in an integral part of the social fabric. The socio-cultural landscape in India has promoted/ing volunteerism, civil societies, and community based organiszations...

In the future, the NGOs will have to play a major role alongside with the governments at different levels and private sectors, only then can we accomplish this Herculean task (NCEDP-2001).

Idiosyncratic Development of NGO's

In Table 1, we see the analyses about 580 NGOs, is in terms of their geographical and sectoral operations. This data reveals some interesting factors. For example, we find NGOs genesis and growth is not independent of the needs. This is evident from large size states such as Madhya Pradesh having few voluntary organizations and states such as Kerala having more number of NGOs. This data is though limited in size still throws light on the idiosyncratic development of NGO's in India.

According to a study by NCEDP (sample of 180 organizations), less than 25 per cent NGOs receive any financial help from the government. The growth of NGOs in urban areas and the scanty growth of NGO's in remote rural areas can be attributed to this factor. Having said this it is important to see the new trend in the growth of CBOs/self-help groups in the rural areas which is *Promoted* by the organizations who may or may not be local based.

A comparison of Tables 1 and 2 also shows that NGO's growth in different states is not proportionate with the need. This does not mean that there are more NGOs in a few states but it means that there is a need to promote NGOs in states with scarce number of NGO's.

Need for Organized Growth of NGO's

Therefore, there is a need to promote NGOs based on the need. This does not mean that government should promote NGO formation. NGO's strength lies in their commitments and close contact with grass roots. However, the government should advertise the need in different districts/tehshils. This information would help NGOs in selection of the geographical area and prevention of duplication of efforts.

Needless to say, such an initiative from the government will also help in fair distribution of services instead of concentration in urban areas.

Need for Policy Guidelines for Sustainability

NGOs initiate projects based on inspiration by other NGO's or by the government supported grant in aid schemes or as per the priorities of International donors. The important issues for the sustenance of such projects by NGO's are:

1. Who will sustain centrally sponsored schemes once the scheme is closed down?
2. To what extent will the State Governments sustain the centrally sponsored programmes?
3. Who will sustain projects supported by the international donors after the project period?
4. How can small Community Based Organizations /Self-

Help mutual aid groups sustain with the help of local resources?

These are some of the burning issues that is to be addressed by the NGO sector. At one end there is an increased expansion in terms of NGO's scope and range of services but on the other hand there is very little support in the area of sustainability of the programmes.

Enhancing the Impact of NGO's Work

Governments also seem at crossroads regarding its policy about the NGOs in the rehabilitation sector. Should the government leave NGO's genesis and growth as a social activity and support only if these organizations are helpful to fulfill the government goals and objectives? or Should the government work with NGOs on an equal partnership basis as an integral part to outsource responsibilities to NGOs? This kind of relationship between NGO's and Government needs a sound system. In fact it calls for a total reform in the government and NGO's to address issues concerning disability in a way which leads to optimum impact.

NGO'S SCOPE OF WORK

NGOs in rehabilitation sector in India are addressing almost all issues concerning disability. Such issues include early childhood development, special, integrated and inclusive education, vocational education, employment and placements. They are actively leading advocacy and networking movements. NGOs' role in human resource development is evident by more than 100 NGOs actively collaborating with the Rehabilitation Council of India in training the necessary personnel. National Institutes which was started primarily for the HRD development and research could not achieve the desired results on their own and RCI is working in collaboration with NGOs. It is evident that NGOs are longer confined to a few sectors such as running special schools but vibrantly understanding, exploring and translating global concerns into local actions.

NEEDS MORE SUPPORT

NGOs in disability sector have expanded their scope of operation and have emerged as the major contributors in providing new services and strengthening the existing services. They are willing to reach every person with disability in India. They are constantly learning from the local and global experiences, which are evident by the large growth of cross-disability NGOs, activist movement and networking initiatives. *However, the goodwill of NGOs cannot sustain on mere commitment, enthusiasm and vitality.* It must be supported with adequate financial back up from the communities, government and corporate. If the potential need for the NGOs is properly utilized it is not too far for us to see a day where every child, woman, youth and a senior citizen with special needs living with dignity and respect.

Some Suggestions to Strengthen the NGO's in India

- NGOs should choose geographical area of operation based on the actual needs. Government must publish the need for NGO's in different districts/tehsils.
- NGOs need to stress on the process documentation.
- There is a definite need to involve disabled people and to include women with disabilities in the Executive Bodies of NGOs working in the disability sector.
- NGOs should have a policy for employing disabled people in their professional and non-professional workforce.
- The Government's needs to review its funding policy. There is a definite need for a need-based and fair distribution of fund.
- NGOs should increase the number of professional staff and review their methods of working to increase the impact and cost-effectiveness.
- There is a definite need for better accountability system.
- The relationship of NGO's in disability sector and Panchyati Raj System need be defined and strengthened.

CONCLUDING REMARKS

This historic convention of the NGOs has come to a close but a new era of "Collaboration" is just to begin.

The "Summit of the Mind" has brought together all the minds to propagate in one voice "The need for providing quality services to persons with disabilities in India".

The convention has brought out the message of "Synergy" in disability sector.

The summit has given an opportunity for the NGOs to make a thorough introspection of what is needed for persons with disabilities in the country and I am sure they have all peaked to the summit of understanding and realization, which will definitely improve their work with persons with disabilities in the future.

This unique summit has brought together professionals, policy makers, grass roots level workers, religious people, and administrators, and the result is that all spoke in one voice to improve the services for persons with disabilities in India.

Some vital recommendations of the deliberations have implications for the overhauling of our approach, delivery, and management of services for persons with disabilities in the country. The recommendations include:

- Development of a perspective Plan at the national level
- Development of database of NGOs in the country
- Networking between NGOs, ZACs, RCI and Government
- Involving parents as partners in disability services
- Mechanism for promoting ICT in disability sector
- Undertaking quality developmental research
- Promoting cross-disability approach in services
- Mobilization of community resources

RCI is your partner in putting the recommendations into action.

Please tell us where you need our help.

Let this collaboration strengthen services for persons with disabilities in the country.

We have reached the summit of realization of our strengths and limitations. Let us make a SWOT analysis to improve our work.

Let us see where our Strength lies.

Let us identify our Weakness through introspection and try to convert them as Strengths.

Let us use the Opportunities wherever possible to improve our quality of services.

Let us understand the internal and external Threats and use our strategies to convert them as opportunities and strengths.

In short, let us mediate on the summit of our mind and we will get solutions which we have been looking for.

23

ORGANISING SELF HELP GROUPS FOR THE WOMEN WITH DISABILITIES

S. Jaya

INTRODUCTION

Self Help Groups (SHGs) are fast emerging as powerful tool of socio-economic empowerment of the poor in our rural areas. The self help group is a small body formed by the people for meeting their specific objectives, particularly credit. It is managed by the rules and regulations formed by them and functions on democratic principles. In self help groups, it is assumed that all poor households need to save and have the inherent capacity to save small amounts regularly; easy access to credit is more important than cheap subsidized credit which involves intricate bureaucratic procedures; the poor are the best judge of their credit needs and are good users and re-payers of credit when formed in groups. Studies have revealed that the linkage of SHG with banks has improved the socio-economic conditions of its members by way of positive impact on income, savings, and self-confidence. The impact is more pronounced in the case of SHGs linked through NGOs. SHGs have proved to be successful in addressing the interests of women in a sustained manner. They are extremely useful in generating savings, ensuring successful delivery of credit to individual women and effecting recovery. Hence it is a small economical and voluntary association of rural and urban poor, which functions democratically and accountably, for the upliftment of their families.

NEED FOR SELF HELP GROUP

Self help groups for disabled women are necessary to overcome exploitation, create confidence for the economic self-reliance of rural poor, particularly among women who are mostly invisible in the social structure. These groups enable them to come together for a common objective and gain strength from each other to deal with exploitation which they are facing in several forms. A group becomes the basis for action and change. It also helps building of relationship for mutual trust between the promoting organization and the rural poor to constant contact and genuine efforts. Self help group can be started to assist people with disabilities to live a little more independently, to live with their families and in their communities. The assistance includes mobility aids, assistive devices, integration with schools and other vocational training centres, self-employment, income generation activities and so on. It is not enough to be merely independent, but it is also necessary to have a group that supports and provides a Co-ordinator, Co-operative and empathetic relationship. Such a group acts as a forum to meet, to discuss and to represent their interests and needs to the outside world. Now that the state administration has begun to recognise the special needs of disabled people, such a group can also work collectively to seek the support services from those in authority, more as a right than a benefit to improve on their existing situation.

Organising people in self help groups serves different purposes, depending on the situation and the need. Such a forum can help people to be visible members in the larger community. Members can support one another through sharing information on referral services and other available resources, help make decisions on family and individual matters etc. Self help groups with the support of other such groups, can advocate jointly to obtain services, aids and equipment, and for integration in the larger community.

This is a need to generate self-employment opportunities for disabled people. Instead of selling the raw products to traders at meagre rates, they can prepare finished/semi-finished products and sell them to the Government/Semi-Government/Co-operatives/ Trading Agencies to fetch better prices.

SOME CHARACTERISTICS OF SELF HELP GROUPS

- Groups generate a common fund where each member contribute his/her savings on a regular basis.
- Groups meet periodically to discuss their transactions.
- Loanees are decided by consensus.
- Loans cover a variety of purposes including non-traditional ones also.
- Loan amounts are small and for short duration.
- Loan procedure is very simple and flex.
- Defaults are negligible.
- Groups are mobilizing savings from their members and are effectively rotating the some among their members.

OBJECTIVES

The objectives of the SHGs is to inculcate the habit of thrift, savings, banking culture, that is availing loan and repaying the same over a given period of time and in the process, gain economic prosperity through credit. The principles underlying the SHGs are financing the poorest of the poor, ensuring excellent recovery level, and empowering disabled women not just by meeting their needs for consumption and productive loans but also through more holistic educative programmes.

GUIDING PRINCIPLES FOR SELF HELP GROUPS (SHGs)

- Any type of disabled woman can be join as a member in

the Self Help Group. But member should be resident in the same area. Be homogenous, and number at least five disabled women any time.

- SHGs should promote savings mobilization.
- Savings should be linked to credit savings first, credit next.
- The development of financial disciplines and systems should be encouraged.
- SHGs begin with a simple book-keeping system.
- They should hold regular meetings once a week in a regular place.
- They should have basic rules or by laws (written or unwritten).
- Group leaders should be elected by the members, with group functions or positions being related among the members.
- Transparency in business operations and the overall conduct of group activities should be maintained at all times.
- Basic training and guidance for the disabled women should be provided regularly.
- The autonomy of SHGs should be respected.
- Group liability should be the substitutes for colateral.
- Loans should be kept small initially and repayments made frequently and regularly.
- Transaction costs should be kept to a minimum through simplified group procedures and control.
- Market rates of interest should apply to both savings and credit, to achieve financial liability as soon as possible.
- Commercial banks should be asked to provide appropriate advances or lines of credit to supplement the group's is financial resources and to enable it to be lent for productive purposes.

THE NEW SHG FOR DISABLED WOMEN

The formation of new SHG for disabled women involve basically two stages, namely pre-group formation stage and the promotion stage.

Pre-group Formation Stage

In this stage, it is important that the SHGs promoter, (NGO's) visits the disabled people in the locality/area frequently gathers information about various facts of the disabled people, their life, and its environment. During the stage the promoter also builds up rapport with the members.

Promotion Stage

There are four stages in this phase

1. *Forming*: In this stage different types of women with disability come together informally and meet. They are encouraged to talk about their problems and solutions. During this stage, based on the felt need, homogenous groups emerge naturally.
2. *Storming*: During this stage, conflicts between individual interest and group interest may be dealt with. The leaderships emerges. The procedures, rules and roles are established.
3. *Norming*: Trust develops among group members leading to cohesiveness in the group.
4. *Performing*: This is the final stage when the group becomes operational and starts functioning for the benefit of its members.

MODUS OPERANDI OF SHG

The Self Help Group (SHG) generally has members not exceeding so and each group selects among its members a leader called 'animator'. Then 1st and 2nd members called Representative -I,

Representative-II elected, to carry out activities of the group. The animator conducts three to four meetings in every month. The group members save regular amount of Rs.10 to Rs.100 and more in every week. The group rotates the money to the needy members for various purposes at a specified low interest rate. As the repayment is cent per cent and the recycling is very fast, the saving amount increases faster owing to the accumulation of income from saving habits which help the members to escape from the clutches of moneylenders. This activity also paves the way for the socio-economic empowerment of disabled women and builds confidence in them that they could stand on their own.

BOOKS AND REGISTERS TO BE MAINTAINED BY EVERY GROUP

1. Attendance Register
2. Minutes Book
3. Savings Ledger
4. Load Ledger
5. General Ledger
6. Cash Book
7. Individual Pass Book
8. Receipt Book
9. Payment Vouchers

CREDIT RATING

Minimum eligibility criteria as evaluated as per last six months performance of SHG

1. SHG should have been in existence for over six months (date of opening of the group's bank account is taken as date of SHG establishment).
2. Size of the SHG should be in the range of 5-20 members. In any case, it should not exceed 20.
3. SHG meetings should have been conducted at regular interval (a minimum at one meeting per month) with a minimum overall attendance of 75 per cent.

4. For 6 months or more SHG should not be a defaulter with any institution. The defaults by few members of SHGs and/or their family members to the financing bank should not ordinarily come in the way of financing SHGs *per-se* by banks, provided the SHG is not in default to it. However, a condition may be imposed that the bank loan should not be utilized by the SHG for financing a defaulter member to the bank. This will also help the bank recover its earlier dues, as opposed to a negative approach.
5. The recovery of internal loans and external loans (both principle and interest due) should not be less than 85 per cent.
6. Atleast, 50 per cent of group members should have taken internal loans from group fund.
7. Savings by all members in the group fund should be on a regular basis. The savings amount and frequency of savings are left to the decision of group/members.
8. The group should have maintained proper books of accounts.
9. The group must have well defined rules and regulations approved by proper resolution.

CREDIT RATINGS OF GROUPS

Once the group fulfils all eligibility norms, the NGO shall ascertain willingness to SHG to access bank credit. If the SHG is inclined to apply for credit, NGO/PIU will organize joint appraisal committee meetings at group level for credit rating of groups. Such meetings can be conducted at block level in the longer run. The committee will discuss with the group, verify books of accounts and assess its performance. For village Panchayat the committee consist of the branch Manager, the Co-ordinator from the NGO and the Assistant Project Officer from DRDA. After rating the group, the fund amount of Rs. 25,000 (15,000 from Bank and 10,000 from DRDA) as revolving fund will be realised to do any activity for the group. For the town Panchayat the committee members were the branch Manager, Assistant

Project Officer from Mahalir Thittam and NGO's Co-ordinator, NABARD will fund for the rated group, the amount will vary according to their activities. After one year, for both the village and town Panchayat, second credit rating is done and economic assistance (5,000 to 2.5 lakhs) is given to the group from DRDA.

LINKAGES WITH DEVELOPMENTAL DEPARTMENTS

Figure 1 depicts the linkages of SHGs with other developmental institutions and departments

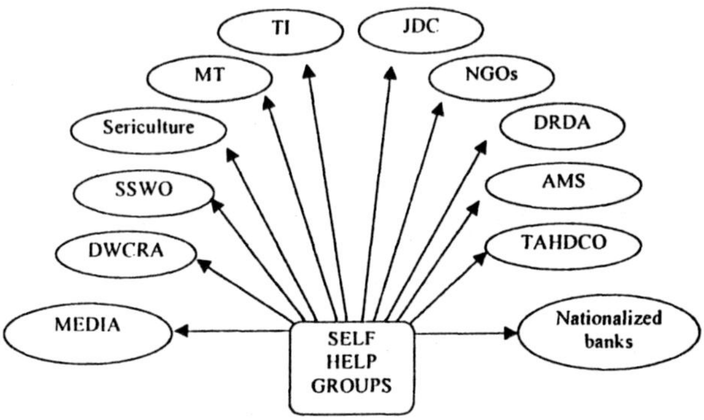

Fig. 1: Linkages of SHGs with Other Institutions

DWCRA —Development Women and Child in Rural Areas
DRDA —District Rural Development Agency
MT —Mahalir Thittam
SSWO —State Social Welfare Officer
AMS —Avin Milk Society
TAHDCO —Tamil Nadu Adi Dravidar Housing and Development Corporation
JDC —Jute Diversification Centre
TI —Training Institutes
NGO —Non-Governmental Organization

ACTIVITIES FOR THE WOMEN WITH DISABILITIES IN SHG

The following are the various activities can be imparted for the women with different types of disabilities. They are as follows:

Soap powder making, Candle making, Wiring furniture, Tailoring, Embroidery, Preparation of different items, Agarbathi, Soft toy making, Phenyle, Liquid blue, Selling snacks, Vermi composing, Mosquito coil, Selling flowers, STD booth, Avin Milk booth, Stationery stores, Petty shop, Ready made garments, Typing, Sericulture, Dairy, Cattle feed, Maintenance of public toilets, Handicrafts, Mat-making, and Wire-bag making.

The following table gives us the clear idea regarding Credit Rating System for Self Help Groups:

Composition of the Credit Rating Index

S. No.	*SHG Parameter*	*Marks for 6m-2yr SHGs*	*Marks for over 2yr SHGs*
1.	*Frequency of Group Meetings (during last l6 months)*		
(i)	4 meetings per month	10	10
(ii)	2-3 meetings per month	7	7
(iii)	2 meetings per month	5	5
(iv)	1 meeting per month	2	2
2.	*Attendance at Group meetings (during last 6 months)*		
(i)	More than 90%	10	10
(ii)	75% to 90%	5	5
(iii)	Less than 75%	0	0
3.	*Member's involvement in Group meeting/activities*		
(i)	High (above 80%)	10	10
(ii)	Medium (above 60%)	5	5
(iii)	Low (Below 50%)	0	0
4.	*Savings Frequency*		
(i)	4 times per month	5	4
(ii)	3 times per month	4	4
(iii)	1 time per month	3	3
(iv)	1 time per month	2	2
5.	*Savings Methodology*		
(i)	Optional rate	5	5
(ii)	Fixed rate	–	–
6.	*Average Savings per member per month*		
(i)	Rs.20/- and Above	5	5
(ii)	Rs. 10-19/-	3	3
(iii)	Less than Rs. 10/-	2	2
7.	*Interest rate on internal loans*		
(i)	Differential rate of interest (different rates are charged for different purposes)	5	5

(*Contd.*)

(*Contd.*)

S. No.	*SHG Parameter*	*Marks for 6m-2yr SHGs*	*Marks for over 2yr SHGs*
8.	*Degree of rotation of Savings*		
(i)	One time or more	5	5
(ii)	0.5-1.0	3	3
9.	*Adequacy of group reserve fund*		
(i)	Fully adequate (adequate for maintenance and other needs)	–	5
(ii)	Partly adequate (adequate for maintenance needs only)	–	3
(iii)	Inadequate (Not adequate even for maintenance needs)	–	2
(iv)	No Existence	–	0
10.	*Repayment of internal loans*		
(i)	Repayment level at 100%	10	10
(ii)	Repayment level at 90-99%	7	7
(iii)	Repayment level at 85-89%	3	3
(iv)	Repayment level at <85%	0	0
11.	*Repayment of all external loans*		
(i)	Repayment level at 100%	10	10
(ii)	Repayment level at 90-99%	7	7
(iii)	Repayment level at 85-89%	3	3
(iv)	Repayment level at <85%	0	0
12.	*Book-keeping (double entry)*		
(i)	All 7 books maintained and updated	10	10
(ii)	Less than 7 books maintained and updated	5	5
(iii)	Single entry Book-keeping done or No books maintained	0	0
13.	*Auditing of group accounts. (book marks 6 months-2 year old groups)*		
(i)	Audited up to date (as on March of every year)	–	5
(ii)	Audited up to last year (one year accounts not audited)	–	3
(iii)	More than one year accounts not audited or accounts not at all audited since inception	–	0
14.	*Clearly defined SHG rules and regulations*		
(i)	Clear rules and regulations for SHG in force by a resolution	5	5
(ii)	No rules or rules are vague or not used	0	0
	Total Score	90	100

CONCLUSION

Now the time has come to implement Self Help Groups and spread it to all phases of development. Hence efforts can be made so intensively to channelise disabled women into groups for group cohesion and dynamism. If this effort proves a success, disabled women would be empowered economically, and scientifically in its true perspective.

24

REVIEW OF QUALITY OF LIFE INSTRUMENTS

S. A. Jayavant & Dr. B.D. Athani

Quality of Life (QOL) is an important, possibly the ultimate outcome measure. QOL encompasses not only disease symptoms and functional consequences but also subjective life satisfaction, happiness and the overall value one places on life at any given time. The importance of including a consideration of the patients QOL in treatment decisions, programme evaluation and resource allocation is immediately apparent and has been extensively documented.

QOL is defined as individual's perception of their position in life in the context of the culture and value systems in which they live and in relation to their goals, expectations, standards and concerns. It is a broad ranging concept incorporating in a complex way individuals physical health, psychological state, level of independence, social relationships, personal beliefs and their relationships to salient features of the environment. QOL includes both positive and negative facets of life.

QOL has two components: Multidimensionality relates to the need to assess life experience broadly (physical, functional, emotional or mental and social aspects). Subjectivity refers to the fact that QOL can be understood only from the patient's perspective. QOL essentially involves appraisal of life or aspects of life by the persons by using his/her own criteria. The very same disease process can have quite different effects on different people. Although it is important to monitor disease and treatment effects using objective measures, only the patient's perspective provides a full understanding of the effect of disease or treatment on the patient.

There is considerable need to prove the value of rehabilitation in practice. Measures of functional ability have become core instruments in rehabilitation medicine. QOL is critical to understanding the benefits of rehabilitation medicine service delivery. Without good methods of assessing QOL, we are hampered in our ability to prioritize interventions according to their likely impact on the QOL of patients.

Health Related Quality of Life (HRQOL) refers to the extent to which ones usual or expected physical, emotional and social well-being are affected by a medical condition or its treatment. HRQOL is an important measure of the performance of health care because it incorporates multiple domains and generally involves the patient's own perspective. HRQOL incorporates health status (*e.g.* physical, psychological, social functioning) impairment, symptoms, disability, perceptions, role functions, social health, general well-being and even aspects of spirituality, sexual function, satisfaction, and environment. By definition, HRQOL is narrower than overall QOL.

The process of developing HRQOL instruments has been criticised because of the failure to involve a sufficient number of disabled people in the design stage. HRQOL measures when applied to disabled people run the risk of placing too much reliance on items that assess only physical functioning. Though many reliable and valid instruments to evaluate HRQOL are available none has emerged as the criterion standard for use in all situations. The selection of the most appropriate instrument depends upon the population, the outcomes of interest, and the purpose of assessment and characteristics of the instrument. Assessments of

HRQOL for PwD could be improved by using information about the environment to supplement individual clinical data.

A fundamental distinction between HRQOL measures is whether they are generic or targeted.

Generic HRQOL Measures

Generic HRQOL measures ask questions that are usually general enough to be applicable to almost everyone including those without health conditions. So they can provide population norms or benchmarks of healthy HRQOL to which HRQOL in disease can be compared. In addition they permit comparisons across different diseases and conditions and across interventions. Generic measures are useful for policy analysis and health care decision-making. General measures of HRQOL can be used for disabilities outcomes research but caution applies to each available tool. Some problems and limits are common to all these measures to varying degrees.

Targeted HRQOL Measures

Disease targeted HRQOL are designed to be applicable and relevant to a particular disease. Targeted measures are directed at some attribute of a group of people and they have the advantage of being more relevant and sensitive to small but important differences. There are several categories of targeted instruments:

1. *Disease specific measures*: Focus on concerns, symptoms and effects related to either the disease or its treatment *e.g.* the Arthritis Impact Measurement Scale (AIMS).
2. *Condition specific*: Designed to assess specific symptoms, such as pain, fatigue and depression common to many different kinds of illnesses *e.g.* The Brief Pain inventory.
3. *Treatment specific*: Assess those symptoms that occur in association with particular treatments, but which may be common to several diseases *e.g.* specific questionnaires to assess peripheral neuropathy from cancer chemotherapy.

Strengths and Limitations of Generic and Targeted Measures

	Generic	*Targeted*
Applicable across all populations	x	
Provides benchmarks	x	
Cross disease and intervention comparisons	x	
Valid indicator of overall health status	x	
Identification of unsuspected findings	x	
Sensitivity to comorbid conditions	x	
Focus on relevant areas		x
Senses changes in clinical status-over time		x
Describe specific problems due to disease and benefit due to treatment		x
Strong relation to physical disease findings		x
More relevant and practical		x

It might be a good idea to supplement generic measures with a targeted measure.

APPROACHES TO ASSESSMENT OF QOL IN REHABILITATION

Function or Activity Approaches

Rehabilitation has always focused on improving activity or function as the key to improving the life of persons with disability. Whether health impairment is rated as better or worse than death depends on the degree to which it is perceived to interfere with individual's most valued activities. Valued activities are clearly crucial to QOL.

Activity related QOL an emerging approach in health related rehabilitation is defined as an approach to assessment of the quality of everyday life that assesses both the activities function, community participation and behaviours of persons and their feelings about or appraisals of them. The relative importance of activities may be ranked, weighted, or evaluated by the person. The premise is that both activity and individual's feelings about them must be assessed to understand whether a successful outcome has been attained. The approach is meant to be particularly valuable in medical rehabilitation therapies, such as occupational therapy, physical therapy, speech and language pathology, rehabilitation counselling and the planning of priorities for comprehensive rehabilitation programmes for individuals; it may be useful set in rehabilitation psychology.

Even though activity is part of experienced QOL, measures of activity or functional status do no tell us about the person' s affective QOL or whether the person feels satisfied with his/her activity level, extended ADLs such as household management, childcare, financial management, recreational activities, work skills and other community and social activities and even in basic activities of daily living (ADLs). The relevance of these items, however, varies greatly by gender, age, culture, circumstance and personal lifestyle. Conventional scales of function assess patients on the same array of activities or items, as if each is of equal significance to the subject. The assumption can be questioned Systematic methods of assessing the varying relevance of activities across individuals are needed.

Subjective Well-being and Life Satisfaction Approaches

Subjective well-being, life satisfaction and subjective QOL all involve an appraisal of the affective tenor of life by the person. It is a different domain, and affective QOL needs to be separately assessed to evaluate outcomes.

Subjective ratings are as close as we can come to the essence of QOL. No one knows the person's experience, feelings, or values better than the person does. Persons "define" their own QOL by using criteria, which are inferred rather than directly measured, and the process of change in QOL is only partly understood. Subjective assessments of QOL frequently yield results that are strikingly different from results of objective or normative assessments. Subjective QOL is related to whether a person meets his/her own expectations as well as those of others. However, subjective assessments of QOL have limitations. Ratings of subjective QOL tend to be unstable, subject to variations from day to day. Conventional QOL measures fail entirely with aphasic, very confused, and minimally responsive persons. Research to develop and validate assessments of affective QOL in patients with severe limitations in communication, orientation and arousal are long overdue.

Health Status and Mixed Approaches

There are approaches to assessment of QOL and experience that allow a degree of objectivity into their largely subjective items. These approaches query specific aspects of life experience that are more objective than global life satisfaction or general feelings. The items may reference specific aspects of health or the experience of illness or need fulfillment's that are potentially observable. The respondent may be asked about "problems" or "difficulties" in aspects of functioning, health, illness, symptoms or needs. Such items are still in part subjective, not just because self-report is involved but also because the respondent provides the standards by which the person rates the "problem". There are also aspects of life experience that in them have objective and subjective implications, or both functional and affective implications. Examples include items dealing with vitality, fatigue and frequency of problems.

Needs-based Approaches

Human beings have needs and QOL is associated with need fulfillment. The strength of association and how to define and assess needs has been controversial. Needs based models are highly successful in predicting global QOL, better than approaches based on injury or disability and so provide essential insight into sources of QOL or its lack. Objective measures of functioning are needed to supplement indices of people well-being and *vice versa.* Both objective activity level and subjective well-being need to be measured to evaluate the outcomes of rehabilitation. Conventionally, objective function and subjective QOL are assessed as separate and independent variables. New approaches are emerging that attempt to relate activity and QOL more closely: activities are weighted by the person's evaluations or feelings about them.

Individualisation and weighted approaches

There are variations in the relevance of individuals activities. Except for assessment of basic survival activities and ADLs problems exist with the assumption that items in a functional scale are equally important or even applicable across individuals. The problem of varying relevance may exist across ADL scales as well. Individuals vary in the degree to which activities make them happy or sad. These variations may prove to be important to understanding QOL. HRQOL questionnaires are now weighing items according to an evaluation by the individual or otherwise allow the individual to express his/her concern. These systematically weigh objective outcome items with varying individual values and needs. Research is needed to understand relationships between the more objective items in standard outcome scales and individual feelings, values and lifestyle preferences.

SOME STANDARD SCALES OF HRQOL

Sickness Impact Profile (SIP)

The SIP, developed as a generic measure of health status contains 136 severity weighted statements to which a subject responds only if the statement is true because his/her health on the day the SIP is completed. Health is explicitly defined for respondents as including disability. The SIP has very high acceptability ratings in-spite of the apparent theoretical mismatch with differences in health and disability for PwD. The domains and scales of the SIP are comprehensive but do not include positive aspects of health, like vitality. The statements represent a wide range of negative health impacts including emotional, social, role and physical functions. Scales measure health impacts very specifically *e.g.,* there are scales for work, eating, recreation and pastimes, sleep and rest. Statements are arranged into 12 scales and 2 dimensions (physical, psychosocial), each of which yields a score: in addition, the SIP yields an overall index measure composed of all items. All scores are computed by adding "weights" assigned to each statement (statements with greater dysfunction have greater weights) and are expressed as a percentage of the total dysfunction possible. Scores range from 0 to 1 usually expressed as a percentage with higher scores indicating higher disability or lower health status. The SIP is fairly easy to use (arithmetic scoring), and takes between 15 and 45 minutes to administer depending on the communication ability of subjects and mode of administration. It has impressive test-retest reliability and has been studied extensively for its validity in disease specific populations.

Nottingham Health Profile

The Nottingham Health Profile (NHP) is based on the SIP. The NHP includes 36 yes/no items about health symptoms in 6 domains and scales (energy, pain, emotional reactions, sleep, social isolation, physical mobility) that are weighted for severity; it also includes a 2nd part that asks a single question about health related interference in each of 7 activities. Activities include employment, social relationships and activities, household activities, and sexual activity. The NHP scores are calculated to represent a continuum of 0 (best health) to 100 (worst health). There is no summary score. It has been used in both interview and self- administered modes. The NHP has also been used to examine rehabilitation outcomes.

WHOQOL

The problem of cultural comparability has been explicitly dealt with in the development of the 100-item HRQOL tool WHOQOL-100. The tool was developed simultaneously across a broad range of member countries, assuring that it could be used more multiculturally and multilingually than any other existing HRQOL tool. The WHOQOL consists of 100 items measuring 6 domains (physical and psychological health, level of independence, social relationships, environment and spiritual) each with a set of "facets" for these domains. Countries may add modules that are important to their-own cultures. A briefer version, the WHOQOL BREF has also been developed.

Short Form 36

The SF-36 is increasingly used to assess health status in survey and clinical research and to monitor medical care outcomes. It contains 8 scales and 2 summary scales based on 36 items derived from longer instruments developed by the Medical Outcomes Study. There is also an abbreviated form the SF-12, which yields 2 summary scales. Responses to each item are scored from 0 (negative health) to 100 (positive health) and yield scale and summary scores from 1 to 100 where higher scores represent better health status. The SF-36 was developed for use in general populations and it has been used in an extensive variety of research and clinical settings, mobility limitations, musculo-skeletal problems and neurologic conditions

CONCLUSIONS

From the standpoint of assessing the outcomes of rehabilitation service delivery or the efficacy of certain rehabilitation interventions, it seems more appropriate to use functional outcome as a measure of QOL, with due weight age to subjective affect and weighting of activities to account for the relative relevance of activities for the particular individual. It is also important to note that all standard instruments for assessment of QOL have been designed field tested and applied to populations in other countries. Considerable international effort has been devoted to the development of a generic HRQOL instrument the WHOQOL, which provides a culturally sensitive means of quantifying patient reported health perceptions. This instrument which has also been field tested in India, at the present time appears most appropriate for use locally. There is however a need for developing instruments for assessment of QOL in the Indian context, which can be valid and reliable for use here.

25

INTEGRATION OF MENTALLY RETARDED CHILDREN WITH THOSE WITH NORMAL INTELLIGENCE

S.S. Jayalakshmi

Education for children including the disabled upto the age of 14 years has had national focus since independence. But special education for the disabled children in special schools gives them more attention to learn better, providing them opportunities to be with non-disabled children.

Birth of Vidya Vikasini Opportunity School

The school was started in 1981, IYDP (International Year for the Disabled Persons), with 2 children aged 6 years who were admitted to Nursery School in U.K.G. and the strength of the class was 12 only. The teacher found out that ***two children*** were different from others. The parents requested the management to keep them in regular school. They did not want to admit them in a special school because of some disadvantages like they might get some undesired behaviour from others. In addition there was not much choice of special schools with special teachers in Coimbatore.

Education

The teacher with B.A. Psychology background took it as a challenge and had these children in the class. A small resource room was created with the necessary materials and were given special care and attention wherever needed. Gradually, the number of children increased.

Advantages of this System

Majority of teachers including the director and the principal involved in this educational system, did not face much problem to educate because they had Early Childhood Education as the background. They had a thorough knowledge about human development and helping them with self help, Social, Cognitive and Language areas. Readiness Activities in the resource room was done without much difficulty.

Problems and Solutions

In spite of the fear of social stigma a few parents of non-disabled children had their apprehension towards this because their children were likely to get certain behaviour patterns from them. It was noted with delight to see the children talking to their parents about these disabled children, they said they were also like other children but they lack in certain things due to some reasons. The parents understood well and congratulated the school for taking it up. The children went to that extent of asking their parents to bring back their disabled sibling from the hostel telling they would take care of them. The representatives from NCERT came and observed our set-up, videographed and published through the T.V. media.

Research

A research study was taken with the assistance of UNICEF to learn about the acceptance of normal and mentally retarded children by each other. The non-disabled and disabled (Mentally Retarded) children of 3rd standard from 3 different schools were the subjects.

The duration of this study was one year. Two groups were exposed to audio/video exposures and one was control group. After a gap (retention period) the Mentally Retarded child was sent to the classroom for one month. The child wanted to stay back in the class. The children of the class also wished the same.

Regular School

There is great support and appreciation from the school for normal children though education department or government did not give any recognition. The interactors from Rotary Club and Leo's from Lions Club helped the special children in academics as well as sports and other extra curricular activities. The teachers who teach special children and children with normal intelligence are all well-equipped with knowledge to assess the behaviour modifications of normals. They also devised methods to teach the slow learners and those with learning disabilities. The teachers knowledge has widened by attending seminars and workshops to deal with these special children.

Opportunity Section

The students of Opportunity Section move well with normal children compete with them, in sports and competitions including quiz.

Training Centre

Lots of advantages are there for Vidya Vikasini Society as it is a popular training centre for pre-service and in-service training courses for teachers of schools from Coimbatore and Nilgiris districts. There is a demand for workshops. Every year many workshops are conducted sponsored by different authorities from State and Centre. So the school has a resource bank in terms of experts and materials.

CURRICULUM

The students are grouped as Pre-Primary, Primary, Secondary and Pre-Vocational. As the curriculum is totally function-oriented and the activities are tested for age appropriateness it is easy to select objectives and teach the children. Yogasana is also a part of the curriculum. Dance and music are used as a therapy for those children. The Opportunity Section integrates the children for academic areas depending on their ability. These children are offered education through computer and also computer education. The children who complete 15 years and introduced to academics appear for National Open School Examination equal to school final. They have come out with many prizes at national level. They are also trained in drawing, painting and to prepare greeting cards.

Vocational Rehabilitation

The children who cannot be academically integrated will be trained in few vocations like detergent making, book binding, paper binding, paper ruling, envelope making, canteen running and selling small eatables like biscuits etc., tailoring, office assistance, home training and gardening, popcorn, candy, floss making etc.

Placement

We have a follow up of these children and happy to record that six of our old students assisting in their family business, four in their farms, and five in different factories. Few Mentally Retarded adults are given jobs in our schools working with physically handicapped adults along with adults with normal intelligence.

The institution has been recognized by all the service clubs, State and Central Government also. The Tamil Nadu State award as 'Best Employer of the Handicapped' and President Award as 'Outstanding Employer of the Handicapped' have been received. Now that inclusive education in the anvil, we plan to do much more for the children and teachers.

26

PROMOTING CROSS-DISABILITY APPROACH IN REHABILITATION

Sumitra Mishra

What is Cross-Disability Approach?

- Term used in describing an approach which involves all categories of disability and promotes collective planning for each category.
- This approach seeks co-operation and networking of non-governmental organisations working on various categories of disabilities.

What is Rehabilitation?

Rehabilitation is the process of helping an individual, achieve the highest level of function, independence, and quality of life possible. Rehabilitation does not reverse or undo the damage caused by disease or trauma, but rather helps restore the individual to optimal health, functioning, and well-being.

We all believe that

The Rehabilitation

- Must be comprehensive
- Leading to Mainstreaming

- Building self-reliance and independence. Social integration with dignity. Satisfying emotional needs
- Improving quality of life through:
  1. Education—Integrated/Special
  2. Medical Care—Correction and appropriate therapy
  3. Vocational Training
  4. Income Generation
  5. Community Organization

We can Safely Conclude that

REHABILITATION *is empowerment because* it is a process which enables an individual to fulfill his/her duties and responsibilities and protect his/her rights in society.

People with disabilities are enabled to get—

- access to health care, education, work, housing, emotional security, family bonds, marriage, leisure, recreation;
- right to choose;
- full participation in decision-making on issues concerning self, family and community.

LET US FACE THE REALITY NOW AND SEE THE CURRENT SCENARIO

SITUATION 1

(*As seen by able bodied people*)

Some words/feelings expressed for disability or a person with disability are—

Sense of pity;
Patronizing Attitude;
Seen as Objects of Charity; Prejudices; Avoidance; Tragedy;
Law of Retribution; Discrimination;
Economic and Social Burden;
Non-People or Lesser Beings;
Overprotection;
Admiration as some super natural qualities

SITUATION 2

(*As seen by persons with disabilities*)

How they feel about attitudes of society or their condition—

Rejected by Society
Resignation
Anger
Despair; Helplessness
Dehumanized
Acceptance

SITUATION 3

(*As persons with disabilities would like to be seen*)

People with different abilities
Have control over own lives
Participants—not recipients
Equal opportunities
Equal members of the Society

Respect for the individual
Equal Rights of persons with disabilities.

To make the above situation a reality, we all will have to work towards Cross-Disability approach as there are some positive benefits of Cross-Disability Approach

Some of the Key benefits can be—

- To further the productivity, independence, full citizenship, and total integration of.
- People with disabilities into all aspects of society and the natural environment. To foster leadership among people with disabilities.
- To support the full implementation and enforcement of disability related laws, particularly the Persons with Disabilities Act of 1995 and the National Trust Act of 1999.
- To conduct programmes to enhance the lives of people with disabilities, including programmes to reduce poverty and unemployment.
- To assure that every disabled person has the right to live and that every child or adult with a disability has access to and funding for assistive technology.
- To educate the public and government policy makers regarding issues affecting people with disabilities.

How can we initiate the process?

By introducing Changes in Models—

- Uniformity in Terminology of Disability
- Networking among Organisation "Of' And "For" disability. Emphasis on H.R.D.
- Cross-Disability Programmes
- Young and Professionally Qualified Staff. Integration and Inclusion
- Co-operation and Networking across Organisations. Government Initiatives Rights Issues

- Self Help Groups
- Modernisation of Programmes
- Increasing Public involvement and support
- Full Spectrum of Rehabilitation. Accountability. Transparency.
- Zero Rejection policy

In Conclusion. I would Like to Suggest the Golden "Dos and Don'ts

DON'T

Just Inform Parents that the Child has a Disability/Impairment

DO

Tell them, "I can't help you But I know Someone Who Can"

Make an extra effort of Referring the Child to an appropriate Rehabilitation Centre/programme for Advice and further Intervention and Follow it up.

LET US ALL WORK TOGETHER

27

DEVELOPMENT OF COMMUNICATIVE COMPETENCE AND LITERACY IN COMMUNICATION DISORDERS
A Challenge in the New Millennium

Usha Dalvi

Communicative Competence

Fundamental to the concept of communicative competence is the ability to produce and understand ideas appropriate to the social context in which they occur, with emphasis on accuracy of idea transfer rather than mere correctness of language form or delivery.

Communication disorders include both speech and language impairments. Speech impairments interfere with message transmission and may involve: articulation errors in sound production, voice deviations in pitch, loudness and quality, fluency deviations and various combinations of the above which may result into severe unintelligible speech. Language impairments interfere with both message transmission and reception. Language development may be absent with no recognizable receptive or expressive language. It may be delayed with language acquired later and more slowly, or interrupted with partial loss of language ability, or qualitatively disordered with bizarre or meaningless language.

Speech and language impairments may also occur in combination. They are significant when they affect the individuals, social, economic and/or physical well-being including their learning abilities. A conservative estimate is that at least five per cent of the world's child population need specialist help to acquire communicative competence. As per report of UNICEF (1994) less than one per cent of these children even attend school/or enrolled in any type of intervention programmes.

So it can be said that communication disorders are massively diverse in type, severity and prognosis. Mostly of unknown etiology and often occur in association with other disabilities.

Generally children in this group have been misunderstood, ridiculed, marginalized and mistreated to greater or lesser degree by the community at large. Only recently has society started to accept the goal of all individuals with communication impairment exercising their full societal rights and responsibilities.

The philosophy of normalization and social role valorization appears to have major influence on the lives of children with communication impairment. Normalization, or the goal of making the lives of people with disabilities as much as possible like that of others, originated in Scandinavia and has been attributed to Bank-Mikkelsen (1969). Wolfensberger (1984) developed the term social role valorization to emphasize the valuing of people in society. In the United States of America, these philosophies have been enshrined in the 1975 Public Law 94-142, the Education of the Handicapped Act, and its subsequent amendments. The Act is based on the principle that a student with disability must receive educational services with zero rejection, non-discriminatory evaluation, individualized education plans, in a least restrictive environment, subject to due process, and with parental involvement. If mandated free, appropriate education, which is easily accessible, ensures equal opportunity, encourages highest potential, and enables self-sufficiency. Similar policies have been adopted in India with the implementation of Persons with

Disabilities Act 1995 and with positive approach towards inclusive education.

The resultant goal is to empower the child and usually involves extensive collaboration between child, family, regular class teacher, special teacher, specialists from other disciplines including speech language pathologists, and targeted community representatives. Emphasis is on quality of life issues, from early childhood to transition from school to adult life.

Even though there is no accurate data on how many children with disabilities come to regular and special school there is increase in figures of these children attending school. These children are receiving more clinical and educational services than before. These services are however, inadequate or inappropriate due to lack of training programmes for professionals/teachers, and poor transition of acquired skills.

NSSO (1994) survey also reported that in rural India about 70 per cent of the physically disabled are not literate as against 46 per cent in urban India and literacy among the disabled in India was 42 per cent in 1991, of which 16 per cent was middle school level and above and 7% was secondary level and above. NSSO considered physically disabled to be multiply handicapped if he or she had one or more of the four types of disability (visual, hearing, speech and locomotor). This group vary widely in their abilities and in their rehabilitation and educational needs coupled with poor communicative competence and literacy skills. They need Augmentative and alternative communication strategies to promote and enhance the communicative and literacy skills.

Light (1989b) proposed a definition of communicative competence for people who use AAC. She states that the development of communicative competence is a complex process that relies on knowledge, judgment, and skills in four domains: linguistic, operational, social and strategic. Linguistically, AAC users need to learn the language(s) spoken in their homes and social communities as well as the linguistic code(s) of their AAC systems (e.g., Blis-symbols, manual signs). Operationally, AAC users must learn the technical skills needed to operate their AAC systems, where the systems are manual sign based, low tech, or electronic. Social domain skills include those related to discourse strategies such as initiating, maintaining, and terminating conversations as well as those needed for functional speech acts such as choice making, requesting, and rejecting. Social domain skills also include those that relate to interpersonal dynamics, such as knowing how to put partners at ease, actively participate in conversations, and so forth.

Literacy

Literacy is used as an umbrella term for both reading and writing.

To be literate is to be able to gather and to construct meaning using written language. All four modes of language—listening, speaking, reading and writing—develop concurrently and code pertinently when these methods of communication are used in real life settings to accomplish real goals. Learning to read and write is a natural step in language development. Literacy learning is interactive, constructive, strategic, and meaning based. It is far more than recognizing or proficiently using a set of print based skills such as better sound recognition or developing specific written vocabulary knowledge.

These skills allow individuals to use literacy as a tool for communication, critical thinking and the attainment of social and cultural power.

For AAC user with severe communication impairments (multiply handicaps) literacy skills at multiple levels, facilitate successful participation in a variety of environments home, work place, school and social settings as it is a critical component for fostering communicative self-expression and independence.

At a communicative level, literacy skills improve their ability to participate successfully in face-to-face interactions by providing them with access to language, allow far more than conventional reading and writing by providing access to a means of self-expression in order to communicate thoughts and opinions and to foster personal independence (DeCoste, 1997b).

When developing literacy programmes for individuals who have multiple disabilities, whose primary impairments include hearing impairments, cognitive impairments, and/or visual impairments, it is important to consider alternative access to literacy materials and use of assistive technology.

Multiple Disability

Smith (1992) noted that many individual factors influence literacy learning for these individuals. These include:

- Physical difficulties
- Limited word knowledge and vocabulary
- Language impairments
- Perceptual difficulties (e.g., visual, auditory)
- Discrepancies between reading achievement, receptive language, and IQ score
- Poor self-esteem
- Passive learning patterns

Individuals with Severe Speech and Physical Impairments (SSPI) often learn to write slowly and with great difficulty. Typically, they experience an uneven profile of strengths and weaknesses that persists into adulthood. The greatest barrier to literacy learning may be limited access to formal instruction and lack of exposure to the general curriculum.

Hearing Impairments

It is a well-known fact that hearing impaired individuals have poor reading and writing skills below their normal hearing peers due to difficulty in understanding the syntax of the teaching language, various semantic difficulties, (Kretschmer, R.E. 1982) understanding and use of figurative language and contexts. Hence it is accepted that they have difficulty not only at lexical and sentential level but also at higher levels.

To understand fully the challenges faced by deaf students in the literacy arena, it is important to take into account several factors, the variation among deaf children as language learners, the influences of early language environments, interactions of hearing loss and access to reading-relevant information. Unfortunately, previous curriculum adopted for developing literacy skills of deaf children have focussed on strategies that work for hearing children, even though deaf and hearing children often have very different background knowledge and learning strategies.

To be in a position to learn the structure and function of preferred language, a deaf learner has to have access to that target language. Therefore first, students must be provided with natural and accurate models of the preferred language. Second, deaf students must have available written materials that are authentic and well-documented. Third, the language used in instruction must be clear and accurate. That is, both the first and the second languages must be accessible to the learner, something that is not always true for deaf children.

There are consistent findings, however, indicating that early exposure to both ASL and English provides the strongest support for the acquisition of literacy skills. Hearing children and deaf children of deaf parents or deaf children of hearing parents may differ in the component skills underlying reading, even when their overall reading levels are the same. Alternatively, they may be similar on particular dimensions that create overall differences in reading level. Several alternatives to straightforward ASL-English bilingual programmes also have been suggested. In any case, without broad evaluations of bilingual education programmes and their influences on literacy and academic achievement, there is a strongly felt need to expose the deaf child to both sign language and preferred language. This will aid in promoting and facilitating acquisition of richer language which in turn will enable the deaf to pursue higher education.

The limited improvement in literacy skills of deaf students of the past several decades is disheartening to some. From the perspective of most researchers and teachers, however, this is not necessarily the case. More progress has been made in this domain during the last 15 years than in the previous 150 years. As we better understand how deaf children learn, we can more appropriately tailor our educational methods with regard to literacy and other domains. Reading programmes in which stories are presented in both sign language and spoken language, where young children all have copies of the same story book, and where parents share with their children stories first presented at school, for example, all appear to have a positive impact on both language growth and literacy.

Having children retell stories at home, collect or draw relevant pictures, and act out portions of the stories all help to establish links between the written word, meaning, and the language used in one-on-one communication. Strategies used by deaf adults in reading to children should also be used by hearing teachers, even if deaf teachers and deaf teacher aids are available.

Cognitive Impairments

Individuals with cognitive impairments are at risk of being held to reduced expectations and lacking exposure to literacy materials, both at home and at school. Individuals with cognitive impairments can and should engage in the same emergent literacy activities as their peers without disabilities (e.g., listening repeatedly to stories, having access to writing tools). We cannot overemphasize the importance of intensive exposure to literacy materials in the early years.

When professionals make decisions about literacy instruction for individuals with cognitive impairments, they should consider not only the impairment itself but also any additional learning needs that might be present. For example, many individuals may experience difficulty in understanding and expressing language, maintaining attention, and interpreting perceptual patterns. Thus, they may require additional scaffolding or educational adaptations to literacy materials to achieve success. With the appropriate instructional support, many individuals with cognitive impairments may experience the same rewards from literacy experiences (e.g., composing personal letters to a friend or relative) as their classmates without disabilities.

Visual Impairments

The incidence of visual impairment is much higher among people with multiple disabilities than in the general population (Brett, 1983; Schorr, 1983). Approximately 50%-60% of school-age individuals with visual impairments have additional impairments, with physical and/or cognitive disabilities concurrently (Gates, 1985; Sacks and Silberman, 1998; Sadowsky, 1985). Approximately 46% of people with cerebral palsy have concurrent visual problems that may include eye muscle imbalance (e.g. strabismus), visual field cuts, visual-perceptual problems, and/or loss of visual acuity, any of which can significantly affect literacy learning (Batshaw, 1997). In addition, research has suggested that as many as 75%-90% of individuals with severe or profound cognitive disabilities also have visual impairments (Cress *et al.*, 1981).

Given the high incidence of visual impairments in people with special needs, professionals should consider the degree and type of the individual's visual problem when providing access to reading and writing. Assessment of an individual's visual status involves specialized vision tests that evaluate a number of components including visual acuity, visual field magnitude, oculomotor functioning, light and colour sensitivity, and visual stability. From a literacy perspective, it is important to use information about an individual's visual needs to determine the appropriate educational adaptations. Some adaptations may include (1) use of enlarged keyboards, print, and/or word processing text; (2) individualized location of the computer monitor; (3) attention to the visual glare on liquid crystal displays; and (4) use of Braille as an alternative symbol set.

Challenges in the New Millennium

The biggest challenge for communication impairment group is Multilingualism, Assessment and Intervention.

Multilingualism

India with a multilingual and multicultural population and a federal policy, one finds a wide variation in medium, content and duration of the programmes conducted in different states and schools. The heterogeneity of communication patterns in schools, the unequal cultivation of different languages for use as medium of instruction, the demand of elegant versions of mother tongue for formal purposes and non-availability of personnel with adequate communication over the text book language, and the switching over to another medium in the multi-tier media without adequate preparation are some of the difficulties faced by the learners who are initiated into education through mother tongue medium (learn in English write in Hindi).

Today many education programmes are geared to facilitate the scope of communication with the prevailing socialization values in a community. Many states have introduced bilingual education policy or three-language formula. (Khubchandani, 1978)

In multilingual society the "ideal claim" and the "real function" of a language there is a wide gap between the language policies professed and actual practice in the classroom. It is not unusual to find many teachers and the taught interact in one language, classes are conducted in another, textbooks are written in a third language and the answers are given in a fourth language/style. This milieu promotes a good deal of code switching and hybridization of true or more contact languages.

Given the scenario of educational policy implementation of PwD Act promoting inclusive education is posing a great challenge to all the professionals involved in rehabilitation.

For a country like ours, with multilingualism and multiculturalism, the need of the hour is to consider developing a programme to promote communicative competence and literacy skills of universal nature.

Assessment

At present there is dearth of language specific tests. The available tests are generally:

1. using tests that are on normal on/or developed on general population, (minority groups are not considered separately)
2. using adaptations of various western tests/translated tests.

Alternative Assessment Procedures

Because of the prior difficulty, professionals and clinicians must recognize that there are a number of cultural and linguistic factors that can potentially impact the nature, accuracy and extent of information obtained during the interview and assessment process. This applies regardless of the disability groups presenting communication problems.

The alternate assessment procedures suggested are:

1. Understand the cultural parameter associated with the particular child being evaluated.
2. Observe normal age peers in natural settings to determine culturally appropriate behaviour and communication behaviour.
3. Observe the child in natural settings similar to those that served as the normal referent.
4. Teachers' report.
5. Involve parents and families in the assessment.
6. Modification of standardized testing as follows:
   — eliminating potentially culturally traced items,
   — recording test instructions,
   — allowing extra time for response,

— increasing the number of practice items,
— recording all responses, particularly when a client changes a response, explains comments, or uses non-verbal gestures to respond,
— using alternative scoring procedures,
— continuing to test beyond ceiling.

7. Developing check lists
— which would facilitate in drawing up more accurate profile depicting the areas of strength and the weakness of the person.

Interventiom

As this group exhibits considerable intra and interindividual difference in both receptive and expressive language, there is no single approach suitable to all. Early intervention programmes should focus on individualized instruction in language based educational orientation within a highly structured learning environment where linguistic and semantic input matches child's comprehension. Successful intervention will enable entry into regular school.

With the implementation of PwD Act and inclusive education, intervention, rehabilitation team should promote whole family involvement in intervention within a context of respect for the rights and freedom of family members, self-determination and quality of life. There has to be a paradigmatic shift in the intervention strategy to include collaborative consultation, contextual pragmatic approach, curriculum-based, strategy-based and whole language approach.

Technology has the potential to both disenfranchise and empower individuals with communication impairments. This not only will greatly expand leisure options and improve quality of life considerations but also enhance their literacy skills.

A computer can serve as a writing aid, learning tool, work station and communication device with its multiple modes of output (voice, visual screen and print, Ferrier and Shane 1987) which will enable them to compete with the non-disabled peers in educational as well as vocational settings.

Today's technology gives software developer the capability to present text interactively in a range of interesting formats. No other medium todate has the capability of interacting with students quite like the computer.

Computer provides:

— Assistive technology for speech access.
— Assistive technology for physical access.
— Literacy software.

Future Direction:

1. To develop language specific assessment protocols.
2. To develop training modules for professionals, parents/ caretakers, gross roots level workers etc.
3. Empowering hearing impaired with rich language' through two-language paradigm *i.e.* preferred language and sign language.
4. Collaborative research with IT for assistive and adaptive aids.

I am extremely grateful to Mr. Rangasayee, Director, A YJNIHH, for guiding and permitting to present the paper.

REFERENCES

Bank-Hakkelsen, N. (1969). "*A Metropolitan Area in Denmark: Copenhagen*", in R. Kugel and W. Wolfenberger (eds) Issues in special education cited in Wodak R. & Carson. D. (eds) Encyclopedia of Language and Education, Vol. 1.

Brett, E.M. (1983). *The Blind Retarded Child.* In K. Wybar & D. Taylor (eds). Pediatric Opthomology: Current Aspects. New York: Marcel Dekkar Schorr G. (1983). Visual Impairments. In J. Blackman (ed). Medical aspects of developmental disabilities in children birth to three (p. 227-231) Iowa City: The University of Iowa.

Cress. P. *et al.*; (1981). *Vision Screening for Persons with Severe Handicap.* Journal of The Association for Persons with Severe Handicaps, 6 (3), pp. 41-50.

De Coste, D.C. 1997b. *The Role of Literacy in Augmentative and Alternative Communication.* In S.L. Glennen & D.C. De Coste (eds). The Handbook of Augmentative and Alternative Communication. San Diego Singular Publishing Group.

Gates, C. (1985). *Survey of Multiply Handicapped Visually Impaired Children in the Rocky Mountain/Great Plains Region.* Journal of Visual Impairment & Blindness, 79, pp. 385-91.

Khubchandani, M. (1978). *Multilingual Education in India,* in B. Spolsky & R. Cooper (eds.) Case Studies in Bilingual Education, Vol. II, Newberry House, Rowley Mass.

Kretshmer R.E., (1982). *Reading and the Hearing Impaired Individual Summation and Application.* Volta Review 85, pp.107-22.

Light, J. (1989b). *Toward a Definition of Communicative Competence for Individuals Using AAC Systems.* Augmentative and Alternative Communication, 5, pp. 137-44.

NSSO, 1994. *Disability in India,* NSS 47th Round in Sarvekshana. July-Dec. 1991, New Delhi. Govt. of India.

Smith, (1992). *Reading Abilities of Non-Speaking Students.* Two case studies. Augmentative and Alternative Communication 3, pp. 12-17.

Wolfensberger, W. (1984). *A Reconceptualization of Normalization as Social Role Valorization,* Mental Retardation 34, pp. 22-27.

IN CONCLUSION

Major H.P.S. Ahluwalia

We are very grateful to the Hon'ble Minister* for agreeing to our request to be present with us today and I am also grateful to Mrs. Sarita Prasad for being with us. This is a very busy period for them because of Parliament Questions. Sir, this is the first time a Convention with NGOs of such a large number is present has been organized. Some have solution to problems while others don't. Secondly, when we thought of convening this Convention, our budget was coming to a very huge amount, so we requested the participants to come on their own and make their own stay arrangements and also pay registration fee of Rs.500 each so that we can hold this Convention at a better place. I want to thank the NGOs for their overwhelming presence and response. They have made very good suggestions after detailed discussions. It was also informed to the Hon'ble Minister that a declaration should be made and he had assured that he will give consideration to all the recommendations. There should be a data base of NGOs. There should also be a networking of NGOs, RCI and government. Another good suggestion has come that parents associations should be involved in all the Committees. Use of Information Communication Technology and promotion of cross-disability were also emphasized. Someone has asked when the next meeting will be held and such meetings should be held regularly. Community mobilisation was also discussed along with how the States and other

---

* Dr. Sanjay Paswan, Hon'ble Minister of State for Social Justice and Empowerment.

agencies should be involved with RCI so that our programmes can reach the grass roots level. Long-term and short-term goals should be fixed so that the benefit can reach to the grass roots level at the earliest. We have centres but we do not have teachers. How we can increase the number of teachers to man these centres? Though education is made compulsory it should be implemented. Unless the child is taken to the school, how will he study. We need the support and co-operation of parents to take the disabled child to the school. We need a course for parents which RCI is going to launch in collaboration with IGNOU. Even if the child is taken to school but the teacher is not sensitized to the needs of disabled child, he will not learn anything. Yesterday, Secretary, Elementary Education, Shri S.C. Tripathi gave detailed information about the schemes of the Ministry of HRD like Sarva Shiksha Abhiyaan. I once again thank you Sir and Mrs. Sarita Prasad, for being with us.

Prof. P Jeyachandran

Actually we were trying to have a session about the recommendations. Dr. Hanumantha Rao was ready with all the recommendations but your enthusiasm in interaction with the Chairman, RCI has taken the allotted time. Sir, since the Hon'ble Minister is here, we thought we would just brief him what we have been doing for the last three days.

Sir, we have agreed all the NGOs are with the government, we have decided we will be networking, a greater networking amongst ourselves and we will work together. We will also demonstrate to the world that we can produce better result with all the limited resources and we will be second to none in providing services for the disabled. We will also take into consideration all the international standards, recommendations into our consideration when we try to evolve any programme and we will also work very closely with other disability sectors across all the disability. We have decided what we have been doing will be strengthened, that we will work with the Parivaar closely and try to satisfy the needs, rather rights. We will do that. We also learnt that we will not blame others for our lapses and we will always ask a question if my programme is not such successful where I have failed in planning, operation and execution. That is what we have decided.

When we talk about cross-disability, we have so many instances in the country in the ancient past to say that people with other disabilities can work together. Sir, from Tamil Nadu in the Tengum periods, there were two poets. One person was with visual impairment and the other was with locomotor impairment. The visual impairment person was carrying this period everywhere. The person with locomotor impairment was guiding him. So we have also learnt in these few days that across the disability, there is a lot of technology available. For example, for technologies hearing impaired, locomotor impaired, those technologies will be used by us, for people with mental retardation. We have developed some good teaching strategies using all the psychological principles which will be shared with other disability areas. We have decided judiciously we will throw away our useless programmes and judiciously we will do our programme.

I must also take this opportunity, to follow our tradition, when Maharaja visits the citizens will appeal. We will also appeal to the Hon'ble Minister that there was a discussion that we should have a separate Ministry because the population may have a special attention if we have a Ministry. Then there was another good suggestion given before forming a Ministry we should form a Commission to go into the details and take necessary action and also the Commission should have a stipulated time frame within that they have to give a report to the Ministry based on that things will be implemented. The other suggestion in the group is allocation has been increased leaps and bounds but the group discussed the allocation should be in parity with the population in the country. It is not simply saying that the money has been increased from 10 crores to 20 crores but as a right they say it should be on parity with the population.

Sir, there was a discussion about the DPEP programme. In

one word I would like to tell if the person who executed the DPEP programme with all its guidelines it is a thundering success. I stand by this because in Tamil Nadu one district is given to one NGO. I am incharge of one of the most backward area, 2,161 disabled children have been integrated. We have submitted the report and the disabled children's attendance is 100 per cent. They may say because the parents have to go to work that is why the children are there. Very good. No drop-out comparing the regular school there are drop-outs or failures but here comparing our disabled friends with visual, locomotor and hearing, they excel there. The reason may be that they were given the individual attention. All the disabled children in Tamil Nadu will have good case history after following the DPEP programme. But the DPEP programme has opened the eyes of the mainstream education and I think the SSA will be a great success based on the observations made. It was also decided that vocational programmes should be given importance. We should have inclusion among the different categories of disability. We will do it. One thing about RCI I must commend. It is a kind of greatest occasion across the disability, we met in the capital that too on an auspicious day. I think things will go auspiciously for us. Someone was talking about early intervention. RCI has prepared curriculum for hearing impaired and mentally retarded in early intervention that is being implemented in different places and those who are interested in starting a training programme, special educators for early intervention you can take the curriculum and go ahead and start the training programme. Research, yes, we have to take RCI scheme to do that. The Ministry has given special allocation to improve North East. The Ministry has also said that this National Institute will do work in this region and this national institute will do work in this region. RCI is totally collaborating with them.

Major Sahib conquered Mount Everest on 29th May, 1965. He was delirious. He could not speak to people for three days I believe. Sir, all the NGOs in collaborating with you will make you delirious. Once Major Sahib told me, after conquering Mount

Everest what is on this earth to conquer. Sir, that is why the Ministry has given the disability sector to you and say conquer it and hoist your flag across the disability and we will do it.

Mrs. Sarita Prasad

First of all let me begin by thanking the Hon'ble Minister of State for finding time to be here today as we know that today was particularly a busy day for him. I am glad to be here today coming to his valedictory function of the All India Cross-Disability Convention and even more glad to learn that about 300 representatives from NGOs, government agencies, institutions and eminent experts in the area of disability and rehabilitation have come to participate in this mega event organized by RCI. I understand that a number of useful recommendations have been made which will go a long way in providing a base for providing education, training and rehabilitation to persons with disabilities. India has passed the most progressive Act in the world. As you know in the past people with disabilities were hidden away and were beyond the periphery of social consciousness. But now disability is becoming more visible and that in itself is an achievement. Although no reliable data is available regarding prevalence of disability but it is generally estimated that almost 3 per cent of our population suffers from some physical disability and another 2 per cent suffers from some form of mental disability. However, history has many examples of people with disabilities having made significant contributions to the social, cultural and political life of nations. This is so not only now but from thousands of years ago. Surdas occupies a pride place in Hindi literature and is almost a buy word in the country. Hommer is still remembered as the most honoured Greek poet. John Molten has immortal place in the British History and literature. Who does not know the name of Dr. Hellen Keller. This suffices to show that disability does not destroy the productive potential and this is a fact which needs to be widely propagated and people have to be made aware that people with disabilities are also to be treated with respect and dignity.

What I would like to emphasize most is that able bodied people have so much to learn from the disabled. The courage and bravery that is shown by them in dealing with life in facing with every day task which we may find very easy but which for them is really a Herculean task. They form a very big lesson for us. Disability is of many kinds. People may have difficulty in hearing, seeing, moving, muscular coordination, intellectual retardation. Each disability needs special techniques, technologies and strategies for education and rehabilitation. Gone are the days when they were clubbed together in one category. Now, Rehabilitation Council of India, as you know, has been charged with the responsibility of standardizing and regulating the training of 16 categories of professionals required for education and rehabilitation of children and adults with disabilities. In the last decade, RCI has greatly expanded the base of available human resources to provide competent services to people with disabilities. Without this base no work can be undertaken. Rehabilitation and special education are both dynamic processes and are undergoing continual change. Science and Technology has contributed to the development of aids and appliances to enhance the functional abilities of persons with disabilities. As science progresses, the rehabilitation strategies also undergo significant changes.

The major purpose of this Convention was to take the holistic view of rehabilitation so that a viable plan of developing human resources, creating a referral base in the rural areas and reach the unreached could be developed. I am happy that the Convention has considered all the relevant issues in detail. I am sure the representatives from NGOs and other agencies when they go back to their respective places will carry with them the concern expressed in the forum and work for the betterment of the lives of people with disabilities in their respective areas with renewed commitment and vigour.

Dr. Sanjay Paswan*

Disability especially in the post ninety period, has come up as a major issue in India also and in our country friends, we are very much aware of the Ashtavakra and Surdas of the medieval period. The philosophy of Ashtavakra has not only benefited the handicapped persons of that period or this period but the philosophy is still relevant and the Bhakti cult in the teachings of Surdas is still important for each and every one. In the present time what Major Ahluwalia is doing for disability is not only for the disabled fellows but for the entire Indian community. Such a gathering of almost all State NGOs is a very good initiative taken by the RCI. But for the NGOs initiative, the NGOs efforts, alone it is not going to deliver anything. Government, Ministry can help, can facilitate the things. So for any problem there is a Ministry. What I am seeing these days that Monastery is more important than Ministry. Not only Monastery is coming to the humanity and mankind that is really imitated to be followed. I am seeing so many sisters are there. Marvelous job they are doing and that must be taken as a model.

So every problem can be helped if we bring a different Ministry, bring a different Commission, that will be done with the passage of time. But what we are having at present times. We are running a Finance Corporation but how many people are being benefited by these financial corporations. That I would like to know. But how the existing resources can be harnessed in totality. The entire globe may not have full resources to provide and fulfill everybody's needs. It is difficult. The existing resources are utilized in a proper way and how more can be covered. So whatever facilities, whatever schemes we are having, if it is being made, if it is being provided, if it is being delivered, in a very nice way, certainly the targeted group may not be deprived. So you must be aware friends that in such a pious task, there may not be any hindrance form black sheep.

---

* Hon'ble Minister of State for Social Justice and Empowerment.

Government alone can not do everything. Institutions are working, Ashram people are doing, Sisters are doing. They all are doing good work within their limited resources. It is a model how they are working. We should ensure that in such a holy work anti-social elements or institution do not enter to spoil the entire work. We have to be careful from manipulators, conspirators and others, who work in the name of disability, in the name of weaker sections. We can reduce our problems, if we deal with such bad persons on time and we can cover the uncovered areas. The government should introduce more schemes, community resources should be utilized, social resources should be increased. Therefore, I would appeal to all of you that such people should be taken to task. Major Ahluwalia, Madam Tuli know all these things.

I am happy that such a Convention has been organized. The findings, the conclusions of the Convention, the recommendations should be discussed at the national and international forum and in the Ministry. We should organize a meeting of all concerned, both the Ministers, Additional Secretary, Chairman, RCI, Dr. Uma Tuli and others to officially discuss the recommendations of this Convention in the Ministry.

The role of government is changing from provider to the facilitator. The recommendations which can be accepted, which cannot be accepted, it should be discussed. Networking and monitoring is necessary. What are your plans, what are your ideas, what is your vision, what are your problems? I am in this Ministry for the last five or six months. I have seen that the same beneficiaries are taking again and again the aids and appliances. There is no restriction. Apart from disabled persons, there are regions in this country which are disabled. So what would happen to the disabled in those regions. If all the facilities are limited only to main cities or headquarters, who will provide facilities to the rural people, who are inaccessible. If you expect something from the government we also expect something from you. The aids and appliances should reach them who are really needy. There should be a check on monitoring of the distribution of aids and appliances so that only the needy and uncovered people receive the aids and appliances. Ours is such a big country with so much population, we must ensure that the resources are utilized properly and fully. This will be our endeavour. Let us try to be realistic than populistic. People expect that the Minister Sahib will make some announcement. But there is no use of any announcement without its implementation. But there should be a chain of communication, it should be further discussed. We should discuss how we can increase our social resources, how can we bring global resources. We have lot of expectations from NGOs. Government's policy is to involve more and more NGOs. This is the trust which NGOs have reposed. You should maintain this trust. I assure you on behalf of the Ministry to do whatever is possible within our resources, within our reach.

Dr. J.P. Singh, Member Secretary

This historic Convention has to come to an end but our collaboration has just begun. We started the Summit of the Mind reaching our own height. This has really brought us all together to propagate in one voice the need for providing quality services to persons with disabilities in India. The Convention has brought out the message of synergy in the disability sector. The summit has given an opportunity to the NGOs to give a thorough retrospection of what is needed for persons with disabilities in the country. I am sure, they will peak to the summit of understanding and realization which will definitely improve their work for persons with disabilities in future. This unique summit has brought together professionals, policy makers, grass roots workers, religious people and administrators and the result is that they spoke in one voice to improve the services for persons with disabilities in India. You have gone through the vital recommendations and definitely it will be taken into account. Hon'ble Minister said that no announcement should be made. But he has made an announcement that the recommendations of this Convention should be discussed in the

Ministry. This is a very good announcement and we hope that this meeting will be held soon.

Expressing my deepest gratitude to every one who has contributed to the success of this Convention. The love and affection which I got from the participants for the last three days was tremendous. Let me start by expressing my gratitude to the Hon'ble Minister Dr. Satyanarayan Jatiya Ji. His inspiring inaugural address set the tone for our deliberations. Equally important were the remarks of Mrs. Rajwant Sandhu, Joint Secretary to the Government of India, Ministry of Social Justice & Empowerment. Prof. V.K. Gangarade's words of practical wisdom one can ill afford to forget. He has given us the philosophy of Gandhi, that is our charkha philosophy. He has been talking about the vocational programme. Some vocation has to be done. Why can't we think of those philosophies also. I would also like to convey our deepest gratitude to Hon'ble Minister of State for Social Justice. He has mentioned about the philosophy of Ashtavakra. He has mentioned about monastery, sisters, Swamijis coming here. This is the way, Sir, this field has grown. They were the pioneers in this and I really salute them. They are coming forward to have a partnership with RCI. I need them to expand my services. Without their help I cannot reach. Out of my 160 institutions, 80 per cent are NGOs who have taken up the challenge to train manpower. Without quality trained manpower you can't provide quality services. Whatever we say will be lip services only.

I would like to thank all the Chairpersons and Co-chairpersons, various speakers who have made very excellent presentations. The presentations will help us to shape new programmes for education and rehabilitation of persons with disabilities throughout the country. The resource persons, the drafting committee, and Prof. P. Jeyachandran who has presented the recommendations deserve special thanks from the Rehabilitation Council of India.

I will be failing in my duty if I do not express my sincerest appreciation to the 500 delegates from 286 NGOs who have spent their own money and showed interest to come and participate in this Convention. The interest shows that rehabilitation in India is in safe hands. We will march ahead hand in hand to provide relief and succour to every person with disability throughout his life cycle. We have received continued co-operation from the Madhya Pradesh Bhoj (Open) University, Indira Gandhi National Open University, other NGOs who have contributed for specific events. CBM, it is not the non-governmental organization, international non-governmental organizations are coming to RCI. I really thank them for this.

I would like to thank the staff of Rehabilitation Council of India who have worked day and night, got firing from me for certain aspects but it is their love and affection that they toiled hard till the end. Thanks are also due to the management of India Habitat Centre for providing many facilities to us. We have got their concessional rates for this Convention and they have not charged any thing for this Auditorium. I just want to thank them.

You have seen Dr. Trikha here and Mr. Arun Rao and his small kid Anand yesterday, I would like to thank them for the sign language interpretation. There are many volunteers who have made this Convention a success making it convenient for the blind and other disabled persons to participate in this Convention.

I cannot forget my Chairman. I convey my sincere thanks. He has been pushing me all the time to do something in this area because he has seen life. He understands the meaning of the Summit of the Mind. I was reading his book that every inch as you go up there is lot of difficulty, challenges are there which have to be overcome, then only you can reach to the peak. I thank you for guiding me.

At the end the media, TV and electronics, they deserve our thanks. They have been covering this Conference and I have seen in the TV the way they have highlighted the programme, it is really excellent. The coverage in the media is very good. I would like to thank them again. I would like to thank each and every one, who have contributed to make this Convention resounding success, whether his name has appeared or not.

RECOMMENDATIONS OF THE ALL INDIA CROSS-DISABILITY CONVENTION

SUMMIT OF MINDS MAY 7-9, 2003

1. At present Rehabilitation of the disabled finds no mention in the Constitution except relief of the Disabled and unemployable in entry nine (9) of the State List. It is strongly recommended that Rehabilitation should be made a Fundamental Right of every person with disability and the Constitution should be appropriately amended and the subject should be placed on the Concurrent List.
2. RCI should develop a document setting forth types of Rehabilitation Services to be provided in the new millennium.
3. In view of the growing realization of the potential of person with disability for national development, it is strongly recommended that a separate Ministry for the Disabled should be formed.
4. Government of India should encourage organisation for Disabled through umbrella schemes of Grants-in-aid to introduce Training in Information Communication Technology and other vocational trades at all stages and also encourage Programmed Learning. RCI should develop various skill development courses for professionals in the field.
5. The Government of India should authorize and provide funds to RCI to develop a complete Data base of all organisations and institutions serving people with various disabilities at all ages and in all parts of the country.
6. In view of the increasing importance of networking as a

means of serving people with disabilities it is recommended that NGO's may be encouraged to set up a Common Cross-Disabilities organisation to undertake advocacy, liaison and other promotive functions on behalf of the disabled.

7. RCI should prepare a 20 year perspective plan in the field of human resource development in Special Education and Rehabilitation. The plan should include Short-Term and Long-Term as well as Distance Courses in all areas impinging on Special Education or Rehabilitation.
8. As parents are becoming vital partners in the successful rehabilitation of persons with disabilities, the NGOs at the regional level and the Zonal Advisory Committees (ZACs) should closely work with the Parent's Organisations for improving the quality of services to persons with disabilities.
9. As the present scenario in the country is changing with regard to the prevalence and incidence of single disability categories, the convention resolved that the organisations working for persons with disabilities in India should adopt cross-disability approach to provide comprehensive services in the country. To make this a reality, RCI needs to develop credit based courses for enabling professionals of one disability to acquire skills in other disability areas.
10. The existing scheme of Sarva Shiksha Abhiyaan has a provision to include all children with disabilities under the umbrella of "Education for All" and therefore, the NGOs and ZACs should ensure that this provision is effectively used to include children with disabilities in schools and also ensure that they are given educational opportunities on par with those of non-disabled children. In view of their zero rejection policy they should adopt a selective educational placement of children in the most appropriate environment as mandated by the PwD Act, 1995.
11. In view of the overriding importance of research in Special

Education and Rehabilitation, the Government of India in the Ministry of Social Justice & Empowerment should give liberal grants to NGO's and others for undertaking meaningful action research to enhance understanding and enrichment of services for people with disabilities. The Government of India should also reconsider giving 100 per cent assistance for good action research projects in Special Education & Rehabilitation.

12. NGO's should do their best to mobilize community resources including those from the corporate sector but the final responsibility for ensuring that every person with disability is actually served is that of the State since rehabilitation should be treated as a fundamental right of every individual with disability.
13. It is recommended that the Voice of Parent Organisations should be heard with greater attention and they should be treated as partners in the development of Rehabilitation Services.
14. RCI should undertake the development of manuals for various courses as well as the writing of independent textbooks and audio-visual materials on different aspects of disability.
15. RCI should be entrusted the task of developing the minimum standards for the provision of Special Education and Rehabilitation Services for person with disability.
16. The Convention laid considerable stress on vocationalization of Special Education and recommended that the Government of India should use its grants-in-aid scheme to promote vocationalization of all Special Education and Rehabilitation programme.
17. The Convention recommended that the predominant mode of educating children with special needs should be Inclusive Education.
18. The Convention also recommended that teaching strategies and suitable institutions should be developed

to meet the needs of hither to neglected sections of children with Special needs like Children with Special Learning Difficulties, Autism and Multiple Impairments.

19. C.B.R. approach should be adopted extensively particularly for disabled adults.
20. Government of India should devise procedures to enhance co-operation between NGO's and Panchayati Raj Institutions.
21. The Government of India in partnership with NGO's should intensify efforts to generate employment opportunities for Persons with Disability in all sectors of the economy and particularly in the rural areas by fully utilizing the Swarna Jayanti Swa Rojgar Yojana of the Ministry of Rural Development as well as by making fuller use of the funds earmarked in all poverty alleviation programmes and also pay particular attention to the needs of the severely disabled by creating schemes of Home Workers, Sheltered Workshops and enclaves in Public Sector Undertakings.
22. From time to time RCI should bring to the notice of all affiliated institutions innovative and proven teaching practices as well as Low Cost Teaching Learning material to enhance concept building.
23. RCI should initiate experiments to train multi-category teachers on the lines of the experiment undertaken by NCERT some year ago.
24. RCI should adopt a life cycle approach to rehabilitation and all services should be age and contextually appropriate.
25. RCI should tap resources of various NGO's and UN specialized agencies to improve its training programmes.

LIST OF PARTICIPANTS

Sl. No.	Name of Participant	Institution Name
1.	Mr. S.M.Wright Registration No.:-002	Rangammal Memorial Higher Secondary School for the Hearing Impaired, Sambanthanur Village, Somasipadi Post, Tiruvannamalai Taluka, Tiruvannamalai Distt.
2.	Mr. N. Vijayan Registration No.:-002A	Rangammal Memorial Higher Secondary School for the Hearing Impaired, Sambanthanur Village, Somasipadi Post, Tiruvannamalai Taluka, Tiruvannamalai Distt.
3.	Brig. A.A.S. Sinha, Registration No.:-003	RAPHAEL, P.O. Box No. 157 Dehradun, Uttaranchal
4.	Ms. Priyo Lall Registration No.:-003A	RAPHAEL, P.O. Box No. 157 Dehradun, Uttaranchal
5.	Mr. Paras Nath Yadav Registration No.:-004	Yaduvanshi Janta Sikshan Sanstha, Malikpura, Jahrabad, Gajipur, Uttar Pradesh
6.	Lalji Yadav Registration No.:-004A	Yaduvanshi Janta Sikshan Sanstha, Malikpura, Jahrabad, Gajipur, Uttar Pradesh
7.	Mr. J.P.Gadkari Registration No.:-005	Karnataka Parents Association for Mentally Retarded Citizens, AMC Compound, Off. Hosur Road, Near Kidwai Memorial Hospital, Bangalore
8.	Mr. S. Suresh Registration No:-005A	Karnataka Parents Association for Mentally Retarded Citizens, AMC Compound, Off. Hosur Road, Near Kidwai Memorial Hospital, Bangalore
9.	Dr. Dilip Kumar Singh Registration No.:-006	Swargiya Dr. Ymuna Prasad Singh Seva Nidhi, Pirpainti, Bhagalpur, Bihar
10.	Swami Jnanatmananda Registration No.:-007	Bharat Sevashram Sangha, River's Meet Road, Sonari, Jamshedpur
11.	Mr. P.S. Sinha Registration No.:-007A	Bharat Sevashram Sangha, River's Meet Road, Sonari, Jamshedpur
12.	Mr. Gurupadappa Shivappa Javali Registration No.:-008	Shri Jagadguru Gurusiddeshwar Vidyavardhak & Sanskritika Samashe, Tq-Badami, Distt. Bagalkot, Guledgudd, Karnataka
13.	Mr. Iranna Sanganabasappa Sheka Registration No.:-008A	Shri Jagadguru Gurusiddeshwar Vidyavardhak & Sanskritika Samashe, Tq-Badami, Distt Bagalkot, Guledgudd

Sl. No.	Name of Participant	Institution Name
14.	Dr. P. Hanumantha Rao Registration No.:-009	Sweekar, Rehabilitation Instittue for Handicapped, Upkaar Complex, Upkaar Junction, Secunderabad
15.	Ms. Nisha Grover Registration No.:-011	Akshar Trust, Meghdoot, R.C Dutt Road, Alkapuri, Baroda
16.	Mr. Snehlata Varnekar Registration No.:-014	Suhrud Mandal, 'Smruti', 805, Bhandarkar Road, Shivajinagar, Pune
17.	Ms. Sunita Dahke Registration No.:-014A	Suhrud Mandal, 'Smruti', 805, Bhandarkar Road, Shivajinagar, Pune
18.	Ms. Snehlata Prabha Registration No.:-015	Pandurang Shamrao Mulgaonkar Vishesh Shikshan, Adhyapak Mahavidyalaya, 805, 'Smruti', Bhandarkar Road, Shivaji Nagar, Pune
19.	Mr. Onkar Nath Sachar Registration No.:-016A	Sh. Dina Nath Kohli Charitable Trust, CMC Complex, Puran Vihar, Jagadhri, Distt. Yamuna Nagar
20.	Dr. S.K. Sharma Registration No.:-017	Dr. Sheela Sharma Memorial Charitable Trust, 2517, Rani Mandi, Vrindaban Road, Mahura (Uttar Pradesh)
21.	Smt. Sunita Sharma Registration No.:-017A	Dr. Sheela Sharma Memorial Charitable Trust, 2517, Rani Mandi Vrindaban Road, Mahura (Uttar Pradesh)
22.	Mr. Labhubhai T. Sonani Registration No.:-019	Smt. Parasanben Narandas Ramji Shahd (Talajawala), Pragnachakshu Vidyalaya, Opp. New Filter, Vidyanagar, Bhavanagar
23.	Kishorbhai K. Pandya Registration No.:-019A	Smt. Parasanben Narandas Ramji Shahd (Talajawala), Pragnachakshu Vidyalaya, Opp. New Filter, Vidyanagar, Bhavanagar
24.	Mr. Pyare Lal Registration No.:-020	K. Velayudhan Memorial Trust, Post Box No. 30, Cherthala, Alappuzha Distt., Kerala
25.	Mr. P.K. Bhargo Registration No.:-021	Institute of Applied Research, HIG 424 E7 Arera Colony, Bhopal (M.P)
26.	Mr. R.K. Sharma Registration No.:-021A	Institute of Applied Research, HIG 424 E7 Arera Colony, Bhopal (M.P)
27.	Ms. Upma Chopra Registration No.:-023	Air Force Golden Jubilee Institute, Subroto Park, New Delhi
28.	Mrs. C.M. Malhotra Registration No.:-023A	Air Force Golden Jubilee Institute, Subroto Park, New Delhi
29.	Mr. N.D. Wahane Registration No.:-024	Bodhisatwa Dr. Babasaheb Ambedkar Sanskritik Mandal, 80(A) and 80(1) Naveen Subedar Nagar, Nagpur

Sl. No.	*Name of Participant*	*Institution Name*
30.	Mr. S.C. Jodape Registration No.:-024A	Bodhisatwa Dr. Babasaheb Ambedkar Sanskritik Mandal, 80(A) and 80(1) Naveen Subedar Nagar, Nagpur
31.	Mr. Subhash Mahant Registration No.:-026	Bharat Vikas Parishad Charitable Trust Punjab, P.O. Viklang Sahayata Kendar, C-Block, Rishi Nagar, Ludhiana
32.	Mr. Puran Chand Registration No.:-026A	Bharat Vikas Parishad Charitable Trust Punjab, P.O. Viklang Sahayata Kendar, C-Block, Rishi Nagar, Ludhiana
33.	Mr. Shankerbhai N. Patel Registration No.:-028	Gram Manglam- Sultanpur, At P.O. Bhudasan Via-Akarund, Ta-Bayad, Distt.Sabarkantha, Gujarat
34.	Mr. Subir Debhi Registration No.:-028A	Gram Manglam-Sultanpur, At P.O. Bhudasan, Via-Akarund, Ta-Bayad, Distt. Sabarkantha, Gujarat
35.	Mr. Jagdish Registration No.:-029	Shree Jay Khodiyar Education Trust, C/11, Anand Tenament, Opp. But Bhawani Temple, Vejalpur, Ahmedabad, Gujarat
36.	Mr. Dilip Bhiwaji Bhondekar Registration No.:-030	Shri Sant Ravidas Sikshan Sanstha, Mata Nagar, Tumsar, Distt. Bhandara, Maharashtra
37.	Wg. Cdr. B.C. Prabhakar Registration No.:-033	J.S.S. Mahavidyapeetha, Ramanuja Road, Mysore
38.	Dr. Mruthyunjaya Registration No.:-033A	J.S.S. Mahavidyapeetha, Ramanuja Road, Mysore
39.	Mr. Satyendra Kumar Pathak Registration No.:-034	Sachchidanand Shiksha Evam Samaj Kalyan Sansthan, Karpi, Jehanabad, Bihar
40.	Mr. S.P. Reddy Registration No.:-035	Uma Education & Technical Society, 4-54, Manovikas Nagar, Rayudupalem, Kakinada, A.P.
41.	Mr. D. Dharma Rao Registration No.:-036	Lepra Society, P.B No. 1518, Krishnapuri Colony, West Marredapally, Secunderabad
42.	Mr. Jayaram Registration No.:-036A	Lepra Society, P.B No. 1518 Krishnapuri Colony, West Marredapally, Secunderabad
43.	Mr. S. Jeyaraj Registration No.:-038	Rural Institute for Development Education, 46, Periyar Nagar, PO Box 31, Little Kanchipuram, Kanchipuram District, Tamilnadu

Sl. No.	*Name of Participant*	*Institution Name*
44.	Mr. R.C. Behera Registration No.:-039	National Institute of Social Rehabilitation and Rural Development, Village–Tikatal, P.O. Chakapada, Via–Begunia, Distt. Khurda, Orissa
45.	Ms. Debakanta Sarangi Registration No.:-042	Arun Institute of Rural Affairs, At–Aswakhola, P.O. Karamul, Via–Mahimagadi, Distt.–Dhenkanal, Orissa
46.	Ms. Sumitra Gupta Registration No.:-043	The Central Institute of Teachers of the Deaf, 3rd Floor, Municipal School Building, Opp. YMCA Swimming Pool, Farook S. Umarbhoy Path, Agripada, Mumbai
47.	Ms. Sudha S. Burde Registration No.:-043A	The Central Institute of Teachers of the Deaf, 3rd Floor, Municipal School Building, Opp. YMCA Swimming Pool, Farook S. Umarbhoy Path, Agripada, Mumbai
48.	Ln K. Moorthi Registration No.:-044	Mother Teresa Dt. Physically Handicapped Rehabilitation Society, 32, Flower Bazaar, Post Box No. 118, Vaniyambadi
49.	L.N.J Dharmi Chand Registration No.:-044A	Mother Teresa Dt. Physically Handicapped Rehabilitation Society, 32, Flower Bazaar, Post Box No. 118, Vaniyambadi
50.	Mr. S.P. Sundaram Registration No.:-044B	Mother Teresa Dt. Physically Handicapped Rehabilitation Society, 32, Flower Bazaar, Post Box No. 118, Vaniyambadi
51.	Mr. K. Ananda Registration No.:-046	Ganjam District Orthopaedically Handicapped Welfare Association, Netaji Subhash Marg, Near S.P. Residence, Chatrapur (Ganjam)
52.	Mr. Hemant Kumar Subudi Registration No.:-046A	Ganjam District Orthopaedically Handicapped Welfare Association, Netaji Subhash Marg, Near S.P. Residence, Chatrapur (Ganjam)
53.	Mr. Kapil Kumar Aggarwal Registration No.:-047	Viklang Sahara Samiti, G–Block, Basti Vikash Kendre, Mangol Puri, New Delhi
54.	Mr. Hanif Shaikh Registration No.:-048	Bhoruka Charitable Trust, V.P.O. Bhorugram, Tehsil Rajgarh, Distt. Churu, Rajasthan
55.	Ms. Basanti Gupta Registration No.:-048A	Bhoruka Charitable Trust, V.P.O. Bhorugram, Tehsil Rajgarh, Distt. Churu, Rajasthan

Sl. No.	*Name of Participant*	*Institution Name*
56.	Swami Biswanathananda Registration No.:-049	Vivekananda Mission Asram, Vivek Nagar, P.O. Chaitanyapur (Haldia), Distt. Medinipur, West Bengal
57.	Ms. Gita Jana Registration No.:-049A	Vivekananda Mission Asram, Vivek Nagar, P.O. Chaitanyapur (Haldia), Distt. Medinipur, West Bengal
58.	Sr. Glory Registration No.:-050	Nirmala Sadan, Teacher's Trianing Centre (DSE-MR) Muvattupuzha, Ernakulam (Dt.) Kerala
59.	Sr. Tessy Maria Registration No.:-050A	Nirmala Sadan, Teacher's Trianing Centre (DSE-MR) Muvattupuzha, Ernakulam (Dt.) Kerala
60.	Mr. Ranchod Soni Registration No.:-053	Blind People's Association (INDIA), Dr. Vikram Sarabhai Road, Vastrapur, Ahmedabad, Gujarat
61.	Ms. Jasmine Sajit Registration No.:-053A	Blind People's Association (INDIA), Dr. Vikram Sarabhai Road, Vastrapur, Ahmedabad, Gujarat
62.	Mr. F.J. Porwal Registration No.:-054	National Association for the Blind, Dr. Vikram Sarabhai Road, Vastrapur, Ahmedabad, Gujarat
63.	Jasubhai B. Kavi Registration No.:-054A	National Association for the Blind, Dr. Vikram Sarabhai Road, Vastrapur, Ahmedabad, Gujarat
64.	Mr. Braj Kishore Sharma Registration No.:-055	Shri Rajiv Gandhi Sarvodaya Vikas Sansthan, Nangal House, Chobbey Para, Pandit Bhawan, Hindon City, Distt.–Karoli, Rajasthan
65.	Mr. Yogendra Sharma Registration No.:-055A	Shri Rajiv Gandhi Sarvodaya Vikas Sansthan, Nangal House, Chobbey Para, Pandit Bhawan, Hindon City, Distt.–Karoli, Rajasthan
66.	Mr. Kanubhai H. Tailor Registration No.:-056	Disabled Welfare Trust of India, 1058, Dhobi Sheri, Nanpura, Surat, Gujarat
67.	Mohd. Aslam, Cycle Wala Registration No.:-056A	Disabled Welfare Trust of India, 1058, Dhobi Sheri, Nanpura, Surat, Gujarat
68.	Sri Narottam Parida Registration No.:-057	Orissa Multipurpose Development Centre, 9/22, MIG-II, BDA Colony, Chandrasakharpur, Bhubaneswar–16, Orissa
69.	Mr. Pratap Kumar Barik Registration No.:-057A	Orissa Multipurpose Development Centre, 9/22, MIG-II, BDA Colony, Chandrasakharpur, Bhubaneswar–16, Orissa

Sl. No.	*Name of Participant*	*Institution Name*
70.	Ms. Antara Sarkar Registration No.:-059	Alakendu Both Niketan, FC-53, Narayantala (West), P.O.- D.B. Nagar, Kolkata
71.	Mr. Annas. C.P. Registration No.:-060	SILENT VALLEY, Residential Vocational Training Centre for Deaf Women, Paravattany, Thrissur, Kerala
72.	Mr. Roy Antony Registration No.:-060A	SILENT VALLEY, Residential Vocational Training Centre for Deaf Women, Paravattany, Thrissur, Kerala
73.	Mr. Jose Mannikathan Varghese Registration No.:-061	AMICI DI RAOUL FOLIEREAU, 58, Kavery Layout, 4th Cross, Thavarekere Main Road, Dharamaram College, Bangalore
74.	Mr. Jayanth Kumar Registration No.:-061A	AMICI DI RAOUL FOLIEREAU, 58, Kavery Layout, 4th Cross, Thavarekere Main Road, Dharamaram College, Bangalore
75.	Mr. Pradeep Registration No.:-062	Training Centre for the Teachers of the Visually Handicapped, Braille Bhawan, Jamalpur, Ludhiana, Punjab
76.	Mr. Shashi Kant Sharma Registration No.:-063	Maharana Pratap Vikas Shiksha Samiti, Village–Nagla Manka, P.O. Cair The Bayana, Distt.–Bharatpur, Rajasthan
77.	Mr. Binod Kumar Sharma Registration No.:-063A	Maharana Pratap Vikas Shiksha Samiti, Village–Nagla Manka, P.O. Cair The Bayana, Distt.–Bharatpur, Rajasthan
78.	Mr. Kagne Laxman Ekanathrao Registration No.:-065	Ayodhya Charitable Trust, S.No. 51/2, Near S.R.P. Gate No. 2, Vikas Nagar, Wanawadi Village, Pune
79.	Mr. Vinod Sharma Registration No.:-066	Sri Sri Bijoykrishna Ashram Relief Society, Delhi Correspondence Office, B-4/74, Paschim Vihar, New Delhi
80.	Mr. Naba Kumar Majumdar Registration No.:-066A	Sri Sri Bijoykrishna Ashram Relief Society, Delhi Correspondence Office, B-4/74, Paschim Vihar, New Delhi
81.	Mr. Sudeep Goyal Registration No.:-067	ASHA KA JHARNA, Harlalka Kothi, Nawalgarh, Rajasthan
82.	Mrs. Yohavathi Narendiran Registration No.:-068	Kovai Rehabilitation & Information Services for the Handicapped, 34, Tatabad First St. (Near Indian Bank), Sivananda Colony, Coimbatore, Tamilnadu
83.	Mr. K. Narendiran Registration No.:-068A	Kovai Rehabilitation & Information Services for the Handicapped, 34, Tatabad First St. (Near Indian Bank), Sivananda Colony, Coimbatore, Tamilnadu

Sl. No.	*Name of Participant*	*Institution Name*
84.	Mr. Santosh Ku. Dash Registration No.:-069	BIKALPA BIKASH, ORISSA, Tukuda, Angul, Orissa
85.	Ms. Lipipuspa Behera Registration No.:-069A	BIKALPA BIKASH, ORISSA, Tukuda, Angul, Orissa
86.	Mr. R.S, Sharma Registration No.:-070	MINU SHARMA VIKLANG RELIEF SOCIETY, Kuraoli, Distt. Mainpuri (U.P.)
87.	Mr. Uma Shankar Pandey Registration No.:-070A	MINU SHARMA VIKLANG RELIEF SOCIETY, Kuraoli, Distt. Mainpuri (U.P.)
88.	Mrs. R.N. Limaye Registration No.:-071	Prbondhini Teachers' Training Centre, Nasik, Behind I.T.I., Opp. Mutha Hospital, Satpur, Nashik
89.	A.S Chakrabarty Registration No.:-071A	Prbondhini Teachers' Training Centre, Nasik, Behind I.T.I., Opp. Mutha Hospital, Satpur, Nashik
90.	Ms. S.S. Jayalakshmi Registration No.:-074	VIDYA VIKASINI OPPORTUNITY SCHOOL, 66-D, Mettupalayam Road, Thudiyalur Post, Coimbatore
91.	Praful N. Vyas Registration No.:-076	Andhajan Kalyan Trust, Yogeshwar, A-55, Anand Nagar Dhoraji, Gujarat
92.	Bhasker Yogendra Mehta Registration No.:-077	National Association for the Blind, Near Satyam Auto Service, Shreenagar Rd. 10 At & P.O. Idar, Distt. Sabarkantha, Idar
93.	Ms. Pravina Bhasker Mehta Registration No.:-077A	National Association for the Blind, Near Satyam Auto Service, Shreenagar Rd. 10 At & P.O. Idar, Distt.–Sabarkantha, Idar
94.	Mr. Brijmohan Sharma Registration No.:-078	Social Work and Environment for Rural Advancement Swera Sanstha Farkiya, Village/Post–Farkiya, Vaya–Shrinagar, Distt. Ajmer, Rajasthan
95.	Ms. Prabha Gehlot Registration No.:-079	Medical Care Centre Trust, K.G.P Children Hospital, Kareli Baugh, Vadodara, Gujarat
96.	Brig. S.N.Datt V.S.M Registration No.:-080	Pritam Spiritual Foundation, Bachitter Nagar Near Radio Station, Poonch, J & K
97.	Mrs. Aabha Dutt Registration No.:-080A	Pritam Spiritual Foundation, Bachitter Nagar Near Radio Station, Poonch, J & K
98.	Mr. S. Chandrasekaran Registration No.:-081	Rural Education and Environment Development Service (REEDS), Plot No. 10, Sivasakthi Nagar Ellisnagar Post, Dharapuram, Erode Distt., Tamil Nadu

Sl. No.	*Name of Participant*	*Institution Name*
99.	Mr. I. Jayseelan Registration No.:-081A	Rural Education and Environment Development Service (REEDS), Plot No. 10, Sivasakthi Nagar Ellisnagar Post, Dharapuram, Erode Distt., Tamil Nadu
100.	Mr. T.N. Shethulinkhan Registration No.:-082	The Poor Up-LIET Organization (PULO), I.D. Network, 159, M.G.R Nagar Vengamedu, Karur, Tamil Nadu
101.	Dr. Sanjay A. Mall Registration No.:-084	World Vision of India, C/o YMCA Cultural Building, 1, Jaisingh Road, New Delhi
102.	Dr. Rita Malhotra Registration No.:-085	Centre for Special Education & Child Guidance, Amar Jyoti Rehabilitation and Research Centre, Amar Jyoti Charitable Trust, Karkardooma Vikas Marg, Delhi
103.	Mr. Natubhai R. Barot Registration No.:-086	Sarvangin Gram Vikas Sanstha, 1st Floor, Riddhi Siddhi Complex, Near Gurjar Pole, Prantij, Distt. Sabarkantha, Gujarat
104.	Mr. Udayan B. Desai Registration No.:-086A	Sarvangin Gram Vikas Sanstha, 1st Floor, Riddhi Siddhi Complex, Near Gurjar Pole, Prantij, Distt. Sabarkantha, Gujarat
105.	Mrs. Saswati Singh Registration No.:-087	INSPIRATION, AGI-123D Vikas Puri, New Delhi
106.	Mr. Pankaj Khajanchi Registration No.:-087A	INSPIRATION, AGI-123D Vikas Puri, New Delhi
107.	Mr. Ram Prakash Gupta Registration No.:-088	Society for the Rehabilitation of Physically Handicapped and Mentally Backward (Regd.), 34, Kotla Road, New Delhi
108.	Mr. Ramesh Kumar Mandal Registration No.:-089	Sahyog Kushth Yagna Trust, Rajendra Nagar Choukdi, Dist Sabarkantha, Gujarat
109.	Mr. Rameshbhai Gajvi Registration No.:-089A	Sahyog Kushth Yagna Trust, Rajendra Nagar Choukdi, Dist Sabarkantha, Gujarat
110.	Mr. Yusufi. S. Kapadia Registration No.:-090	Blind Welfare Council, Mission Hospital Road, Nr. Railway over Bridge, Dahod, Gujarat
111.	Mr. Tapan Kumar Pandit Registration No.:-091	Dr. Ambedkar Society for Socio-Economic Welfare and Development, Nabinabagh, P.O. Midnapore, Distt. Paschim Midinipure, West Bengal
112.	Mrs. K. Vijaya Lakshmi Registration No.:-092	Vamsi Mahila Mandali, 1-120, VNR Peta, Bitragunta, Bogolu Mandal Nellore Distt., Andhra Pradesh

Sl. No.	*Name of Participant*	*Institution Name*
113.	Ms. P. Swarna Latha Registration No.:-092A	Vamsi Mahila Mandali, 1-120, VNR Peta, Bitragunta, Bogolu Mandal Nellore Distt., Andhra Pradesh
114.	Mr. Asok Chakraborty Registration No.:-093	SHELTER (Society for Help Education Love Training and Employment for the Retarded), 3, Kalbati Lane, Bhadreswar, Hooghly, West Bengal
115.	Mr. Debasis Rath Registration No.:-094	Rural and Urban Socio- Cultural Help. (Rush), 25, Upper NUA Sahi, Puri, Orissa
116.	Dr. R..N. Sharma Registration No.:-097	Medicare and Research Foundation, 172, Zone II Maharana Pratap Nagar (Near Sargam Talkies) Bhopal
117.	Dr. J.S. Ahluwalia Registration No.:-097A	Medicare and Research Foundation, 172, Zone II Maharana Pratap Nagar (Near Sargam Talkies) Bhopal
118.	Mr. Subhasisi Sinha Registration No.:-098	Anandiketan Society for Mental Health Care, P.O. and Village Khajurdihi Via–Katwa, Distt. Burdwan
119.	Shri Subrata Sinha Registration No.:-098A	Anandiketan Society for Mental Health Care, P.O. and Village Khajurdihi Via–Katwa, Distt. Burdwan
120.	Dr. G.N. Karna Registration No.:-099	Society for Disability and Rehabilitation Studies, A-2/144, Sector 17 Rohini, New Delhi
121.	Mr. Ramesh Kumar Registration No.:-099A	Society for Disability and Rehabilitation Studies, A-2/144, Sector 17 Rohini, New Delhi
122.	Dr. Sharada Fatehpuria Registration No.:-100	Manovikas Kendra Rehabilitation and Research Institute for the Handicapped, 482, Madudah, Plot-I 24, Sec. J. Eastern Metropolitan Bypass, Kolkata, West Bengal
123.	Mr. Ashish Kumar Sanyal Registration No.:-100A	Manovikas Kendra Rehabilitation and Research Institute for the Handicapped, 482, Madudah, Plot-I 24, Sec. J. Eastern Metropolitan Bypass, Kolkata, West Bengal
124.	Prof. (Dr.) Bishnupada Nanda Registration No.:-100B	Manovikas Kendra Rehabilitation and Research Institute for the Handicapped, 482, Madudah, Plot-I 24, Sec. J. Eastern Metropolitan Bypass, Kolkata, West Bengal
125.	Dr. Sudha Kaul Registration No.:-102	Indian Institute of Cerebral Palasy, P-35/1 Taratolla Road, Kolkata, West Bengal

Sl. No.	*Name of Participant*	*Institution Name*
126.	Ms. Swati Lahiri Registration No.:-102A	Indian Institute of Cerebral Palasy, P-35/1 Taratolla Road, Kolkata, West Bengal
127.	Ms. Smita Worah Registration No.:-102B	Indian Institute of Cerebral Palasy, P-35/1 Taratolla Road, Kolkata, West Bengal
128.	Mr. Nand Kishore Singh Registration No.:-103	Gramin Vikas Anusanshadhan Evam Prasikshan Sangathan Janardan Path, Mahisouri Jamui, Dist Jamul, Bihar
129.	Dr. Veena Singh Registration No.:-106	Isaraji Devi Sikshan Sanstha, 23, B Park Road Allahabad, Uttar Pradesh
130.	Ms. Poona Jaishwal Registration No.:-106A	Isaraji Devi Sikshan Sanstha, 23, B Park Road Allahabad, Uttar Pradesh
131.	Mr. M. Ramaswami Registration No.:-107	Mangalam Adj., Old R.S. Gardens Post Office Tirupati
132.	Ms. M. Varalakshmi Registration No.:-107A	Mangalam Adj., Old R.S. Gardens Post Office Tirupati
133.	Mohd. Majhar Alam Registration No.:-108	Shama Vikas Samiti Ansar Nagar, Malah Bogha, Islampur, Dist. Nalanda, Bihar
134.	Registration No.:-108A	– do –
135.	Dr. M. Manivannan Registration No.:-110	International Human Resource Development Centre for the Disabled, Sri Ramakrishna Vidyalaya Post Coimbatore, Tamil Nadu
136.	Shri V.R. Mathivanan Registration No.:-110A	International Human Resource Development Centre for the Disabled, Sri Ramakrishna Vidyalaya Post Coimbatore, Tamil Nadu
137.	Dr. C. Tulsi Das Registration No.:-111	Deva Integrated School for the Handicapped, B21/100, Bind Bhavan, Kamachh Chungi, Varanasi, Uttar Pradesh
138.	Mr. Shyam Lal Registration No.:-111A	Deva Integrated School for the Handicapped, B21/100, Bind Bhavan, Kamachh Chungi, Varanasi, Uttar Pradesh
139.	Mr. Sukant Kumar Khatoi Registration No.:-112	Netajee Club, At- Arilo, P.O. Ratilo Via–Revah, Distt. Puri, Orissa
140.	Dr. Dev Yogi Registration No.:-113	Mamta Kendra Nani Kadi, Ta–Kadi Distt. Mehsana, Gujarat Pin
141.	Ms. Dudharejiyu Hetalben Bharutlal Registration No.:-113A	Mamta Kendra Nani Kadi, Ta–Kadi Distt. Mehsana, Gujarat
142.	Mr. Patel Alkesh Kumar Ishwarlal Registration No.:-114	Mangal Jeevan Trust, Siddhpur, Kakosi Road, At & P.O.–Sedrana, Ta–Sidhpur Distt. Patan

Sl. No.	*Name of Participant*	*Institution Name*
143.	Ms. Patel Gavariben Natavar Lal Registration No.:-114A	Mangal Jeevan Trust, Siddhpur, Kakosi Road, At & P.O.–Sedrana, Ta–Sidhpur, Distt. Patan
144.	Mr. N.M. Kanabar Registration No.:-115	The Society for the Mentally Retarded, Opp. B.T. Savani Kidney Hospital Sau. University Road, Rajkot
145.	Mr. Hitesh N. Kanabar Registration No.:-115A	The Society for the Mentally Retarded, Opp. B.T. Savani Kidney Hospital, Sau. University Road, Rajkot, Gujarat
146.	Nurul Islam Registration No.:-117	Rampurhat Spastics and Handicapped Society Rampurhat Chamragodam, P.O. P.S. Rampurhat Distt. Birbhum, West Bengal
147.	Ms. Bandana Banerjee Registration No.:-117A	Rampurhat Spastics and Handicapped, Society Rampurhat Chamragodam, P.O. P.S. Rampurhat Distt. Birbhum, West Bengal
148.	Mr. Shish Ram Registration No.:-118	Shri Krishna Vikas Sansthan Vill. Phusapur, P.O. Sarai Kalan Distt. Alwar, Rajasthan
149.	Mr. Mehta Dinesh Keshavlal Registration No.:-119	Andhajan Talim Kendra, Aerodrome Road, Jamnagar
150.	Punjani Navinchandra Pranshanker Registration No.:-119A	Andhajan Talim Kendra, Aerodrome Road, Jamnagar
151.	Ms. Jacintha Saldanha Registration No.:-120	Pre School and Service Centre for the Hearing Handicapped, Tripolia Social Service Centre, P.O. Gulzarbagh, Patna, Bihar
152.	Sr. Lissy Mathew Registration No.:-121	Asha Deep Rehabilitation Centre for the Handicapped, Fair Field Colony, Digha Ghat, Patna, Bihar
153.	Dr. E.M. Johnson Registration No.:-122	Vocational Rehabilitation Training Centre (Regd.) for Blind/Disabled, Habowal Road, Opp. Kitchlu Nagar, Ludhiana, Punjab
154.	Mrs. Sara Johnson Registration No.:-122A	Vocational Rehabilitation Training Centre (Regd.) for Blind/Disabled, Habowal Road, Opp. Kitchlu Nagar, Ludhiana, Punjab
155.	Mr. Somnath Munshi Registration No.:-123	Bikashayan 40, Bonhooghly Govt. Colony, Kolkata, West Bengal
156.	Mr. Amresh Chandra Registration No.:-124A	Shikshit Yuva Sewa Samiti, Pandey Bazar, Basti, Uttar Pradesh
157.	Mr. S.K. Bhatnagar Registration No.:-125A	Sanjeevani Seva Sangam Insitute for Hearing Impaired and Research, Centre Scheme No. 54, Behind Satya Sai Vidya Vihar, A.B. Road, Indore, Madhya Pradesh

Sl. No.	*Name of Participant*	*Institution Name*
158.	Mr. Uma Shankar Prasad Registration No.:-126	Krishak Vikas Samiti, New Chandmari Tarkulwa Road, Motihari, East Champaran Bihar
159.	Mr. Krishana Kanhaiya Kumar Registration No.:-126A	Krishak Vikas Samiti, New Chandmari Tarkulwa Road, Motihari, East Champaran, Bihar
160.	Ms. Nibha Devi Registration No.:-127	Ram Wati Prasikshan Kendra, P.O. Khaira, Distt. Jamui, Bihar
161.	Mr. Dayanidhi Dubey Registration No.:-128	Uttar Pradesh Gram Vikas Santh, Opp. Thana Kotwali, Dehat, Ramaipatti Distt. Mirzapur, Uttar Pradesh
162.	Dr. Gyanendra Dhar Dubey Registration No.:-128A	Uttar Pradesh Gram Vikas Santh, Opp. Thana Kotwali, Dehat, Ramaipatti Distt. Mirzapur, Uttar Pradesh
163.	Mr. Devraj Mishra Registration No.:-128B	Uttar Pradesh Gram Vikas Santh, Opp. Thana Kotwali, Dehat, Ramaipatti, Distt. Mirzapur, Uttar Pradesh
164.	Dr. R. Ranganathan Registration No.:-129	Department of Special Education, Andhra Univeristy Vishakha Patnam, Andhra Pradesh
165.	Mr. Ravindra Gokhale Registration No.:-130	Sweekar, 9 Kasturba Gandhi Bhawan, 349/2 Bajaj Nagar, Nagpur, Maharashtra
166.	Mr. Joshi Anil Upendra Registration No.:-130A	Sweekar, 9 Kasturba Gandhi Bhawan, 349/2 Bajaj Nagar, Nagpur, Maharashtra
167.	Mr. Vijay Kumar Registration No.:-131	ECOVIC, Enivironment Consultancy Vikas Centre, 278, Nehru Nagar, Patna
168.	Ms. Sujata Kumar Registration No.:-131A	ECOVIC, Environment Consultancy Vikas Centre, 278, Nehru Nagar, Patna
169.	Mr. Jagannath Panda Registration No.:-133	The Institute for Helping the Disabled, 203, Sahidnagar, Bhubaneswar, Orissa
170.	Mr. Bhagirathi Panda Registration No.:-133B	The Institute for Helping the Disabled, 203, Sahidnagar, Bhubaneswar, Orissa
171.	Mr. B.L. Jain Registration No.:-134	Lata Gramin Mahila Utthan Samiti, In front of Ganga Vishan Bada, Dattpura, Muraina, Madhya Pradesh
172.	Mr. N.C. Bose Croos Registration No.:-135	CBR Forum, Apartment 001, Ground Floor, "Lourdesville", No. 39, North Road, St. Thomas Town Post Cooke Town, Bangalore
173.	Mr. Ronak V. Chavada Registration No.:-138	Jay Shri Hiral Mahila Vikas Charitable Sanstha, Plot No. 38/2, Sec-14, Gandhinagar, Gujarat

Sl. No.	*Name of Participant*	*Institution Name*
174.	Mr. G.K. Parmar Registration No.:-138A	Jay Shri Hiral Mahila Vikas Charitable Sanstha, Plot No. 38/2, Sec-14, Gandhinagar, Gujarat
175.	Mr. Prakash J. Mankodi Registration No.:-140	National Association for the Blind, Jamnagar Distt. Branch, Aerodrome Road, Jamnagar
176.	Mr. Surender Kumar Rai Registration No.:-143	SRIJANAA, Minto Road, Opp. Govt. of India Press, New Delhi
177.	Mr. Asis Kr. Singha Roy Registration No.:-144	Adarsha Pratibandhi Samity, Lenin Sarani, Bahrghat Dakshin Dinajpur, West Bengal
178.	Mr. Rajkishor Sabut Registration No.:-145	Pingalakhi Public Welfare Organisation, At/P.O. Nimapara, Ganesh Bazar Distt. Puri, Orissa
179.	Mr. Gagan Bihari Das Registration No.:-145A	Pingalakhi Public Welfare Organisation, At/P.O. Nimapara, Ganesh Bazar Distt. Puri, Orissa
180.	Mr. Niranjan Ghosh Registration No.:-148	Pratibondhee Shanghaa, 32/1, Lake View Park Kolkata, West Bengal
181.	Mr. Peter Abraham Registration No.:-148A	Pratibondhee Shanghaa, 32/1, Lake View Park Kolkata, West Bengal
182.	Mr. V.Krishnaswmay Registration No.:-149	Madhuram Narayanan Centre for Exceptional Children, 126, G.N. Chetty Road, T. Nagar, Chennai, Tamil Nadu
183.	Mrs. Jaya Krishnasmay Registration No.:-149A	Madhuram Narayanan Centre for Exceptional Children, 126, G.N. Chetty Road, T. Nagar, Chennai, Tamil Nadu
184.	Mr. Rambir K. Patel Registration No.:-152	National Association for the Blind, In Front of Civil Hospital Road, Nonawada, Distt. Valsad, Gujarat
185.	Mr. Kamal Registration No.:-152A	National Association for the Blind, In Front of Civil Hospital Road, Nonawada, Distt. Valsad, Gujarat
186.	Mr. John Rock Registration No.:-153A	Sociat Education for Development, Arockiyapuram, Neyyoor, Kanyakumari Distt. Karnataka
187.	Mr. Shyamal Deb Registration No.:-154	All Tripura Scheduled Castes Tribes & Minority Upliftment Council, Ramnagar Rd. No. 1, P.O. Ramnagar, Agartala, Tripura(W)
188.	Mr. D. Shibu Registration No.:-155A	Balavikas Teachers Training Centre, Opp. Hindustan Latex, Peroorkada P.O. Thiruvananthapuram

Sl. No.	*Name of Participant*	*Institution Name*
189.	Mr. Souren Sur Registration No.:-156	North Calcutta Pratibandhi Seva Kendra, 63/1 Paik Para 1st Row, Kolkata, West Bengal
190.	Mr. Atanu Ghosh Registration No.:-157	Korak Pratibandhi Kalyan Kendra, 1/25, Gorakashabasi Road, Nagerbazar, Dum Dum, Kolkata
191.	Mr. Mithlesh Kumar Verma Registration No.:-158	Sarvodaya Gramin Vikas Sansthan, "Shanti Kunj" Bharoapar, Ramchandrapur Road, Biharsharif
192.	Mr. Ram Prakash Singh Registration No.:-158A	Sarvodaya Gramin Vikas Sansthan, "Shanti Kunj" Bharoapar, Ramchandrapur Road, Biharsharif
193.	Mrs. M. Sheela Rani Registration No.:-160	Durgabai Deshmukh Vocational Training and Rehabilitation Centre, Andhra Mahila Sabha, Vidyanagar, Hyderabad, Andhra Pradesh
194.	Dr. Ganga Dayal Shakya Registration No.:-162	Buddh Shikshan Prashikshan Samiti, Moh. Mool Chand, Ganjdundwara, Etah, Uttar Pradesh
195.	Smt. Asha Rathour Registration No.:-162A	Buddh Shikshan Prashikshan Samiti, Moh. Mool Chand, Ganjdundwara, Etah, Uttar Pradesh
196.	Dr. P. Patchaimal Registration No.:-163	Centre for Development and Communication Trust, Kamatchipuram (S.O.) Theni Distt., Tamil Nadu
197.	Mr. Deb Kumar Paul Registration No.:-167	Ajodhya Pur Palli Mangal Samiti, Vill & P.O. Ajodhyapur, Distt. Purba Medinipur, West Bengal
198.	Mr. K. Kathiresan Registration No.:-168	Akshaya Rehabilitation Trust, No. 1, Ashinasapuram, 3rd Street, Sellur, Madurai, Tamil Nadu
199.	Mr. Ramalingam Registration No.:-168A	Akshaya Rehabilitation Trust, No. 1, Ashinasapuram, 3rd Street, Sellur, Madurai, Tamil Nadu
200.	Mr. K. Raman Shankar Registration No.:-169	National Association for the Blind, 124-127, Cotton Depot., R.M. Alpaiwalla Complex, Cotton Green, Mumbai
201.	Mr. Biswajit Dhar Registration No.:-170	Ramakrishna Vivekananda Mission School for Deaf & Blind Girls, Barrackpore, North 24 Parganas, West Bengal

Sl. No.	*Name of Participant*	*Institution Name*
202.	Mr. Ankur Saxena Registration No.:-171	P.G Dept of Social Work, C/o A-3/7, Urmi Apts. Behind Convent School, Fatehgunj, Baroda, Gujarat
203.	Mr. Bhagaban Sarma Registration No.:-172	Assam Mental Welfare Society, Vill.–Malikuchi, (Degheli) P.O. Bar Degheli, Distt. Nalbari, Assam
204.	Sr. Gynthia Santhmayor Registration No.:-173	Holy Cross Hearing Impaired School, Holy Cross Hospital, Ambikapur Post, Distt. Surguja, Chhattisgarh
205.	Dr. Marita Adam Registration No.:-174	SANGATH, Sangath Centre for Child Development and Family Guidance, 841/1, Behind Electricity Department Alto-Porvorim, Bardez, Goa
206.	Ms. Yogita Joshi Registration No.:-174A	SANGATH, Sangath Centre for Child Development and Family Guidance, 841/1, Behind Electricity Department Alto-Porvorim, Bardez, Goa
207.	Dr. Jasphool Singh Registration No.:-175	Haryana Nav Yuvak Kala Sangam, 48, Sec-1, Rohtak, Haryana
208.	Ms. Renu Singh Registration No.:-176	The Spastics Society of Northern India, Balbir Saxena Marg, New Delhi
209.	Mr. Rajesh Kumar Mansell Registration No.:-177	Masih Social Decvelopment Society Lower Chopra, Pauri Garwal, Utranchal
210.	Mr. Georgekutty Kareparampil Registration No.:-178	Kerela Federation of the Blind, Kunnukuzhi P.O. Thiruvananthapuram, Kerala
211.	Mr. C.K. Aboobacket Registration No.:-178A	Kerela Federation of the Blind, Kunnukuzhi P.O. Thiruvananthapuram, Kerala
212.	Dr. H.T. Dholakia Registration No.:-181	Parivaa–NFPA 4, Madhu Niketan, 21, West Avenue, Santacruz (W) Mumbai, Maharashtra
213.	Mr.Bhal Korgaonkar Registration No.:-181A	Parivaa–NFPA 4, Madhu Niketan, 21, West Avenue, Santacruz (W) Mumbai, Maharashtra
214.	Mr. Ndranath Mukherjee Registration No.:-182	Voice World, 4 Nrishngha Dutta Road Kolkata, West Bengal
215.	Mrs. Dolly Dutta Registration No.:-182A	Voice World, 4 Nrishngha Dutta Road, Kolkata, West Bengal
216.	Prof. Binod Kumar Registration No.:-183	Centre of Integrated Development and Research, Sahadev Khunta, Baleshwar, Orissa

Sl. No.	*Name of Participant*	*Institution Name*
217.	Mr. Subrat Kumar Dash Registration No.:-183A	Centre of Integrated Development and Research, Sahadev Khunta, Baleshwar, Orissa
218.	Mr. N. Satyanarayana Registration No.:-184	Disabled Welfare and Child Development Rural Youth Association, Vill–Bhavani Nagar Post–Maghavaram Via–Naupada, Distt. Srikakulam, Andhra Pradesh
219.	Ms. Sebababrata De Registration No.:-186	Pratibandhi Purnavas Samiti, P.O. Abhoynagar, Agartala, Tripura (W)
220.	Mr. Arun Kumar Registration No.:-187	The Delhi Society for the Welfare of Mentally Retarded Children, Yahso Bhawan, Okhla Marg, New Delhi
221.	Dr. Gaurav Deep Singh Registration No.:-188	Sardar Bhagwan Singh (Ph) Institute of Biomedical Sciences, Balawala, Dehradun, Uttaranchal
222.	Dr. Narkesh Arumugam Registration No.:-188A	Sardar Bhagwan Singh (Ph) Institute of Biomedical Sciences, Balawala, Dehradun, Uttaranchal
223.	S.A. Mundle Registration No.:-189	COSMOS, 24, Bose Para Road, Kolkata, West Bengal
224.	Mr. M.A. Malik Registration No.:-190	A.K. Model Public School, Samiti Mohalla Nai Basti, (B-14) Bijnor, Uttar Pradesh
225.	Mr. Aijaz Alam Registration No.:-190A	A.K. Model Public School, Samiti Mohalla Nai Basti, (B-14) Bijnor, Uttar Pradesh
226.	Mr. Kanhai Lal Yadav Registration No.:-191	Shivam Gram Utthan Seva Sansthan, Village–Maddhupur P.O. Maharajpur Distt. Azamgarh (U.P.)
227.	Mr. Shivlal Yadav Registration No.:-191A	Shivam Gram Utthan Seva Sansthan, Village–Maddhupur P.O. Maharajpur Distt. Azamgarh (U.P.)
228.	Mr. Ram Prakash Napit Registration No.:-192	Viklang Seva Sangh, Narguda Darwaja Tikamgarh, Madhya Pradesh
229.	Mr. Santohs Kumar Sen Registration No.:-192A	Viklang Seva Sangh, Narguda Darwaja Tikamgarh, Madhya Pradesh
230.	Ms. Nirmalaben C. Raval Registration No.:-193	Manthan Apang Kanya Seva Sankul, At & P.O. Hajipur Ta Kalol, Distt. Gandhi Nagar
231.	Mr. Girishbhai N. Patel Registration No.:-193A	Manthan Apang Kanya Seva Sankul, At & P.O. Hajipur Ta Kalol, Distt. Gandhi Nagar
232.	Ms. Aruna Devi Registration No.:-194	Shrirampur Child Guidance Centre Rajbati, 16, Raja K.L. Coswami Street, Shrirampur, Hooghly

Sl. No.	*Name of Participant*	*Institution Name*
233.	Dr. Manoj Kumar Registration No.:-195	J.M. Institute of Speech and Hearing, Indrapuri P.O. Keshri Nagar, Patna, Bihar
234.	Mr. Prem Lal Ray Registration No.:-195A	J.M. Institute of Speech and Hearing, Indrapuri P.O. Keshri Nagar, Patna, Bihar
235.	Ms. Indu Bhushan Kochgaway Registration No.:-196	Sharp Memorial School for the Blind, Rajpur, Dehradun
236.	Mr. Vivek Dilawar Registration No.:-196A	Sharp Memorial School for the Blind, Rajpur, Dehradun
237.	Dr. Bhushan Punani Registration No.:-200	Blind Peoples Association, Jagdish Patel Chowk, Surdas Marg, Ahmedabad
238.	Mr. Alakh Deo Paswan Registration No.:-201	Composite Regional Centre for Persons with Disabilities, Bemina Bye Pass, Opp. J & K Bank, Karan Nagar, Srinagar
239.	Dr. Abudus Salam Registration No.:-201A	Composite Regional Centre for Persons with Disabilities, Bemina Bye Pass, Opp. J & K Bank, Karan Nagar, Srinagar
240.	Mr. S.A. Raja Registration No.:-202	Sankalp Natya Sansthan, Ajmal Khan Road Najibabad, Bijnor, Uttar Pradesh
241.	Mr. Anil Sharma Registration No.:-202A	Sankalp Natya Sansthan, Ajmal Khan Road, Najibabad, Bijnor, Uttar Pradesh
242.	Mrs. Kasturi Mohapatra Registration No.:-204	Open Learning System, Plot No. G-3, A/1, Gadakana Mouza, Bhubaneswar
243.	Anil Saxena Registration No.:-205	Anchal Charitable Trust, No. 167-A, Mansarovar Park, Shahdara, Delhi
244.	Mr. S. Mukherjee Registration No.:-207	Centre for Integrated Human Development, (CIHI) Main Road, Vivekanand Nagar, Ghaziabad, Uttar Pradesh
245.	Er. Y.K. Goel Registration No.:-207A	Centre for Integrated Human Development, (CIHI) Main Road, Vivekanand Nagar, Ghaziabad, Uttar Pradesh
246.	Mr. Haribhai Sitaram Pandya Registration No.:-208	North Gujarat Handicap Help Union and Social Dev. Centre, Brahmpole, Sidhpur, North Gujarat
247.	Registration No.:-208A	– do –
248.	Ms. Lina Bardhan Registration No.:-209	Noble Mission of South Calcutta, 122/1/1/4 A, Manohar Pukur Road, Kolkata, West Bengal
249.	Ms. Kaberi Sinha Registration No.:-210	Antaranga Mansik Pratibandhi Mahila Vidyaniketan, P.O. Pujali, Budge Budge, Distt. South 24 Parganas, West Bengal

Sl. No.	*Name of Participant*	*Institution Name*
250.	Mr. Chander Shekhar Sharma Registration No.:-212	Matri Bhumi Social Welfare Society, 46/10 Chobata Bazar Mandi, Himachal Pradesh
251.	Mr. Prafulla Kumar Deep Registration No.:-213	Palli Vikash Parisad, Kanharpada (Sagada), Distt. Boudh, Orissa
252.	Mr. Suraj Pal Singh Registration No.:-214	Doon Research and Rehabilitation Institute for the Mentally Handicapped, 26, Ramesh Nagar, Beside Roshan Di Hatti, New Delhi
253.	Mr. Kanubhai J. Shelar Registration No.:-215	The Society for Physically Handicapped, 6, Marut Nandan Complex (Sudama House), Pritamnagar's 1st Slope, Ellisbridge, Ahmedabad
254.	Mr. Bhupesh P. Modi Registration No.:-215A	The Society for Physically Handicapped, 6, Marut Nandan Complex (Sudama House), Pritamnagar's 1st Slope, Ellisbridge, Ahmedabad
255.	Mr. Namdeo Sadashio Lambkane Registration No.:-216	Nirashrit Kalyankari Sanstha, C/o Dr. C.M. Chaudhari Nurses Colony, Near Govt. Hospital, Bhandara, Maharashtra
256.	Mr. J. Sudhakaran Registration No.:-217	J.K. Maas Foundation Trustee, 85-A, Arunachalam Street, S.S. Colony, Madurai, Tamil Nadu
257.	Mrs. Snigdha Sarkar Registration No.:-218	PARTNER, Hooghly, C/o Pratibandhi Kalyan Kendra, Abinash Mukherjee Road, P.O. & Distt. Hooghly, West Bengal
258.	Mr. Anil Pateriya Registration No.:-219	Society for Pragati Bharat, 113, Gandhi Nagar, Lalitpur
259.	Mr. Ajay Shrivastava Registration No.:-219A	Society for Pragati Bharat, 113, Gandhi Nagar, Lalitpur
260.	Dr. C.D. Parasher Registration No.:-220	P.M.R. Research Centre, 6-104, Kaushalya Park, Hauz Khas, New Delhi
261.	Ms. Asha Sethi Registration No.:-221	NIMH, Regional Centre, Kasturba Niketan, Lajpat Nagar, New Delhi
262.	Ms. Usha Grover Registration No.:-221A	NIMH, Regional Centre, Kasturba Niketan, Lajpat Nagar, New Delhi
263.	Mr. M. B. Jha Registration No.:-222	Parwarish- CDHCI, 10, Shahjahani Market, Kala Darwaza, Opp. Gandhi Medical College, Bhopal, Madhya Pradesh
264.	Mr. B. Showri Reddy Registration No.:-224	Voluntary Organization of Rural Development Society, Pedda Kottala, Nandyal

Sl. No.	*Name of Participant*	*Institution Name*
265.	Mr. G. Paul Registration No.:-224A	Voluntary Organization of Rural Development Society, Pedda Kottala, Nandyal
266.	Mr. Purusottam Sahoo Registration No.:-225	Project India, Social Service Dedicated for National Building, Baniapat, P.O. & Distt. Keonjhar, Orissa
267.	Mr. Vidhu Prakash Rout Registration No.:-225A	Project India, Social Service Dedicated for National Building, Baniapat, P.O. & Distt. Keonjhar, Orissa
268.	Mr. Abnishranjan Registration No.:-226	Indian Institute of Health Eduication and Research, Health Institute Road, Beur, Patna, Bihar
269.	Mr. Jagdish Saran Registration No.:-227	Vishal Samaj Vikas Sansthan, Moh. Roshan Bag, Civil Line Rampur, Uttar Pradesh
270.	Mr. Sukanta Chhotaray Registration No.:-228	Bhairabi Special School for the Handicapped, Bhairabi Club, Kurumpada, P.O. Hadapada Distt. Khurda
271.	Mr. Kumaresh Ch. Kar Registration No.:-229	Dum Dum Reliant Handicapped Welfare Society, 48/1, Kamalapur (West) Dum Dum, Kolkata, West Bengal
272.	Mr. Neerpal Singh Registration No.:-230	Gram Jyoti Sansthan, D-96, Pratap Nagar Saboli Village, Nand Nagri, Delhi
273.	Mrs. Neelam Masson Registration No.:-230A	Gram Jyoti Sansthan, D-96, Pratap Nagar, Saboli Village, Nand Nagri, Delhi
274.	Ms. Rita Chatterjee Registration No.:-231	Aanchal (NDMC's Special School for Mentally Handicapped), Kautilya Marg, Chanakya Puri, New Delhi
275.	Ms. Chitra Gupta Registration No.:-231A	Aanchal (NDMC's Special School for Mentally Handicapped), Kautilya Marg, Chanakya Puri, New Delhi
276.	Mr. Thakur V. Vijay Prasad Registration No.:-233	Rehabilitaton Coordination India, C/o Thakur Hari Prasad Institute Campus, Vivekanandnagar, Dilsukhnagar, Hyderabad, Andhra Pradesh
277.	Sri Krishna Samanta Registration No.:-235	Midnapore Rehabilitation Centre for Children, Gitanjali, Vidyasagar Road, Midnapore, West Bengal
278.	Mr. Pragnasheela Samanta Registration No.:-235A	Midnapore Rehabilitation Centre for Children, Gitanjali, Vidyasagar Road, Midnapore, West Bengal

Sl. No.	*Name of Participant*	*Institution Name*
279.	Mr. Hotilal Pipil Registration No.:-237	Shri Manpower, 44-A/1, Mayur Vihar-1, New Delhi
280.	Sailen Chowdhury Registration No.:-238	Paschim Banga Rajya Pratibandhi Sammilani, 4, Santoshpur Avenue, Kolkata, West Bengal
281.	Shri Madan Das Registration No.:-238A	Paschim Banga Rajya Pratibandhi Sammilani, 4, Santoshpur Avenue, Kolkata, West Bengal
282.	Ms. Deepika Jain Registration No.:-241	AVSAR, 245, Keshavganj, Choti Payaga, Sagar, Madhya Pradesh
283.	Mrs. Sushila Sinha "Grihmata Registration No.:-242	Santal Pargana Vikas and Seva Sansthan, Karnibag Road, B. Deoghar
284.	Mrs. Arati Shah Registration No.:-243	Ambika Sishu Kendra, 44-91, Prakash Nagar, 3rd Lane, Kurnool, Andhra Pradesh
285.	Ms. E.V.K. Bhagya Lakshmi Registration No.:-243A	Ambika Sishu Kendra, 44-91, Prakash Nagar, 3rd Lane, Kurnool, Andhra Pradesh
286.	Mrs. Jharna Bhattacharya Registration No.:-244	Kulachi Manovikas Kendra, Kulachi Hansraj Model School, "G" Block, Phase-I, Ashok Vihar, New Delhi
287.	Mr. K. Gopalkrishnan Registration No.:-244A	Kulachi Manovikas Kendra, Kulachi Hansraj Model School, "G" Block, Phase-I, Ashok Vihar, Delhi
288.	Mr. V.S. Choudhary Registration No.:-245	Indira Rashtriya Chetna Evam Samajotthan Sansthan, Hoshiyari Mandir Raiwala, Dehradun, Uttaranchal
289.	Mr. Madan Pal Registration No.:-245A	Indira Rashtriya Chetna Evam Samajotthan Sansthan, Hoshiyari Mandir Raiwala, Dehradun, Uttaranchal
290.	Mr. Raj Bahadur Singh Registration No.:-246	Lokoudyog Sewa Sansthan, Vill. & P.O. Sikraura, Distt. Azamgarh P.O. Sikraura, Uttar Pradesh
291.	Mr. Sanjeev Kumar Registration No.:-246A	Lokoudyog Sewa Sansthan, Vill. & P.O. Sikraura, Distt. Azamgarh P.O. Sikraura, Uttar Pradesh
292.	Mr. Gourang Charan Nayak Registration No.:-247	Utkal Sanskruti Bikash Parishad, Kalyani Nagar, Cuttack, Orissa
293.	Mr. Satya Gopal Parija Registration No.:-247A	Utkal Sanskruti Bikash Parishad, Kalyani Nagar, Cuttack, Orissa
294.	Mr. J. Senthil Kumar Registration No.:-248	J.S. Trust, No. 162, Red Hill Road, Ambattur, Chennai, Tamil Nadu
295.	Mr. S. Veera Raghavan Registration No.:-248A	J.S. Trust, No. 162, Red Hill Road, Ambattur, Chennai, Tamil Nadu

Sl. No.	*Name of Participant*	*Institution Name*
296.	Major R.L Grover (Retd.) Registration No.:-249	International Society for Human Welfare and Rehabilitation Centre, A-4, Naraina Industrial Area Phase-1, New Delhi
297.	Registration No.:-249A	– do –
298.	Ms. Vandana Garware Registration No.:-250	The Spastics Society of India, Sion, Trombay Road, Chembur, Mumbai, Maharashtra
299.	Mr. Abad Surendra Registration No.:-251	Vikalang Vihar, Ambedkar Social Welfare Minority Society, Vill. Shahpur Afgan, P.O. Telma, Distt. Balia, Uttar Pradesh
300.	Ms. Manjula A. Kalyaan Registration No.:-252	Swayamkrushi, 265, New Vasavi Nagar, Secunderabad, Andhra Pradesh
301.	Mr. Kusumakar Sukul Registration No.:-253	Bhagirath Sewa Sansthan, R10/144, Raj Nagar, Ghaziabad, Uttar Pradesh
302.	Mr. Manoj Kumar Mathur Registration No.:-253A	Bhagirath Sewa Sansthan, R10/144, Raj Nagar, Ghaziabad, Uttar Pradesh
303.	Mr. Vivekananda Ghosh Registration No.:-254	Anubhav, A Unit of Sabhuj Sangha, Vill. & P.O. Keshabpur, Distt. Hooghly, West Bengal
304.	Mrs. Vasandhara Avinash Kelkar Registration No.:-256	V.R. Ruia Mook Badhir Vidyalaya, S.P. College Campus, Pune, Maharashtra
305.	Ms. Meenakshi Srivastav Registration No.:-257	DISHA, Centre for Special Education, Vocational and Rehabilitation Centre, 450, AB, Nirman Nagar, Jaipur, Rajasthan
306.	Mr. Ravi Hooja Registration No.:-257A	DISHA, Centre for Special Education, Vocational and Rehabilitation Centre, 450, AB, Nirman Nagar, Jaipur, Rajasthan
307.	Ms. Kavita Choudhrie Registration No.:-259	Sneh Niketan School, Post Box No. 43, Near Gorakhpur Police Station, Jabalpur, Madhya Pradesh
308.	Mr. Jagdish Krishnarao Harde Registration No.:-260	Maharashtra State Govt & Semi Govt. Handicapped Employees Organization, C/o Flat No. 6/2 Bhagirathi Apartment, Bharat Nagar, Amravati Road, Nagpur, Maharashtra
309.	Mr. Suhas Rangrao Kale Registration No.:-261	Individual P.W. Disability, "ASRA" Vijjsnehi Colony, Kathora Road, Amravati
310.	Sau. Megha Suhas Kale Registration No.:-261A	Individual P.W. Disability, "ASRA" Vijjsnehi Colony, Kathora Road, Amravati
311.	Mr. Mukesh Jha Registration No.:-262	Bateshwar Seva Sansthan, Nahar Chowk, Godda, Jharkhand

Sl. No.	*Name of Participant*	*Institution Name*
312.	Mr. Sanjeev Kumar Registration No.:-262A	Bateshwar Seva Sansthan, Nahar Chowk, Godda, Jharkhand
313.	Ms. Tina Mendis Registration No.:-263	The Leprosy Mission Trust India, Church of North India 16, Pandit Pant Marg, New Delhi
314.	Mr. Upahar Pramanik Registration No.:-263A	The Leprosy Mission Trust India, Church of North India 16, Pandit Pant Marg, New Delhi
315.	Mr. Satish Bhardwaj Registration No.:-264	"SANTUSHTI", 19, Shastri Nagar, Lane No. 1, Haridwar Road, Dehradun
316.	Mr. Uma Shankar Pandey Registration No.:-264A	"SANTUSHTI", 19, Shastri Nagar, Lane No. 1, Haridwar Road, Dehradun
317.	Mr. Ashok Kumar Mishra Registration No.:-265	Indian National Disability Development Society, Sneha Bhavan, P.O. Barachana, Distt. Jaipur
318.	Mr. Ranjeet Lenka Registration No.:-265A	Indian National Disability Development Society, Sneha Bhavan, P.O. Barachana, Distt. Jaipur
319.	Dr. B.P. Dhakal Registration No.:-267	Spastic Society of Sikkim, Government of Sikkim, Department of Health & Family Welfare, Gangtok
320.	Ms. Geetanjali Naik Registration No.:-268	Jai Durga Club, Sialrama, P.O. Gudi Gaon Distt. Jharsuguda, Orissa
321.	Mr. Ishwar Prasad Deheri Registration No.:-268A	Jai Durga Club, Sialrama, P.O. Gudi Gaon Distt. Jharsuguda, Orissa
322.	Dr. J.B.Banerji Registration No.:-269	Viklang Kendra, Secretary's Office, 13, Lukergang Allahabad, U.P.
323.	Smt. Uttara Ratna Registration No.:-269A	Viklang Kendra, Secretary's Office, 13, Lukergang Allahabad, U.P.
324.	Ms. Usha Dalvi Registration No.:-270	Ali Yavar Jung National Institute for the Hearing Handicapped, Northern Regional Centre, Kasturba Niketan, Lajpat Nagar-II, New Delhi
325.	Ms. Anuradha Registration No.:-270A	Ali Yavar Jung National Institute for the Hearing Handicapped, Northern Regional Centre, Kasturba Niketan, Lajpat Nagar-II, New Delhi
326.	Mr. R.. Bhattacharya Registration No.:-270B	Ali Yavar Jung National Institute for the Hearing Handicapped, Northern Regional Centre, Kasturba Niketan, Lajpat Nagar-II, New Delhi

Sl. No.	*Name of Participant*	*Institution Name*
327.	Mr. V.P. Sah Registration No.:-270C	Ali Yavar Jung National Institute for the Hearing Handicapped, Northern Regional Centre, Kasturba Niketan, Lajpat Nagar-II, New Delhi
328.	Mrs. Kamini Zohra Mustafi Registration No.:-271	The Learning Centre, Bishop Cotton School Shimla, (H.P.)
329.	Mrs. Neerja Shukla Registration No.:-271A	The Learning Centre, Bishop Cotton School Shimla, (H.P.)
330.	Ms. Pradeep Kumar Singh Registration No.:-272	INDCARE Trust, Plot No. 66, Green Avenue, Colonel Bhatia Road, Vikas Nagar, Hastsal, New Delhi
331.	Ms. Reeva Sood Registration No.:-272A	INDCARE Trust, Plot No. 66, Green Avenue, Colonel Bhatia Road, Vikas Nagar, Hastsal, New Delhi
332.	Mr. R.A.Joseph Registration No.:-273	Integrated Institute for the Disabled, Karaundi, B.H.U., Varanasi, Uttar Pradesh
333.	Mr. Jayshri Ghosh Registration No.:-273A	Viklang Kendra, Lukerganj, Allahabad, Uttar Pradesh
334.	Mr. Srinwas Redu Registration No.:-274	Nav Yuvak Mandal Sansthan, Mithi Reduwali, District Project Office, Near New Idgah Ward No. 3, Churu, Rajasthan
335.	Mr. Santosh Gupta Registration No.:-276	Red Cross Hindu Institute for Education and Rehabilitation of M.R.C., Red Cross Bhawan, Near D.C. Residence, Sonipat
336.	Mr. G.B. Singh Registration No.:-277	Chandra Bhushan Singh Memorial Mahila, Bal Evam Shravan Viklang Shiksha Evam Punarvas Sansthan, 124, Rama Krishna Vihar, Plot No. 29, I.P. Extn., Delhi
337.	Dr. Heera R.V. Registration No.:-278	Institute for Communicative & Cognitive Neuro Sciences, Under the Society for Rehabilitation of Cognitive & Communicative Disorders T.C. 06/1969, Prasanth Nagar, Thiruvananthapuram, Kerala
338.	Mrs. Nandini Jayachandran Registration No.:-278A	Institute for Communicative & Cognitive Neuro Sciences, Under the Society for Rehabilitation of Cognitive & Communicative Disorders, T.C. 06/1969, Prasanth Nagar, Thiruvananthapuram, Kerala
339.	Dr. Kunh Ahammed Kutty Registration No.:-279	Association for Welfare of the Handicapped, M.Square Complex, Padmani Road, P.B. 59 Calicut, Kerala

Sl. No.	*Name of Participant*	*Institution Name*
340.	Mr. Deepak P. Sahay Registration No.:-282	All India Federation of the Deaf, AIFD, 18 Northend Complex, R.K. Ashram Marg, New Delhi
341.	Mr. Samir Ray Registration No.:-282A	All India Federation of the Deaf, AIFD, 18 Northend Complex, R.K. Ashram Marg, New Delhi
342.	Ms. Amita Dubey Registration No.:-283	National Association for the Blind, L.K.O. Baba Bhootnath Mandir, Indira Nagar, Lucknow, Uttar Pradesh
343.	Dr. Basudeb Giri Registration No.:-284	Akshayanagar Pallisri Sangha, Vill. & P.O. Akshaynagar Block & P.S. Kakdwip Distt. South 24 Parganas, West Bengal
344.	Mr. A. Banerjee Registration No.:-285	Liberal Association for Mevement of People, 66, Surya Sen Street, Kolkata
345.	Mr. Prasant Rath Registration No.:-286	AHINSA, Kumbharsahi, Dhenkanal, Orissa
346.	Mr. Ramesh Kumar Das Registration No.:-287	Better Institute for Rural Development and Action (Birds), Kankalanda, P.O. Mahimagadi, Distt. Dhenkanad, Orissa
347.	Mr. Pramod Kumar Mishra Registration No.:-288	TYAGA, Chhatratota P.O. Mahanga Cuttack, Orissa
348.	Mr. Jogen Chandra Das Registration No.:-289	Durpang Pichala Anchalic Bikalanga Anusthan, Vill. Balipukhuri, P.O. Durpang, Via–Bhogpur, Distt. Lakhimpur, Assam
349.	Shri Dhanti Das Registration No.:-289A	Durpang Pichala Anchalic Bikalanga Anusthan, Vill. Balipukhuri, P.O. Durpang, Via–Bhogpur, Distt. Lakhimpur, Assam
350.	Mr. Gopal Paul Registration No.:-290	Rajapur Vivekananda Gram Unnayan Kendra, Vill. Rajapur, P.O. Karabera, P.S. Ulberia, Distt. Howrah, West Bengal
351.	Mr. Tapan Kumar Dey Registration No.:-290A	Rajapur Vivekananda Gram Unnayan Kendra, Vill. Rajapur, P.O. Karabera, P.S. Ulberia, Distt. Howrah, West Bengal
352.	Mr. Ashwani Kumar Aggarwal Registration No.:-291	NAB, New Delhi
353.	Mr. Prasanna Kumar Pincha Registration No.:-292	Action Aid, Assam
354.	Mr. Mahendra Maiti Registration No.:-293	Pratibandhi Shayak Samiti, At & P.O. Panskura, Distt. Purba Medinipore, West Bengal

Sl. No.	*Name of Participant*	*Institution Name*
355.	Mr. Pravat Das Registration No.:-293A	Pratibandhi Shayak Samiti, At & P.O. Panskura, Distt. Purba Medinipore, West Bengal
356.	Ms. Sunita Bhandari Registration No.:-294	Prayas Sansthan, Udaipur, Rajasthan
357.	Mr. Raja Bhandari Registration No.:-294A	Prayas Sansthan, Udaipur, Rajasthan
358.	Ms. Jyotsna Registration No.:-295	Gauri Shanker Mandbuddhi Kalyan Va Mahila Sansthan, C-135, Mangal Marg, Bapur Nagar, Jaipur
359.	Mr. Damodar Dash Registration No.:-296	Open Learning System, Bhubaneshwar, Orissa
360.	Mrs. Anuradha Naidu Registration No.:-297	SABLA, Action Aid, New Delhi
361.	Mr. Pankaj Kumar Das Registration No.:-298	Louis Braille Memorial School for the Sightless, Birla Road, P.O. Makhla, Distt. Hooghly, West Bengal
362.	Mr. Bansidhar Jena Registration No.:-298A	Louis Braille Memorial School for the Sightless, Birla Road, P.O. Makhla, Distt. Hooghly, West Bengal
363.	Mr. Somnath Ghosh Registration No.:-299	Koleghat Lok Siksha Niketan
364.	Mr. A.K.Biswas Registration No.:-299A	– do –
365.	Mr. Manoj Sharma Registration No.:-300	Progressive Youth Society, Ramngar, Jammu & Kashmir
366.	Mr. A.G. Mohan Registration No.:-301	Special School for the Mental Retardation
367.	M. Latha Registration No.:-301A	– do –
368.	Mr. Mukul Chandra Goswami Registration No.:-302	Ashadeep, Islampur Road, Gandhi Basti, Guwahati
369.	Ms. Ketaki Baradalai Registration No.:-303	Shishu Sarothi, Guwahati
370.	Ms. Pratibha Goel Registration No.:-304	Research Scholor Dept. of Education, University of Delhi, 33 Chhatra Marg, Delhi
371.	Md. Jashir Hussain Khan Registration No.:-304A	University of Delhi, 33 Chhatra Marg, Delhi
372.	Sh. Mukut Moni Roy Registration No.:-305	Dharaninagar Rural Development Society, P.O. Mollarpur, Distt. Birbhum, West Bengal

Sl. No.	*Name of Participant*	*Institution Name*
373.	Mr. G.C. Upadhay Registration No.:-306	Deva Integrated School for the Handicapped, Varanasi
374.	Mr. Rajesh Kumar Singh Registration No.:-307	Rashtriya Mahila Sahara Samiti, Begusarai, Goregaon Sahar P.O. Suhird Nagar, Distt. Begusarai, Bihar
375.	Mr. Uday Marendi Registration No.:-308	Van Uden Badhir Kalyan Vidyalay, Dhobi Jharna, Micro Wave Tower, Sahibganj (S.P), Jharkhand
376.	S.T. Gaiki Registration No.:-309	Lehri Seva Mandal, Sarak Arjuni Distt. Gondia, Maharashtra
377.	Ms. Ritu Ghosh Registration No.:-310	Mobility India, 1st and 1st A Cross, J.P. Nagar, Second Phase, Bangalore
378.	Ms. Albina Shankar Registration No.:-310A	Mobility India, 1st and 1st A Cross, J.P. Nagar, Second Phase, Bangalore
379.	Ms. Chitra Kataria Registration No.:-311	ISIC, New Delhi
380.	Ms. Subi Menon Registration No.:-311A	ISIC, New Delhi
381.	Mr. Krupanandam Y Registration No.:-312	N.I.V.H, 116 Rajpur Road, Dehradun
382.	P. Eswaramoorthi Registration No.:-313	Sun Educational Trust, 42-CKC Complex, Vijayamagalam Road, Uttukuli, Distt. Erode, Tamil Nadu
383.	Dr. P.Chandra Das CBR Registration No.:-313A	Sun Educational Trust, 42-CKC Complex Vijayamagalam Road, Uttukuli, Distt. Erode, Tamil Nadu
384.	Ms. Gitanjali Kamra Registration No.:-314	Vasant Valley School, Special Section, Sec-C, Mahipalpur, Mehrauli Road, Vasant Kunj, New Delhi
385.	Ms. Suman Bajaj Registration No.:-314A	Vasant Valley School, Special Section, Sec-C, Mahipalpur, Mehrauli Road, Vasant Kunj, New Delhi
386.	Ms. Sumitra Mishra Registration No.:-315	Sense International (India), Row House, E/2, Tarun Nagar, Part-II, Gurukul Road, Memnagar, Ahmedabad
387.	Mr. Pawan Kumar Registration No.:-316	Prem Jyoti Society, Vill & P.O. Chiraigaon, Varanasi, Uttar Pradesh
388.	Dr. (Mrs.) S. Hamal Registration No.:-317	Health & Family Welfare, Sikkim Viklang Sahitya Samiti, Sikkim

Sl. No.	*Name of Participant*	*Institution Name*
389.	Mr. Kanhekar Vijay Kumar V. Registration No.:-318	Mahatma Gandhi Seva Sangh, "Rakhan" 9, Yogksham Colony, Jintoor Road, Parbhani, Maharashtra
390.	Ms. Kamala Singh Registration No.:-319	Premjyoti Society, Vill- Bhabanpura, P.O. Kamauli Varanasi, Uttar Pradesh
391.	Mr. Lal Bhai Registration No.:-320	Gram Seva Sansthan, Dhaparh: P.O. Bhattgaon, Gongarh, Tehri Gahrwal, Uttaranchal
392.	Mr. Mani Graces V.J. Registration No.:-321	Daleview Punnalal, Punnalal, P.O. Puvachal, Trivandrum, Kerala
393.	Mrs. Radhika D.K. Registration No.:-322	DALEVIEW, Vikas Puri, New Delhi
394.	Mr. G. Shankar Registration No.:-322A	DALEVIEW, Vikas Puri, New Delhi
395.	Dr. (Smt.) Priti G. Chouksey Registration No.:-323	NIRAKARAN Physical Medicine & Rehabilitation Centre, 1116 Wright Town, Near Maharashtra High School, Jabalpur, Madhya Pradesh
396.	Ms. Alana Registration No.:-324	Handicap International, P.O. Box 3837, Andrews Ganj, New Delhi
397.	Mr. Dillip Kumar Registration No.:-325	– do –
398.	Mr. Rakesh Goswami Registration No.:-326	Vanchit Pratisthan
399.	Mr. Sudhir Prashad Registration No.:-327	Uthan Bharti
400.	Mr. Krishna Kumar Registration No.:-328	Uthan Bharti
401.	Mr. Dillip Kumar Sahoo Registration No.:-329	Project Swarajya, Ganesh Ghat, Bakharabad, Cuttack, Orissa
402.	L.Ş Sudandara Doss Registration No.:-330	Ajay Memorial Foundation, 6, Officers Colony, Anna Nagar, West Exstension, Chennai
403.	Mr. Khushal Visvanath Thalal Registration No.:-331	Viklang Sewa Sansta, Shriram Panherkar, E-1/2, Urjanagar, Chandrapur, Maharashtra
404.	Mr. Badu Tukaram Pawai Registration No.:-331A	Viklang Sewa Sansta, Shriram Panherkar, E-1/2, Urjanagar, Chandrapur, Maharashtra
405.	Dr. O.P. Bharadwaj Registration No.:-332	Om Keshav Swachik Sansthan, 9 Gandhi Road, Dehradun, Uttaranchal